Java™ and XSLT

Other Java™ Titles from O'Reilly

Creating Effective JavaHelp™

Database Programming with JDBC™
  and Java™

Developing JavaBeans™

Enterprise JavaBeans™

Java™ 2D Graphics

Java™ & XML

Java™ Cryptography

Java™ Distributed Computing

Java™ Enterprise in a Nutshell

The Java™ Enterprise CD Bookshelf

Java™ Examples in a Nutshell

Java™ Foundation Classes in a Nutshell

Java™ I/O

Java™ in a Nutshell

Java™ Internationalization

Java™ Message Service

Java™ Network Programming

Java™ Performance Tuning

Java™ Professional Library

Java™ Security

JavaServer™ Pages

Java™ Servlet Programming

Java™ Swing

Java™ Threads

Jini™ in a Nutshell

Learning Java™

Java™ Cookbook

Java™ and XSLT

Eric M. Burke

O'REILLY®

Beijing · Cambridge · Farnham · Köln · Paris · Sebastopol · Taipei · Tokyo

Java™ and XSLT
by Eric M. Burke

Published by O'Reilly & Associates, Inc., 101 Morris Street, Sebastopol, CA 95472.

Editor: Mike Loukides

Production Editor: Matt Hutchinson

Cover Designer: Ellie Volckhausen

Printing History:

> September 2001:   First Edition.

ISBN: 0-596-00143-6

For Jennifer and Aidan

Table of Contents

Preface

Java and Extensible Stylesheet Language Transformations (XSLT) are very different technologies that complement one another, rather than compete. Java's strengths are portability, its vast collection of standard libraries, and widespread acceptance by most companies. One weakness of Java, however, is in its ability to process text. For instance, Java may not be the best technology for merely converting XML files into another format such as XHTML or Wireless Markup Language (WML). Using Java for such a task requires skilled programmers who understand APIs such as DOM, SAX, or JDOM. For web sites in particular, it is desirable to simplify the page generation process so nonprogrammers can participate.

XSLT is explicitly designed for XML transformations. With XSLT, XML data can be transformed into any other text format, including HTML, XHTML, WML, and even unexpected formats such as Java source code. In terms of complexity and sophistication, XSLT is harder than HTML but easier than Java. This means that page authors can probably learn how to use XSLT successfully but will require assistance from programmers as pages are developed.

XSLT processors are required to interpret and execute the instructions found in XSLT stylesheets. Many of these processors are written in Java, making Java an excellent choice for applications that must interoperate with XML and XSLT. For web sites that utilize XSLT, Java servlets and EJBs are still required to intercept client requests, fetch data from databases, and implement business logic. XSLT may be used to generate each of the XHTML web pages, but this cannot be done without a language like Java acting as the coordinator.

This book explains the most important concepts behind the XSLT markup language but is not a comprehensive reference on that subject. Instead, the focus is on interoperability with Java, with particular emphasis on servlets and web applications.

Every concept is backed by working examples, all of which work on widely available, free tools.

Audience

Java programmers who want to learn how to use XSLT comprise the target audience for this book. Java programming experience is essential, and basic familiarity with XML terminology is helpful, but not required. Since so many of the examples revolve around web applications and servlets, Chapters 4 and 6 are devoted to this topic, offering a fast-paced tutorial to servlet technology. Chapters 2 and 3 contain a detailed XSLT tutorial, so no prior knowledge of XSLT is required.

This book is particularly well-suited for readers who may have read a lot about these technologies but have not used everything together in a complete application. Chapter 7, for example, presents the implementation of a web-based discussion forum from start to finish. Fully worked examples can be found in every chapter, ranging from an Ant build file documentation stylesheet in Chapter 3 to internationalization techniques in Chapter 8.

Software and Versions

Keeping up with the latest technologies is always a challenge, particularly when writing about XML-related tools. The set of tools listed in Table P-1 is sufficient to run just about every example in this book.

Table P-1. Software and versions

Tool	URL	Description
Crimson	Included with JAXP 1.1	XML parser from Apache
JAXP 1.1	*http://java.sun.com/xml*	Java API for XML Processing
JDK 1.2.x	*http://java.sun.com*	Any Java 2 Standard Edition SDK
JDOM beta 6	*http://www.jdom.org*	Open source alternative to DOM
JUnit 3.7	*http://www.junit.org*	Open source unit testing framework
Tomcat 4.0	*http://jakarta.apache.org*	Open source servlet container
Xalan	Included with JAXP 1.1	XSLT processor

There are certainly other tools, most notably the SAXON XSLT processor available from *http://users.iclway.co.uk/mhkay/saxon*. This can easily be substituted for Xalan because of the vendor-independence that JAXP offers.

All of the examples, as well as JAR files for the tools listed in Table P-1, are available for download from *http://www.javaxslt.com* and from the O'Reilly web site at *http://www.oreilly.com/catalog/javaxslt.* The included *README.txt* file contains instructions for compiling and running the examples.

Organization

This book consists of 10 chapters and 3 appendixes, as follows:

Chapter 1, Introduction

Provides a broad overview of the technologies covered in this book and explains how XML, XSLT, Java, and other APIs are related. Also reviews basic XML concepts for readers who are familiar with Java but do not have a lot of XML experience.

Chapter 2, XSLT Part 1—The Basics

Introduces XSLT syntax through a series of small examples and descriptions. Describes how to produce HTML and XHTML output and explains how XSLT works as a language. XPath syntax is also introduced in this chapter.

Chapter 3, XSLT Part 2— Beyond the Basics

Continues with material presented in the previous chapter, covering more sophisticated XSLT language features such as conditional logic, parameters and variables, text and number formatting, and producing XML output. This chapter concludes with a more sophisticated example that produces summary reports for Ant build files.

Chapter 4, Java-Based Web Technologies

Offers comparisons between popular web development technologies, comparing each with the Java and XSLT approach. The model-view-controller architecture is discussed in detail, and the relationship between XSLT web applications and EJB is touched upon.

Chapter 5, XSLT Processing with Java

Shows how to use XSLT processors with Java applications and servlets. Older Xalan and SAXON APIs are mentioned, but the primary focus is on Sun's JAXP. Key examples show how to use XSLT and SAX to transform non-XML files and data sources, how to improve performance through caching techniques, and how to interoperate with DOM and JDOM.

Chapter 6, Servlet Basics and XSLT

Provides a detailed review of Java servlet programming techniques. Shows how to create web applications and WAR files, how to deploy XML and XSLT files within these web applications, and how to perform XSLT transformations from servlets.

Chapter 7, Discussion Forum

Implements a complete web application from start to finish. In this chapter, a web-based discussion forum is designed and implemented using Java, XML, and XSLT techniques. The relationship between CSS and XSLT is presented, and XHTML Strict is used for all web pages.

Chapter 8, Additional Techniques

Covers important Java and XSLT programming techniques that build upon concepts presented in earlier chapters, concluding with a detailed discussion of XSLT internationalization. Other topics include XSLT page layout templates, servlet session tracking without cookies, browser identification, and servlet filters.

Chapter 9, Development Environment, Testing, and Performance

Offers practical advice for making a wide range of XML parsers, XSLT processors, and various other Java tools work together. Shows how to resolve conflicts with incompatible XML JAR files, how to write simple unit tests with JUnit, and how to write custom JAXP error handlers. Also discusses performance techniques and the relationship between XSLT and EJB.

Chapter 10, Wireless Applications

Describes the world of wireless technologies, with emphasis on Wireless Markup Language (WML). Shows how to detect wireless devices from a servlet, how to write XSLT stylesheets for these devices, and how to test using a variety of cell phone simulators. An online movie theater application is developed to reinforce the concepts.

Appendix A, Discussion Forum Code

Contains all of the remaining code from the discussion forum example presented in Chapter 7.

Appendix B, JAXP API Reference

Lists and briefly describes each of the classes in Version 1.1 of the JAXP API.

Appendix C, XSLT Quick Reference

Contains a quick reference for the XSLT language. Lists all XSLT elements along with required and optional attributes and allowable content within each element. Also cross references each element with the W3C XSLT specification.

Conventions Used in This Book

Italic is used for:

* Pathnames, filenames, and program names

* New terms where they are defined

* Internet addresses, such as domain names and URLs

`Constant width` is used for:

- Anything that appears literally in a Java program, including keywords, datatypes, constants, method names, variables, class names, and interface names

- All Java code listings

- HTML, XML, and XSLT documents, tags, and attributes

`Constant width italic` is used for:

- General placeholders that indicate that an item is replaced by some actual value in your own program

`Constant width bold` is used for:

- Command-line entries

- Emphasis within a Java or XML source file

How to Contact Us

We have tested and verified the information in this book to the best of our ability, but you may find that features have changed (or even that we have made mistakes!). Please let us know about any errors you find, as well as your suggestions for future editions, by writing to:

O'Reilly & Associates, Inc.
101 Morris Street
Sebastopol, CA 95472
(800) 998-9938 (in the U.S. or Canada)
(707) 829-0515 (international/local)
(707) 829-0104 (FAX)

There is a web page for this book, which lists errata, examples, or any additional information. You can access this page at:

http://www.oreilly.com/catalog/javaxslt

To comment or ask technical questions about this book, send email to:

bookquestions@oreilly.com

For more information about books, conferences, software, Resource Centers, and the O'Reilly Network, see the O'Reilly web site at:

http://www.oreilly.com

Acknowledgments

I would like to thank my wife Jennifer for tolerating my absence during the past six months, as I have locked myself in the basement researching, writing, and thinking. I also feel fortunate that my two-year-old son Aidan goes to bed early; a vast majority of this book was written well after 8:30 P.M.!

Coming up with a list of people to thank is a difficult job because so many have influenced the material in this book. I only hope that I do not leave anyone out. All of the technical reviewers did an amazing amount of work, each offering a unique perspective and useful advice. The official reviewers were Dean Wette, Kevin Heifner, Paul Jensen, Shane Curcuru, and Tim Brown.

I would also like to thank Weiqi Gao, Shu Zhu, Santosh Shanbhag, and Suman Ganesh for help with the internationalization example in Chapter 8. A technical article by Dan Troesser inspired my servlet filter implementation, and Justin Michel and Brent Roberts reviewed some of the first chapters that I wrote.

There are two companies that I really want to thank. O'Reilly has this little link on their home page called "Write for Us." This book came into existence because I casually clicked on that link one day and decided to submit a proposal. Although my original idea was not accepted, Mike Loukides and I exchanged several emails after that in a virtual brainstorming session, and eventually the proposal for this book emerged. I am still amazed that an unknown visitor to a web site can become an O'Reilly author.

The other company I would like to thank is Object Computing, Inc. (OCI), my employer. They have a remarkable group of highly talented software engineers, all of whom are always available to answer questions, offer advice, and inspire me to learn more. These people are the reason I work for OCI and are the reason this book was possible.

Finally, I would like to thank Mark Volkmann of OCI for teaching me about XML in the first place and for answering countless questions during the past five years.

1

Introduction

When XML first appeared, people widely believed that it was the imminent successor to HTML. This viewpoint was influenced by a variety of factors, including media hype, wishful thinking, and simple confusion about the number of new technologies associated with XML. The reality is that millions of web sites are written in HTML, and no widely used browser fully supports XML and its related standards. Even when browser vendors incorporate full support for XML and its family of related technologies, it will take years before enough people use these new versions to justify rewriting most web sites in XML. Although maintaining compatibility with older browsers is essential, companies should not hesitate to move forward with XML and related technologies on the server.

From the browser perspective, HTML will remain dominant on the Web for many years to come. Looking beneath the hood will reveal a much different picture, however, in which HTML is used only during the last instant of presentation. Web applications must support a multitude of browsers, and the easiest way to do this is to simply *transform* data into HTML before sending it to the client. On the server side, XML is the preferred way to process and exchange data because it is portable, standard, and easy to work with. This is where Java and XSLT enter the picture.

Java, XSLT, and the Web

Extensible Stylesheet Language Transformations (XSLT) is designed to transform XML data into some other form, most commonly HTML, XHTML, or another XML format. An *XSLT processor*, such as Apache's Xalan, performs transformations using one or more XSLT *stylesheets*, which are also XML documents. As Figure 1-1 illustrates, XSLT can be utilized on the web tier while web browsers on the client tier deal only with HTML.

1

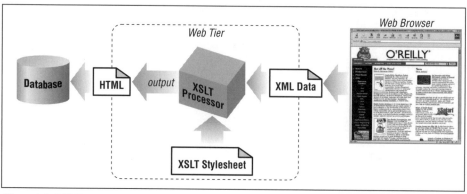

Figure 1-1. XSLT transformation

Typically in an XSLT- and Java-based web application, XML data is generated dynamically based on database queries. Although some newer databases can export data directly as XML, you will often write custom Java code to extract data using JDBC and convert it to XML. This XML data, such as a customized list of benefit elections or perhaps an airline schedule for a specific time window, may be different for each client using the application. In order to display this XML data on most browsers, it must first be converted to HTML. As Figure 1-1 shows, the XML data is fed into the processor as one input, and an XSLT stylesheet is provided as a second input. The output is then sent directly to the web browser as a stream of HTML. The XSLT stylesheet produces HTML formatting instructions, while the XML provides raw data.

What's Wrong with HTML?

One of the fundamental problems with HTML is its haphazard implementation. Although the specification for HTML is available from the World Wide Web Consortium (W3C), its evolution was driven mostly by competition between Netscape and Microsoft rather than a thoughtful design process and open standards. This resulted in a bloated language littered with browser-specific tags and varying support for standards. Since no two browsers support the exact same set of HTML features, web authors often limit themselves to a subset of HTML. Another approach is to create and maintain separate copies of each web page, which take advantage of the unique features found in a particular browser. The limitations of HTML are compounded for dynamic sites, in which Java programs are often responsible for accessing enterprise data sources and presenting that information through the browser.

Extracting information from back-end data sources is much more difficult than simple web page authoring. This requires skilled developers who know how to interact with Enterprise JavaBeans or relational databases. Since skilled Java developers are a scarce and expensive resource, it makes sense to let them work on the back-end data sources and business logic while web page developers and less experi-enced programmers work on the HTML user interface. As we will see in Chapter 4, this can be difficult with traditional Java servlet approaches because Java code is often cluttered with HTML generation code.

Keeping Data and Presentation Separate

HTML does not separate data from presentation. For example, the following frag-ment of HTML displays some information about a customer. In it, data fields such as "Aidan" and "Burke" are clearly intertwined with formatting elements such as `<tr>` and `<td>`:

```
<h3>Customer Information</h3>
<table border="1" cellpadding="2" cellspacing="0">
  <tr><td>First Name:</td><td>Aidan</td></tr>
  <tr><td>Last Name:</td><td>Burke</td></tr>
  <!-- etc... -->
</table>
```

Traditionally, this sort of HTML is generated dynamically using `println()` state-ments in a servlet, or perhaps through a JavaServer Page (JSP). Both require Java programmers, and neither technology explicitly keeps business logic and data sep-arated from the HTML generation code. To support multiple incompatible brows-ers, you have to be careful to avoid duplication of a lot of Java code and the HTML itself. This places additional burdens on Java developers who should be working on more important problems.

There are ways to keep programming logic separate from the HTML generation, but *extracting* meaningful data from HTML pages is next to impossible. This is because the HTML does not clearly indicate how its data is structured. A human can look at HTML and determine what its fields mean, but it is quite difficult to write a computer program that can reliably extract meaningful data. Although you can search for text patterns such as `First   Name:` followed by `<td>`, this approach* fails as soon as the presentation is modified. For example, changing the page as follows would cause this approach to fail:

```
<tr><td>Full Name:</td><td>Aidan Burke</td></tr>
```

The XSLT Solution

XSLT makes it possible to define clearly the roles of Java, XML, XSLT, and HTML. Java is used for business logic, database queries and updates, and for creat-ing XML data. The XML is responsible for raw data, while XSLT transforms the

---

* This approach is commonly known as "screen scraping."

XML into HTML for viewing by a browser. A key advantage of this approach is the clean separation between the XML data and the HTML views. In order to support multiple browsers, multiple XSLT stylesheets are written, but the same XML data is reused on the server. In the previous example, the XML data for the customer did not contain any formatting instructions:

```
<customer>
  <firstName>Aidan</firstName>
  <lastName>Burke</lastName>
</customer>
```

Since XML contains only data, it is almost always much simpler than HTML. Additionally, XML can be created using a Java API such as JDOM (*http://www.jdom.org*). This facilitates error checking and validation, something that cannot be achieved if you are simply printing HTML as text using `PrintWriter` and `println()` statements in a servlet.

Best of all, the XML-generation code has to be written only once. The XML data can then be transformed by any number of XSLT stylesheets in order to support different browsers, alternate languages, or even nonbrowser devices such as web-enabled cell phones.

XML Review

In a nutshell, XML is a format for storing structured data. Although it looks a lot like HTML, XML is much more strict with quotes, properly terminated tags, and other such details. XML does not define tag names, so document authors must invent their own set of tags or look towards a standards organization that defines a suitable XML *markup language*. A markup language is essentially a set of custom tags with semantic meaning behind each tag; XSLT is one such markup language, since it is expressed using XML syntax.

The terms *element* and *tag* are often used interchangeably, and both are used in this book. Speaking from a more technical viewpoint, element refers to the concept being modeled, while tag refers to the actual markup that appears in the XML document. So <account> is a tag that represents an account element in a computer program.

SGML, XML, and Markup Languages

Standard Generalized Markup Language (SGML) forms the basis for HTML, XHTML, XML, and XSLT, but in very different ways for each. Figure 1-2 illustrates the relationships between these technologies.

SGML is a very sophisticated *metalanguage* designed for large and complex documentation. As a metalanguage, it defines syntax rules for tags but does not define

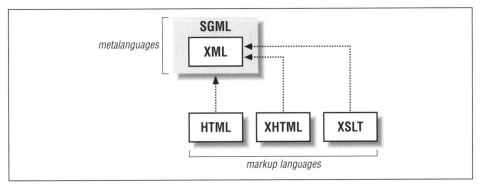

Figure 1-2. SGML heritage

any specific tags. HTML, on the other hand, is a specific markup language implemented using SGML. A markup language defines its own set of tags, such as <h1> and <p>. Because HTML is a markup language instead of a metalanguage, you cannot add new tags and are at the mercy of the browser vendor to properly implement those tags.

XML, as shown in Figure 1-2, is a subset of SGML. XML documents are compatible with SGML documents, however XML is a much smaller language. A key goal of XML is simplicity, since it has to work well on the Web where bandwidth and limited client processing power is a concern. Because of its simplicity, XML is easier to parse and validate, making it a better performer than SGML. XML is also a metalanguage, which explains why XML does not define any tags of its own. XSLT is a particular markup language implemented using XML, and will be covered in detail in the next two chapters.

XHTML, like XSLT, is also an XML-based markup language. XHTML is designed to be a replacement for HTML and is almost completely compatible with existing web browsers. Unlike HTML, however, XHTML is based strictly on XML, and the rules for well-formed documents are very clearly defined. This means that it is much easier for vendors to develop editors and programming tools to deal with XHTML, because the syntax is much more predictable and can be validated just like any other XML document. Many of the examples in this book use XHTML instead of HTML, although XSLT can easily handle either format.

As we look at more advanced techniques for processing XML with XSLT, we will see that XML is not always dealt with in terms of a text file containing tags. From a certain perspective, XML files and their tags are really just a serialized representation of the underlying XML elements. This serialized form is good for storing XML data in files but may not be the most efficient format for exchanging data between systems or programmatically modifying the underlying data. For particularly large documents, a relational or object database offers far better scalability and performance than native XML text files.

XHTML Basics

XHTML is a W3C Recommendation that represents the future of HTML. Based on HTML 4.0, XHTML is designed to be compatible with existing web browsers while complying fully with XML. This means that a properly written XHTML document is always a well-formed XML document. Furthermore, XHTML documents must adhere to one or more of the XHTML DTDs, therefore XHTML pages can be validated using today's XML parsers such as Apache's Crimson.

XHTML is designed to be modular; therefore, subsets can be extracted and utilized for wireless devices such as cell phones. XHTML Basic, also a W3C Recommendation, is one such modularization effort, and will likely become a force to be reckoned with in the wireless space.

Here is an example XHTML document:

```
<?xml version="1.0" encoding="UTF-8"?>
<!DOCTYPE html PUBLIC "-//W3C//DTD XHTML 1.0 Strict//EN"
  "http://www.w3.org/TR/xhtml1/DTD/xhtml1-strict.dtd">
<html xmlns="http://www.w3.org/1999/xhtml">
  <head>
    <title>Hello, World!</title>
  </head>
  <body>
    <p>Hello, World!</p>
  </body>
</html>
```

Some of the most important XHTML rules include:

- XHTML documents must be well-formed XML and must adhere to one of the XHTML DTDs. As expected with XML, all elements must be properly terminated, attribute values must be quoted, and elements must be properly nested.

- The `<!DOCTYPE ...>` tag is required.

- Unlike HTML, tags must be lowercase.

- The root element must be `<html>` and must designate the XHTML namespace as shown in the previous example.

- `<head>` and `<body>` are required.

The preceding document adheres to the *strict* DTD, which eliminates deprecated HTML tags and many style-related tags. Two other DTDs, *transitional* and *frameset*, provide more compatibility with existing web browsers but should be avoided when possible. For full information, refer to the W3C's specifications and documentation at *http://www.w3.org*.

XML Syntax

Example 1-1 shows a sample XML document that contains data about U.S. Presidents. This document is said to be *well-formed* because it adheres to several basic rules about proper XML formatting.

Example 1-1. presidents.xml

```xml
<?xml version="1.0" encoding="UTF-8"?>
<!DOCTYPE presidents SYSTEM "presidents.dtd">
<presidents>
  <president>
    <term from="1789" to="1797"/>
    <name>
      <first>George</first>
      <last>Washington</last>
    </name>
    <party>Federalist</party>
    <vicePresident>
      <name>
        <first>John</first>
        <last>Adams</last>
      </name>
    </vicePresident>
  </president>
  <president>
    <term from="1797" to="1801"/>
    <name>
      <first>John</first>
      <last>Adams</last>
    </name>
    <party>Federalist</party>
    <vicePresident>
      <name>
        <first>Thomas</first>
        <last>Jefferson</last>
      </name>
    </vicePresident>
  </president>

  <!-- remaining presidents omitted -->

</presidents>
```

In HTML, a missing tag here and there or mismatched quotes are not disastrous. Browsers make every effort to go ahead and display these poorly formatted documents anyway. This makes the Web a much more enjoyable environment because users are not bombarded with constant syntax errors.

Since the primary role of XML is to represent structured data, being well-formed is very important. When two banking systems exchange data, if the message is corrupted in any way, the receiving system must reject the message altogether or risk making the wrong assumptions. This is important for XSLT programmers to understand because XSLT itself is expressed using XML. When writing stylesheets, you must always adhere to the basic rules for well-formed documents.

All well-formed XML documents must have exactly one *root element*. In Example 1-1, the root element is `<presidents>`. This forms the base of a tree data structure in which every other element has exactly one parent and zero or more children. Elements must also be properly terminated and nested:

```
<name>
  <first>George</first>
  <last>Washington</last>
</name>
```

Although *whitespace* (spaces, tabs, and linefeeds) between elements is typically irrelevant, it can make documents more readable if you take the time to indent consistently. Although XML parsers preserve whitespace, it does not affect the meaning of the underlying elements. In this example, the `<first>` tag must be terminated with a corresponding `</first>`. The following XML would be illegal because the tags are not properly nested:

```
<name>
  <first>George
    <last>Washington</first>
  </last>
</name>
```

XML provides an alternate syntax for terminating elements that do not have children, formally known as *empty elements*. The `<term>` element is one such example:

```
<term from="1797" to="1801"/>
```

The closing slash indicates that this element does not contain any *content*, although it may contain *attributes*. An attribute is a name/value pair, such as `from="1797"`. Another requirement for well-formed XML is that all attribute values be enclosed in quotes (`""`) or apostrophes (`' '`).

Most presidents had middle names, some did not have vice presidents, and others had several vice presidents. For our example XML file, these are known as *optional elements*. Ulysses Grant, for example, had two vice presidents. He also had a middle name:

```
<president>
  <term from="1869" to="1877"/>
  <name>
    <first>Ulysses</first>
```

```
      <middle>Simpson</middle>
        <last>Grant</last>
    </name>
    <party>Republican</party>
    <vicePresident>
      <name>
        <first>Schuyler</first>
        <last>Colfax</last>
      </name>
    </vicePresident>
    <vicePresident>
      <name>
        <first>Henry</first>
        <last>Wilson</last>
      </name>
    </vicePresident>
  </president>
```

Capitalization is also important in XML. Unlike HTML, all XML tags are case sensitive. This means that `<president>` is not the same as `<PRESIDENT>`. It does not matter which capitalization scheme you use, provided you are consistent. As you might guess, since XHTML documents are also XML documents, they too are case sensitive. In XHTML, all tags must be lowercase, such as `<html>`, `<body>`, and `<head>`.

The following list summarizes the basic rules for a well-formed XML document:

*   It must contain exactly one root element; the remainder of the document forms a tree structure, in which every element is contained within exactly one parent.

*   All elements must be properly terminated. For example, `<name>Eric</name>` is properly terminated because the `<name>` tag is terminated with `</name>`. In XML, you can also create empty elements like `<married/>`.

*   Elements must be properly nested. This is legal:

    ```
    <b><i>bold and italic</i></b>
    ```
    But this is illegal:

    ```
    <b><i>bold and italic</b></i>
    ```

*   Attributes must be quoted using either quotes or apostrophes. For example:

    ```
    <date month="march" day='01' year="1971"/>
    ```

*   Attributes must contain name/value pairs. Some HTML elements contain marker attributes, such as `<td nowrap>`. In XHTML, you would write this as `<td nowrap="nowrap"/>`. This is compatible with XML and should work in existing web browsers.

This is not the complete list of rules but is sufficient to get you through the examples in this book. Clearly, most HTML documents are not well-formed. Many tags, such as <br> or <hr>, violate the rule that all elements must be properly terminated. In addition, browsers do not complain when attribute values are not quoted. This will have interesting ramifications for us when we write XSLT stylesheets, which are themselves written in XML but often produce HTML. What this basically means is that the stylesheet must contain well-formed XML, so it is difficult to produce HTML that is not well-formed. XHTML is certainly a more natural fit because it is also XML, just like the XSLT stylesheet.

Validation

A well-formed XML document adheres to the basic syntax guidelines just outlined. A *valid* XML document goes one step further by adhering to either a Document Type Definition (DTD) or an XML Schema. In order to be considered valid, an XML document must first be well-formed. Stated simply, DTDs are the traditional approach to validation, and XML Schemas are the logical successor. XML Schema is another specification from the W3C and offers much more sophisticated validation capabilities than DTDs. Since XML Schema is very new, DTDs will continue to be used for quite some time. You can learn more about XML Schema at *http://www.w3.org/XML/Schema*.

The second line of Example 1-1 contains the following *document type declaration*:

```
<!DOCTYPE presidents SYSTEM "presidents.dtd">
```

This refers to the DTD that exists in the same directory as the *presidents.xml* file. In many cases, the DTD will be referenced by a URI instead:

```
<!DOCTYPE presidents SYSTEM "http://www.javaxslt.com/dtds/presidents.dtd">
```

Regardless of where the DTD is located, it contains rules that define the allowable structure of the XML data. Example 1-2 shows the DTD for our list of presidents.

Example 1-2. presidents.dtd

```
<!ELEMENT presidents (president+)>
<!ELEMENT president (term, name, party, vicePresident*)>
<!ELEMENT name (first, middle*, last, nickname?)>
<!ELEMENT vicePresident (name)>
<!ELEMENT first (#PCDATA)>
<!ELEMENT last (#PCDATA)>
<!ELEMENT middle (#PCDATA)>
<!ELEMENT nickname (#PCDATA)>
<!ELEMENT party (#PCDATA)>
<!ELEMENT term EMPTY>
```

Example 1-2. presidents.dtd (continued)

```
<!ATTLIST term
    from CDATA #REQUIRED
    to CDATA #REQUIRED
>
```

The first line in the DTD says that the `<presidents>` element can contain one or more `<president>` elements as children. The `<president>`, in turn, contains one each of `<term>`, `<name>`, and `<party>` in that order. It then may contain zero or more `<vicePresident>` elements. If the XML data did not adhere to these rules, the XML parser would have rejected it as invalid.

The `<name>` element can contain the following content: exactly one `<first>`, followed by zero or more `<middle>`, followed by exactly one `<last>`, followed by zero or one `<nickname>`. If you are wondering why `<middle>` can occur many times, consider this former president:

```
<name>
  <first>George</first>
  <middle>Herbert</middle>
  <middle>Walker</middle>
  <last>Bush</last>
</name>
```

Elements such as `<first>George</first>` are said to contain `#PCDATA`, which stands for *parsed character data*. This is ordinary text that can contain markup, such as nested tags. The `CDATA` type, which is used for attribute values, cannot contain markup. This means that `<` characters appearing in attribute values will have to be encoded in your XML documents as `&lt;`. The `<term>` element is `EMPTY`, meaning that it cannot have content. This is not to say that it cannot contain attributes, however. This DTD specifies that `<term>` must have `from` and `to` attributes:

```
<term from="1869" to="1877"/>
```

We will not cover the remaining syntax rules for DTDs in this book, primarily because they do not have much impact on our code as we apply XSLT stylesheets. DTDs are primarily used during the parsing process, when XML data is read from a file into memory. When generating XML for a web site, you generally produce new XML rather than parse existing XML, so there is much less need to validate. One area where we will use DTDs, however, is when we examine how to write unit tests for our Java and XSLT code. This will be covered in Chapter 9.

Java and XML

Java APIs for XML such as SAX, DOM, and JDOM will be used throughout this book. Although we will not go into a great deal of detail on specific parsing APIs, the Java-based XSLT tools do build on these technologies, so it is important to have a basic understanding of what each API does and where it fits into the XML landscape. For in-depth information on any of these topics, you might want to pick up a copy of *Java & XML* by Brett McLaughlin (O'Reilly).

A parser is a tool that reads XML data into memory. The most common pattern is to parse the XML data from a text file, although Java XML parsers can also read XML from any Java `InputStream` or even a URL. If a DTD or Schema is used, then validating parsers will ensure that the XML is valid during the parsing process. This means that once your XML files have been successfully parsed into memory, a lot less custom Java validation code has to be written.

SAX

In the Java community, Simple API for XML (SAX) is the most commonly used XML parsing method today. SAX is a free API available from David Megginson and members of the XML-DEV mailing list (*http://www.xml.org/xml-dev*). It can be downloaded* from *http://www.megginson.com/SAX*. Although SAX has been ported to several other languages, we will focus on the Java features. SAX is only responsible for scanning through XML data top to bottom and sending event notifications as elements, text, and other items are encountered; it is up to the recipient of these events to process the data. SAX parsers do not store the entire document in memory, therefore they have the potential to be very fast for even huge files.

Currently, there are two versions of SAX: 1.0 and 2.0. Many changes were made in version 2.0, and the SAX examples in this book use this version. Most SAX parsers should support the older 1.0 classes and interfaces, however, you will receive deprecation warnings from the Java compiler if you use these older features.

Java SAX parsers are implemented using a series of interfaces. The most important interface is `org.xml.sax.ContentHandler`, which has methods such as `startDocument()`, `startElement()`, `characters()`, `endElement()`, and `endDocument()`. During the parsing process, `startDocument()` is called once, then `startElement()` and `endElement()` are called once for each tag in the XML data. For the following XML:

```
<first>George</first>
```

the `startElement()` method will be called, followed by `characters()`, followed by `endElement()`. The `characters()` method provides the text `"George"` in this example. This basic process continues until the end of the document, at which time `endDocument()` is called.

---

* One does not generally need to download SAX directly because it is supported by and included with all of the popular XML parsers.

TIP   Depending on the SAX implementation, the characters()
             method may break up contiguous character data into several chunks
             of data. In this case, the characters() method will be called sev-
             eral times until the character data is entirely parsed.

Since ContentHandler is an interface, it is up to your application code to somehow implement this interface and subsequently do something when the parser
invokes its methods. SAX does provide a class called DefaultHandler that implements the ContentHandler interface. To use DefaultHandler, create a subclass
and override the methods that interest you. The other methods can safely be
ignored, since they are just empty methods. If you are familiar with AWT programming, you may recognize that this idiom is identical to event adapter classes such
as java.awt.event.WindowAdapter.

Getting back to XSLT, you may be wondering where SAX fits into the picture. It
turns out that XSLT processors typically have the ability to gather input from a
series of SAX events as an alternative to static XML files. Somewhat nonintuitively,
it also turns out that you can generate your own series of SAX events rather easily—without using a SAX parser. Since a SAX parser just calls a series of methods
on the ContentHandler interface, you can write your own pseudo-parser that
does the same thing. We will explore this in Chapter 5 when we talk about using
SAX and an XSLT processor to apply transformations to non-XML data, such as
results from a database query or content of a comma separated values (CSV) file.

DOM

The Document Object Model (DOM) is an API that allows computer programs to
manipulate the underlying data structure of an XML document. DOM is a W3C
Recommendation, and implementations are available for many programming languages. The in-memory representation of XML is typically referred to as a *DOM
tree* because DOM is a tree data structure. The root of the tree represents the XML
document itself, using the org.w3c.dom.Document interface. The *document root
element*, on the other hand, is represented using the org.w3c.dom.Element interface. In the presidents example, the <presidents> element is the document root
element. In DOM, almost every interface extends from the org.w3c.dom.Node
interface; Document and Element are no exception. The Node interface provides
numerous methods to navigate and modify the DOM tree consistently.

Strangely enough, the DOM Level 2 Recommendation does not provide standard
mechanisms for reading or writing XML data. Instead, each vendor implementation does this a little bit differently. This is generally not a big problem because
every DOM implementation out there provides some mechanism for both parsing
and *serializing*, or writing out XML files. The unfortunate result, however, is that

reading and writing XML will cause vendor-specific code to creep into any application you write.

TIP At the time of this writing, a new W3C document called "Document Object Model (DOM) Level 3 Content Models and Load and Save Specification" was in the working draft status. Once this specification reaches the recommendation status, DOM will provide a standard mechanism for reading and writing XML.

Since DOM does not specify a standard way to read XML data into memory, most DOM (if not all) implementations delegate this task to a dedicated parser. In the case of Java, SAX is the preferred parsing technology. Figure 1-3 illustrates the typical interaction between SAX parsers and DOM implementations.

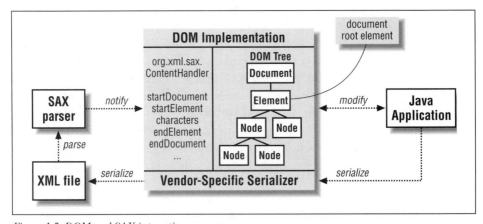

Figure 1-3. DOM and SAX interaction

Although it is important to understand how these pieces fit together, we will not go into detailed parsing syntax in this book. As we progress to more sophisticated topics, we will almost always be generating XML dynamically rather than parsing in static XML data files. For this reason, let's look at how DOM can be used to generate a new document from scratch. Example 1-3 contains XML for a personal library.

Example 1-3. library.xml

```
<?xml version="1.0" encoding="UTF-8"?>
<!DOCTYPE library SYSTEM "library.dtd">
<library>
  <!-- This is an XML comment -->
  <publisher id="oreilly">
    <name>O'Reilly</name>
    <street>101 Morris Street</street>
```

Example 1-3. library.xml (continued)

```
    <city>Sebastopol</city>
    <state>CA</state>
    <postal>95472</postal>
  </publisher>
  <book publisher="oreilly" isbn="1-56592-709-5">
    <edition>1</edition>
    <publicationDate mm="10" yy="1999"/>
    <title>XML Pocket Reference</title>
    <author>Robert Eckstein</author>
  </book>
  <book publisher="oreilly" isbn="0-596-00016-2">
    <edition>1</edition>
    <publicationDate mm="06" yy="2000"/>
    <title>Java and XML</title>
    <author>Brett McLaughlin</author>
  </book>
</library>
```

As shown in *library.xml*, a `<library>` consists of `<publisher>` elements and `<book>` elements. To generate this XML, we will use Java classes called `Library`, `Book`, and `Publisher`. These classes are not shown here, but they are really simple. For example, here is a portion of the Book class:

```
public class Book {
    private String author;
    private String title;
    ...

    public String getAuthor() {
        return this.author;
    }

    public String getTitle() {
        return this.title;
    }
    ...
}
```

Each of these three helper classes is merely used to hold data. The code that creates XML is encapsulated in a separate class called `LibraryDOMCreator`, which is shown in Example 1-4.

Example 1-4. XML generation using DOM

```
package chap1;

import java.io.*;
import java.util.*;
```

Example 1-4. XML generation using DOM (continued)

```java
import org.w3c.dom.Document;
import org.w3c.dom.Element;

/**
 * An example from Chapter 1. Creates the library XML file using the
 * DOM API.
 */
public class LibraryDOMCreator {

    /**
     * Create a new DOM org.w3c.dom.Document object from the specified
     * Library object.
     *
     * @param library an application defined class that
     * provides a list of publishers and books.
     * @return a new DOM document.
     */
    public Document createDocument(Library library)
            throws javax.xml.parsers.ParserConfigurationException {
        // Use Sun's Java API for XML Parsing to create the
        // DOM Document
        javax.xml.parsers.DocumentBuilderFactory dbf =
            javax.xml.parsers.DocumentBuilderFactory.newInstance();
        javax.xml.parsers.DocumentBuilder docBuilder =
            dbf.newDocumentBuilder();
        Document doc = docBuilder.newDocument();

        // NOTE: DOM does not provide a factory method for creating:
        //    <!DOCTYPE library SYSTEM "library.dtd">
        // Apache's Xerces provides the createDocumentType method
        // on their DocumentImpl class for doing this.  Not used here.

        // create the <library> document root element
        Element root = doc.createElement("library");
        doc.appendChild(root);

        // add <publisher> children to the <library> element
        Iterator publisherIter = library.getPublishers().iterator();
        while (publisherIter.hasNext()) {
            Publisher pub = (Publisher) publisherIter.next();
            Element pubElem = createPublisherElement(doc, pub);
            root.appendChild(pubElem);
        }

        // now add <book> children to the <library> element
        Iterator bookIter = library.getBooks().iterator();
        while (bookIter.hasNext()) {
            Book book = (Book) bookIter.next();
```

Example 1-4. XML generation using DOM (continued)

```
            Element bookElem = createBookElement(doc, book);
            root.appendChild(bookElem);
        }

        return doc;
    }

    private Element createPublisherElement(Document doc, Publisher pub) {
        Element pubElem = doc.createElement("publisher");

        // set id="oreilly" attribute
        pubElem.setAttribute("id", pub.getId());

        Element name = doc.createElement("name");
        name.appendChild(doc.createTextNode(pub.getName()));
        pubElem.appendChild(name);

        Element street = doc.createElement("street");
        street.appendChild(doc.createTextNode(pub.getStreet()));
        pubElem.appendChild(street);

        Element city = doc.createElement("city");
        city.appendChild(doc.createTextNode(pub.getCity()));
        pubElem.appendChild(city);

        Element state= doc.createElement("state");
        state.appendChild(doc.createTextNode(pub.getState()));
        pubElem.appendChild(state);

        Element postal = doc.createElement("postal");
        postal.appendChild(doc.createTextNode(pub.getPostal()));
        pubElem.appendChild(postal);

        return pubElem;
    }

    private Element createBookElement(Document doc, Book book) {
        Element bookElem = doc.createElement("book");

        bookElem.setAttribute("publisher", book.getPublisher().getId());
        bookElem.setAttribute("isbn", book.getISBN());

        Element edition = doc.createElement("edition");
        edition.appendChild(doc.createTextNode(
                Integer.toString(book.getEdition())));
        bookElem.appendChild(edition);

        Element publicationDate = doc.createElement("publicationDate");
```

Example 1-4. XML generation using DOM (continued)

```
        publicationDate.setAttribute("mm",
                Integer.toString(book.getPublicationMonth()));
        publicationDate.setAttribute("yy",
                Integer.toString(book.getPublicationYear()));
        bookElem.appendChild(publicationDate);

        Element title = doc.createElement("title");
        title.appendChild(doc.createTextNode(book.getTitle()));
        bookElem.appendChild(title);

        Element author = doc.createElement("author");
        author.appendChild(doc.createTextNode(book.getAuthor()));
        bookElem.appendChild(author);

        return bookElem;
    }

    public static void main(String[] args) throws IOException,
            javax.xml.parsers.ParserConfigurationException {
        Library lib = new Library();
        LibraryDOMCreator ldc = new LibraryDOMCreator();
        Document doc = ldc.createDocument(lib);

        // write the Document using Apache Xerces
        // output the Document with UTF-8 encoding; indent each line
        org.apache.xml.serialize.OutputFormat fmt =
            new org.apache.xml.serialize.OutputFormat(doc, "UTF-8", true);
        org.apache.xml.serialize.XMLSerializer serial =
            new org.apache.xml.serialize.XMLSerializer(System.out, fmt);
        serial.serialize(doc.getDocumentElement());
    }
}
```

This example starts with the usual series of `import` statements. Notice that `org.w3c.dom.*` is imported, but packages such as `org.apache.xml.serialize.*` are not. The code is written this way in order to make it obvious that many of the classes you will use are not part of the standard DOM API. These nonstandard classes all use fully qualified class and package names in the code. Although DOM itself is a W3C recommendation, many common tasks are not covered by the spec and can only be accomplished by reverting to vendor-specific code.

The workhorse of this class is the `createDocument` method, which takes a `Library` as a parameter and returns an `org.w3c.dom.Document` object. This method could throw a `ParserConfigurationException`, which indicates that Sun's Java API for XML Parsing (JAXP) could not locate an XML parser:

```
    public Document createDocument(Library library)
            throws javax.xml.parsers.ParserConfigurationException {
```

The Library class simply stores data representing a personal library of books. In a real application, the Library class might also be responsible for connecting to a back-end data source. This arrangement provides a clear separation between XML generation code and the underlying database. The sole purpose of LibraryDOMCreator is to crank out DOM trees, making it easy for one programmer to work on this class while another focuses on the implementation of Library, Book, and Publisher.

The next step is to begin constructing a DOM Document object:

```
javax.xml.parsers.DocumentBuilderFactory dbf =
    javax.xml.parsers.DocumentBuilderFactory.newInstance();
javax.xml.parsers.DocumentBuilder docBuilder =
    dbf.newDocumentBuilder();
Document doc = docBuilder.newDocument();
```

This code relies on JAXP because the standard DOM API does not provide any support for creating a new Document object in a standard way. Different parsers have their own proprietary way of doing this, which brings us to the whole point of JAXP: it encapsulates differences between various XML parsers, allowing Java programmers to use a consistent API regardless of which parser they use. As we will see in Chapter 5, JAXP 1.1 adds a consistent wrapper around various XSLT processors in addition to standard SAX and DOM parsers.

JAXP provides a DocumentBuilderFactory to construct a DocumentBuilder, which is then used to construct new Document objects. The Document class is a part of DOM, so most of the remaining code is defined by the DOM specification.

In DOM, new XML elements must always be created using factory methods, such as createElement(...), on an instance of Document. These elements must then be added to either the document itself or one of the elements within the document before they actually become part of the XML:

```
// create the <library> document root element
Element root = doc.createElement("library");
doc.appendChild(root);
```

At this point, the <library/> element is empty, but it has been added to the document. The code then proceeds to add all <publisher> children:

```
// add <publisher> children to the <library> element
Iterator publisherIter = library.getPublishers().iterator();
while (publisherIter.hasNext()) {
    Publisher pub = (Publisher) publisherIter.next();
    Element pubElem = createPublisherElement(doc, pub);
    root.appendChild(pubElem);
}
```

For each instance of Publisher, a <publisher> Element is created and then added to <library>. The createPublisherElement method is a private helper method that simply goes through the tedious DOM steps required to create each XML element. One thing that may not seem entirely obvious is the way that text is added to elements, such as O'Reilly in the <name>O'Reilly</name> tag:

```
Element name = doc.createElement("name");
name.appendChild(doc.createTextNode(pub.getName()));
pubElem.appendChild(name);
```

The first line is pretty obvious, simply creating an empty <name/> element. The next line then adds a new text node as a child of the name object rather than setting the value directly on the name. This is indicative of the way that DOM represents XML: any parsed character data is considered to be a child of a node, rather than part of the node itself. DOM uses the org.w3c.dom.Text interface, which extends from org.w3c.dom.Node, to represent text nodes. This is often a nuisance because it results in at least one extra line of code for each element you wish to generate.

The main() method in Example 1-4 creates a Library object, converts it into a DOM tree, then prints the XML text to System.out. Since the standard DOM API does not provide a standard way to convert a DOM tree to XML, we introduce Xerces specific code to convert the DOM tree to text form:

```
// write the document using Apache Xerces
// output the document with UTF-8 encoding; indent each line
org.apache.xml.serialize.OutputFormat fmt =
    new org.apache.xml.serialize.OutputFormat(doc, "UTF-8", true);
org.apache.xml.serialize.XMLSerializer serial =
    new org.apache.xml.serialize.XMLSerializer(System.out, fmt);
serial.serialize(doc.getDocumentElement());
```

As we will see in Chapter 5, JAXP 1.1 does provide a mechanism to perform this task using its transformation APIs, so we do not technically have to use the Xerces code listed here. The JAXP approach maximizes portability but introduces the overhead of an XSLT processor when all we really need is DOM.

JDOM

DOM is specified in the language independent Common Object Request Broker Architecture Interface Definition Language (CORBA IDL), allowing the same interfaces and concepts to be utilized by many different programming languages. Though valuable from a specification perspective, this approach does not take advantage of specific Java language features. JDOM is a Java-only API that can be used to create and modify XML documents in a more natural way. By taking advantage of Java features, JDOM aims to simplify some of the more tedious aspects of DOM programming.

JDOM is not a W3C specification, but is open source software* available at *http:// www.jdom.org*. JDOM is great from a programming perspective because it results in much cleaner, more maintainable code. Since JDOM has the ability to convert its data into a standard DOM tree, it integrates nicely with any other XML tool. JDOM can also utilize whatever XML parser you specify and can write out XML to any Java output stream or file. It even features a class called SAXOutputter that allows the JDOM data to be integrated with any tool that expects a series of SAX events.

The code in Example 1-5 shows how much easier JDOM is than DOM; it does the same thing as the DOM example, but is about fifty lines shorter. This difference would be greater for more complex applications.

Example 1-5. XML generation using JDOM

```
package com.oreilly.javaxslt.chap1;

import java.io.*;
import java.util.*;
import org.jdom.DocType;
import org.jdom.Document;
import org.jdom.Element;
import org.jdom.output.XMLOutputter;

/**
 * An example from Chapter 1. Creates the library XML file.
 */
public class LibraryJDOMCreator {

    public Document createDocument(Library library) {
        Element root = new Element("library");
        // JDOM supports the <!DOCTYPE...>
        DocType dt = new DocType("library", "library.dtd");
        Document doc = new Document(root, dt);

        // add <publisher> children to the <library> element
        Iterator publisherIter = library.getPublishers().iterator();
        while (publisherIter.hasNext()) {
            Publisher pub = (Publisher) publisherIter.next();
            Element pubElem = createPublisherElement(pub);
            root.addContent(pubElem);
        }
```

---

* Sun has accepted JDOM as Java Specification Request (JSR) 000102; see *http://java.sun.com/aboutJava/ communityprocess/*.

Example 1-5. XML generation using JDOM (continued)

```
        // now add <book> children to the <library> element
        Iterator bookIter = library.getBooks().iterator();
        while (bookIter.hasNext()) {
            Book book = (Book) bookIter.next();
            Element bookElem = createBookElement(book);
            root.addContent(bookElem);
        }

        return doc;
    }

    private Element createPublisherElement(Publisher pub) {
        Element pubElem = new Element("publisher");

        pubElem.addAttribute("id", pub.getId());
        pubElem.addContent(new Element("name").setText(pub.getName()));
        pubElem.addContent(new Element("street").setText(pub.getStreet()));
        pubElem.addContent(new Element("city").setText(pub.getCity()));
        pubElem.addContent(new Element("state").setText(pub.getState()));
        pubElem.addContent(new Element("postal").setText(pub.getPostal()));

        return pubElem;
    }

    private Element createBookElement(Book book) {
        Element bookElem = new Element("book");

        // add publisher="oreilly" and isbn="1234567" attributes
        // to the <book> element
        bookElem.addAttribute("publisher", book.getPublisher().getId())
                .addAttribute("isbn", book.getISBN());

        // now add an <edition> element to <book>
        bookElem.addContent(new Element("edition").setText(
                Integer.toString(book.getEdition())));

        Element pubDate = new Element("publicationDate");
        pubDate.addAttribute("mm",
                Integer.toString(book.getPublicationMonth()));
        pubDate.addAttribute("yy",
                Integer.toString(book.getPublicationYear()));
        bookElem.addContent(pubDate);

        bookElem.addContent(new Element("title").setText(book.getTitle()));
        bookElem.addContent(new Element("author").setText(book.getAuthor()));

        return bookElem;
    }
```

Example 1-5. XML generation using JDOM (continued)

```
public static void main(String[] args) throws IOException {
    Library lib = new Library();
    LibraryJDOMCreator ljc = new LibraryJDOMCreator();
    Document doc = ljc.createDocument(lib);

    // Write the XML to System.out, indent two spaces, include
    // newlines after each element
    new XMLOutputter("  ", true, "UTF-8").output(doc, System.out);
}
```

The JDOM example is structured just like the DOM example, beginning with a method that converts a Library object into a JDOM Document:

```
public Document createDocument(Library library) {
```

The most striking difference in this particular method is the way in which the Document and its Elements are created. In JDOM, you simply create Java objects to represent items in your XML data. This contrasts with the DOM approach, which relies on interfaces and factory methods. Creating the Document is also easy in JDOM:

```
Element root = new Element("library");
// JDOM supports the <!DOCTYPE...>
DocType dt = new DocType("library", "library.dtd");
Document doc = new Document(root, dt);
```

As this comment indicates, JDOM allows you to refer to a DTD, while DOM does not. This is just another odd limitation of DOM that forces you to include implementation-specific code in your Java applications. Another area where JDOM shines is in its ability to create new elements. Unlike DOM, text is set directly on the Element objects, which is more intuitive to Java programmers:

```
private Element createPublisherElement(Publisher pub) {
    Element pubElem = new Element("publisher");

    pubElem.addAttribute("id", pub.getId());
    pubElem.addContent(new Element("name").setText(pub.getName()));
    pubElem.addContent(new Element("street").setText(pub.getStreet()));
    pubElem.addContent(new Element("city").setText(pub.getCity()));
    pubElem.addContent(new Element("state").setText(pub.getState()));
    pubElem.addContent(new Element("postal").setText(pub.getPostal()));

    return pubElem;
}
```

Since methods such as addContent() and addAttribute() return a reference to the Element instance, the code shown here could have been written as one

long line. This is similar to `StringBuffer.append()`, which can also be
"chained" together:

```
buf.append("a").append("b").append("c");
```

In an effort to keep the JDOM code more readable, however, our example adds
one element per line.

The final piece of this pie is the ability to print out the contents of JDOM as an
XML file. JDOM includes a class called `XMLOutputter`, which allows us to generate the XML for a `Document` object in a single line of code:

```
new XMLOutputter("  ", true, "UTF-8").output(doc, System.out);
```

The three arguments to `XMLOutputter` indicate that it should use two spaces for
indentation, include linefeeds, and encode its output using UTF-8.

JDOM and DOM interoperability

Current XSLT processors are very flexible, generally supporting any of the following sources for XML or XSLT input:

*   a DOM tree or output from a SAX parser

*   any Java `InputStream` or `Reader`

*   a URI, file name, or `java.io.File` object

JDOM is not directly supported by some XSLT processors, although this is changing fast.* For this reason, it is typical to convert a JDOM `Document` instance to
some other format so it can be fed into an XSLT processor for transformation.
Fortunately, the JDOM package provides a class called `DOMOutputter` that can easily make the transformation:

```
org.jdom.output.DOMOutputter outputter =
        new org.jdom.output.DOMOutputter();
org.w3c.dom.Document domDoc = outputter.output(jdomDoc);
```

The DOM `Document` object can then be used with any of the XSLT processors or a
whole host of other XML libraries and tools. JDOM also includes a class that can
convert a `Document` into a series of SAX events and another that can send XML
data to an `OutputStream` or `Writer`. In time, it seems likely that tools will begin
offering native support for JDOM, making extra conversions unnecessary. The
details of all these techniques are covered in Chapter 5.

---

* As this book went to press, Version 6.4 of SAXON was released with beta support for transforming
  JDOM trees. Additionally, JDOM beta 7 introduces two new classes, `JDOMSource` and `JDOMResult`,
  that interoperate with any JAXP-compliant XSLT processor.

Beyond Dynamic Web Pages

You probably know a little bit about servlets already. Essentially, they are Java classes that run on the web tier, offering a high-performance, portable alternative to CGI scripts. Java servlets are great for extracting data from a database and then generating XHTML for the browser. They are also good for validating HTTP POST or GET requests from browsers, allowing people to fill out job applications or order books online. But more powerful techniques are required when you create web *applications* instead of simple web *sites*.

Web Development Challenges

When compared to GUI applications based on Swing or AWT, developing for the Web can be much more difficult. Most of the difficulties you will encounter can be traced to one of the following:

- Hypertext Transfer Protocol (HTTP)
- HTML limitations
- browser compatibility problems
- concurrency issues

HTTP is a fairly simple protocol that enables a client to communicate with a server. Web browsers almost always use HTTP to communicate with web servers, although they may use other protocols such as HTTPS for secure connections or even FTP for file downloads. HTTP is a request/response protocol, and the browser must initiate the request. Each time you click on a hyperlink, your browser issues a new request to a web server. The server processes the request and sends a response, thus finishing the exchange.

This request/response cycle is easy to understand but makes it tedious to develop an application that maintains *state information* as the user moves through a complex web application. For example, as a user adds items to a shopping cart, a servlet must store that data somewhere while waiting for the client to make another request. When that request arrives, the servlet has to associate the cart with that particular client, since the servlet could be dealing with hundreds or thousands of concurrent clients. Other than establishing a timeout period, the servlet has no idea when the client abandons the cart, deciding to shop on a competitor's site instead. The HTTP protocol makes it impossible for the server to initiate a conversation with the client, so the servlet cannot periodically ping the client as it can with a "normal" client/server application.

HTML itself can be another hindrance to web application development. It was not designed to compete with feature-rich GUI toolkits, yet customers are increasingly demanding that applications of all sorts become "web enabled." This presents a significant challenge because HTML offers only a small set of primitive GUI components. Sophisticated HTML generation is not the subject of this book, but we will see how to use XSLT to separate complex HTML generation code from underlying programming logic and servlet code. As HTML grows ever more complex, the benefits of a clean separation become increasingly obvious.

As you probably well know, browsers are not entirely compatible with one another. As a web application developer, this generally means that you have to test on a wide variety of platforms. XSLT offers support in this area because you can write reusable stylesheets for the consistent parts of HTML and import or include browser-specific stylesheet fragments to work around browser incompatibilities. Of course, the underlying XML data and programming logic is shared across all browsers, even though you may have multiple stylesheets.

Finally, we have the issue of concurrency. In the servlet model, a single servlet instance must handle multiple concurrent requests. Although you can explicitly synchronize access to a servlet, this often results in performance degradation as individual client requests queue up, waiting for their turn. Processing requests in parallel will be an important part of our XSLT-based servlet designs in later chapters.

Web Applications

The difference between a "web site" and a "web application" is subjective. Although some of the technologies are the same, web applications tend to be far more interactive and more difficult to create than typical web sites. For example, a web site is mostly read-only, with occasional forms for submitting information. For this, simple technologies such as HTML combined with JavaServer Pages (JSPs) can do the job. A web application, on the other hand, is typically a custom application intended to perform a specific business or technical function. They are often written as replacements for existing systems in an effort to enable browser-based access. When replacing existing systems, developers are typically asked to duplicate all of the existing functionality, using a web browser and HTML. This is difficult at best because of HTML's limited support for sophisticated GUI components. Most of the screens in a web application are dynamically generated and customized on a per-user basis, while many pages on a typical web site are static.

Java, XML, and XSLT are suitable for web applications because of the high degree of modularity they offer. While one programmer develops the back-end data access code, a graphic designer can be working on the HTML user interface. Yet another servlet expert can be working on the web tier, while someone else is defining and creating the XML data. Programmers and graphic designers will typically work together to define the XSLT stylesheets, although the current lack of interactive tools may make this more of a programming task.

Another reason XML is suitable for web applications is its unique ability to interoperate with back-end business systems and databases. Once an XML layer has been added to your data tier, the web tier can extract that data in XML form regardless of which operating system or hardware platform is used. XSLT can then convert that XML into HTML without a great deal of custom coding, resulting in less work for your development team.

Nonbrowser Clients

While web sites typically deliver HTML to browsers, web applications may be asked to interoperate with applications other than browsers. It is typical to provide feature-rich Swing GUI clients for use within a company, while remote workers access the system via an XHTML interface through a web browser. An XML approach is key in this environment because the raw XML can be sent to the Swing client, while XSLT can be used to generate the XHTML views from the same XML data.

If your XML is not in the correct format, XSLT can also be used to transform it into another variant of XML. For example, a client application may expect to see:

```
<name>Eric Burke</name>
```

But the XML data on the web tier deals with the data as:

```
<firstName>Eric</firstName><lastName>Burke</lastName>
```

In this case, XSLT can be used to transform the XML into the simplified format that the client expects.

SOAP

Sending raw XML data to clients is a good approach because it interoperates with any operating system, hardware platform, or programming language. Allowing Visual Basic clients to extract XML data from a web application allows existing client software to be salvaged while enabling remote access to enterprise data using a more portable solution such as Java. But defining a custom XML format is tedious because it requires you to manually write code that encodes and decodes messages between the client and the web application.

Simple Object Access Protocol (SOAP) is a standardized protocol for exchanging data using XML messages. SOAP was originally introduced by Microsoft but has been submitted to the W3C for standardization and is endorsed by many companies. SOAP is fairly simple, allowing vendors to quickly create tools that simplify data exchange between web applications and any type of client.

Since SOAP messages are implemented using XML, they can be created and updated using XSLT stylesheets. This means that data can be extracted from a relational database as XML, transformed with XSLT into a standard SOAP message, and then delivered to a client application written in any language. For more information on SOAP standardization efforts, visit *http://www.w3.org/TR/SOAP*.

Wireless

Cell phones, personal digital assistants (PDAs), and other handheld devices seem to be the next big thing. From a marketing perspective, it is not entirely clear how the business model of the Web will translate to the world of wireless. It is also unclear which technologies will be used for this new generation of devices. One currently popular technology is Wireless Application Protocol (WAP), which uses an XML markup language called Wireless Markup Language (WML) to render pages. Other languages have been proposed, such as Compact HTML (CHTML), but perhaps the most promising prospect is XHTML Basic. XHTML Basic is backed by the W3C and is primarily based on several XHTML modules. Its designers had the luxury of coming after WML, so they could incorporate many WML concepts and build on that experience.

Because of the uncertainties in the wireless arena, an XML and XSLT approach is the safest available today. Encoding your data in XML enables flexibility to support any markup language or protocol on the client, hopefully without rewriting major pieces of Java code. Instead, new XSLT stylesheets are written to support new devices and protocols. An added benefit of XSLT is its ability to support both traditional browser clients and newer wireless clients from the same underlying XML data and Java business logic.

Getting Started

The best way to get started with new technologies is to experiment. For example, if you do not know XSLT, you should experiment with plenty of stylesheets as you work through the next two chapters. Aside from trying out the examples that appear in this book, you may want to invent a simple XML data file that represents something of interest to you, such as your personal music collection or family tree. Using XSLT stylesheets, try to create web pages that show your data in many different formats.

Once the basics of XSLT are out of the way, servlets will be your next big challenge. Although the servlet API is not particularly difficult to learn, configuration and deployment issues can make it difficult to debug and test your applications. The best advice is to start small, writing a very basic application that proves your environment is configured correctly before moving on to more sophisticated examples. Apache's Tomcat is probably the best *servlet container* for beginners because it is free, easy to configure, and is the official reference implementation for Sun's servlet API. A servlet container is the server that runs servlets. Chapter 6 covers the essentials of the servlet API, but for all the details you will want to pick up a copy of *Java Servlet Programming* by Jason Hunter (O'Reilly). You definitely want to get the second edition because it covers the dramatic changes that were introduced in Version 2.2 of the servlet API.

Java XSLT Processor Choices

Although this book uses primarily Sun's JAXP and Apache's Xalan, many other XSLT processors are available. Processors based on other languages may offer much higher performance when invoked from the command line, primarily because they do not incur the overhead of a Java Virtual Machine (JVM) at application startup time. When using XSLT from a servlet, however, the JVM is already running, so startup time is no longer an issue. Pure Java processors are great for servlets because of the ease with which they can be embedded into the web application. Simply adding a JAR file to the CLASSPATH is generally all that must be done.

Putting an up-to-date list of XSLT processors into a book is futile because the market is maturing too fast. Some of the currently popular Java-based processors are listed here, but a quick web search for "XSLT Processors" would be prudent before you decide to standardize on a particular tool, as new processors are constantly appearing. We will see how to use Xalan in the next chapter; a few other choices are listed here.

XT

XT was one of the earliest XSLT processors, written by James Clark. If you read the XSLT specification, you may recognize him as the editor of the XSLT specification. As the XSLT specification evolved, XT followed a parallel path of evolution, making it a leader in terms of standards compliance. At the time of this writing, however, XT had not been updated as recently as some of the other Java-based processors. Version 19991105 of XT implements the W3C's proposed-recommendation (PR-xslt-19991008) version of XSLT and is available at *http://www. jclark.com/xml/xt.html.* Like the other processors listed here, XT is free.

LotusXSL

LotusXSL is a Java XSLT processor from IBM Alphaworks available at *http://www. alphaworks.ibm.com.* In November 1999 IBM donated LotusXSL to Apache, forming the basis for Xalan. LotusXSL continued to exist as a separate product. However, it is currently a thin wrapper around the Xalan processor. Future versions of

LotusXSL may add features above and beyond those offered by Xalan, but there doesn't seem to be a compelling reason to choose LotusXSL unless you are already using it.

SAXON

The SAXON XSLT processor from Michael Kay is available at *http://saxon. sourceforge.net*. SAXON is open source software in accordance with the Mozilla Public License and is a very popular alternative to Xalan. SAXON provides full support for the current XSLT specification and is very well documented. It also provides several value-added features such as the ability to output multiple result trees from the same transformation and update the values of variables within stylesheets.

To transform a document using SAXON, first include *saxon.jar* in your CLASS-PATH. Then type **java com.icl.saxon.StyleSheet -?** to list all available options. The basic syntax for transforming a stylesheet is as follows:

```
java com.icl.saxon.StyleSheet [options] source-doc style-doc [ params...]
```

To transform the *presidents.xml* file and send the results to standard output, type the following:

```
java com.icl.saxon.StyleSheet presidents.xml presidents.xslt
```

JAXP

Version 1.1 of Sun's Java API for XML Processing (JAXP) contains support for XSLT transformations, a notable omission from earlier versions of JAXP. It can be downloaded from *http://java.sun.com/xml*. Parsing XML and transforming XSLT are not the primary focus of JAXP. Instead, the key goal is to provide a standard Java interface to a wide variety of XML parsers and XSLT processors. Although JAXP does include reference implementations of XML parsers and an XSLT processor, its key benefit is the choice of tools afforded to Java developers. Vendor lock-in should be much less of an issue thanks to JAXP.

Since JAXP is primarily a Java-based API, we will cover its programmatic interfaces in depth as we talk about XSLT programming techniques in Chapter 5. JAXP currently includes Apache's Xalan as its default XSLT processor, so the Xalan instructions presented in Chapter 2 will also apply to JAXP.

Web Browser Support for XSLT

In a web application environment, performing XSLT transformations on the client instead of the server is valuable for a number of reasons. Most importantly, it reduces the workload on the server machine, allowing a greater number of clients to be served. Once a stylesheet is downloaded to the client, subsequent requests will presumably use a cached copy, therefore only the raw XML data will need to be transmitted with each request. This has the potential to greatly reduce bandwidth requirements.

Even more interesting tricks are possible when JavaScript is introduced into the equation. You can programmatically modify either the XML data or the XSLT stylesheet on the client side, reapply the stylesheet, and see the results immediately without requesting a new document from the server.

Microsoft introduced XSLT support into Version 5.0 of Internet Explorer, but the XSLT specification was not finalized at the time. Unfortunately, significant changes were made to XSLT before it was finally promoted to a W3C Recommendation, but IE had already shipped using the older version of the specification. Although Microsoft has done a good job updating its MSXML parser with full support for the final XSLT Recommendation, millions of users will probably stick to IE 5.0 or 5.5 for quite some time, making it very difficult to perform portable XSLT transformations on the client. For IE 5.0 or 5.5 users, the MSXML parser is available as a separate download from Microsoft. Once downloaded, installed, and configured using a separate program called *xmlinst*, the browser will be compliant with Version 1.0 of the XSLT recommendation. This is something that developers will want to do, but probably very few end users will have the technical skills to go through these steps.

At the time of this writing, Netscape had not introduced support for XSLT into its browsers. We hope this changes by the time this book is published. Although their implementation will be released much later than Microsoft's, it should be compliant with the latest XSLT Recommendation.

Yet another alternative is to utilize a browser plug-in that supports XSLT, although this approach is probably most effective within the confines of a corporation. In this environment, the browser can be controlled to a certain extent, allowing client-side transformations much sooner than possible on public web sites.

Because XSLT transformation on the client will likely be mired in browser compatibility issues for several years, the role of Java with respect to XSLT will continue to be important. One use will be to detect the browser using a Java servlet, and then deliver the appropriate stylesheet to the client only if a compliant browser is in use. Otherwise, the servlet will drive the transformation process by invoking the XSLT processor on the web server. Once we finish with XSLT syntax in the next two chapters, the role of Java and XSLT will be covered throughout the remainder of this book.

2

XSLT Part 1—The Basics

Extensible Stylesheet Language (XSL) is a specification from the World Wide Web Consortium (W3C) and is broken down into two complementary technologies: XSL Formatting Objects and XSL Transformations (XSLT). XSL Formatting Objects, a language for defining formatting such as fonts and page layout, is not covered in this book. XSLT, on the other hand, was primarily designed to transform a well-formed XML document into XSL Formatting Objects.

Even though XSLT was designed to support XSL Formatting Objects, it has emerged as the preferred technology for all sorts of transformations. Transformation from XML to HTML is the most common, but XSLT can also be used to transform well-formed XML into just about any text file format. This will give XML- and XSLT-based web sites a major leg up as wireless devices become more prevalent because XSLT can also be used to transform XML into Wireless Markup Language or some other stripped-down format that wireless devices will require.

XSLT Introduction

Why is transformation so important? XML provides a simple syntax for defining markup, but it is up to individuals and organizations to define specific markup languages. There is no guarantee that two organizations will use the exact same markup; in fact, you may struggle to agree on consistent formats within the same group or company. One group may use <employee>, while others may use <worker> or <associate>. In order to share data, the XML data has to be transformed into a common format. This is where XSLT shines—it eliminates the need to write custom computer programs to transform data. Instead, you simply create one or more XSLT stylesheets.

An XSLT processor is an application that applies an XSLT stylesheet to an XML data source. Instead of modifying the original XML data, the result of the transformation is copied into something called a *result tree*, which can be directed to a static file, sent directly to an output stream, or even piped into another XSLT processor for further transformations. Figure 2-1 illustrates the transformation process, showing how the XML input, XSLT stylesheet, XSLT processor, and result tree relate to one another.

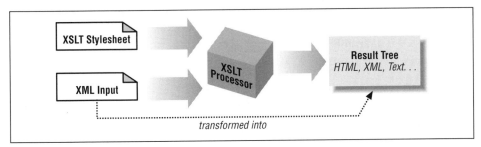

Figure 2-1. XSLT transformation

The XML input and XSLT stylesheet are normally two separate entities.* For the examples in this chapter, the XML will always reside in a text file. In future chapters, however, we will see how to improve performance by dealing with the XML as an in-memory object tree. This makes sense from a Java/XSLT perspective because most web applications will generate XML dynamically rather than deal with a series of static files. Since the XML data and XSLT stylesheet are clearly separated, it is very plausible to write several different stylesheets that convert the same XML into radically different formats.

XSLT transformation can occur on either the client or server, although server-side transformations are currently dominant. Since a vast majority of Internet users do not use XSLT-compliant browsers (at the time of this writing), the typical model is to transform XML into HTML on the web server so the browser sees only the resulting HTML. In a closed corporate environment where the browser feature set can be controlled, moving the XSLT transformation process to the browser can improve scalability and reduce network traffic.

It should be noted that XSLT stylesheets do not perform the same function as Cascading Style Sheets (CSS), which you may be familiar with. In the CSS model, style elements are applied to HTML or XML on the web browser, affecting formatting such as fonts and colors. CSS do not produce a separate result tree and cannot be applied in advance using a standalone processor as XSLT can. The CSS processing model operates on the underlying data in a top down fashion in a single pass,

---

* Section 2.7 of the XSLT specification covers embedded stylesheets.

while XSLT can iterate and perform conditional logic on the XML data. Although XSLT can produce style instructions, its true role is that of a transformation language rather than a style language. XSL Formatting Objects, on the other hand, is a style language that is much more comparable to CSS.

For wireless applications, HTML is not typically generated. Instead, Wireless Markup Language (WML) is the current standard for cell phones and other wireless devices. In the future, new standards such as XHTML Basic may be used. When using an XSLT approach, the same XML data can be transformed into many forms, all via different stylesheets. Regardless of how many stylesheets are used, the XML data will remain unchanged. A typical web site might have the following stylesheets for a single XML home page:

homeBasic.xslt
> For older web browsers

homeIE5.xslt
> Takes advantage of newer Internet Explorer features

homeMozilla.xslt
> Takes advantage of newer Netscape features

homeWML.xslt
> Transforms into Wireless Markup Language

homeB2B.xslt
> Transforms the XML into another XML format, suitable for "B2B-style" XML data feeds to customers

Schema evolution implies an upgrade to an existing data source where the structure of the data must be modified. When the data is stored in XML format, XSLT can be used to support schema evolution. For example, Version 1.0 of your application may store all of its files in XML format, but Version 2.0 might add new features that cannot be supported by the old 1.0 file format. A perfect solution is to write a single stylesheet to transform all of the old 1.0 XML files to the new 2.0 file format.

An XSLT Example

You need three components to perform XSLT transformations: an XML data source, an XSLT stylesheet, and an XSLT processor. The XSLT stylesheet is actually a well-formed XML document, so the XSLT processor will also include or use an XML parser. Apache's Xalan is used for most of the examples in this book; the previous chapter listed several other processors that you may want to investigate. You can download Xalan from *http://xml.apache.org*. It uses and includes Apache's Xerces parser, but can be configured to use other parsers. The ability to swap out parsers is important because this gives you the flexibility to use the latest innovations as competing (and perhaps faster) parsers are released.

Example 2-1 represents an early prototype of a discussion forum home page. The complete discussion forum application will be developed in Chapter 7. This is the raw XML data, without any formatting instructions or HTML. As you can see, the home page simply lists the message boards that the user can choose to view.

Example 2-1. discussionForumHome.xml

```
<?xml version="1.0" encoding="UTF-8"?>
<discussionForumHome>
  <messageBoard id="1" name="Java Programming"/>
  <messageBoard id="2" name="XML Programming"/>
  <messageBoard id="3" name="XSLT Questions"/>
</discussionForumHome>
```

It is assumed that this data will be generated dynamically as the result of a database query, rather than hardcoded as a static XML file. Regardless of its origin, the XML data says nothing about how to actually display the web page. For clarity, we will keep the XSLT stylesheet fairly simple at this point. The beauty of an XML/ XSLT approach is that you can beef up the stylesheet later on without compromising any of the underlying XML data structures. Even more importantly, the Java code that will generate the XML data does not have to be cluttered up with HTML and user interface logic; it just produces the basic XML data. Once the format of the data has been defined, a Java programmer can begin working on the database logic and XML generation code, while another team member begins writing the XSLT stylesheets.

Example 2-2 lists the XSLT stylesheet that produces the home page. Don't worry if not everything in this first example makes sense. XSLT is, after all, a completely new language. We will cover everything in detail throughout the remainder of this and the next chapter.

Example 2-2. discussionForumHome.xslt

```
<?xml version="1.0" encoding="UTF-8"?>
<xsl:stylesheet
    version="1.0"
    xmlns:xsl="http://www.w3.org/1999/XSL/Transform">
  <xsl:output method="html"/>

  <!-- match the document root -->
  <xsl:template match="/">
    <html>
      <head>
        <title>Discussion Forum Home Page</title>
```

Example 2-2. discussionForumHome.xslt (continued)

```
      </head>
      <body>
        <h1>Discussion Forum Home Page</h1>
        <h3>Please select a message board to view:</h3>
        <ul>
          <xsl:apply-templates select="discussionForumHome/messageBoard"/>
        </ul>
      </body>
    </html>
  </xsl:template>


  <!-- match a <messageBoard> element -->
  <xsl:template match="messageBoard">
    <li>
      <a href="viewForum?id={@id}">
        <xsl:value-of select="@name"/>
      </a>
    </li>
  </xsl:template>
</xsl:stylesheet>
```

TIP   The filename extension for XSLT stylesheets is irrelevant. In this
               book, .xslt is used. Many stylesheet authors prefer .xsl.

The first thing that should jump out immediately is the fact that the XSLT
stylesheet is also a well-formed XML document. Do not let the xsl: namespace
prefix fool you—everything in this document adheres to the same basic rules that
every other XML document must follow. Like other XML files, the first line of the
stylesheet is an XML declaration:

```
    <?xml version="1.0" encoding="UTF-8"?>
```

Unless you are dealing with internationalization issues, this will remain unchanged
for every stylesheet you write. This line is immediately followed by the document
root element, which contains the remainder of the stylesheet:

```
    <xsl:stylesheet
        version="1.0"
        xmlns:xsl="http://www.w3.org/1999/XSL/Transform">
```

The <xsl:stylesheet> element has two attributes in this case. The first,
version="1.0", specifies the version of the XSLT specification. Although this is
the current version at the time of this writing, the next version of the XSLT specification is well underway and may be finished by the time you read this. You can stay
abreast of the latest XSLT developments by visiting the W3C home page at *http://
www.w3.org*.

The next attribute declares the XML namespace, defining the meaning of the `xsl:` prefix you see on all of the XSLT elements. The prefix `xsl` is conventional, but could be anything you choose. This is useful if your document already uses the `xsl` prefix for other elements, and you do not want to introduce a naming conflict. This is really the entire point of namespaces: they help to avoid name conflicts. In XML, `<a:book>` and `<b:book>` can be discerned from one another because each book has a different namespace prefix. Since you pick the namespace prefix, this avoids the possibility that two vendors will use conflicting prefixes.

In the case of XSLT, the namespace prefix does not have to be `xsl`, but the value does have to be *http://www.w3.org/1999/XSL/Transform*. The value of a namespace is not necessarily a real web site, but the syntax is convenient because it helps ensure uniqueness. In the case of XSLT, 1999 represents the year that the URL was allocated for this purpose, and is not related to the version number. It is almost certain that future versions of XSLT will continue to use this same URL.

WARNING   Even the slightest typo in the namespace will render the stylesheet useless for most processors. The text must match *http://www.w3.org/1999/XSL/Transform* exactly, or your stylesheet will not be processed. Spelling or capitalization errors are a common mistake and should be the first thing you check when things are not working as you expect.

The next line of the stylesheet simply indicates that the result tree should be treated as an HTML document instead of an XML document:

```
<xsl:output method="html"/>
```

In Version 1.0 of XSLT, processors are not required to fully support this element. Xalan does, however, so we will include this in all of our stylesheets. Since the XSLT stylesheet itself must be written as well-formed XML, some HTML tags are difficult to include. Instead of writing `<hr>`, you must write `<hr/>` in your stylesheet. When the output method is html, processors such as Xalan will remove the slash (/) character from the result tree, which produces HTML that typical web browsers expect.

The remainder of our stylesheet consists of two *templates*. Each matches some pattern in the XML input document and is responsible for producing output to the result tree. The first template is repeated as follows:

```
<xsl:template match="/">
  <html>
    <head>
      <title>Discussion Forum Home Page</title>
    </head>
```

```
    <body>
      <h1>Discussion Forum Home Page</h1>
      <h3>Please select a message board to view:</h3>
      <ul>
        <xsl:apply-templates select="discussionForumHome/messageBoard"/>
      </ul>
    </body>
  </html>
</xsl:template>
```

When the XSLT processor begins its transformation process, it looks in your
stylesheet for a template that matches the "/" pattern. This pattern matches the
source XML document that is being transformed. You may recall from Chapter 1
that DOM uses the Document interface to represent the document, which is what
we are matching here. This is always the starting point for processing, so nearly
every stylesheet you write will contain a template similar to this one. Since this is
the first template to be instantiated, it is also where we create the framework for
the resulting HTML document. The second template, which matches the
"messageBoard" pattern, is currently ignored. This is because the processor is
only looking at the root of the XML document, and the <messageBoard> element is nested beneath the <discussionForumHome> element.

Most of the tags in this template do not start with <xsl:, so they are simply copied
to the result tree. In fact, the only dynamic content in this particular template is the
following line, which tells the processor to continue the transformation process:

```
    <xsl:apply-templates select="discussionForumHome/messageBoard"/>
```

Without this line, the transformation process would be complete because the "/"
pattern was already located and a corresponding template was instantiated. The
<xsl:apply-templates> element tells the XSLT processor to begin a new
search for elements in the source XML document that match the
"discussionForumHome/messageBoard" pattern and to instantiate an additional template that matches. As we will see shortly, the transformation process is
recursive and must be driven by XSLT elements such as <xsl:apply-
templates>. Simply including one or more <xsl:template> elements in a
stylesheet does not mean that they will be instantiated.

In this example, the <xsl:apply-templates> element tells the XSLT processor
to first select all <discussionForumHome> elements of the *current node*. The current node is "/", or the top of the document, so it only selects the
<discussionForumHome> element that occurs at the document's root level. If
another <discussionForumHome> element is deeply nested within the XML document, it will not be selected by this pattern. Assuming that the processor locates
the <discussionForumHome> element, it then searches for all of its
<messageBoard> children.

TIP   The select attribute in `<xsl:apply-templates>` does not have to
             be the same as the match attribute in `<xsl:template>`. Although
             the stylesheet presented in Example 2-2 could have specified `<xsl:`
             `template   match="discussionForumHome/messageBoard">` for
             the second template, this would limit the reusability of the template.
             Specifically, it could only be applied to `<messageBoard>` elements
             that occur as direct children of `<discussionForumHome>` elements.
             Since our template matches only `"messageBoard"`, it can be reused
             for `<messageBoard>` elements that appear anywhere in the XML
             document.

For each `<messageBoard>` child, the processor looks for the template in your
stylesheet that provides the best match. Since our stylesheet contains a template
that matches the `"messageBoard"` pattern exactly, it is instantiated for each of the
`<messageBoard>` elements. The job of this template is to produce a single HTML
list item tag for each `<messageBoard>` element:

```
<xsl:template match="messageBoard">
  <li>
    <a href="viewForum?id={@id}">
      <xsl:value-of select="@name"/>
    </a>
  </li>
</xsl:template>
```

As you can see, the list item must be properly terminated; HTML-style standalone
`<li>` tags are not allowed because they break the requirement that XSLT
stylesheets be well-formed XML. Terminating the element with `</li>` also works
with HTML, so this is the approach you must take. The hyperlink is a best guess at
this point in the design process because the servlet has not been defined yet.
Later, when we develop a servlet to actually process this web page, we will update
the link to point to the correct servlet.

In the stylesheet, @ is used to select the values of attributes. Curly braces (`{}`) are
known as an *attribute value template* and will be discussed in Chapter 3. If you look
back at Example 2-1, you will see that each message board has two attributes, id
and name:

```
<messageBoard id="1" name="Java Programming"/>
```

When the stylesheet processor is executed and the result tree generated, we end
up with the HTML shown in Example 2-3. The HTML is minimal at this point,
which is exactly what you want. Fancy changes to the page layout can be added
later; the important concept is that programmers can get started right away with
the underlying application logic because of the clean separation between data and
presentation that XML and XSLT provide.

Example 2-3. discussionForumHome.html

```html
<html>
  <head>
    <title>Discussion Forum Home Page</title>
  </head>
  <body>
    <h1>Discussion Forum Home Page</h1>
    <h3>Please select a message board to view:</h3>
    <ul>
      <li>
        <a href="viewForum?id=1">Java Programming</a>
      </li>
      <li>
        <a href="viewForum?id=2">XML Programming</a>
      </li>
      <li>
        <a href="viewForum?id=3">XSLT Questions</a>
      </li>
    </ul>
  </body>
</html>
```

Trying It Out

To try things out, download the examples for this book and locate
discussionForumHome.xml and *discussionForumHome.xslt*. They can be found in the
chap1 directory. If you would rather type in the examples, you can use any text editor or a dedicated XML editor such as Altova's XML Spy (*http://www.xmlspy.com*).
After downloading and unzipping the Xalan distribution from Apache, simply add
xalan.jar and *erces.jar* to your CLASSPATH. The transformation can then be initiated with the following command:

```
java org.apache.xalan.xslt.Process -IN discussionForumHome.xml -XSL
discussionForumHome.xslt
```

This will apply the stylesheet, sending the resulting HTML content to standard
output. Adding **-OUT** *filename* to the command will cause Xalan to send the
result tree directly to a file. To see the complete list of Xalan options, just type
java org.apache.xalan.xslt.Process. For example, the -TT option allows
you to see (trace) which templates are being called.

TIP   Xalan's -IN and -XSL parameters accept URLs as arguments rather
              than as file names. A simple filename will work if the files are in the
              current working directory, but you may need to use a full URL syn-
              tax, such as *file:///path/file.ext*, when the file is located elsewhere.

In Chapter 5, we will show how to invoke Xalan and other XSLT processors from Java code, which is far more efficient because a separate Java Virtual Machine (JVM) does not have to be invoked for each transformation. Although it can take several seconds to start the JVM, the actual XSLT transformations will usually occur in milliseconds.

Another option is to find a web browser that supports XSLT, which allows you to edit your stylesheet and hit the "Reload" button to view the transformation.

Transformation Process

Now that we have seen an example, let's back up and talk about some basics. In particular, it is important to understand the relationship between `<xsl:template match=...>` and `<xsl:apply-templates select=...>`. This should help to solidify your understanding of the previous example and lay the groundwork for more sophisticated processing. Although XSLT is a language, it is not intended to be a general-purpose programming language. Because of its specialized mission as a transformation language,* the design of XSLT works in the way that XML is structured, which is fundamentally a tree data structure.

XML Tree Data Structure

Every well-formed XML document forms a tree data structure. The document itself is always the root of the tree, and every element within the document has exactly one parent. Since the document itself is the root, it has no parent. As you learn XSLT, it can be helpful to draw pictures of your XML data that show its tree structure. Figure 2-2 illustrates the tree structure for *discussionForumHome.xml.*

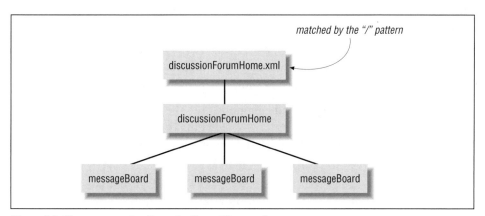

Figure 2-2. Tree structure for discussionForumHome.xml

---

* XSLT is declarative in nature, while mainstream programming languages tend to be more procedural.

The document itself is the root of the tree and may contain processing instructions, the document root element, and even comments. XSLT has the ability to select any of these items, although you will probably want to select elements and attributes when transforming to HTML. As mentioned earlier, the "/" pattern matches the document itself, which is the root node of the entire tree.

A tree data structure is fundamentally recursive because it consists of leaf nodes and smaller trees. Each of these smaller trees, in turn, also consist of leaf nodes and still smaller trees. Algorithms that deal with tree structures can almost always be expressed recursively, and XSLT is no exception. The processing model adopted by XSLT is explicitly designed to take advantage of the recursive nature of every well-formed XML document. This means that most stylesheets can be broken down into highly modular, easily understandable pieces, each of which processes a subset of the overall tree (i.e., a subtree).

Two important concepts in XSLT are the *current node* and *current node list*. The current node is comparable to the current working directory on a file system. The `<xsl:value-of select="."/>` element is similar to printing the name of the current working directory. The current node list is similar to the list of subdirectories. The key difference is that in XSLT, the current node appears in your source XML document. The current node list is a collection of nodes. As processing proceeds, the current node and current node list are constantly changing as you traverse the source tree, looking for patterns in the data.

Recursive Processing with Templates

Most transformation in XSLT is driven by two elements: `<xsl:template>` and `<xsl:apply-templates>`. In XSLT lingo, a node can represent anything that appears within your XML data. Nodes are typically elements such as `<message>` or element attributes such as `id="123"`. Nodes can also be XML processing instructions, text, or even comments. XSLT transformation begins with a current node list that contains a single entry: the root node. This is the XML document and is represented by the "/" pattern. Processing proceeds as follows:

- For each node "X" in the current node list, the processor searches for all `<xsl:template match="pattern">` elements in your stylesheet that potentially match that node. From this list of templates, the one with the *best match**
  is selected.

- The selected `<xsl:template match="pattern">` is instantiated using node "X" as its current node. This template typically copies data from the source

---

* See section 5.5 of the XSLT specification for conflict-resolution rules.

document to the result tree or produces brand new content in combination with data from the source.

- If the template contains `<xsl:apply-templates select="newPattern"/>`, a new current node list is created and the process repeats recursively. The `select` pattern is relative to node "X", rather than the document root.

As the XSLT transformation process continues, the current node and current node list are constantly changing. This is a good thing, since you do not want to constantly search for patterns beginning from the document root element. You are not limited to traversing down the tree, however; you can iterate over portions of the XML data many times or navigate back up through the document tree structure. This gives XSLT a huge advantage over CSS because CSS is limited to displaying the XML in the order in which it appears in the document.

Let's suppose that your source document contains the following XML:

```
<school>
  <name>SIUC</name>
  <city>Carbondale</city>
  <state>Illinois</state>
</school>
```

The following template could be used to match the `<school>` element and output its contents:

```
<xsl:template match="school">
  <b><xsl:value-of select="name"/> is located in
  <xsl:value-of select="city"/>, <xsl:value-of select="state"/>.</b>
</xsl:template>
```

The result will be something like:

```
<b>SIUC is located in Carbondale, Illinois.</b>
```

As you can see, elements that do not start with `xsl:` are simply copied to the result tree, as is plain text such as "is located in."* We do not show this here, but if you try the example you will see that whitespace characters (spaces, tabs, and linefeeds) are also copied to the result tree. When the destination is HTML, it is usually safe to ignore this issue because the browser will collapse that whitespace. If you view the actual source code of the generated HTML, it can look pretty ugly. An alternative to simply including "is located in" is to use:

```
<xsl:text> is located in </xsl:text>.
```

This provides explicit control over how whitespace and linefeeds are treated.

---

* Technically, elements that do not belong to the XSLT namespace are simply copied to the result tree; the namespace prefix might not be `xsl:`.

Comparing `<xsl:template>` to `<xsl:apply-templates>`

One way to understand the difference between `<xsl:template>` and `<xsl:apply-templates>` is to think about the difference between a Java method and the code that invokes the method. For example, a method in Java is declared as follows:

```
public void printMessageBoard(MessageBoard board) {
    // print information about the message board
}
```

In XSLT, the template plays a similar role:

```
<xsl:template match="messageBoard">
  <!-- print information about the message board -->
</xsl:template>
```

In order to invoke the Java method, use the following Java code:

```
someObject.printMessageBoard(currentBoard);
```

And in XSLT, use:

```
<xsl:apply-templates select="..."/>
```

to instantiate the template using the current `<messageBoard>` node.

While this is a good comparison to help illustrate the difference between `<xsl:template>` and `<xsl:apply-templates>`, it is important to remember that the XSLT model is not really a method call. Instead, `<xsl:apply-templates>` instructs the processor to scan through the XML document again, looking for nodes that match a pattern. If matching nodes are found, the best matching template is instantiated.

In the next chapter, we will see that XSLT also has `<xsl:call-template>`, which works similarly to a Java method call.

`<xsl:value-of>` copies the value of something in the XML source tree to the result tree. In this case, the current node is `<school>`, so `<xsl:value-of select="name"/>` selects the text content of the `<name>` element contained within `<school>`. This is the simplest usage of XPath, which will be introduced shortly. XPath is not limited to the current node, so it can also be used to locate elements in other parts of the source document. It can even select attributes, processing instructions, or anything else that can occur in XML.

Built-in Template Rules

All XSLT processors must include four built-in template rules that have lower precedence than any other rules, so they can be overridden by simply writing a new template rule that matches the same pattern. The best way to think about built-in rules is to assume they are always in the background, ready to be applied if no other rule is found that matches a node.

The first rule allows recursive processing to continue in case an explicit rule does not match the current node or the root node:

```
<xsl:template match="*|/">
  <xsl:apply-templates/>
</xsl:template>
```

This template matches all elements (*) and the root node (/), i.e., the document itself. It will not match processing instructions, comments, attributes, or text. The <xsl:apply-templates/> causes all children that are not attribute nodes or processing instruction nodes to be processed.

The second built-in rule is identical to the first, except it applies to each *mode* used in the stylesheet:

```
<xsl:template match="*|/" mode="m">
  <xsl:apply-templates mode="m"/>
</xsl:template>
```

Template modes are discussed in the next chapter, so we will not go into details here. The third built-in rule simply copies all text and attribute nodes to the result tree:

```
<xsl:template match="text()|@*">
  <xsl:value-of select="."/>
</xsl:template>
```

And finally, the built-in rule for processing instructions and comments does nothing. This is why comments and processing instructions in the input XML data do not automatically show up in the result tree:

```
<xsl:template match="processing-instruction()|comment()"/>
```

A Skeleton Stylesheet

As your XML documents get more complex, you will most likely want to break up your stylesheets into several templates. The starting point is a template that matches the "/" pattern:

```
<xsl:template match="/">
...content
</xsl:template>
```

This template matches the document itself and is usually where you output the basic <html>, <head>, and <body> elements. Somewhere within this template, you must tell the processor to continue searching for additional patterns, thus beginning the recursive transformation process. In a typical stylesheet, `<xsl:apply-templates>` is used for this purpose, instructing the processor to search for additional content in the XML data.

It should be stressed that this is not the only way to write a stylesheet, but it is a very natural way to handle the recursive nature of XML. Example 2-4 contains a skeleton XSLT stylesheet that you can use as a starting point for most of your projects.

Example 2-4. Skeleton stylesheet

```
<?xml version="1.0" encoding="UTF-8"?>
<xsl:stylesheet
    version="1.0"
    xmlns:xsl="http://www.w3.org/1999/XSL/Transform">
  <xsl:output method="html"/>
  <!--****************************************************************
      ** "/" template matches the document and is the starting point
      ****************************************************************-->
  <xsl:template match="/">
    <html>
      <head>
        <title>[title goes here]</title>
      </head>
      <body>
          <xsl:apply-templates select="[some XPath expression]"/>
      </body>
    </html>
  </xsl:template>
  <!--****************************************************************
      ** "[???]" template
      ****************************************************************-->
  <xsl:template match="???">
    [continue the process...]
    <xsl:apply-templates select="[another XPath expression]"/>
    [you can also include more content here...or even include
     multiple apply-templates...]
  </xsl:template>
</xsl:stylesheet>
```

Deciding how to modularize the stylesheet is a subjective process. One suggestion is to look for moderately sized chunks of XML data repeated numerous times throughout a document. For example, a `<customer>` element may contain a name, address, and phone number. Creating a template that matches `"customer"` is probably a good idea. You may even want to create another template for the `<name>` element, particularly if the name is broken down into subelements, or if the name is reused in other contexts such as `<employee>` and `<manager>`.

When you need to produce HTML tables or unordered lists in the result tree, two
templates (instead of one) can make the job very easy. The first template will produce the `<table>` or `<ul>` element, and the second will produce each table row
or list item. The following fragment illustrates this basic pattern:

```
<!-- the outer template produces the unordered list -->
<!-- (note: plural 'customers') -->
<xsl:template match="customers">
  <ul>
    <xsl:apply-templates select="customer"/>
  </ul>
</xsl:template>

<!-- the inner template is repeated for each customer -->
<xsl:template match="customer">
  <li><xsl:value-of select="name"/></li>
</xsl:template>
```

Another XSLT Example, Using XHTML

Example 2-5 contains XML data from an imaginary scheduling program. A schedule has an owner followed by a list of appointments. Each appointment has a date,
start time, end time, subject, location, and optional notes. Needless to say, a true
scheduling application probably has a lot more data, such as repeating appointments, alarms, categories, and many other bells and whistles. Assuming that the
scheduler stores its data in XML files, we can easily add features later by writing a
stylesheet to convert the existing XML files to some new format.

Example 2-5. schedule.xml

```
<?xml version="1.0" encoding="UTF-8"?>
<?xml-stylesheet type="text/xsl" href="schedule.xslt"?>
<schedule>
  <owner>
    <name>
      <first>Eric</first>
      <last>Burke</last>
    </name>
  </owner>
  <appointment>
    <when>
      <date month="03" day="15" year="2001"/>
      <startTime hour="09" minute="30"/>
      <endTime hour="10" minute="30"/>
    </when>
    <subject>Interview potential new hire</subject>
    <location>Rm 103</location>
    <note>Ask Bob for an updated resume.</note>
```

Example 2-5. schedule.xml (continued)

```
    </appointment>
    <appointment>
      <when>
        <date month="03" day="15" year="2001"/>
        <startTime hour="15" minute="30"/>
        <endTime hour="16" minute="30"/>
      </when>
      <subject>Dr. Appointment</subject>
      <location>1532 Main Street</location>
    </appointment>
    <appointment>
      <when>
        <date month="03" day="16" year="2001"/>
        <startTime hour="11" minute="30"/>
        <endTime hour="12" minute="30"/>
      </when>
      <subject>Lunch w/Boss</subject>
      <location>Pizza Place on First Capitol Drive</location>
    </appointment>
</schedule>
```

As you can see, the XML document uses both attributes (`month="03"`) and child elements to represent its data. XSLT has the ability to search for and transform both types of data, as well as comments, processing instructions, and text. In our current document, the appointments are stored in chronological order. Later, we will see how to change the sort order using `<xsl:sort>`.

Unlike the earlier example, the second line of Example 2-5 contains a reference to the XSLT stylesheet:

```
<?xml-stylesheet type="text/xsl" href="schedule.xslt"?>
```

This processing instruction is entirely optional. When viewing the XML document in a web browser that supports XSLT, this is the stylesheet that is used. If you apply the stylesheet from the command line or from a server-side process, however, you normally specify both the XML document and the XSLT document as parameters to the processor. Because of this capability, the processing instruction shown does not force that particular stylesheet to be used. From a development perspective, including this line quickly displays your work because you simply load the XML document into a compatible web browser, and the stylesheet is loaded automatically.

TIP   In this book, the `xml-stylesheet` processing instruction uses
             `type="text/xsl"`. However, some processors use `type="text/
             xml"`, which does not work with Microsoft Internet Explorer. The
             XSLT specification contains one example, which uses `"text/xml"`.

Figure 2-3 shows the XHTML output from an XSLT transformation of *schedule.xml*. As you can see, the stylesheet is capable of producing content that does not appear in the original XML data, such as `"Subject:"`. It can also selectively copy element content and attribute values from the XML source to the result tree; nothing requires every piece of data to be copied.

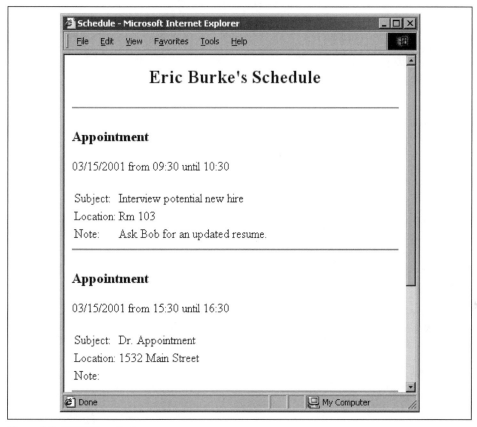

Figure 2-3. XHTML output

The XSLT stylesheet that produces this output is shown in Example 2-6. As mentioned previously, XSLT stylesheets must be well-formed XML documents. Once again, we use *.xslt* as the filename extension, but *.xsl* is also common. This stylesheet is based on the skeleton document presented in Example 2-4. However, it produces XHTML instead of HTML.

Example 2-6. schedule.xslt

```
<?xml version="1.0" encoding="UTF-8"?>
<xsl:stylesheet
    version="1.0"
    xmlns:xsl="http://www.w3.org/1999/XSL/Transform">
```

Example 2-6. schedule.xslt (continued)

```
<xsl:output method="xml"
    doctype-public="-//W3C//DTD XHTML 1.0 Transitional//EN"
    doctype-system="http://www.w3.org/TR/xhtml1/DTD/xhtml1-transitional.dtd"/>
<!--************************************************************
    ** "/" template
    ************************************************************-->
<xsl:template match="/">
  <html xmlns="http://www.w3.org/1999/xhtml">
    <head>
      <title>Schedule</title>
    </head>
    <body>
      <h2 align="center">
        <xsl:value-of select="schedule/owner/name/first"/>
        <xsl:text disable-output-escaping="yes"> </xsl:text>
        <xsl:value-of select="schedule/owner/name/last"/>'s Schedule</h2>
      <xsl:apply-templates select="schedule/appointment"/>
    </body>
  </html>
</xsl:template>
<!--************************************************************
    ** "appointment" template
    ************************************************************-->
<xsl:template match="appointment">
  <hr/>
  <h3>Appointment</h3>
  <xsl:apply-templates select="when"/>
  <table>
    <tr>
      <td>Subject:</td>
      <td>
        <xsl:value-of select="subject"/>
      </td>
    </tr>
    <tr>
      <td>Location:</td>
      <td>
        <xsl:value-of select="location"/>
      </td>
    </tr>
    <tr>
      <td>Note:</td>
      <td>
        <xsl:value-of select="note"/>
      </td>
    </tr>
  </table>
</xsl:template>
```

Example 2-6. schedule.xslt (continued)

```
  <!--*********************************************************
      ** "when" template
      *******************************************************-->
  <xsl:template match="when">
    <p>
      <xsl:value-of select="date/@month"/>
      <xsl:text>/</xsl:text>
      <xsl:value-of select="date/@day"/>
      <xsl:text>/</xsl:text>
      <xsl:value-of select="date/@year"/>
      from
      <xsl:value-of select="startTime/@hour"/>
      <xsl:text>:</xsl:text>
      <xsl:value-of select="startTime/@minute"/>
      until
      <xsl:value-of select="endTime/@hour"/>
      <xsl:text>:</xsl:text>
      <xsl:value-of select="endTime/@minute"/>
    </p>
  </xsl:template>
</xsl:stylesheet>
```

The first part of this stylesheet should look familiar. The first four lines are typical of just about any stylesheet you will write. Next, the output method is specified as xml because this stylesheet is producing XHTML instead of HTML:

```
<xsl:output method="xml"
    doctype-public="-//W3C//DTD XHTML 1.0 Transitional//EN"
    doctype-system="http://www.w3.org/TR/xhtml1/DTD/xhtml1-transitional.dtd"/>
```

The <xsl:output> element produces the following XHTML content:

```
<?xml version="1.0" encoding="UTF-16"?>
<!DOCTYPE html PUBLIC
  "-//W3C//DTD XHTML 1.0 Transitional//EN"
  "http://www.w3.org/TR/xhtml1/DTD/xhtml1-transitional.dtd">
```

Moving on, the first template in the stylesheet matches "/" and outputs the skeleton for the XHTML document. Another requirement for XHTML is the namespace attribute on the <html> element:

```
<html xmlns="http://www.w3.org/1999/xhtml">
```

The remainder of *schedule.xslt* consists of additional templates, each of which matches a particular pattern in the XML input.

The `<xsl:text>` element is used to insert additional text into the result tree.
Although plain text is allowed in XSLT stylesheets, the `<xsl:text>` element
allows more explicit control over whitespace handling. As shown here, a nonbreaking space is inserted into the result tree:

```
<xsl:text disable-output-escaping="yes"> </xsl:text>
```

Unfortunately, the following syntax does not work:

```
<!-- does not work... -->
<xsl:text> </xsl:text>
```

This is because ` ` is not one of the five built-in entities supported by XML.
Since XSLT stylesheets are always well-formed XML, the parser complains when
` ` is found in the stylesheet. Replacing the first ampersand character with
`&amp;` allows the XML parser to read the stylesheet into memory. The XML parser
interprets this entity and sends the following markup to the XSLT processor:

```
<!-- this is what the XSLT processor sees, after the XML parser
     interprets the &amp; entity -->
<xsl:text disable-output-escaping="yes"> </xsl:text>
```

The second piece of this solution is the `disable-output-escaping="yes"`
attribute. Without this attribute the XSLT processor may attempt to escape the
nonbreaking space by converting it into an actual character. This causes many web
browsers to display question marks because they cannot interpret the character.
Disabling output escaping tells the XSLT processor to pass ` ` to the result
tree. Web browsers then interpret and display the nonbreaking space properly.

In the final template shown in Example 2-6, you may notice the element `<xsl:
value-of select="date/@month"/>`. The @ character represents an attribute,
so in this case the stylesheet is outputting the value of the month attribute on the
date element. For this element:

```
<date month="03" day="15" year="2001"/>,
```

the value `"03"` is copied to the result tree.

XPath Basics

XPath is another recommendation from the W3C and is designed for use by XSLT and another technology called XPointer. The primary goal of XPath is to define a mechanism for addressing portions of an XML document, which means it is used for locating element nodes, attribute nodes, text nodes, and anything else that can occur in an XML document. XPath treats these nodes as part of a tree structure rather than dealing with XML as a text string. XSLT also relies on the tree structure that XPath defines. In addition to addressing, XPath contains a set of functions to format text, convert to and from numbers, and deal with booleans.

Unlike XSLT, XPath itself is not expressed using XML syntax. A simplified syntax makes sense when you consider that XPath is most commonly used inside of attribute values within other XML documents. XPath includes both a verbose syntax and a set of abbreviations, which end up looking a lot like path names on a file system or web site.

How XSLT Uses XPath

XSLT uses XPath in three basic ways:

- To select and match patterns in the original XML data. Using XPath in this manner is the focus of this chapter. You see this most often in `<xsl:template match="pattern">` and `<xsl:apply-templates select="node-set-expression"/>`. In either case, XPath syntax is used to locate various types of nodes.

- To support conditional processing. We will see the exact syntax of `<xsl:if>` and `<xsl:choose>` in the next chapter, both of which rely on XPath's ability to represent boolean values of `true` and `false`.

- To generate text. A number of string formatting instructions are provided, giving you the ability to concatenate strings, manipulate substrings, and convert from other data types to strings. Again, this will be covered in the next chapter.

Axes

Whenever XSLT uses XPath, something in the XML data is considered to be the current context node. XPath defines seven different types of nodes, each representing a different part of the XML data. These are the document root, elements, text, attributes, processing instructions, comments, and nodes representing namespaces. An axis represents a relationship to the current context node, which may be any one of the preceding seven items.

A few examples should clear things up. One axis is `child`, representing all immediate children of the context node. From our earlier *schedule.xml* example, the
`child` axis of `<name>` includes the `<first>` and `<last>` elements. Another axis is
`parent`, which represents the immediate parent of the context node. In many
cases the axis is empty. For example, the document root node has no `parent` axis.
Figure 2-4 illustrates some of the other axes.

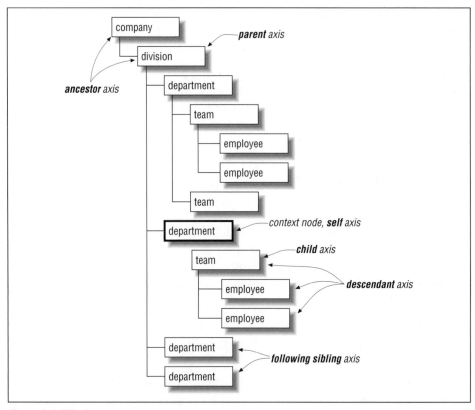

Figure 2-4. XPath axes

As you can see, the second `<department>` element is the context node. The diagram illustrates how some of the more common axes relate to this node. Although
the names are singular, in most cases the axes represent node sets rather than
individual nodes. The code:

```
<xsl:apply-templates select="child::team"/>
```

selects all `<team>` children, not just the first one. Table 2-1 lists the available axes
in alphabetical order, along with a brief description of each.

Table 2-1. Axes summary

Axis name	Description
ancestor	The parent of the context node, its parent, and so on until the root node is reached. The ancestor of the root is an empty node set.
ancestor-or-self	The same as ancestor, with the addition of the context node. The root node is always included.
attribute	All attributes of the context node.
child	All immediate children of the context node. Attributes and namespace nodes are not included.
descendant	All children, grandchildren, and so forth. Attribute and namespace nodes are not considered descendants of element nodes.
descendant-or-self	Same as descendant, with the addition of the context node.
following	All elements in the document that occur after the context node. Descendants of the context node are not included.
following-sibling	All following nodes in the document that have the same parent as the context node.
namespace	The namespace nodes of the context node.
parent	The immediate parent of the context node, if a parent exists.
preceding	All nodes in the document that occur before the context node, except for ancestors, attribute nodes, and namespace nodes.
preceding-sibling	All nodes in the document that occur before the context node and have the same parent. This axis is empty if the context node is an attribute node or a namespace node.
self	The context node itself.

Location Steps

As you may have guessed, an axis alone is only a piece of the puzzle. A *location step* is a more complex construct used by XPath and XSLT to select a node set from the XML data. Location steps have the following syntax:

```
axis::node-test[predicate-1]...[predicate-n]
```

The axis and node-test are separated by double colons and are followed by zero or more predicates. As mentioned, the job of the axis is to specify the relationship between the context node and the node-test. The node-test allows you to specify the type of node that will be selected, and the predicates filter the resulting node set.

Once again, discussion of XSLT and XPath tends to sound overly technical until you see a few basic examples. Let's start with a basic fragment of XML:

```
<message>
  <header> <!-- the context node -->
    <subject>Hello, World</subject>
    <date mm="03" dd="01" yy="2002"/>
    <sender>pres@whitehouse.gov</sender>
    <recipient>burke_e@ociweb.com</recipient>
    <recipient>burke_e@yahoo.com</recipient>
    <recipient>aidan@burke.com</recipient>
  </header>
  <body>
    ...
  </body>
</message>
```

If the <header> is the context node, then `child::subject` will select the <subject> node, `child::recipient` will select the set of all <recipient> nodes, and `child::*` will select all children of <header>. The asterisk (*) character is a wildcard that represents all nodes of the *principal node type*. Each axis has a principal node type, which is always `element` unless the axis is `attribute` or `namespace`. If <date> is the context node, then `attribute::yy` will select the `yy` attribute, and `attribute::*` will select all attributes of the <date> element.

Without any predicates, a location step can result in zero or more nodes. Adding a predicate simply filters the resulting node set, generally reducing the size of the resulting node set. Adding additional predicates applies additional filters. For example, `child::recipient[position()=1]` will initially select all <recipient> elements from the previous example then filter (reduce) the list down to the first one: `burke_e@ociweb.com`. Positions start at 1, rather than 0. As Example 2-8 will show, predicates can contain any XPath expression and can become quite sophisticated.

Location Paths

Location paths consist of one or more location steps, separated by slash (/) characters. An absolute location path begins with the slash (/) character and is relative to the document root. All other types of location paths are relative to the context node. Paths are evaluated from left to right, just like a path in a file system or a web site. The XML shown in Example 2-7 is a portion of a larger file containing basic information about U.S. presidents. This is used to demonstrate a few more XSLT and XPath examples.

Example 2-7. presidents.xml

```
<?xml version="1.0" encoding="UTF-8"?>
<?xml-stylesheet type="text/xsl" href="xpathExamples.xslt"?>
<presidents>
  <president>
    <term from="1789" to="1797"/>
    <name>
      <first>George</first>
      <last>Washington</last>
    </name>
    <party>Federalist</party>
    <vicePresident>
      <name>
        <first>John</first>
        <last>Adams</last>
      </name>
    </vicePresident>
  </president>
  <president>
    <term from="1797" to="1801"/>
    <name>
      <first>John</first>
      <last>Adams</last>
    </name>
    <party>Federalist</party>
    <vicePresident>
      <name>
        <first>Thomas</first>
        <last>Jefferson</last>
      </name>
    </vicePresident>
  </president>
    /**
    * remaining presidents omitted
    */
```

The complete file is too long to list here but is included with the downloadable files for this book. The `<vicePresident>` element can occur many times or not at all because some presidents did not have vice presidents. Names can also contain optional `<middle>` elements. Using this XML data, the XSLT stylesheet in Example 2-8 shows several location paths.

Example 2-8. Location paths

```
<?xml version="1.0" encoding="UTF-8"?>
<xsl:stylesheet version="1.0" xmlns:xsl="http://www.w3.org/1999/XSL/Transform">
  <xsl:output method="html" />
  <xsl:template match="/">
```

Example 2-8. Location paths (continued)

```
<html>
<body>
<h1>XPath Examples</h1>

The third president was:
<ul>
  <xsl:apply-templates select="presidents/president[position() = 3]/name"/>
</ul>

Presidents without vice presidents were:
<ul>
  <xsl:apply-templates
      select="presidents/president[count(vicePresident) = 0]/name"/>
</ul>

Presidents elected before 1800 were:
<ul>
  <xsl:apply-templates
      select="presidents/president[term/@from &lt; 1800]/name"/>
</ul>

Presidents with more than one vice president were:
<ul>
  <xsl:apply-templates
      select="descendant::president[count(vicePresident) > 1]/name"/>
</ul>

Presidents named John were:
<ul>
  <xsl:apply-templates
      select="presidents/president/name[child::first='John']"/>
</ul>

Presidents elected between 1800 and 1850 were:
<ul>
  <xsl:apply-templates
      select="presidents/president[(term/@from > 1800) and
              (term/@from &lt; 1850)]/name"/>
</ul>

</body>
</html>
</xsl:template>


<xsl:template match="name">
  <li>
    <xsl:value-of select="first"/>
```

Example 2-8. Location paths (continued)

```
      <xsl:text> </xsl:text>
      <xsl:value-of select="middle"/>
      <xsl:text> </xsl:text>
      <xsl:value-of select="last"/>
    </li>
  </xsl:template>
</xsl:stylesheet>
```

In the first `<xsl:apply-templates>` element, the location path is as follows:

```
presidents/president[position() = 3]/name
```

This path consists of three location steps separated by slash (/) characters, but the final step is what we want to select. This path is read from left to right, so it first selects the `<presidents>` children of the current context. The next step is relative to the `<presidents>` context and selects all `<president>` children. It then filters the list according to the predicate. The third `<president>` element is now the context, and its `<name>` children are selected. Since each president has only one `<name>`, the template that matches `"name"` is instantiated only once.

This location path shows how to perform basic numeric comparisons:

```
presidents/president[term/@from &lt; 1800]/name
```

Since the less-than (<) character cannot appear in an XML attribute value, the `&lt;` entity must be substituted. In this particular example, we use the @ abbreviated syntax to represent the attribute axis.

Abbreviated Syntax

Using `descendant::`, `child::`, `parent::`, and other axes is very verbose, requiring a lot of typing. Fortunately, XPath supports an abbreviated syntax for many of these axes that requires a lot less effort. The abbreviated syntax has the added advantage in that it looks like you are navigating the file system, so it tends to be somewhat more intuitive. Table 2-2 compares the abbreviated syntax to the verbose syntax. The abbreviated syntax is almost always used and will be used throughout the remainder of this book.

Table 2-2. Abbreviated syntax

Abbreviation	Axis
//	descendant
.	self
..	parent
@	attribute
	child

In the last row, the abbreviation for the child axis is blank, indicating that `child::` is an implicit part of a location step. This means that `vicePresident/name` is equivalent to `child::vicePresident/child::name`. Additional explanations follow:

- `vicePresident` selects the `vicePresident` children of the context node.

- `vicePresident/name` selects all `name` children of `vicePresident` children of the context node.

- `//name` selects all `name` descendants of the context node.

- `.` selects the context node.

- `../term/@from` selects the `from` attribute of `term` children of the context node's parent.

Looping and Sorting

As shown throughout this chapter, you can use `<xsl:apply-templates ...>` to search for patterns in an XML document. This type of processing is sometimes referred to as a "data driven" approach because the data of the XML file drives the selection process. Another style of XSLT programming is called "template driven," which means that the template's code tends to drive the selection process.

Looping with `<xsl:for-each>`

Sometimes it is convenient to explicitly drive the selection process with an `<xsl:for-each>` element, which is reminiscent of traditional programming techniques. In this approach, you explicitly loop over a collection of nodes without instantiating a separate template as `<xsl:apply-templates>` does. The syntax for `<xsl:for-each>` is as follows:

```
<xsl:for-each select="president">
  ...content for each president element
</xsl:for-each>
```

The `select` attribute can contain any XPath location path, and the loop will iterate over each element in the resulting node set. In this example, the context is `<president>` for all content within the loop. Nested loops are possible and could be used to loop over the list of `<vicePresident>` elements.

Sorting

Sorting can be applied in either a data-driven or template-driven approach. In either case, `<xsl:sort>` is added as a child element to something else. By adding several consecutive `<xsl:sort>` elements, you can accomplish multifield sorting.

Each sort can be in ascending or descending order, and the data type for sorting is either `"number"` or `"text"`. The sort order defaults to ascending. Some examples of <xsl:sort> include:

```
<xsl:sort select="first"/>
<xsl:sort select="last" order="descending"/>
<xsl:sort select="term/@from" order="descending" data-type="number"/>
<xsl:sort select="name/first" data-type="text" case-order="upper-first"/>
```

In the last line, the `case-order` attribute specifies that uppercase letters should be alphabetized before lowercase letters. The other accepted value for this attribute is `lower-first`. According to the specification, the default behavior is "language dependent."

Looping and Sorting Examples

The easiest way to learn about looping and sorting is to play around with a lot of small examples. The code in Example 2-9 applies numerous different looping and sorting strategies to our list of presidents. Comments in the code indicate what is happening at each step.

Example 2-9. Looping and sorting

```
<?xml version="1.0" encoding="UTF-8"?>
<xsl:stylesheet version="1.0"
      xmlns:xsl="http://www.w3.org/1999/XSL/Transform">
  <xsl:output method="html"/>
  <xsl:template match="/">
    <html>
      <body>
        <h1>Sorting Examples</h1>
        <xsl:apply-templates select="presidents"/>
      </body>
    </html>
  </xsl:template>
  <!--*****************************************************************
      ** presidents template
      *****************************************************************-->
  <xsl:template match="presidents">
    <!--*****************************************************************
        ** Sorting using xsl:for-each
        *****************************************************************-->
    <h2>All presidents sorted by first name using xsl:for-each</h2>
    <xsl:for-each select="president">
      <xsl:sort select="name/first"/>
      <xsl:apply-templates select="name"/>
    </xsl:for-each>
```

Example 2-9. Looping and sorting (continued)

```
<!--**************************************************************
     ** Sorting using xsl:apply-templates
     **************************************************************-->
<h2>All presidents sorted by first name using xsl:apply-templates</h2>
<xsl:apply-templates select="president/name">
  <xsl:sort select="first"/>
</xsl:apply-templates>
<h2>All presidents sorted by date using xsl:apply-templates</h2>
<xsl:apply-templates select="president/name">
  <xsl:sort select="../term/@from" data-type="number" order="descending"/>
</xsl:apply-templates>
<!--**************************************************************
     ** Multi-field sorting
     **************************************************************-->
<h2>Multi-field sorting example</h2>
<xsl:apply-templates select="president/name">
  <xsl:sort select="last"/>
  <xsl:sort select="first" order="descending"/>
</xsl:apply-templates>
<!--**************************************************************
     ** Nested xsl:for-each loops
     **************************************************************-->
<h2>All presidents and vice presidents using xsl:for-each</h2>
<ul>
  <xsl:for-each select="president">
    <xsl:sort select="name/first" order="descending"/>
    <li>
      <xsl:apply-templates select="name"/>
    </li>
    <ul>
      <xsl:for-each select="vicePresident">
        <xsl:sort select="name/first"/>
        <li>
          <xsl:apply-templates select="name"/>
        </li>
      </xsl:for-each>
    </ul>
  </xsl:for-each>
</ul>
<!--**************************************************************
     ** Same as previous, only using xsl:apply-templates
     **************************************************************-->
<h2>All presidents and vice presidents using xsl:apply-templates</h2>
<ul>
  <xsl:apply-templates select="president">
    <xsl:sort select="name/first" order="descending"/>
  </xsl:apply-templates>
</ul>
```

Example 2-9. Looping and sorting (continued)

```
    </xsl:template>
    <!--*****************************************************************
        ** 'president' template, outputs the president's name and vice
        **                 president's name.
        *****************************************************************-->
    <xsl:template match="president">
      <li>
        <xsl:apply-templates select="name"/>
      </li>
      <ul>
        <xsl:for-each select="vicePresident">
          <xsl:sort select="name/first"/>
          <li>
            <xsl:apply-templates select="name"/>
          </li>
        </xsl:for-each>
      </ul>
    </xsl:template>
    <!--*****************************************************************
        ** name template, outputs first, middle, and last name
        *****************************************************************-->
    <xsl:template match="name">
      <xsl:text disable-output-escaping="yes"> </xsl:text>
      <xsl:value-of select="first"/>
      <xsl:text disable-output-escaping="yes"> </xsl:text>
      <xsl:value-of select="middle"/>
      <xsl:text disable-output-escaping="yes"> </xsl:text>
      <xsl:value-of select="last"/>
      <br/>
    </xsl:template>
</xsl:stylesheet>
```

Notice that when applying a sort to `<xsl:apply-templates>`, that element can
no longer be an empty element. Instead, one or more `<xsl:sort>` elements are
added as children of `<xsl:apply-templates>`. You should also note that sorting
cannot occur in the `<xsl:template match="name">` element. The reason for
this is simple: at the `<xsl:apply-templates>` end, you have a list of nodes to
sort. By the time the processing reaches `<xsl:template match="name">`, the
search has narrowed down to a single `<name>`, so there is no node list left to sort.

Outputting Dynamic Attributes

Let's assume we have an XML document that lists books in a personal library, and
we want to create an HTML document with links to these books on *Amazon.com*. In
order to generate the hyperlink, the href attribute must contain the ISBN of the

book, which can be found in our original XML data. An example of the URL we would like to generate is as follows:

```
<a href="http://www.amazon.com/exec/obidos/ASIN/0596000162">Java and XML</a>
```

One thought is to include `<xsl:value-of select="isbn"/>` directly inside of the attribute. However, XML does not allow you to insert the less-than (<) character inside of an attribute value:

```
<!-- won't work... -->
<a href="<xsl:value-of select="isbn"/>">Java and XML</a>
```

We also need to consider that the attribute value is dynamic rather than static. XSLT does not automatically recognize content of the `href="..."` attribute as an XPath expression, since the `<a>` tag is not part of XSLT. There are two possible solutions to this problem.

<xsl:attribute>

In the first approach, `<xsl:attribute>` is used to add one or more attributes to elements. In the following template, an `href` attribute is added to an `<a>` element:

```
<xsl:template match="book">
  <li>
    <a> <!-- the href attribute is generated below -->
      <xsl:attribute name="href">
        <xsl:text>http://www.amazon.com/exec/obidos/ASIN/</xsl:text>
        <xsl:value-of select="@isbn"/>
      </xsl:attribute>
      <xsl:value-of select="title"/>
    </a>
  </li>
</xsl:template>
```

The `<li>` tag is used because this is part of a larger stylesheet that presents a bulleted list of links to each book. The `<a>` tag, as you can see, is missing its `href` attribute. The `<xsl:attribute>` element adds the missing `href`. Any child content of `<xsl:attribute>` is added to the attribute value. Because we do not want to introduce any unnecessary whitespace, `<xsl:text>` is used. Finally, `<xsl:value-of>` is used to select the `isbn` attribute.

Attribute Value Templates

Using `<xsl:attribute>` can be quite complex for a simple attribute value. Fortunately, XSLT provides a much simpler syntax called attribute value templates (AVT). The next example uses an AVT to achieve the identical result:

```
<xsl:template match="book">
  <li>
```

```
        <a href="http://www.amazon.com/exec/obidos/ASIN/{@isbn}">
          <xsl:value-of select="title"/>
        </a>
      </li>
    </xsl:template>
```

The curly braces ({}) inside of the attribute value cause the magic to happen. Normally, when the stylesheet encounters attribute values for HTML elements, it treats them as static text. The braces tell the processor to treat a portion of the attribute dynamically.

In the case of {@isbn}, the contents of the curly braces is treated exactly as <xsl:value-of select="@isbn"/> in the previous approach. This is obviously much simpler. The text inside of the {} characters can be any location path, so you are not limited to selecting attributes. For example, to select the title of the book, simply change the value to {title}.

So where do you use AVTs and where don't you? Well, whenever you need to treat an attribute value as an XPath expression rather than static text, you may need to use an AVT. But for standard XSLT elements, such as <xsl:template match="pattern">, you don't need to use the AVT syntax. For nonXSLT elements, such as any HTML tag, AVT syntax is required.

<xsl:attribute-set>

There are times when you may want to define a group of attributes that can be reused. For this task, XSLT provides the <xsl:attribute-set> element. Using this element allows you to define a named group of attributes that can be referenced from other points in a stylesheet. The following stylesheet fragment shows how to define an attribute set:

```
<xsl:attribute-set name="body-style">
  <xsl:attribute name="bgcolor">yellow</xsl:attribute>
  <xsl:attribute name="text">green</xsl:attribute>
  <xsl:attribute name="link">navy</xsl:attribute>
  <xsl:attribute name="vlink">red</xsl:attribute>
</xsl:attribute-set>
```

This is a "top level element," which means that it can occur as a direct child of the <xsl:stylesheet> element. The definition of an attribute set does not have to come before templates that use it. The attribute set can be referenced from another <xsl:attribute-set>, from <xsl:element>, or from <xsl:copy> elements. We will talk about <xsl:copy> in the next chapter, but here is how <xsl:element> is used:

```
<xsl:template match="/">
  <html>
```

```
    <head>
      <title>Demo of attribute-set</title>
    </head>
    <xsl:element name="body" use-attribute-sets="body-style">
      <h1>Books in my library...</h1>
      <ul>
        <xsl:apply-templates select="library/book"/>
      </ul>
    </xsl:element>
  </html>
</xsl:template>
```

As you can probably guess, the code shown here will output an HTML body tag that looks like this:

```
<body bgcolor="yellow" text="green" link="navy" vlink="red">
...body content
</body>
```

In this particular example, the <xsl:attribute-set> was used only once, so its value is minimal. It is possible for one stylesheet to include another, however, as we will see in the next chapter. In this way, you can define the <xsl:attribute-set> in a fragment of XSLT included in many other stylesheets. Changes to the shared fragment are immediately reflected in all of your other stylesheets.

3

XSLT Part 2—
Beyond the Basics

As you may have guessed, this chapter is a continuation of the material presented in the previous chapter. The basic syntax of XSLT should make sense by now. If not, it is probably a good idea to sit down and write a few stylesheets to gain some basic familiarity with the technology. What we have seen so far covers the basic mechanics of XSLT but does not take full advantage of the programming capabilities this language has to offer. In particular, this chapter will show how to write more reusable, modular code through features such as named templates, parameters, and variables.

The chapter concludes with a real-world example that uses XSLT to produce HTML documentation for Ant build files. Ant is a Java build tool that uses XML files instead of *Makefiles* to drive the compilation process. Since XML is used, XSLT is a natural choice for producing documentation about the build process.

Conditional Processing

In the previous chapter, we saw a template that output the name of a president or vice president. Its basic job was to display the first name, middle name, and last name. A nonbreaking space was printed between each piece of data so the fields did not run into each other. What we did not see was that many presidents do not have middle names, so our template ended up printing the first name, followed by two spaces, followed by the last name. To fix this, we need to check for the existence of a middle name before simply outputting its content and a space. This requires *conditional logic*, a feature found in just about every programming language in existence.

XSLT provides two mechanisms that support conditional logic: <xsl:if> and <xsl:choose>. These allow a stylesheet to produce different output depending on the results of a *boolean expression*, which must yield `true` or `false` as defined by the XPath specification.

<xsl:if>

The behavior of the `<xsl:if>` element is comparable to the following Java code:

```
if (boolean-expression) {
  // do something
}
```

In XSLT, the syntax is as follows:

```
<xsl:if test="boolean-expression">
  <!-- Content: template -->
</xsl:if>
```

The `test` attribute is required and must contain a boolean expression. If the result is `true`, the content of this element is instantiated; otherwise, it is skipped. The code in Example 3-1 illustrates several uses of `<xsl:if>` and related XPath expressions. Code that is highlighted will be discussed in the next several paragraphs.

Example 3-1. <xsl:if> examples

```
<?xml version="1.0" encoding="UTF-8"?>
<xsl:stylesheet version="1.0"
  xmlns:xsl="http://www.w3.org/1999/XSL/Transform">
  <xsl:output method="html"/>
  <!--*******************************************************
      ** "/" template
      *******************************************************-->
  <xsl:template match="/">
    <html>
      <body>
        <h1>Conditional Processing Examples</h1>
        <xsl:apply-templates select="presidents"/>
      </body>
    </html>
  </xsl:template>
  <!--*******************************************************
      ** "presidents" template
      *******************************************************-->
  <xsl:template match="presidents">
    <h3>
      List of
        <xsl:value-of select="count(president)"/>
      Presidents
    </h3>
    <ul>
```

Example 3-1. <xsl:if> examples (continued)

```
      <xsl:for-each select="president">
        <li>
          <!-- display every other row in bold -->
          <xsl:if test="(position() mod 2) = 0">
            <xsl:attribute name="style">
              <xsl:text>font-weight: bold;</xsl:text>
            </xsl:attribute>
          </xsl:if>
          <xsl:apply-templates select="name"/>
          <!-- display some text after the last element -->
          <xsl:if test="position() = last()">
            <xsl:text> (current president)</xsl:text>
          </xsl:if>
        </li>
      </xsl:for-each>
    </ul>
  </xsl:template>
  <!--*******************************************************
      ** "name" template
      *******************************************************-->
  <xsl:template match="name">
    <xsl:value-of select="last"/>
    <xsl:text>, </xsl:text>
    <xsl:value-of select="first"/>
    <xsl:if test="middle">
      <xsl:text> disable-output-escaping="yes"> </xsl:text>
      <xsl:value-of select="middle"/>
    </xsl:if>
  </xsl:template>
</xsl:stylesheet>
```

The first thing the match="presidents" template outputs is a heading that displays the number of presidents:

```
List of
  <xsl:value-of select="count(president)"/>
Presidents
```

The count() function is an XPath *node set* function and returns the number of
elements in a node set. In this case, the node set is the list of <president> elements that are direct children of the <presidents> element, so the number of
presidents in the XML file is displayed. The next block of code does the bulk of
the work in this stylesheet, outputting each president as a list item using a loop:

```
      <xsl:for-each select="president">
        <li>
          <!-- display every other row in bold -->
          <xsl:if test="(position() mod 2) = 0">
```

```
    <xsl:attribute name="style">
      <xsl:text>font-weight: bold;</xsl:text>
    </xsl:attribute>
  </xsl:if>
```

In this example, the `<xsl:for-each>` loop first selects all `<president>` elements that are immediate children of the `<presidents>` element. As the loop iterates over this node set, the `position()` function returns an integer representing the current node position within the current node list, beginning with index 1. The mod operator computes the remainder following a truncating division, just as Java and ECMAScript do for their % operator. The XPath expression `(position() mod 2) = 0` will return `true` for even numbers; therefore the style attribute will be added to the `<li>` tag for every other president, making that list item bold.

This template continues as follows:

```
<xsl:apply-templates select="name"/>
<!-- display some text after the last element -->
<xsl:if test="position() = last()">
  <xsl:text> (current president)</xsl:text>
</xsl:if>
</li>
</xsl:for-each>
```

The `last()` function returns an integer indicating the size of the current context; in this case, it returns the number of presidents. When the position is equal to this count, the additional text (`current president`) is appended to the result tree. Java programmers should note that XPath uses a single = character for comparisons instead of ==, as Java does. A portion of the HTML for our list ends up looking like this:

```
<li>Washington, George</li>
<li style="font-weight: bold;">Adams, John</li>
<li>Jefferson, Thomas</li>
<li style="font-weight: bold;">Madison, James</li>
<li>Monroe, James</li>
<li style="font-weight: bold;">Adams, John Quincy</li>
<li>Jackson, Andrew</li>
...remaining HTML omitted
<li>Bush, George (current president)</li>
```

The name output has been improved from the previous chapter and now uses `<xsl:if>` to determine if the middle name is present:

```
<xsl:template match="name">
  <xsl:value-of select="last"/>
  <xsl:text>, </xsl:text>
  <xsl:value-of select="first"/>
  <xsl:if test="middle">
```

```
      <xsl:text> disable-output-escaping="yes"> </xsl:text>
      <xsl:value-of select="middle"/>
   </xsl:if>
  </xsl:template>
```

In this case, `<xsl:if test="middle">` checks for the existence of a node set rather than for a boolean value. If any `<middle>` elements are found, the content of `<xsl:if>` is instantiated. The test does not have to be this simplistic; any of the XPath location paths from the previous chapter would work here as well.

As written here, if any `<middle>` elements are found, the first one is printed. Later, in Example 3-7, `<xsl:for-each>` will be used to print all middle names for presidents, such as George Herbert Walker Bush.

Checking for the existence of an attribute is very similar to checking for the existence of an element. For example:

```
<xsl:if test="@someAttribute">
  ...execute this code if "someAttribute" is present
</xsl:if>
```

Unlike most programming languages, `<xsl:if>` does not have a corresponding `else` or `otherwise` clause. This is only a minor inconvenience[*] because the `<xsl:choose>` element provides this functionality.

<xsl:choose>, <xsl:when>, and <xsl:otherwise>

The XSLT equivalent of Java's `switch` statement is `<xsl:choose>`, which is virtually identical[†] in terms of functionality. `<xsl:choose>` must contain one or more `<xsl:when>` elements followed by an optional `<xsl:otherwise>` element. Example 3-2 illustrates how to use this feature. This example also uses `<xsl:variable>`, which will be covered in the next section.

Example 3-2. <xsl:choose>

```
<xsl:template match="presidents">
  <h3>Color Coded by Political Party</h3>
  <ul>
    <xsl:for-each select="president">
      <xsl:variable name="color">
        <!-- define the color value based on political party -->
        <xsl:choose>
          <xsl:when test="party = 'Democratic'">
            <xsl:text>blue</xsl:text>
          </xsl:when>
```

---

* `<xsl:choose>` requires a lot of typing.

† Java's `switch` statement only works with `char`, `byte`, `short`, or `int`.

Example 3-2. <xsl:choose> (continued)

```
          <xsl:when test="party = 'Republican'">
            <xsl:text>green</xsl:text>
          </xsl:when>
          <xsl:when test="party = 'Democratic Republican'">
            <xsl:text>purple</xsl:text>
          </xsl:when>
          <xsl:when test="party = 'Federalist'">
            <xsl:text>brown</xsl:text>
          </xsl:when>
          <xsl:when test="party = 'Whig'">
            <xsl:text>black</xsl:text>
          </xsl:when>
          <!-- never executed in this example -->
          <xsl:otherwise>
            <xsl:text>red</xsl:text>
          </xsl:otherwise>
        </xsl:choose>
      </xsl:variable>
      <li>
        <font color="{$color}">
          <!-- show the party name -->
          <xsl:apply-templates select="name"/>
          <xsl:text> - </xsl:text>
          <xsl:value-of select="party"/>
        </font>
      </li>
    </xsl:for-each>
  </ul>
</xsl:template>
```

In this example, the list of presidents is displayed in order along with the political party of each president. The <xsl:when> elements test for each possible party, setting the value of a variable. This variable, color, is then used in a font tag to set the current color to something different for each party. The <xsl:otherwise> element is never executed because all of the political parties are listed in the <xsl:when> elements. If a new president affiliated with some other political party is ever elected, then none of the <xsl:when> conditions would be true, and the font color would be red.

One difference between the XSLT approach and a pure Java approach is that XSLT does not require break statements between <xsl:when> elements. In XSLT, the <xsl:when> elements are evaluated in the order in which they appear, and the first one with a test expression resulting in true is evaluated. All others are skipped. If no <xsl:when> elements match, then <xsl:otherwise>, if present, is evaluated.

Since `<xsl:if>` has no corresponding `<xsl:else>`, `<xsl:choose>` can be used to mimic the desired functionality as shown here:

```
<xsl:choose>
  <xsl:when test="condition">
    <!-- if condition -->
  </xsl:when>
  <xsl:otherwise>
    <!-- else condition -->
  </xsl:otherwise>
</xsl:choose>
```

As with other parts of XSLT, the XML syntax forces a lot more typing than Java programmers are accustomed to, but the mechanics of `if/else` are faithfully preserved.

Parameters and Variables

As in other programming languages, it is often desirable to set up a variable whose value is reused in several places throughout a stylesheet. If the title of a book is displayed repeatedly, then it makes sense to store that title in a variable rather than scan through the XML data and locate the title repeatedly. It can also be beneficial to set up a variable once and pass it as a parameter to one or more templates. These templates often use `<xsl:if>` or `<xsl:choose>` to produce different content depending on the value of the parameter that was passed.

<xsl:variable>

Variables in XSLT are defined with the `<xsl:variable>` element and can be global or local. A global variable is defined at the "top-level" of a stylesheet, which means that it is defined outside of any templates as a direct child of the `<xsl:stylesheet>` element. Top-level variables are visible throughout the entire stylesheet, even in templates that occur before the variable declaration.

The other place to define a variable is inside of a template. These variables are visible only to elements that follow the `<xsl:variable>` declaration within that template and to their descendants. The code in Example 3-2 showed this form of `<xsl:variable>` as a mechanism to define the font color.

Defining variables

Variables can be defined in one of three ways:

```
<xsl:variable name="homePage">index.html</xsl:variable>
<xsl:variable name="lastPresident"select="president[position() = last()]/name"/>
<xsl:variable name="empty"/>
```

In the first example, the content of <xsl:variable> specifies the variable value. In the simple example listed here, the text index.html is assigned to the homePage variable. More complex content is certainly possible, as shown earlier in Example 3-2.

The second way to define a variable relies on the select attribute. The value is an XPath expression, so in this case we are selecting the name of the last president in the list.

Finally, a variable without a select attribute or content is bound to an empty string. The example shown in item 3 is equivalent to:

```
<xsl:variable name="empty" select="''"/>
```

Using variables

To use a variable, refer to the variable name with a $ character. In the following example, an XPath location path is used to select the name of the last president. This text is then stored in the lastPresident variable:

```
<xsl:variable name="lastPresident" select="president[position() = last()]/name"/>
```

Later in the same stylesheet, the lastPresident variable can be displayed using the following fragment of code:

```
<xsl:value-of select="$lastPresident"/>
```

Since the select attribute of <xsl:value-of> expects to see an XPath expression, $lastPresident is treated as something dynamic, rather than as static text. To use a variable within an HTML attribute value, however, you must use the attribute value template (AVT) syntax, placing braces around the variable reference:

```
<a href="{$homePage}">Click here to return to the home page...</a>
```

Without the braces, the variable would be misinterpreted as literal text rather than treated dynamically.

The primary limitation of variables is that they cannot be changed. It is impossible, for example, to use a variable as a counter in an <xsl:for-each> loop. This can be frustrating to programmers accustomed to variables that can be changed, but can often be overcome with some ingenuity. It usually comes down to passing a parameter to a template instead of using a global variable and then recursively calling the template again with an incremented parameter value. An example of this technique will be presented shortly.

Another XSLT trick involves combining the variable initialization with <xsl: choose>. Since variables cannot be changed, you cannot first declare a variable

and then assign its value later on. The workaround is to place the variable definition as a child of <xsl:variable>, perhaps using <xsl:choose> as follows:

```
<xsl:variable name="midName">
  <xsl:choose>
    <xsl:when test="middleName">
      <xsl:value-of select="middleName"/>
    </xsl:when>
    <xsl:otherwise>
      <xsl:text> </xsl:text>
    </xsl:otherwise>
  </xsl:choose>
</xsl:variable>
```

This code defines a variable called midName. If the <middleName> element is
present, its value is assigned to midName. Otherwise, a blank space is assigned.

<xsl:call-template> and Named Templates

Up until this point, all of the templates have been tightly coupled to the actual
data in the XML source. For example, the following template matches an
<employee> element; therefore, <employee> must be contained within your
XML data:

```
<xsl:template match="employee">
...content, perhaps display the name and SSN for the employee
</xsl:template>
```

But in many cases, you may wish to use this template for types of elements other
than <employee>. In addition to <employee> elements, you may want to use this
same code to output information for a <programmer> or <manager> element. In
these circumstances, <xsl:call-template> can be used to explicitly invoke a
template by name, rather than matching a pattern in the XML data. The template
will have the following form:

```
<xsl:template name="formatSSN">
...content
</xsl:template>
```

This template will be used to support the following XML data, in which both
<manager> and <programmer> elements have ssn attributes. Using a single
named template avoids the necessity to write one template for <manager> and
another for <programmer>. We will see an example XSLT stylesheet when we discuss parameters.

```
<?xml version="1.0" encoding="UTF-8"?>
<team>
  <manager ssn="230568737">
    <name>Aidan Burke</name>
```

```
    </manager>
    <programmer ssn="393776766">
      <name>Jennifer Burke</name>
    </programmer>
    <programmer ssn="993885777">
      <name>Bill Tellam</name>
    </programmer>
  </team>
```

<xsl:param>and <xsl:with-param>

It is difficult to use named templates without parameters, and parameters can also
be used for regular templates. Parameters allow the same template to take on different behavior depending on data the caller provides, resulting in more reusable
code fragments. In the case of a named template, parameters allow data such as a
social security number to be passed into the template. Example 3-3 contains a
complete stylesheet that demonstrates how to pass the ssn parameter into a
named template.

Example 3-3. namedTemplate.xslt

```
<?xml version="1.0" encoding="UTF-8"?>
<xsl:stylesheet version="1.0" xmlns:xsl="http://www.w3.org/1999/XSL/Transform">
  <xsl:output method="html"/>
  <xsl:template match="/">
    <html>
      <body>
        <h3>Team Members</h3>
        <ul>
          <xsl:for-each select="team/manager|team/programmer">
            <xsl:sort select="name"/>
            <li>
              <xsl:value-of select="name"/>
              <xsl:text>, ssn = </xsl:text>
              <xsl:call-template name="formatSSN">
                <xsl:with-param name="ssn" select="@ssn"/>
              </xsl:call-template>
            </li>
          </xsl:for-each>
        </ul>
      </body>
    </html>
  </xsl:template>

  <!-- a named template that formats a 9 digit SSN
       by inserting '-' characters -->
  <xsl:template name="formatSSN">
    <xsl:param name="ssn"/>
```

Example 3-3. namedTemplate.xslt (continued)

```
    <xsl:value-of select="substring($ssn, 1, 3)"/>
    <xsl:text>-</xsl:text>
    <xsl:value-of select="substring($ssn, 4, 2)"/>
    <xsl:text>-</xsl:text>
    <xsl:value-of select="substring($ssn, 6)"/>
  </xsl:template>
</xsl:stylesheet>
```

This stylesheet displays the managers and programmers in a list, sorted by name. The `<xsl:for-each>` element selects the *union* of team/manager and team/ programmer, so all of the managers and programmers are listed. The pipe operator (|) computes the union of its two operands:

```
<xsl:for-each select="team/manager|team/programmer">
```

For each manager or programmer, the content of the <name> element is printed, followed by the value of the ssn attribute, which is passed as a parameter to the formatSSN template. Passing one or more parameters is accomplished by adding `<xsl:with-param>` as a child of `<xsl:call-template>`. To pass additional parameters, simply list additional `<xsl:with-param>` elements, all as children of `<xsl:call-template>`.

At the receiving end, `<xsl:param>` is used as follows:

```
<xsl:template name="formatSSN">
  <xsl:param name="ssn"/>
  ...
```

In this case, the value of the ssn parameter defaults to an empty string if it is not passed. In order to specify a default value for a parameter, use the select attribute. In the following example, the zeros are in apostrophes in order to treat the default value as a string rather than as an XPath expression:

```
<xsl:param name="ssn" select="'000000000'"/>
```

Within the formatSSN template, you can see that the substring() function selects portions of the social security number string. More details on substring() and other string-formatting functions are discussed later in this chapter.

Incrementing Variables

Unfortunately, there is no standard way to increment a variable in XSLT. Once a variable has been defined, it cannot be changed. This is comparable to a final field in Java. In some circumstances, however, recursion combined with template parameters can achieve similar results. The XML shown in Example 3-4 will be used to illustrate one such approach.

Example 3-4. familyTree.xml

```
<?xml version="1.0" encoding="UTF-8"?>
<?xml-stylesheet type="text/xsl" href="familyTree.xslt"?>
<person name="Otto">
  <person name="Sandra">
    <person name="Jeremy">
      <person name="Eliana"/>
    </person>
    <person name="Eric">
      <person name="Aidan"/>
    </person>
    <person name="Philip">
      <person name="Alex"/>
      <person name="Andy"/>
    </person>
  </person>
</person>
```

As you can see, the XML is structured recursively. Each <person> element can
contain any number of <person> children, which in turn can contain additional
<person> children. This is certainly a simplified family tree, but this recursive pat-
tern does occur in many XML documents. When displaying this family tree, it is
desirable to indent the text according to the ancestry. Otto would be at the root,
Sandra would be indented by one space, and her children would be indented by
an additional space. This gives a visual indication of the relationships between the
people. For example:

```
Otto
  Sandra
    Jeremy
      Eliana
    Eric
      Aidan
    Philip
      Alex
      Andy
```

The XSLT stylesheet that produces this output is shown in Example 3-5.

Example 3-5. familyTree.xslt

```
<?xml version="1.0" encoding="UTF-8"?>
<xsl:stylesheet version="1.0" xmlns:xsl="http://www.w3.org/1999/XSL/Transform">
  <xsl:output method="html"/>

  <!-- processing begins here -->
  <xsl:template match="/">
    <html>
      <body>
```

Example 3-5. familyTree.xslt (continued)

```
          <!-- select the top level person -->
          <xsl:apply-templates select="person">
            <xsl:with-param name="level" select="'0'"/>
          </xsl:apply-templates>
        </body>
      </html>
    </xsl:template>


    <!-- Output information for a person and recursively select
         all children. -->
    <xsl:template match="person">
      <xsl:param name="level"/>

      <!-- indent according to the level -->
      <div style="text-indent:{$level}em">
        <xsl:value-of select="@name"/>
      </div>

      <!-- recursively select children, incrementing the level -->
      <xsl:apply-templates select="person">
        <xsl:with-param name="level" select="$level + 1"/>
      </xsl:apply-templates>
    </xsl:template>
</xsl:stylesheet>
```

As usual, this stylesheet begins by matching the document root and outputting a basic HTML document. It then selects the root <person> element, passing level=0 as the parameter to the template that matches person:

```
<xsl:apply-templates select="person">
  <xsl:with-param name="level" select="'0'"/>
</xsl:apply-templates>
```

The person template uses an HTML <div> tag to display each person's name on a new line and specifies a text indent in ems. In Cascading Style Sheets, one em is supposed to be equal to the width of the lowercase letter m in the current font. Finally, the person template is invoked recursively, passing in $level + 1 as the parameter. Although this does not increment an existing variable, it does pass a new local variable to the template with a larger value than before. Other than tricks with recursive processing, there is really no way to increment the values of variables in XSLT.

Template Modes

The final variation on templates is that of the mode. This feature is similar to parameters but a little simpler, sometimes resulting in cleaner code. Modes make it possible for multiple templates to match the same pattern, each using a different mode of operation. One template may display data in verbose mode, while another may display the same data in abbreviated mode. There are no predefined modes; you make them up. The mode attribute looks like this:

```
<xsl:template match="name" mode="verbose">
   ...display the full name
</xsl:template>

<xsl:template match="name" mode="abbreviated">
   ...omit the middle name
</xsl:template>
```

In order to instantiate the appropriate template, a mode attribute must be added to <xsl:apply-templates> as follows:

```
<xsl:apply-templates select="president/name" mode="verbose"/>
```

If the mode attribute is omitted, then the processor searches for a matching template that does not have a mode. In the code shown here, both templates have modes, so you must include a mode on <xsl:apply-templates> in order for one of your templates to be instantiated.

A complete stylesheet is shown in Example 3-6. In this example, the name of a president may occur inside either a table or a list. Instead of passing a parameter to the president template, two modes of operation are defined. In table mode, the template displays the name as a row in a table. In list mode, the name is displayed as an HTML list item.

Example 3-6. Template modes

```
<?xml version="1.0" encoding="UTF-8"?>
<xsl:stylesheet version="1.0" xmlns:xsl="http://www.w3.org/1999/XSL/Transform">
  <xsl:output method="html"/>

  <!--
    ** Demonstrates how to use template modes
    -->
  <xsl:template match="/">
    <html>
      <body>

        <h2>Presidents in an HTML Table</h2>
        <table border="1">
          <tr>
            <th>Last Name</th>
            <th>First Name</th>
          </tr>
          <xsl:apply-templates select="//president" mode="table"/>
        </table>
```

Example 3-6. Template modes (continued)

```
          <h2>Presidents in an Unordered List</h2>
          <ul>
            <xsl:apply-templates select="//president" mode="list"/>
          </ul>
        </body>
      </html>
    </xsl:template>

    <!--
      ** Display a president's name as a table row
      -->
    <xsl:template match="president" mode="table">
      <tr>
        <td>
          <xsl:value-of select="name/last"/>
        </td>
        <td>
          <xsl:value-of select="name/first"/>
        </td>
      </tr>
    </xsl:template>

    <!--
      ** Display a president's name as a list item
      -->
    <xsl:template match="president" mode="list">
      <li>
        <xsl:value-of select="name/last"/>
        <xsl:text>, </xsl:text>
        <xsl:value-of select="name/first"/>
      </li>
    </xsl:template>

</xsl:stylesheet>
```

<xsl:template> Syntax Summary

Sorting through all of the possible variations of <xsl:template> is a seemingly difficult task, but we have really only covered three attributes:

match
>   Specifies the node in the XML data that a template applies to

name
>   Defines an arbitrary name for a template, independent of specific XML data

mode
>   Similar to method overloading in Java, allowing multiple versions of a template that match the same pattern

The only attribute we have not discussed in detail is `priority`, which is used to resolve conflicts when more than one template matches. The XSLT specification defines a very specific set of steps for processors to follow when more than one template rule matches.[*] From a code maintenance perspective, it is a good idea to avoid conflicting template rules within a stylesheet. When combining multiple stylesheets, however, you may find yourself with conflicting template rules. In these cases, specifying a higher numeric priority for one of the conflicting templates can resolve the problem. Table 3-1 provides a few summarized examples of the various forms of `<xsl:template>`.

Table 3-1. Summary of common template syntax

Template example	Notes

`<xsl:template match="president">`
  `...`
`</xsl:template>`
	Matches president nodes in the source XML document

`<xsl:template name="formatName">`
  `<xsl:param name="style"/>`
  `...`
`</xsl:template>`
	Defines a named template; used in conjunction with `<xsl:call-template>` and `<xsl:with-param>`

`<xsl:template match="customer"`
    `mode="myModeName">`
  `...`
`</xsl:template>`
	Matches customer nodes when `<xsl:apply-templates>` also uses `mode="myModeName"`

Combining Multiple Stylesheets

Through template parameters, named templates, and template modes, we have seen how to create more reusable fragments of code that begin to resemble function calls. By combining multiple stylesheets, one can begin to develop libraries of reusable XSLT templates that can dramatically increase productivity.

Productivity gains occur because programmers are not writing the same code over and over for each stylesheet. Reusable code is placed into a single stylesheet and imported or included into other stylesheets. Another advantage of this technique is maintainability. XSLT syntax can get ugly, and modularizing code into small fragments can greatly enhance readability. For example, we have seen several examples related to the list of presidents so far. Since we almost always want to display the name of a president or vice president, name-formatting templates should be broken out into a separate stylesheet. Example 3-7 shows a stylesheet designed for reuse by other stylesheets.

---

[*] See section 5.5 of the XSLT specification at *http://www.w3.org/TR/xslt.*

Example 3-7. nameFormatting.xslt

```
<?xml version="1.0" encoding="UTF-8"?>
<xsl:stylesheet version="1.0" xmlns:xsl="http://www.w3.org/1999/XSL/Transform">
  <xsl:output method="html"/>
  <!--
    ** Show a name formatted like: "Burke, Eric Matthew"
    -->
  <xsl:template match="name" mode="lastFirstMiddle">
    <xsl:value-of select="last"/>
    <xsl:text>, </xsl:text>
    <xsl:value-of select="first"/>
    <xsl:for-each select="middle">
      <xsl:text> disable-output-escaping="yes"> </xsl:text>
      <xsl:value-of select="."/>
    </xsl:for-each>
  </xsl:template>

  <!--
    ** Show a name formatted like: "Eric Matthew Burke"
    -->
  <xsl:template match="name" mode="firstMiddleLast">
    <xsl:value-of select="first"/>
    <xsl:for-each select="middle">
      <xsl:text> disable-output-escaping="yes"> </xsl:text>
      <xsl:value-of select="."/>
    </xsl:for-each>
    <xsl:text> disable-output-escaping="yes"> </xsl:text>
    <xsl:value-of select="last"/>
  </xsl:template>
</xsl:stylesheet>
```

The code in Example 3-7 uses template modes to determine which template is instantiated. Adding additional templates would be simple, and those changes would be available to any stylesheet that included or imported this one. This stylesheet was designed to be reused by other stylesheets, so it does not include a template that matches the root node.

For large web sites, the ability to import or include stylesheets is crucial. It almost goes without saying that every web page on a large site will contain the same navigation bar, footer, and perhaps a common heading region. Standalone stylesheet fragments included by other stylesheets should generate all of these reusable elements. This allows you to modify something like the copyright notice on your page footer in one place, and those changes are reflected across the entire web site without any programming changes.

<xsl:include>

The `<xsl:include>` element allows one stylesheet to include another. It is only allowed as a top-level element, meaning that `<xsl:include>` elements are siblings to `<xsl:template>` elements in the stylesheet structure. The syntax of `<xsl:include>` is:

```
<xsl:include href="uri-reference"/>
```

When a stylesheet includes another, the included stylesheet is effectively inserted in place of the `<xsl:include>` element. Actually, the children of its `<xsl:stylesheet>` element are inserted into the including document. It is possible to include many other stylesheets and for those stylesheets to include others.

Inclusion is a relatively simple mechanism because the resulting stylesheet behaves exactly as if you had typed all included elements into the including stylesheet. This can result in problems when two conflicting template rules are included, so you must be careful to plan ahead to avoid any conflicts. When a conflict occurs, the XSLT processor should report an error and halt.

<xsl:import>

Importing (rather than including) a stylesheet adds some intelligence to the process. When conflicts occur, the importing stylesheet takes precedence over any imported stylesheets. Unlike `<xsl:include>`, `<xsl:import>` elements must occur before any other element children of `<xsl:stylesheet>`, as shown here:

```
<?xml version="1.0" encoding="UTF-8"?>
<xsl:stylesheet version="1.0" xmlns:xsl="http://www.w3.org/1999/XSL/Transform">
  <!-- xsl:import must occur before any other top-level elements -->
  <xsl:import href="pageElements.xslt"/>
  <xsl:import href="globalConstants.xslt"/>
  <xsl:output method="html"/>
  <xsl:template match="/">
    <html>
      ...
    </html>
  </xsl:template>
  <!-- but xsl:include can occur anywhere, provided it is a top-level element -->
  <xsl:include href="nameFormatting.xslt"/>
</xsl:stylesheet>
```

For the purposes of most web sites, the most common usage pattern is for each page to import or include common stylesheet fragments, such as templates to produce page headers, footers, and other reusable elements on a web site. Once a stylesheet has been included or imported, its templates can be used as if they were in the current stylesheet.

The key reason to use <xsl:import> instead of <xsl:include> is to avoid conflicts. If your stylesheet already has a template that matches pageHeader, you will not be able to include *pageElements.xslt* if it also has that template. On the other hand, you can use <xsl:import>. In this case, your own pageHeader template will take priority over the imported pageHeader.

TIP   Changing all <xsl:import> elements to <xsl:include> will help identify any naming conflicts you did not know about.

Formatting Text and Numbers

XSLT and XPath define a small set of functions to manipulate text and numbers. These allow you to concatenate strings, extract substrings, determine the length of a string, and perform other similar tasks. While these features do not approach the capabilities offered by a programming language like Java, they do allow for some of the most common string manipulation tasks.

Number Formatting

The format-number() function is provided by XSLT to convert numbers such as 123 into formatted numbers such as $123.00. The function takes the following form:

```
string format-number(number, string, string?)
```

The first parameter is the number to format, the second is a format string, and the third (optional) is the name of an <xsl:decimal-format> element. We will cover only the first two parameters in this book. Interestingly enough, the behavior of the format-number() function is defined by the JDK 1.1.x version of the java.text.DecimalFormat class. For complete information on the syntax of the second argument, refer to the JavaDocs for JDK 1.1.x.

Outputting currencies is a common use for the format-number() function. The pattern $#,##0.00 can properly format a number into just about any U.S. currency. Table 3-2 demonstrates several possible inputs and results for this pattern.

Table 3-2. Formatting currencies using $#,##0.00

Number	Result
0	$0.00
0.9	$0.90
0.919	$0.92

Table 3-2. Formatting currencies using $#,##0.00 (continued)

Number	Result
10	$10.00
1000	$1,000.00
12345.12345	$12,345.12

The XSLT code to utilize this function may look something like this:

```
<xsl:value-of select="format-number(amt,'$#,##0.00')"/>
```

It is assumed that `amt` is some element in the XML data,[*] such as `<amt>1000</amt>`. The `#` and `0` characters are placeholders for digits and behave exactly as `java.text.DecimalFormat` specifies. Basically, `0` is a placeholder for any digit, while `#` is a placeholder that is absent when the input value is 0.

Besides currencies, another common format is percentages. To output a percentage, end the format pattern with a `%` character. The following XSLT code shows a few examples:

```
<!-- outputs 0% -->
<xsl:value-of select="format-number(0,'0%')"/>


<!-- outputs 10% -->
<xsl:value-of select="format-number(0.1,'0%')"/>


<!-- outputs 100% -->
<xsl:value-of select="format-number(1,'0%')"/>
```

As before, the first parameter to the `format-number()` function is the actual number to be formatted, and the second parameter is the pattern. The 0 in the pattern indicates that at least one digit should always be displayed. The `%` character also has the side effect of multiplying the value by 100 so it is displayed as a percentage. Consequently, 0.15 is displayed as 15%, and 1 is displayed as 100%.

To test more patterns, the XML data shown in Example 3-8 can be used. This works in conjunction with *numberFormatting.xslt* to display every combination of format and number listed in the XML data.

Example 3-8. numberFormatting.xml

```
<?xml version="1.0" encoding="UTF-8"?>
<?xml-stylesheet type="text/xsl" href="numberFormatting.xslt"?>
<numberFormatting>
  <formatSamples>
    <!-- add more <format> elements to test more combinations-->
```

---

[*] The XSLT specification does not define what happens if the XML data does not contain a valid number.

Example 3-8. numberFormatting.xml (continued)

```
      <format>$#,##0.00</format>
      <format>#.#</format>
      <format>0.#</format>
      <format>0.0</format>
      <format>0%</format>
      <format>0.0#</format>
   </formatSamples>
   <numberSamples>
      <!-- add more <number> elements to test more combinations -->
      <number>-10</number>
      <number>-1</number>
      <number>0</number>
      <number>0.000123</number>
      <number>0.1</number>
      <number>0.9</number>
      <number>0.91</number>
      <number>0.919</number>
      <number>1</number>
      <number>10</number>
      <number>100</number>
      <number>1000</number>
      <number>10000</number>
      <number>12345.12345</number>
      <number>55555.55555</number>
   </numberSamples>
</numberFormatting>
```

The stylesheet, *numberFormatting.xslt,* is shown in Example 3-9. Comments in the code explain what happens at each step. To test new patterns and numbers, just edit the XML data and apply the transformation again. Since the XML file references the stylesheet with `<?xml-stylesheet?>`, you can simply load the XML into an XSLT compliant web browser and click on the Reload button to see changes as they are made.

Example 3-9. numberFormatting.xslt

```
<?xml version="1.0" encoding="UTF-8"?>
<xsl:stylesheet version="1.0" xmlns:xsl="http://www.w3.org/1999/XSL/Transform">
  <xsl:output method="html"/>
  <xsl:template match="/">
    <html>
      <body>
        <!-- loop over each of the sample formats -->
        <xsl:for-each select="numberFormatting/formatSamples/format">
          <h2>
            <!-- show the format as a heading -->
            <xsl:value-of select="."/>
```

Example 3-9. numberFormatting.xslt (continued)

```
          </h2>
          <table border="1" cellpadding="2" cellspacing="0">
            <tr>
              <th>Number</th>
              <th>Result</th>
            </tr>

            <!-- pass the format as a parameter to the template that
                 shows each number -->
            <xsl:apply-templates select="/numberFormatting/numberSamples/number">
              <xsl:with-param name="fmt" select="."/>
            </xsl:apply-templates>
          </table>
        </xsl:for-each>
      </body>
    </html>
  </xsl:template>

  <!-- output the number followed by the result of the format-number function -->
  <xsl:template match="number">
    <xsl:param name="fmt"/>
    <tr>
      <td align="right">
        <xsl:value-of select="."/>
      </td>
      <td align="right">
        <!-- the first param is a dot, representing the text content
             of the <number> element -->
        <xsl:value-of select="format-number(.,$fmt)"/>
      </td>
    </tr>
  </xsl:template>
</xsl:stylesheet>
```

This stylesheet first loops over the list of `<format>` elements:

```
<xsl:for-each select="numberFormatting/formatSamples/format">
```

Within the loop, all of the `<number>` elements are selected. This means that every format is applied to every number:

```
<xsl:apply-templates select="/numberFormatting/numberSamples/number">
```

Text Formatting

Several text-formatting functions are defined by the XPath specification, allowing code in an XSLT stylesheet to perform such operations as concatenating two or more strings, extracting a substring, and computing the length of a string. Unlike strings in Java, all strings in XSLT and XPath are indexed from position 1 instead of position 0.

Let's suppose that a stylesheet defines the following variables:

```
<xsl:variable name="firstName" select="'Eric'"/>
<xsl:variable name="lastName" select="'Burke'"/>
<xsl:variable name="middleName" select="'Matthew'"/>
<xsl:variable name="fullName"
    select="concat($firstName, ' ', $middleName, ' ', $lastName)"/>
```

In the first three variables, apostrophes are used to indicate that the values are strings. Without the apostrophes, the XSLT processor would treat these as XPath expressions and attempt to select nodes from the XML input data. The third variable, `fullName`, demonstrates how the `concat()` function is used to concatenate two or more strings together. The function simply takes a comma-separated list of strings as arguments and returns the concatenated results. In this case, the value for `fullName` is "Eric Matthew Burke."

Table 3-3 provides additional examples of string functions. The variables in this table are the same ones from the previous example. In the first column, the return type of the function is listed first, followed by the function name and the list of parameters. The second and third columns provide an example usage and the output from that example.

Table 3-3. String function examples

Function syntax	Example	Output
string concat (string,string,string*)	`concat($firstName, ' ', $lastName)`	Eric Burke
boolean starts-with (string,string)	`starts-with($firstName, 'Er')`	true
boolean contains(string,string)	`contains($fullName, 'Smith')`	false
string substring-before (string,string)	`substring-before($fullName, ' ')`	Eric
string substring-after (string,string)	`substring-after($fullName, ' ')`	Matthew Burke
string substring (string,number,number?)	`substring($middleName,1,1)`	M
number string-length(string?)	`string-length($fullName)`	18
string normalize-space(string?)	`normalize-space(' testing ')`	testing
string translate (string,string,string)	`translate('test','aeiou','AEIOU')`	tEst

All string comparisons, such as `starts-with()` and `contains()`, are case-sensitive. There is no concept of case-insensitive comparison in XSLT. One potential workaround is to convert both strings to upper- or lowercase, and then perform the comparison. Converting a string to upper- or lowercase is not directly supported by a function in the current implementation of XSLT, but the `translate()` function can be used to perform the task. The following XSLT snippet converts a string from lower- to uppercase:

```
translate($text,
    'abcdefghijklmnopqrstuvwxyz',
    'ABCDEFGHIJKLMNOPQRSTUVWXYZ')
```

In the `substring-before()` and `substring-after()` functions, the second argument contains a delimiter string. This delimiter does not have to be a single character, and an empty string is returned if the delimiter is not found. These functions could be used to parse formatted data such as dates:

```
<date>06/25/1999</date>
```

The XSLT used to extract the month, day, and year looks like this:

```
<xsl:variable name="dateStr" select="//date"/>
<xsl:variable name="dayYear" select="substring-after($dateStr, '/')"/>
Month: <xsl:value-of select="substring-before($dateStr, '/')"/> <br/>
Day: <xsl:value-of select="substring-before($dayYear, '/')"/> <br/>
Year: <xsl:value-of select="substring-after($dayYear, '/')"/>
```

In the first line of code, the `dateStr` variable is initialized to contain the full date. The next line then creates the `dayYear` variable, which contains everything after the first / character—at this point, `dateStr=06/25/1999` and `dayYear=25/1999`. In Java, this is slightly easier because you simply create an instance of the `StringTokenizer` class and iterate through the tokens or use the `lastIndexOf()` method of `java.lang.String` to locate the second /. With XSLT, the options are somewhat more limited. The remaining lines continue chopping up the variables into `substring`s, again delimiting on the / character. The output is as follows:

```
Month: 06
Day: 25
Year: 1999
```

Another form of the `substring()` function takes one or two number arguments, indicating the starting index and the optional length of the `substring`. If the second number is omitted, the `substring` continues until the end of the input string. The starting index always begins at position 1, so `substring("abcde",2,3)` returns bcd, and `substring("abcde",2)` returns bcde.

Schema Evolution

Looking beyond HTML generation, a key use for XSLT is transforming one form of XML into another form. In many cases, these are not radical transformations, but minor enhancements such as adding new attributes, changing the order of elements, or removing unused data. If you have only a handful of XML files to transform, it is a lot easier to simply edit the XML directly rather than going through the trouble of writing a stylesheet. But in cases where a large collection of XML documents exist, a single XSLT stylesheet can perform transformations on an entire library of XML files in a single pass. For B2B applications, schema evolution is useful when different customers require the same data, but in different formats.

An Example XML File

Let's suppose that you wrote a logging API for your Java programs. Log files are written in XML and are formatted as shown in Example 3-10.

Example 3-10. Log file before transformation

```
<?xml version="1.0" encoding="UTF-8"?>
<log>
  <message text="input parameter was null">
    <type>ERROR</type>
    <when>
      <year>2000</year>
      <month>01</month>
      <day>15</day>
      <hour>03</hour>
      <minute>12</minute>
      <second>18</second>
    </when>
    <where>
      <class>com.foobar.util.StringUtil</class>
      <method>reverse(String)</method>
    </where>
  </message>
  <message text="cannot read config file">
    <type>WARNING</type>
    <when>
      <year>2000</year>
      <month>01</month>
      <day>15</day>
      <hour>06</hour>
      <minute>35</minute>
      <second>44</second>
    </when>
    <where>
```

Example 3-10. Log file before transformation (continued)

```
        <class>com.foobar.servlet.MainServlet</class>
        <method>init()</method>
      </where>
    </message>
    <!-- more messages ... -->
</log>
```

As you can see from this example, the file format is quite verbose. Of particular concern is how the date and time are written. Since log files can be quite large, it would be a good idea to select a more concise format for this information. Additionally, the text is stored as an attribute on the <message> element, and the type is stored as a child element. It would make more sense to list the type as an attribute and the message as an element. For example:

```
      <message type="WARNING">
        <text>This is the text of a message.
              Multi-line messages are easier when an
              element is used instead of an attribute.</text>
        ...remainder omitted
```

The Identity Transformation

Whenever writing a schema evolution stylesheet, it is a good idea to start with an *identity transformation.* This is a very simple template that simply takes the original XML document and "transforms" it into a new document with the same elements and attributes as the original document. Example 3-11 shows a stylesheet that contains an identity transformation template.

Example 3-11. identityTransformation.xslt

```
<?xml version="1.0" encoding="UTF-8"?>
<xsl:stylesheet version="1.0" xmlns:xsl="http://www.w3.org/1999/XSL/Transform">
  <xsl:output method="xml" version="1.0" encoding="UTF-8" indent="yes"/>

  <xsl:template match="@*|node()">
    <xsl:copy>
      <xsl:apply-templates select="@*|node()"/>
    </xsl:copy>
  </xsl:template>
</xsl:stylesheet>
```

Amazingly, it takes only a single template to perform the identity transformation, regardless of the complexity of the XML data. Our stylesheet encodes the result using UTF-8 and indents lines, regardless of the original XML format. In XPath, node() is a node test that matches all child nodes of the current context. This is fine, but it omits the attributes of the current context. For this reason, `@*` must be unioned with `node()` as follows:

```
<xsl:template match="@*|node()">
```

Translated into English, this means that the template will match any attribute or any child node of the current context. Since `node()` includes elements, comments, processing instructions, and even text, this template will match anything that can occur in the XML document.

Inside of our template, we use `<xsl:copy>`. As you can probably guess, this instructs the XSLT processor to simply copy the current node to the result tree. To continue processing, `<xsl:apply-templates>` then selects all attributes or children of the current context using the following code:

```
<xsl:apply-templates select="@*|node()"/>
```

Transforming Elements and Attributes

Once you have typed in the identity transformation and tested it, it is time to begin adding additional templates that actually perform the schema evolution. In XSLT, it is possible for two or more templates to match a pattern in the XML data. In these cases, the more specific template is instantiated. Without going into a great deal of technical detail, an explicit match such as `<xsl:template match="when">` takes precedence over the identity transformation template, which is essentially a wildcard pattern that matches any attribute or node. To modify specific elements and attributes, simply add more specific templates to the existing identity transformation stylesheet.

In the log file example, a key problem is the quantity of XML data written for each `<when>` element. Instead of representing the date and time using a series of child elements, it would be much more concise to use the following syntax:

```
<timestamp time="06:35:44" day="15" month="01" year="2000"/>
```

The following template will perform the necessary transformation:

```
<xsl:template match="when">
  <!-- change 'when' into 'timestamp', and change its
       child elements into attributes -->
  <timestamp time="{hour}:{minute}:{second}"
    year="{year}" month="{month}" day="{day}"/>
</xsl:template>
```

This template can be added to the identity transformation stylesheet and will take precedence whenever a `<when>` element is encountered. Instead of using `<xsl:copy>`, this template produces a new `<timestamp>` element AVTs are then used to specify attributes for this element, effectively converting element values into attribute values. The AVT syntax {hour} is equivalent to selecting the <hour> child of the <when> element. You may notice that XSLT processors do not necessarily preserve the order of attributes. This is not important because the relative ordering of attributes is meaningless in XML, and you cannot force the order of XML attributes.

The next thing to tackle is the <message> element. As mentioned earlier, we would like to convert the text attribute to an element, and the <type> element to an attribute. Just like before, add a new template that matches the <message> element, which will take precedence over the identity transformation. Comments in the code explain what happens at each step.

```
<!-- locate <message> elements -->
<xsl:template match="message">
  <!-- copy the current node, but not its attributes -->
  <xsl:copy>
    <!-- change the <type> element to an attribute -->
    <xsl:attribute name="type">
      <xsl:value-of select="type"/>
    </xsl:attribute>

    <!-- change the text attribute to a child node -->
    <xsl:element name="text">
      <xsl:value-of select="@text"/>
    </xsl:element>

    <!-- since the select attribute is not present,
         xsl:apply-templates processes all children
         of the current node. (not attributes or processing instructions!) -->
    <xsl:apply-templates/>

  </xsl:copy>
</xsl:template>
```

This almost completes the stylesheet. <xsl:copy> simply copies the <message> element to the result tree but does not copy any of its attributes or children. We can explicitly add new attributes using <xsl:attribute> and explicitly create new child elements using <xsl:element>. <xsl:apply-templates> then tells the processor to continue the transformation process for the children of <message>. One problem right now is that the <type> element has been converted into an attribute but has not been removed from the document. The identity transformation still copies the <type> element to the result tree without modification. To fix this, simply add an *empty template* as follows:

```
<xsl:template match="type"/>
```

The complete schema evolution stylesheet simply contains the previous templates. Without duplicating all of the code, here is its overall structure:

```xml
<?xml version="1.0" encoding="UTF-8"?>
<xsl:stylesheet
    version="1.0"
    xmlns:xsl="http://www.w3.org/1999/XSL/Transform">
    <xsl:output method="xml" version="1.0" encoding="UTF-8" indent="yes"/>

    <!-- the identity transformation -->
    <xsl:template match="@*|node()">
      ...
    </xsl:template>

    <!-- locate <message> elements -->
    <xsl:template match="message">
      ...
    </xsl:template>

    <!-- locate <when> elements -->
    <xsl:template match="when">
      ...
    </xsl:template>

    <!-- suppress the <type> element -->
    <xsl:template match="type"/>
</xsl:stylesheet>
```

The Result File

Now that the stylesheet is complete, it can be applied to all of the existing XML log files using a simple shell script or batch file. The resulting XML file is shown in Example 3-12.

Example 3-12. Result of the transformation

```xml
<?xml version="1.0" encoding="UTF-8"?>
<?xml-stylesheet type="text/xsl" href="schemaChange.xslt"?>
<log>
  <message type="ERROR">
        <text>input parameter was null</text>

    <timestamp time="03:12:18" day="15" month="01" year="2000"/>
    <where>
      <class>com.foobar.util.StringUtil</class>
      <method>reverse(String)</method>
    </where>
  </message>
  <message type="WARNING">
```

Example 3-12. Result of the transformation (continued)

```
        <text>cannot read config file</text>

    <timestamp time="06:35:44" day="15" month="01" year="2000"/>
    <where>
      <class>com.foobar.servlet.MainServlet</class>
      <method>init()</method>
    </where>
  </message>
  <message type="ERROR">
        <text>negative duration is not allowed</text>

    <timestamp time="10:01:49" day="17" month="01" year="2000"/>
    <where>
      <class>com.foobar.util.DateUtil</class>
      <method>getWeek(int)</method>
    </where>
  </message>
</log>
```

Ant Documentation Stylesheet

Apache's Ant has taken the Java development community by storm, supplement-
ing traditional Java IDEs and outright replacing *Makefiles* on most Java development projects. Ant is a build tool, similar to the *make* utility, only it uses XML files
instead of *Makefiles*. In addition to a portable build file based on XML, Ant itself is
written in Java and has few platform-specific dependencies. Finally, since Ant can
reuse the same running instance of the Java Virtual Machine for nearly every step
of the build process, it is blazingly fast. Ant can be downloaded from *http://jakarta.
apache.org* and is open source software.

Ant Basics

Ant is driven by an XML *build file*, which consists of one *project*. This project contains one or more *targets*, and targets can have dependencies on one another. The
project and targets are represented as <project> and <target> in the XML
build file; <project> must be the document root element. It is common to have a
"prepare" target that builds the output directories and a "compile" target that
depends on the "prepare" target. If you tell Ant to execute the "compile" target, it
first checks to see that the "prepare" target has created the necessary directories.
The structure of an Ant build file looks like this:

```
<?xml version="1.0"?>
<project name="SampleProject" default="compile" basedir=".">

    <!-- global properties -->
```

```
<property name="srcdir" value="src"/>
<property name="builddir" value="build"/>

<target name="prepare" description="Creates the output directories">
   ...tasks
</target>

<target name="compile" depends="prepare">
   ...tasks
</target>

<target name="distribute" depends="compile">
   ...tasks
</target>
</project>
```

For each target, Ant is smart enough to know if files have been modified and if it needs to do any work. For compilation, the timestamps of *.class* files are compared to timestamps of *.java* files. Through these dependencies, Ant can avoid unnecessary compilation and perform quite well. Although the targets shown here contain only single dependencies, it is possible for a target to depend on several other targets:

```
<target name="X" depends="A,B,C">
```

Although Ant build files are much simpler than corresponding *Makefiles*, complex projects can introduce many dependencies that are difficult to visualize. It can be helpful to view the complete list of targets with dependencies displayed visually, such as in a hierarchical tree view. XSLT can be used to generate this sort of report.

Stylesheet Functionality

Since the build file is XML, XSLT makes it easy to generate HTML web pages that summarize the targets and dependencies. Our stylesheet also shows a list of *global properties* and can easily be extended to display anything else contained in the build file.

Although this stylesheet creates several useful HTML tables in its report, its most interesting feature is the ability to display a complete dependency graph of all Ant build targets. The output for this graph is shown in Example 3-13.

Example 3-13. Target dependencies

```
clean
   all (depends on clean, dist)
prepare
   tomcat (depends on prepare)
```

Example 3-13. Target dependencies (continued)

```
        j2ee (depends on tomcat)
          j2ee-dist (depends on j2ee)
      main (depends on tomcat, webapps)
          dist (depends on main, webapps)
              dist-zip (depends on dist)
              all (depends on clean, dist)
    webapps (depends on prepare)
        dist (depends on main, webapps)
            dist-zip (depends on dist)
            all (depends on clean, dist)
        main (depends on tomcat, webapps)
            dist (depends on main, webapps)
                dist-zip (depends on dist)
                all (depends on clean, dist)
targets
```

This is actually the output from the Ant build file included with Apache's Tomcat. The list of top-level targets is shown at the root level, and dependent targets are indented and listed next. The targets shown in parentheses list what each target depends on. This tree view is created by recursively analyzing the dependencies, which appear in the Ant build file as follows:

```
<target name="all" depends="clean,dist">
```

Figure 3-1 shows a portion of the output in a web browser. A table listing all targets follows the dependency graph. The output concludes with a table of all global properties defined in the Ant build file.

The comma-separated list of dependencies presents a challenge that is best handled through recursion. For each target in the build file, it is necessary to print a list of targets that depend on that target. It is possible to have many dependencies, so an Ant build file may contain a <target> that looks like this:

```
<target name="docs" depends="clean, prepare.docs, compile">
```

In the first prototype of the Antdoc stylesheet, the algorithm to print the dependency graph uses simple substring operations to determine if another target depends on the current target. This turns out to be a problem because two unrelated targets might have similar names, so some Ant build files cause infinite recursion in the stylesheet. In the preceding example, the original prototype of Antdoc says that "docs" depends on itself because its list of dependencies contains the text prepare.docs.

In the finished version of Antdoc, the list of target dependencies is cleaned up to remove spaces and commas. For example, "clean, prepare.docs, compile" is converted into "|clean|prepare.docs|compile|". By placing the pipe (|)

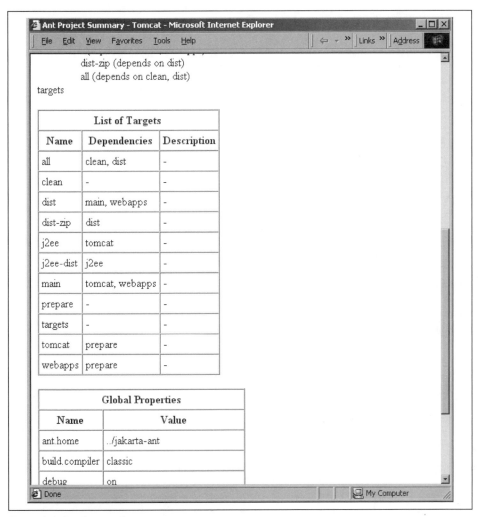

Figure 3-1. Antdoc sample output

character before and after every dependency, it becomes much easier to locate dependencies by searching for strings.

The Complete Example

The complete XSLT stylesheet is listed in Example 3-14. Comments within the code explain what happens in each step. To use this stylesheet, simply invoke your favorite XSLT processor at the command line, passing *antdoc.xslt* and your Ant build file as parameters.

Example 3-14. antdoc.xslt

```xml
<?xml version="1.0" encoding="UTF-8"?>
<!--
  ****************************************************************
  ** Antdoc v1.0
  **
  ** Written by Eric Burke (burke_e@ociweb.com)
  **
  ** Uses XSLT to generate HTML summary reports of Ant build
  ** files.
  ****************************************************************-->
<xsl:stylesheet version="1.0"
    xmlns:xsl="http://www.w3.org/1999/XSL/Transform">
  <xsl:output method="xml"
      doctype-public="-//W3C//DTD XHTML 1.0 Strict//EN"
      doctype-system="http://www.w3.org/TR/xhtml1/DTD/xhtml1-strict.dtd"
      indent="yes" encoding="UTF-8"/>

  <!-- global variable: the project name -->
  <xsl:variable name="projectName" select="/project/@name"/>
  <xsl:template match="/">
    <html xmlns="http://www.w3.org/1999/xhtml">
      <head>
        <title>Ant Project Summary -
            <xsl:value-of select="$projectName"/></title>
      </head>
      <body>
        <h1>Ant Project Summary</h1>
        <xsl:apply-templates select="project"/>
      </body>
    </html>
  </xsl:template>

  <!--
  ****************************************************************
  ** "project" template
  ****************************************************************-->
  <xsl:template match="project">
    <!-- show the project summary table, listing basic info
         such as name, default target, and base directory -->
    <table border="1" cellpadding="4" cellspacing="0">
      <tr><th colspan="2">Project Summary</th></tr>
      <tr>
        <td>Project Name:</td>
        <td><xsl:value-of select="$projectName"/></td>
      </tr>
      <tr>
        <td>Default Target:</td>
        <td><xsl:value-of select="@default"/></td>
```

Example 3-14. antdoc.xslt (continued)

```
      </tr>
      <tr>
        <td>Base Directory:</td>
        <td><xsl:value-of select="@basedir"/></td>
      </tr>
    </table>

    <!-- show all target dependencies as a tree -->
    <h3>Target Dependency Tree</h3>
    <xsl:apply-templates select="target[not(@depends)]" mode="tree">
      <xsl:sort select="@name"/>
    </xsl:apply-templates>
    <p/>

    <!-- Show a table of all targets -->
    <table border="1" cellpadding="4" cellspacing="0">
      <tr><th colspan="3">List of Targets</th></tr>
      <tr>
        <th>Name</th>
        <th>Dependencies</th>
        <th>Description</th>
      </tr>
      <xsl:apply-templates select="target" mode="tableRow">
        <xsl:sort select="count(@description)" order="descending"/>
        <xsl:sort select="@name"/>
      </xsl:apply-templates>
    </table>
    <p/>
    <xsl:call-template name="globalProperties"/>
  </xsl:template>

<!--
  ****************************************************************
  ** Create a table of all global properties.
  ****************************************************************-->
  <xsl:template name="globalProperties">
    <xsl:if test="property">
      <table border="1" cellpadding="4" cellspacing="0">
        <tr><th colspan="2">Global Properties</th></tr>
        <tr>
          <th>Name</th>
          <th>Value</th>
        </tr>
        <xsl:apply-templates select="property" mode="tableRow">
          <xsl:sort select="@name"/>
        </xsl:apply-templates>
      </table>
```

Example 3-14. antdoc.xslt (continued)

```
    </xsl:if>
  </xsl:template>


  <!--
  ****************************************************************
  ** Show an individual property in a table row.
  ****************************************************************-->
  <xsl:template match="property[@name]" mode="tableRow">
    <tr>
      <td><xsl:value-of select="@name"/></td>
      <td>
        <xsl:choose>
          <xsl:when test="not(@value)">
            <xsl:text disable-output-escaping="yes"> </xsl:text>
          </xsl:when>
          <xsl:otherwise>
            <xsl:value-of select="@value"/>
          </xsl:otherwise>
        </xsl:choose>
      </td>
    </tr>
  </xsl:template>


  <!--
  ****************************************************************
  ** "target" template, mode=tableRow
  ** Print a target name and its list of dependencies in a
  ** table row.
  ****************************************************************-->
  <xsl:template match="target" mode="tableRow">
    <tr valign="top">
      <td><xsl:value-of select="@name"/></td>
      <td>
        <xsl:choose>
          <xsl:when test="@depends">
            <xsl:call-template name="parseDepends">
              <xsl:with-param name="depends" select="@depends"/>
            </xsl:call-template>
          </xsl:when>
          <xsl:otherwise>-</xsl:otherwise>
        </xsl:choose>
      </td>
      <td>
        <xsl:if test="@description">
          <xsl:value-of select="@description"/>
        </xsl:if>
        <xsl:if test="not(@description)">
          <xsl:text>-</xsl:text>
```

Example 3-14. antdoc.xslt (continued)

```
        </xsl:if>
      </td>
    </tr>
  </xsl:template>


  <!--
  ****************************************************************
  ** "parseDepends" template
  ** Tokenizes and prints a comma separated list of dependencies.
  ** The first token is printed, and the remaining tokens are
  ** recursively passed to this template.
  ****************************************************************-->
  <xsl:template name="parseDepends">
    <!-- this parameter contains the list of dependencies -->
    <xsl:param name="depends"/>

    <!-- grab everything before the first comma,
         or the entire string if there are no commas -->
    <xsl:variable name="firstToken">
      <xsl:choose>
        <xsl:when test="contains($depends, ',')">
          <xsl:value-of
            select="normalize-space(substring-before($depends, ','))"/>
        </xsl:when>
        <xsl:otherwise>
          <xsl:value-of select="normalize-space($depends)"/>
        </xsl:otherwise>
      </xsl:choose>
    </xsl:variable>

    <xsl:variable name="remainingTokens"
      select="normalize-space(substring-after($depends, ','))"/>

    <!-- output the first dependency -->
    <xsl:value-of select="$firstToken"/>

    <!-- recursively invoke this template with the remainder
         of the comma separated list -->
    <xsl:if test="$remainingTokens">
      <xsl:text>, </xsl:text>
      <xsl:call-template name="parseDepends">
        <xsl:with-param name="depends" select="$remainingTokens"/>
      </xsl:call-template>
    </xsl:if>

  </xsl:template>


  <!--
```

Example 3-14. antdoc.xslt (continued)

```
*****************************************************************
** This template will begin a recursive process that forms a
** dependency graph of all targets.
*****************************************************************-->
<xsl:template match="target" mode="tree">
  <xsl:param name="indentLevel" select="'0'"/>
  <xsl:variable name="curName" select="@name"/>
  <div style="text-indent: {$indentLevel}em;">
    <xsl:value-of select="$curName"/>

    <!-- if the 'depends' attribute is present, show the
         list of dependencies -->
    <xsl:if test="@depends">
      <xsl:text> (depends on </xsl:text>
      <xsl:call-template name="parseDepends">
        <xsl:with-param name="depends" select="@depends"/>
      </xsl:call-template>
      <xsl:text>)</xsl:text>
    </xsl:if>
  </div>

  <!-- set up the indentation -->
  <xsl:variable name="nextLevel" select="$indentLevel+1"/>

  <!-- search all other <target> elements that have "depends"
       attributes -->
  <xsl:for-each select="../target[@depends]">

    <!-- Take the comma-separated list of dependencies and
         "clean it up". See the comments for the "fixDependency"
         template -->
    <xsl:variable name="correctedDependency">
      <xsl:call-template name="fixDependency">
        <xsl:with-param name="depends" select="@depends"/>
      </xsl:call-template>
    </xsl:variable>

    <!-- Now the dependency list is pipe (|) delimited, making
         it easier to reliably search for substrings. Recursively
         instantiate this template for all targets that depend
         on the current target -->
    <xsl:if test="contains($correctedDependency,concat('|',$curName,'|'))">
      <xsl:apply-templates select="." mode="tree">
        <xsl:with-param name="indentLevel" select="$nextLevel"/>
      </xsl:apply-templates>
    </xsl:if>
  </xsl:for-each>
</xsl:template>
```

Example 3-14. antdoc.xslt (continued)

```
<!--
******************************************************************
** This template takes a comma-separated list of dependencies
** and converts all commas to pipe (|) characters. It also
** removes all spaces. For instance:
**
** Input: depends="a, b,c "
** Ouput: |a|b|c|
**
** The resulting text is much easier to parse with XSLT.
******************************************************************-->
<xsl:template name="fixDependency">
  <xsl:param name="depends"/>

  <!-- grab everything before the first comma,
       or the entire string if there are no commas -->
  <xsl:variable name="firstToken">
    <xsl:choose>
      <xsl:when test="contains($depends, ',')">
        <xsl:value-of
          select="normalize-space(substring-before($depends, ','))"/>
      </xsl:when>
      <xsl:otherwise>
        <xsl:value-of select="normalize-space($depends)"/>
      </xsl:otherwise>
    </xsl:choose>
  </xsl:variable>

  <!-- define a variable that contains everything after the
       first comma -->
  <xsl:variable name="remainingTokens"
    select="normalize-space(substring-after($depends, ','))"/>

  <xsl:text>|</xsl:text>
  <xsl:value-of select="$firstToken"/>
  <xsl:choose>
    <xsl:when test="$remainingTokens">
      <xsl:call-template name="fixDependency">
        <xsl:with-param name="depends" select="$remainingTokens"/>
      </xsl:call-template>
    </xsl:when>
    <xsl:otherwise>
      <xsl:text>|</xsl:text>
    </xsl:otherwise>
  </xsl:choose>
</xsl:template>

</xsl:stylesheet>
```

Specifying XHTML output

One of the first things this stylesheet does is set the output method to "xml" because the resulting page will be XHTML instead of HTML. The doctype-public and doctype-system are required for valid XHTML and indicate the strict DTD in this case:

```
<xsl:output method="xml"
    doctype-public="-//W3C//DTD XHTML 1.0 Strict//EN"
    doctype-system="http://www.w3.org/TR/xhtml1/DTD/xhtml1-strict.dtd"
    indent="yes" encoding="UTF-8"/>
```

The remaining XHTML requirement is to declare the namespace of the <html> element:

```
<xsl:template match="/">
  <html xmlns="http://www.w3.org/1999/xhtml">
    ...
  </html>
</xsl:template>
```

Because of these XSLT elements, the result tree will contain the following XHTML:

```
<?xml version="1.0" encoding="UTF-8"?>
<!DOCTYPE html PUBLIC
  "-//W3C//DTD XHTML 1.0 Strict//EN"
  "http://www.w3.org/TR/xhtml1/DTD/xhtml1-strict.dtd">
<html xmlns="http://www.w3.org/1999/xhtml">
  ...
</html>
```

Creating the dependency graph

The most interesting and difficult aspect of this stylesheet is its ability to display the complete dependency graph for all Ant build targets. The first step is to locate all of the targets that do not have any dependencies. As shown in Example 3-13, these targets are named clean, prepare, and targets for the Tomcat build file. They are selected by looking for <target> elements that do not have an attribute named depends:

```
<!-- show all target dependencies as a tree -->
<h3>Target Dependency Tree</h3>
<xsl:apply-templates select="target[not(@depends)]" mode="tree">
  <xsl:sort select="@name"/>
</xsl:apply-templates>
```

The [not(@depends)] predicate will refine the list of <target> elements to include only those that do not have an attribute named depends. The <xsl: apply-templates> will instantiate the following template without any parameters:

```
<xsl:template match="target" mode="tree">
  <xsl:param name="indentLevel" select="'0'"/>
  <xsl:variable name="curName" select="@name"/>
```

If you refer to Example 3-14, you will see that this is the second-to-last template in the stylesheet. Since it is broken up into many pieces here, you may find it easier to refer to the original code as this description progresses. Since the indentLevel parameter is not specified, it defaults to '0', which makes sense for the top-level targets. As this template is instantiated recursively, the level of indentation increases. The curName variable is local to this template and contains the current Ant target name. Lines of text are indented using a style attribute:

```
<div style="text-indent: {$indentLevel}em;">
```

CSS is used to indent everything contained within the <div> tag by the specified number of ems.* The value of the current target name is then printed using the appropriate indentation:

```
<xsl:value-of select="$curName"/>
```

If the current <target> element in the Ant build file has a depends attribute, its dependencies are printed next to the target name as part of the report. The parseDepends template handles this task. This template, also part of Example 3-14, is instantiated using <xsl:call-template>, as shown here:

```
<xsl:if test="@depends">
  <xsl:text> (depends on </xsl:text>
  <xsl:call-template name="parseDepends">
    <xsl:with-param name="depends" select="@depends"/>
  </xsl:call-template>
  <xsl:text>)</xsl:text>
</xsl:if>
```

To continue with the dependency graph, the target template must instantiate itself recursively. Before doing this, the indentation must be increased. Since XSLT does not allow variables to be modified, a new variable is created:

```
<xsl:variable name="nextLevel" select="$indentLevel+1"/>
```

---

* An em is approximately equal to the width of a lowercase letter "m" in the current font.

When the template is recursively instantiated, `nextLevel` will be passed as the value for the `indentLevel` parameter:

```
<xsl:apply-templates select="." mode="tree">
  <xsl:with-param name="indentLevel" select="$nextLevel"/>
</xsl:apply-templates>
```

The remainder of the template is not duplicated here, but is emphasized in Example 3-14. The basic algorithm is as follows:

- Use `<xsl:for-each>` to select all targets that have dependencies.

- Instantiate the "fixDependency" template to replace commas with | characters.

- Recursively instantiate the "target" template for all targets that depend on the current target.

Cleaning up dependency lists

The final template in the Antdoc stylesheet is responsible for tokenizing a comma-separated list of dependencies, inserting pipe (|) characters between each dependency:

```
<xsl:template name="fixDependency">
  <xsl:param name="depends"/>
```

The `depends` parameter may contain text such as "a, b, c." The template tokenizes this text, producing the following output:

```
|a|b|c|
```

Since XSLT does not have an equivalent to Java's `StringTokenizer` class, recursion is required once again. The technique is to process the text before the first comma then recursively process everything after the comma. The following code assigns everything before the first comma to the `firstToken` variable:

```
<xsl:variable name="firstToken">
  <xsl:choose>
    <xsl:when test="contains($depends, ',')">
      <xsl:value-of
        select="normalize-space(substring-before($depends, ','))"/>
    </xsl:when>
    <xsl:otherwise>
      <xsl:value-of select="normalize-space($depends)"/>
    </xsl:otherwise>
  </xsl:choose>
</xsl:variable>
```

If the depends parameter contains a comma, the substring-before() function locates the text before the comma, and normalize-space() trims whitespace. If no commas are found, there must be only one dependency.

Next, any text after the first comma is assigned to the remainingTokens variable. If there are no commas, the remainingTokens variable will contain an empty string:

```
<xsl:variable name="remainingTokens"
  select="normalize-space(substring-after($depends, ','))"/>
```

The template then outputs a pipe character followed by the value of the first token:

```
<xsl:text>|</xsl:text>
<xsl:value-of select="$firstToken"/>
```

Next, if the remainingTokens variable is nonempty, the fixDependency template is instantiated recursively. Otherwise, another pipe character is output at the end:

```
<xsl:choose>
  <xsl:when test="$remainingTokens">
    <xsl:call-template name="fixDependency">
      <xsl:with-param name="depends" select="$remainingTokens"/>
    </xsl:call-template>
  </xsl:when>
  <xsl:otherwise>
    <xsl:text>|</xsl:text>
  </xsl:otherwise>
</xsl:choose>
```

Ideally, these descriptions will help clarify some of the more complex aspects of this stylesheet. The only way to really learn how this all works is to experiment, changing parts of the XSLT stylesheet and then viewing the results in a web browser. You should also make use of a command-line XSLT processor and view the results in a text editor. This is important because browsers may skip over tags they do not understand, so you might not see mistakes until you view the source.

4

Java-Based Web Technologies

In a perfect world, a single web development technology would be inexpensive, easy to maintain, offer rapid response time, and be highly scalable. It would also be portable to any operating system or hardware platform and would adapt well to future requirement changes. It would support access from wireless devices, standalone client applications, and web browsers, all with minimal changes to code.

No perfect solution exists, nor is one likely to exist anytime soon. If it did, many of us would be out of work. A big part of software engineering is recognizing that tradeoffs are inevitable and knowing when to sacrifice one set of goals in order to deliver the maximum value to your customer or business. For example, far too many programmers focus on raw performance metrics without any consideration for ease of development or maintainability by nonexperts. These decisions are hard and are often subjective, based on individual experience and preferences.

The goal of this chapter is to look at the highlights of several popular technologies for web application development using Java and see how each measures up to an XSLT-based approach. The focus is on *architecture*, which implies a high-level viewpoint without emphasis on specific implementation details. Although XSLT offers a good balance between performance, maintainability, and flexibility, it is not the right solution for all applications. It is hoped that the comparisons made here will help you decide if XSLT is the right choice for your web applications.

Traditional Approaches

Before delving into more sophisticated options, let's step back and look at a few basic approaches to web development using Java. For small web applications or moderately dynamic web sites, these approaches may be sufficient. As you might suspect, however, none of these approaches hold up as well as XML and XSLT when your sites get more complex.

CGI

Common Gateway Interface (CGI) is a protocol for interfacing external applications, which can be written in just about any language, with web servers. The most common language choices for CGI are C and Perl. This interface is accomplished in a number of ways, depending on the type of request. For example, parameters associated with an HTTP GET request are passed to the CGI script via the QUERY_ STRING environment variable. HTTP POST data, on the other hand, is piped to the standard input stream of the CGI script. CGI always sends results back to the web server via its standard output.

Ordinary CGI programs are invoked from the web server as external programs, which is the most notable difference when compared with servlets. With each request from the browser, the web server spawns a new process to run the CGI program. Aside from the obvious performance penalty, this also makes it difficult to maintain *state information* between requests. A web-based shopping cart is a perfect example of state information that must be preserved between requests. Figure 4-1 illustrates the CGI process.

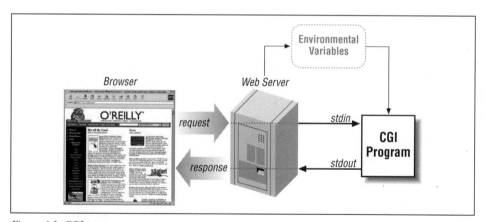

Figure 4-1. CGI process

TIP   FastCGI is an alternative to CGI with two notable differences. First, FastCGI processes do not exit with each request/response cycle. Second, the environment variable and pipe I/O mechanism of CGI has been eschewed in favor of TCP connections, allowing FastCGI programs to be distributed to different servers. The net result is that FastCGI eliminates the most vexing problems of CGI while making it easy to salvage existing CGI programs.

Although technically possible, using Java for CGI programming is not generally a good idea. In fact, it is an awful idea! The Java Virtual Machine (JVM) would have to be launched with each and every request, which would be painfully slow. Any Java programmer knows that application startup time has never been one of the strengths of Java. Servlets had to address this issue first. What was needed was a new approach in which the JVM was loaded a single time and left running even when no requests came in. The term *servlet engine* referred to the JVM that hosted the servlets, often serving a dual role as an HTTP web server.

Servlets as CGI Replacements

Sun's Java servlet API was originally released way back in 1997 when Java was mostly a client-side development language. Servlets were originally marketed and used as replacements for CGI programs. Developers were quick to adopt servlets because of their advantages over CGI.

Since the servlet engine can run for as long as the web server runs, servlets can be loaded into memory once and kept around for subsequent requests. This is easy to accomplish in Java because servlets are really nothing more than Java classes. The JVM simply loads the servlet objects into memory, hanging on to the references for as long as the web application runs.

The persistent nature of servlets results in two additional benefits, both of which push servlets well beyond the capabilities of basic CGI. First, state information can be preserved in memory for long periods of time. Even though the browser loses its connection to the web server after each request/response cycle, servlets can store objects in memory until the browser reconnects for the next page. Secondly, since Java has built-in threading capability, it is possible for numerous clients to share the same servlet instance. Creating additional threads is far more efficient than spawning additional external processes, making servlets very good performers.

Early versions of the Java servlet API did not specify the mechanism for *deployment* (i.e., installation) onto servers. Although the servlet API was consistent, deployment onto different servlet engines was completely vendor specific. With Version 2.2 of the servlet API, however, proprietary servlet engines were dropped in favor of a generic *servlet container* specification. The idea of a container is to formalize the relationship between a servlet and the environment in which it resides. This made it possible to deploy the same servlet on any vendor's container without any changes.

Along with the servlet container came the concept of a *web application*. A web application consists of a collection of servlets, static web pages, images, or any other resources that may be needed. The standard unit of deployment for web applications is the Web Application Archive (WAR) file, which is actually just a

Java Application Archive (JAR) file that uses a standard directory structure and has a *.war* file extension. In fact, you use the *jar* command to create WAR files. Along with the WAR file comes a *deployment descriptor*, which is an XML configuration file that specifies all configuration aspects of a web application. The important details of WAR files and deployment descriptors will be outlined in Chapter 6.

Servlets are simple to implement, portable, can be deployed to any servlet container in a consistent way, and offer high performance. Because of these advantages, servlets are the underlying technology for every other approach discussed in this chapter. When used in isolation, however, servlets do have limitations. These limitations manifest themselves as web applications grow increasingly complex and web pages become more sophisticated.

The screen shot shown in Figure 4-2 shows a simple web page that lists television shows for the current day. In this first implementation, a servlet is used. It will be followed with a JavaServer Pages (JSP) implementation presented later in this chapter.

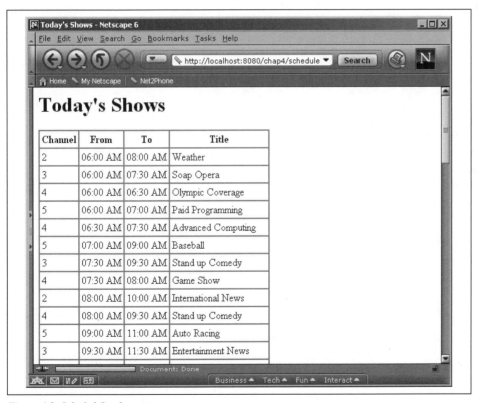

Figure 4-2. ScheduleServlet output

The Schedule Java class has a method called getTodaysShows(), that returns an array of Show objects. The array is already sorted, which reduces the amount of work that the servlet has to do to generate this page. The Schedule and Show classes are used for all of the remaining examples in this chapter. Ideally, this will help demonstrate that no matter which approach you take, keeping business logic and database access code out of the servlet makes it easier to move to new technologies without rewriting all of your code. The code for *ScheduleServlet.java* is shown in Example 4-1. This is typical of a first-generation servlet, generating its output using a series of println() statements.

Example 4-1. ScheduleServlet.java

```
package chap4;

import java.io.*;
import java.text.SimpleDateFormat;
import javax.servlet.*;
import javax.servlet.http.*;

public class ScheduleServlet extends HttpServlet {
    public void doGet(HttpServletRequest request,
            HttpServletResponse response) throws IOException,
            ServletException {

        SimpleDateFormat dateFmt = new SimpleDateFormat("hh:mm a");

        Show[] shows = Schedule.getInstance().getTodaysShows();

        response.setContentType("text/html");
        PrintWriter pw = response.getWriter();
        pw.println("<html><head><title>Today's Shows</title></head><body>");
        pw.println("<h1>Today's Shows</h1>");
        pw.println("<table border=\"1\" cellpadding=\"3\"");
        pw.println(" cellspacing=\"0\">");

        pw.println("<tr><th>Channel</th><th>From</th>");
        pw.println("<th>To</th><th>Title</th></tr>");

        for (int i=0; i<shows.length; i++) {
            pw.println("<tr>");
            pw.print("<td>");
            pw.print(shows[i].getChannel());
            pw.println("</td>");
            pw.print("<td>");
            pw.print(dateFmt.format(shows[i].getStartTime()));
            pw.println("</td>");
            pw.print("<td>");
            pw.print(dateFmt.format(shows[i].getEndTime()));
```

Example 4-1. ScheduleServlet.java (continued)

```
            pw.println("</td>");
            pw.print("<td>");
            pw.print(shows[i].getTitle());
            pw.println("</td>");
            pw.println("</tr>");
        }
        pw.println("</table>");
        pw.println("</body>");
        pw.println("</html>");
    }
}
```

If you are interested in the details of servlet coding, be sure to read Chapter 6. For now, focus on how the HTML is generated. All of those `println()` statements look innocuous enough in this short example, but a "real" web page will have thousands of `println()` statements, resulting in code that is quite difficult to maintain over the years. Generally, you will want to factor that code out into a series of methods or objects that generate fragments of the HTML. However, this approach is still tedious and error prone.

The main problems are development scalability and future maintainability. The code becomes increasingly difficult to write as your pages get more complex, and it becomes very difficult to make changes to the HTML when new requirements arrive. Web content authors and graphic designers are all but locked out of the process since it takes a programmer to create and modify the code. Each minor change requires your programming staff to recompile, test, and deploy to the servlet container.

Beyond the tedious nature of HTML generation, first-generation servlets tend to do too much. It is not clear where error handling, form processing, business logic, and HTML generation are supposed to reside. Although we are able to leverage two helper classes to generate the list of shows, a more rigorous approach will be required for complex web applications. All of the remaining technologies presented in this chapter are designed to address one or more of these issues, which become increasingly important as web applications get more sophisticated.

JSP

You have no doubt heard about JSP. This is a hot area in web development right now with some pretty hefty claims about productivity improvements. The argument is simple: instead of embedding HTML code into Java servlets, which requires a Java programmer, why not start out with static HTML? Then add special tags to this HTML that are dynamically expanded by the JSP engine, thus producing a dynamic web page. Example 4-2 contains a very simple example of JSP that produces exactly the same output as `ScheduleServlet`.

Example 4-2. schedule.jsp

```
<%@ page import="chap4.*,java.text.*" %>
<%! SimpleDateFormat dateFmt = new SimpleDateFormat("hh:mm a"); %>
<html>
  <head>
    <title>Today's Shows</title>
  </head>
<body>
<h1>Today's Shows</h1>
<% Show[] shows = Schedule.getInstance().getTodaysShows(); %>
<table border="1" cellpadding="3" cellspacing="0">
  <tr><th>Channel</th><th>From</th><th>To</th><th>Title</th></tr>

  <% for (int i=0; i<shows.length; i++) { %>
  <tr>
    <td><%= shows[i].getChannel() %></td>
    <td><%= dateFmt.format(shows[i].getStartTime()) %></td>
    <td><%= dateFmt.format(shows[i].getEndTime()) %></td>
    <td><%= shows[i].getTitle() %></td>
  </tr>
  <% } %>
</table>
</body>
</html>
```

As *schedule.jsp* shows, most of the JSP is static HTML with dynamic content sprinkled in here and there using special JSP tags. When a client first requests a JSP, the entire page is translated into source code for a servlet. This generated servlet code is then compiled and loaded into memory for use by subsequent requests. During the translation process, JSP tags are replaced with dynamic content, so the end user only sees the HTML output as if the entire page was static.

Runtime performance of JSP is comparable to hand-coded servlets because the static content in the JSP is generally replaced with a series of `println()` statements in the generated servlet code. The only major performance hit occurs for the first person to visit the JSP, because it will have to be translated and compiled. Most JSP containers provide options to precompile the JSP, so even this hit can be avoided.

Debugging in JSP can be somewhat challenging. Since JSP pages are machine translated into Java classes, method signatures and class names are not always intuitive. When a programming error occurs, you are often faced with ugly stack traces that show up directly in the browser. You do have the option of specifying an error page to be displayed whenever an unexpected condition occurs. This gives the end user a more friendly error message, but does little to help you diagnose the problem.

Here is a portion of what Apache's Tomcat shows in the web browser when the closing curly brace (}) is accidentally omitted from the loop shown in the JSP example:

```
A Servlet Exception Has Occurred
org.apache.jasper.JasperException: Unable to compile class for
JSP..\work\localhost\chap4\_0002fschedule_0002ejspschedule_jsp_2.java:104:
'catch' without 'try'.
           } catch (Throwable t) {
         ^
..\work\localhost\chap4\_0002fschedule_0002ejspschedule_jsp_2.java:112:
'try' without 'catch' or 'finally'.
}
^
..\work\localhost\chap4\_0002fschedule_0002ejspschedule_jsp_2.java:112:
'}' expected.
}
  ^
3 errors

at org.apache.jasper.compiler.Compiler.compile(Compiler.java:294)
at org.apache.jasper.servlet.JspServlet.doLoadJSP(JspServlet.java:478)
...remainder of stack trace omitted
```

The remainder of the stack trace is not very helpful because it simply lists methods that are internal to Tomcat. _0002fschedule_0002ejspschedule_jsp_2 is the name of the Java servlet class that was generated. The line numbers refer to positions in this generated code, rather than in the JSP itself.

Embedding HTML directly into servlets is not appealing because it requires a programmer to maintain. With JSP, you often embed Java code into HTML. Although the embedding is reversed, you still have not cleanly separated HTML generation and programming logic. Think about the problems you encounter when the validation logic in a JSP goes beyond a simple one-page example. Do you really want hundreds of lines of Java code sprinkled throughout your HTML, surrounded by those pretty <% %> tags? Unfortunately, far too many JSP pages have a substantial amount of Java code embedded directly in the HTML.

The first few iterations of JSP did not offer bulletproof approaches for separating Java code from the HTML. Although *JavaBeans tags* were offered in an attempt to remove some Java code, the level of sophistication was quite limited. These tags allow JSPs to interact with helper classes written according to Sun's JavaBeans API (*http://java.sun.com/products/javabeans*). Recent trends in the JSP specification have made substantial improvements. The big push right now is for custom tags,* which finally allow you to remove the Java code from your pages. A web page with custom tags may look like Example 4-3.

Example 4-3. JSP with custom tags

```
<%@ taglib uri="/my_taglib" prefix="abc" %>
<html>
<head>
<title>JSP Tag Library Demonstration</title>
</head>
<body>
  <abc:standardHeader/>
  <abc:companyLogo/>

  <h1>Recent Announcements</h1>
  <abc:announcements filter="recent"/>

  <h1>Job Openings</h1>
  <abc:jobOpenings department="hr"/>
  <abc:standardFooter/>
</body>
</html>
```

As you can see, custom tags look like normal XML tags with a *namespace prefix*. Namespace prefixes are used to give XML tags unique names. Because you select the prefix for each tag library, you can use libraries from many different vendors without fear of naming conflicts. These tags are mapped to Java classes called *tag handlers* that are responsible for the actual work. In fact, the JSP specification does not limit the underlying implementation to Java, so other languages can be used if the JSP container supports it. Using the custom tag approach, programmers in your company can produce a set of approved tags for creating corporate logos, search boxes, navigation bars, and page footers. Nonprogrammers can focus on HTML layout, oblivious to the underlying tag handler code. The main drawback to this approach is the current lack of standard tags. Although several open source projects are underway to develop custom tag libraries, it is unlikely that you will be able to find an existing custom tag for every requirement.

One persistent problem with a pure JSP approach is that of complex validation. Although JSP with custom tags can be an ideal approach for *displaying* pages, the approach falls apart when a JSP is used to validate the input from a complex HTML form. In this situation, it is almost inevitable that Java code—perhaps a lot of it—will creep into the page. This is where a hybrid approach (JSP and servlets), which will be covered in the next section, is desirable.

---

* Technically, programmers create custom actions, which are invoked using custom JSP tags.

Compared with an XML/XSLT approach, JSP requires a lot more effort to cleanly separate presentation from the underlying data and programming logic. For web sites that are mostly static, JSP can be easy for nonprogrammers to create, since they work directly in HTML. When dynamic content becomes more prevalent, your options are to embed lots of Java code into the JSP, create custom tags, or perhaps write Java beans that output fragments of HTML. Embedding code into the JSP is not desirable because of the ugly syntax and maintenance difficulties. The other approaches do hide code from the JSP author, but some part of your web application (to be consistent) is still cranking out HTML from Java code, either in custom tags or JavaBeans components. This still raises serious questions about the ability to make quick changes to your HTML without recompiling and deploying your Java code.

Another weakness of JSPs in comparison with XML and XSLT becomes obvious when you try to test your web application. With JSP, it is virtually impossible to test your code outside the bounds of a web browser and servlet container. In order to write a simple automated unit test against a JSP, you have to start a web server and invoke your JSPs via HTTP requests. With XML and XSLT, on the other hand, you can programmatically generate the XML data without a web browser or server. This XML can then be validated against a DTD or schema. You can also test the XSLT stylesheets using command-line tools without deploying to a servlet container or starting a web server. The result of the transformation can even be validated again with a DTD if you use XHTML instead of HTML.

Template Engines

Before moving on, let's discuss template engines. A quick search on the Internet reveals that template engines are abundant, each claiming to be better than JSP for various reasons. For the most part, template engines have a lot in common with JSP, particularly if you restrict yourself to custom tags. There are some differences, however:

- Template engines typically forbid you from embedding Java code into pages. Although JSP allows Java code along with HTML, it is not considered good form.

- Most template engines are not compiled, so they do not have the same problems that JSP has with error messages. They also start up faster on the first invocation, which can make development easier. The effect on end users is minimal. From a deployment perspective, you do not need a Java compiler on the web server as you do with JSP.

- Template engines come with an existing library of tags or simple scripting languages. JSP does not provide any standard tags, although numerous libraries are available from other vendors and open source projects. The JSP API is open, so you can create your own custom tags with a fair amount of effort. Template engines have their own unique mechanisms for integrating with underlying Java code.

- JSP has the backing of Sun and is pretty much available out of the box on any servlet container. The main benefit of a "standard" is the wide availability of documentation, knowledgeable people, and examples. There are many implementations of JSP to choose from.

The Hybrid Approach

Since JSP now has custom tags, you can remove (hide, actually) all of the Java code when "rendering," or generating a page to send to the browser. When a complex HTML form is posted to the JSP, however, you still have problems. You must verify that all fields are present, verify that the data is within bounds, and clean up the data by checking for null values and trimming all strings. Validation is not particularly difficult, but it can be tedious and requires a lot of custom code. You do not want to embed that code directly into a JSP because of the debugging and maintenance issues.

The solution is a hybrid approach, in which a servlet works in conjunction with a JSP. The servlet API has a nice class called `RequestDispatcher` that allows server-side forwarding and including. This is the normal mechanism for interaction between the servlet and JSP. Figure 4-3 illustrates this design at a high level.

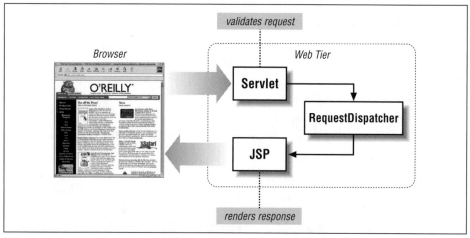

Figure 4-3. Hybrid JSP/servlet approach

This approach combines the best features of servlets with the best features of JSPs. The arrows indicate the flow of control whenever the browser issues a request. The job of the servlet is to intercept the request, validate that the form data is correct, and delegate control to an appropriate JSP. Delegation occurs via `javax.servlet.RequestDispatcher`, which is a standard part of the servlet API. The JSP simply renders the page, ideally using custom tags and no Java code mixed with the HTML.

The main issue with this approach becomes evident when your web site begins to grow beyond a few pages. You must make a decision between one large servlet that intercepts all requests, a separate servlet per page, or helper classes responsible for processing individual pages. This is not a difficult technological challenge, but rather a problem of organization and consistency. This is where web frameworks can lend a helping hand.

The Universal Design

Despite the proliferation of APIs, frameworks, and template engines, most web application approaches seem to be consolidating around the idea of model-view-controller (MVC). Clean separation between data, presentation, and programming logic is a key goal of this design. Most web frameworks implement this pattern, and the hybrid approach of JSP and servlets follows it. XSLT implementations also use this pattern, which leads to the conclusion that model-view-controller is truly a universal approach to development on the web tier.

Web Frameworks

A framework is a value-added class library that makes it easier to develop certain types of applications. For example, an imaging framework may contain APIs for reading, writing, and displaying several image formats. This makes it much easier to build applications because someone else already figured out how to structure your application.

Servlet frameworks are no different. Now that servlets, JSP, and hybrid approaches have been available for a few years, common architectural patterns are emerging as "best practices." These include separation of Java code and HTML generation, using servlets in conjunction with JSP, and other variations. Once basic patterns and themes are understood, it becomes desirable to write common frameworks that automate the mundane tasks of building web applications.

The most important tradeoff you make when selecting a framework is vendor lock-in versus open standards. At this time, there are no open standards for frameworks. Although there are numerous open source frameworks, none is backed by a standards organization or even Sun's Java Community Process. The low-level servlet and JSP APIs are very well defined and widely implemented Java standard extensions. But a framework can offer much more sophisticated features such as enhanced error checking, database connection pooling, custom tag libraries, and other value-added features. As you add more framework-specific features, however, your flexibility to choose another framework or vendor quickly diminishes.

One typical framework is Turbine, which is one of many different frameworks supported by Apache. Turbine is a large framework with many value-added features including:

- Database connection pooling, integration with object to relational mapping tools, and relational database abstractions
- Integration with numerous template engines
- Role-based security and access control lists
- Web browser detection
- Integration with JavaMail

This is only a short list of Turbine's features. At its core, however, the compelling reason to use a framework like Turbine is the underlying object model. The fundamental approach of Turbine is to cleanly separate validation logic, the servlet itself, and page rendering into distinctly different modules. In fact, Turbine uses a single servlet, so your validation and rendering logic have to go elsewhere. The approach is to define helper classes called *actions*, which are responsible for validation of incoming requests. Once an action has validated the inbound request, other classes such as `Layout`, `Page`, and `Navigation` are responsible for rendering a view back to the browser.

When compared to a pure XML/XSLT approach, frameworks have the advantage of value-added features. If you remove all of the non-web features, such as database connection pooling and object-to-relational mapping tools, you will see that the underlying model-view-controller architecture is very easy to implement. You should be wary of any framework that provides too much non-web-related functionality because many of these features should be placed on the application server instead of the web server anyway. The remainder of this chapter is devoted to showing you how to structure a complex web application without committing yourself to a specific framework.

Model-View-Controller

Cleanly separating data and presentation logic is important. What exactly are the benefits? First and foremost, when data is completely isolated from the user interface, changes can be made to the visual appearance of an application without affecting the underlying data. This is particularly important in web applications that have to support multiple incompatible browsers or even WML, XHTML Basic, or HTML. It is much harder to adapt to new user interface requirements when data and presentation are mixed.

Programming logic should also be separated from data and presentation logic. To a certain extent, programming logic must depend in part on both data and presentation. But you can generally isolate business logic, which depends on the data, and presentation logic, which depends on the user interface. Figure 4-4 illustrates these dependencies.

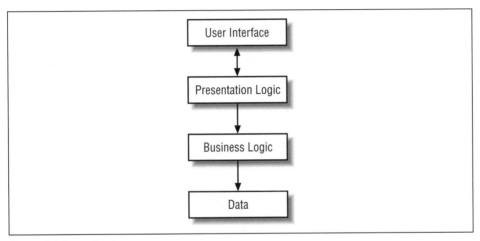

Figure 4-4. Dependencies

The arrows indicate dependencies. For example, if your underlying data changes, then the business logic will probably have to change. However, that does not always flow up and break your presentation logic. In general, if changes are sweeping, it is hard to avoid affecting upper layers, but minor changes can almost always be encapsulated. If the implementation of your business logic changes, however, there is no reason to change the underlying data. Likewise, you should be able to make changes to the presentation logic without breaking the business logic. Later in this chapter, we will see how Java, XML, and XSLT can be utilized to satisfy these dependencies.

The dominant pattern in scalable web sites is model-view-controller. The MVC pattern originated with Smalltalk-80 as a way to develop graphical user interfaces in an object-oriented way. The basics are simple. GUI components represent the view and are responsible for displaying visual information to the user. The model contains application data. The controller is responsible for coordinating between the model and the view. It intercepts events from the view components, queries the model for its current state, makes modifications to the model, and notifies the view of changes to the model. Figure 4-5 illustrates the interaction between these three components.

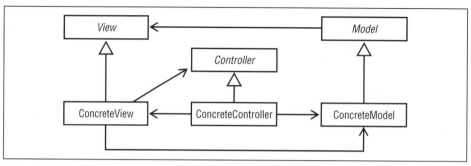

Figure 4-5. Model-view-controller

As shown, the `Model`, `View`, and `Controller` are either abstract classes or interfaces. The concrete classes are application-specific, and the open arrows indicate the direction of association between the various classes. For example, the abstract `Model` sends notifications only to the abstract `View`, but `ConcreteView` knows about its `ConcreteModel`. This makes sense when you consider how hard it would be to create a specific view, such as a customer editor panel, without knowledge of a specific data model like `Customer`. Since the `Model` only knows about `View` instances in an abstract way, however, it can send generic notifications when it changes, allowing new views to be attached later.

It is important to remember that this is just a pattern; specific implementations may vary somewhat and use different class names. One variation is to eliminate the explicit references from `ConcreteView` to `ConcreteModel` and from `Model` to `View`. In this approach, the `Controller` would take a more prevalent role. A common theme in Java is to remove the explicit controller using data models and view components that send notifications to event listeners. Although typically thought of in terms of GUI applications, the MVC architecture is not limited to this domain. For web applications, it is commonly used in:

- The hybrid servlet + JSP approach
- Most servlet frameworks
- The XSLT approach

In the hybrid approach, the servlet is the controller and the JSP is the view. It is assumed that the data will be retrieved from a database or Enterprise JavaBeans (EJB) components, which act as the model. A good framework may make the distinction between model, view, and controller more explicit. Instead of using the servlet as a controller, a common pattern is to use a single servlet that delegates work to helper classes that act as controllers. Each of these classes is equivalent to `ConcreteController` in Figure 4-5 and has knowledge of specific web pages and data.

Although originally intended for Smalltalk GUIs, MVC has always been one of the most frequently used patterns in all sorts of GUIs, from Motif to Java. On the web, MVC is also prevalent, although a few mechanics are slightly different. In a web environment, we are restricted to the HTTP protocol, which is *stateless*. With each click of a hyperlink, the browser must establish a new connection to the web server. Once the page has been delivered, the connection is broken. It is impossible for the server to initiate a conversation with the client, so the server merely waits until the next request arrives.

Implementing MVC in this stateless architecture results in looser coupling between the controller and the view. In a GUI environment, the controller immediately notifies the view of any changes to the underlying model. In a web environment, the controller must maintain state information as it waits for the browser to make another request. As each browser request arrives, it is the controller's job to validate the request and forward commands on to the model. The controller then sends the results back to the view.

This may all sound academic and vague at this point. The next few sections will present much more detailed diagrams that show exactly how MVC is implemented for an XSLT-driven web site.

XSLT Implementation

All of the approaches presented up to this point are, of course, building up to the XSLT approach. In many respects, the XSLT approach is simultaneously the most powerful and the easiest to understand. For a single web page, the XSLT approach is probably harder than a servlet or JSP to configure. Configuration of the XML parser and XSLT processor can be quite difficult, mostly due to CLASSPATH issues.* But as the complexity of a web application increases, the benefits of using XSLT become obvious. Figuring out how to tackle these complex web applications is the real goal of this chapter.

The XSLT approach maps fairly directly to the MVC pattern. The XML represents the model, the servlet represents the controller, and the XSLT produces HTML, which represents the view. The XSLT stylesheets may contain a minimal amount of logic, potentially blurring the line between view and controller. Figure 4-6 represents a conceptual view of how the XSLT approach maps to MVC.

One weakness common to every approach other than XSLT is the HTML-centric viewpoint. In every example presented thus far, it was assumed that we generated HTML. What happens when the requirement to support cellular phones arises? It

---

* This can be a frustrating experience when the servlet container comes with an older XML parser that uses DOM or SAX Version 1. Most XSLT processors require Version 2 parsers.

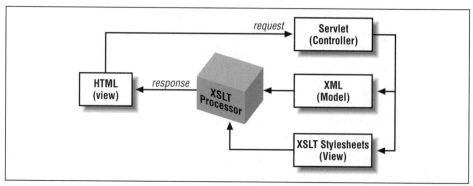

Figure 4-6. XSLT conceptual model

is very likely that these devices will not use HTML. Instead, they will use WML, XHTML Basic, or some other technology that has not been invented yet. For now, consider that you would have to write brand new servlets or JSPs to support these devices when using traditional approaches. Any programming logic embedded into JSP pages would be duplicated or would have to be factored out into common helper classes. In a pure servlet approach, the hardcoded HTML generation logic would have to be completely rewritten.

XSLT offers an elegant solution—simply create a second stylesheet. Instead of transforming XML into HTML, this new stylesheet transforms XML into WML. You can even support different web browsers with the XSLT approach. Again, just write different stylesheets for browser-specific functions. Since XSLT stylesheets can import and include functionality from other stylesheets, much of the code can be shared and reused across a project.

Regardless of what your XSLT will produce, start by producing the XML. For the schedule web application, the XML is dynamic and must be programmatically generated. JDOM code is shown in Example 4-4, which produces the XML necessary to create the schedule web page.

Example 4-4. ScheduleJDOM.java

```
package chap4;

import java.text.SimpleDateFormat;
import org.jdom.*;
import org.jdom.output.*;

/**
 * Produces a JDOM Document for a tv schedule.
 */
public class ScheduleJDOM {
    private SimpleDateFormat dateFmt = new SimpleDateFormat("hh:mm a");
```

Example 4-4. ScheduleJDOM.java (continued)

```java
/**
 * Simple main() method for printing the XML document to System.out,
 * useful for testing.
 */
public static void main(String[] args) throws Exception {
    Document doc = new ScheduleJDOM().getTodaysShows();
    new XMLOutputter("   ", true, "UTF-8").output(doc, System.out);
}


/**
 * @return a new JDOM Document for all TV shows scheduled for today.
 */
public Document getTodaysShows() {
    Schedule sched = Schedule.getInstance();
    Show[] shows = sched.getTodaysShows();

    Element rootElem = new Element("schedule");

    for (int i=0; i<shows.length; i++) {
        rootElem.addContent(createShowElement(shows[i]));
    }
    return new Document(rootElem);
}


/**
 * A helper method to convert a Show object into a JDOM Element.
 */
public Element createShowElement(Show show) {
    Element e = new Element("show");
    e.addContent(new Element("channel").setText(
            Integer.toString(show.getChannel())));
    e.addContent(new Element("from").setText(
            this.dateFmt.format(show.getStartTime())));
    e.addContent(new Element("to").setText(
            this.dateFmt.format(show.getEndTime())));
    e.addContent(new Element("title").setText(show.getTitle()));
    return e;
}
}
```

You might be wondering why this JDOM code is that much better than the servlet code, which also used Java to programmatically produce output. The difference is fundamental and important. With this JDOM example, `println()` statements are not used. Instead, a data structure representing the television schedule is created. By virtue of the JDOM API, the data structure is guaranteed to produce well-formed XML. We could very easily add a DTD, writing a unit test that validates the integrity of the generated data structure.

In addition to ensuring the integrity of the data, the JDOM code will typically be much smaller than the servlet or JSP code. In this basic web page, the servlet and JSP were quite small because the HTML did not contain any significant formatting or layout. In a real-world web page, however, the servlet and JSP will continue to grow in complexity as the HTML layout gets more sophisticated, while the JDOM code remains exactly the same.

Although the XSLT stylesheet will get larger as the HTML gets more complex, this is arguably less of a problem because the presentation logic is completely separated from the underlying XML data. Once fully tested, the XSLT can be deployed to the web server without recompiling the Java code or restarting the servlet. The XML data produced by JDOM is shown in Example 4-5.

Example 4-5. XML for schedule web page

```
<?xml version="1.0" encoding="UTF-8"?>
<?xml-stylesheet type="text/xsl" href="schedule.xslt"?>
<schedule>
  <show>
    <channel>2</channel>
    <from>06:00 AM</from>
    <to>06:30 AM</to>
    <title>Baseball</title>
  </show>
  <show>
    <channel>3</channel>
    <from>06:00 AM</from>
    <to>08:00 AM</to>
    <title>Stand up Comedy</title>
  </show>
  ...remaining XML omitted
</schedule>
```

The stylesheet that produces the exact same output as the JSP and servlet is listed in Example 4-6.

Example 4-6. schedule.xslt

```
<?xml version="1.0" encoding="UTF-8"?>
<xsl:stylesheet version="1.0"
  xmlns:xsl="http://www.w3.org/1999/XSL/Transform">
  <xsl:output method="html"/>

  <!-- ========== Produce the HTML Document ========== -->
  <xsl:template match="/">
    <html>
      <head><title>Today's Shows</title></head>
      <body>
```

Example 4-6. schedule.xslt (continued)

```
          <h1>Today's Shows</h1>
          <table cellpadding="3" border="1" cellspacing="0">
            <tr>
              <th>Channel</th>
              <th>From</th>
              <th>To</th>
              <th>Title</th>
            </tr>

            <!-- ===== select the shows ===== -->
            <xsl:apply-templates select="schedule/show"/>
          </table>
        </body>
      </html>
    </xsl:template>

  <!-- ======== Display each show as a row in the table ======== -->
  <xsl:template match="show">
    <tr>
      <td><xsl:value-of select="channel"/></td>
      <td><xsl:value-of select="from"/></td>
      <td><xsl:value-of select="to"/></td>
      <td><xsl:value-of select="title"/></td>
    </tr>
  </xsl:template>
</xsl:stylesheet>
```

The remaining piece of the puzzle is to write a servlet that combines all of these pieces and delivers the result of the XSLT transformation to the client (see Chapter 6). In a nutshell, the servlet acts as a controller between the various components, doing very little of the actual work. The client request is intercepted by the servlet, which tells ScheduleJDOM to produce the XML data. This XML is then fed into an XSLT processor such as Xalan, along with *schedule.xslt*. Finally, the output is sent to the browser as HTML, XHTML, WML, or some other format.

TIP   Another interesting option made possible by this architecture is allowing the client to request raw XML without any kind of XSLT transformation. This allows your web site to support nonbrowser clients that wish to extract meaningful business data in a portable way.

We examined the weaknesses of other approaches, so it is only fair to take a critical look at the XSLT approach. First, XSLT is a new language that developers or web content authors have to learn. Although the syntax is strange, it can be argued that XSLT is easier to learn than a sophisticated programming language like Java.

There is resistance on this front, however, which is typical of a new technology that is unfamiliar.

The second potential weakness of the XSLT approach is runtime performance. There is a performance penalty associated with XSLT transformation. Fortunately, there are numerous optimizations that can be applied. The most common involves the caching of stylesheets so they do not have to be parsed with each request. This and other techniques for optimization will be covered in later chapters.

Since XSLT stylesheets are actually XML documents, any available XML editor will work for XSLT. But eventually we should see more and more specialized XSLT editors that hide some of the implementation details for nonprogrammers. As with first-generation Java GUI builders, these early tools may not generate stylesheets as cleanly as a handcoded effort.

Development and Maintenance Benefits of XSLT

As mentioned earlier, testing JSPs can be difficult. Since they can be executed only within a JSP container, automated unit tests must start a web server and invoke the JSP via HTTP requests in order to test their output. The XSLT-based web approach does not suffer from this problem.

Referring back to Figure 4-6, you can see that the data model in an XSLT web application is represented as XML. This XML is generated independently of the servlet container, so a unit test can simply create the XML and validate it against a DTD or XML Schema. Tools such as XML Spy make it easy to create XSLT stylesheets and test them interactively against sample XML files long before they are ever deployed to a servlet container. XML Spy is available from *http://www. xmlspy.com*. If you are looking for alternatives, a directory of XML tools can be found at *http://www.xmlsoftware.com*.

The XSLT processor is another piece of the puzzle that is not tied to the servlet in any way. Because the processor is an independent component, additional unit tests can perform transformations by applying the XSLT stylesheets to the XML data, again without any interference from a web server or servlet container. If your stylesheets produce XHTML instead of HTML, the output can be easily validated against one of the W3C DTDs for XHTML. JUnit, an open source unit-testing tool, can be used for all of these tests. It can be downloaded from *http://www.junit.org*.

XSLT and EJB

Now that the options for web tier development have been examined, let's look at how the web tier interacts with other tiers in large enterprise class systems. A typical EJB architecture involves a thin browser client, a servlet-driven web tier, and EJB on an application server tier. Figure 4-7 expands upon the conceptual XSLT model presented earlier.

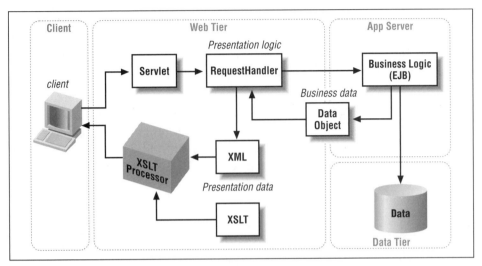

Figure 4-7. XSLT and EJB architecture

This diagram is much closer to the true physical model of a multitier web application that uses XSLT. The arrows indicate the overall flow of a single request, originating with the client. This client is typically a web browser, but it could be a cell phone or some other device. The client request goes to a single servlet and is handed off to something called RequestHandler. In the pattern outlined here, you create numerous subclasses of RequestHandler. Each subclass is responsible for validation and presentation logic for a small set of related functions. One manageable strategy is to design one subclass of RequestHandler for each web page in the application. Another approach is to create fine-grained request handlers that handle one specific task, which can be beneficial if the same piece of functionality is invoked from many different screens in your application.

The request handler interacts with the application server via EJB components. The normal pattern is to execute commands on session beans, which in turn get their data from entity beans. The internal behavior of the EJB layer is irrelevant to the web tier, however. Once the EJB method call is complete, one or more "data objects" are returned to the web tier. From this point, the data object must be converted to XML.

The conversion to XML can be handled in a few different ways. One common approach is to write methods in the data objects themselves that know how to generate a fragment of XML, or perhaps an entire document. Another approach is to write an XML adapter class for each data object. Instead of embedding the XML generation code into the data object, the adapter class generates the XML. This approach has the advantage of keeping the data objects lightweight and clean, but it does result in additional classes to write. In either approach, it is preferable to return XML as a DOM or JDOM tree, rather than raw XML text. If the XML is returned as raw text, it will have to be parsed right back into memory by the XSLT processor. Returning the XML as a data structure allows the tree to be passed directly to the XSLT processor without the additional parsing step.

Yet another approach is to return XML directly from the EJB components, thus eliminating the intermediate data objects. Chapter 9 will examine this in detail, primarily from a performance perspective. The main drawback to consider is that XML tends to be very verbose. Sending large-text XML files from the application server to the web server may be less efficient than sending serialized Java objects. You could compress the data, but that would add processor overhead for compression and decompression.

Regardless of how the XML is generated, the final step shown in Figure 4-7 is to pass the XML and stylesheet to the XSLT processor for transformation. The result tree is sent directly to the client, thus fulfilling the request. If the client is a browser, the XSLT stylesheet will probably transform the XML into HTML or XHTML. For a nonbrowser client, however, it is conceivable that the XML data is delivered directly without any XSLT transformation.

Tradeoffs

Scalability is a key motivation for a multitier EJB architecture. In such an architecture, each tier can execute on a different machine. Additional performance gains are possible when multiple servers are clustered on each tier. Another motivating factor is reliability. If one machine fails, a redundant machine can continue processing. When updates are made, new versions of software can be deployed to one machine at a time, preventing long outages. Security is improved by strictly regulating access to the data tier via EJB components.

Yet another motivation for a distributed system is simplicity, although a basic EJB application is far more complex than a simple two-tier application. Yes, distributed systems are complex, but for highly complex applications this approach simplifies your work by dividing independent tasks across tiers. One group of programmers can work on the EJB components, while another works on the request handler classes on the web tier. Yet another group of designers can work on XML and XSLT, while your database expert focuses on the database.

For simple applications, a multitier EJB approach is overkill and will likely harm performance. If your web site serves only a few hundred visitors per day, then eliminating EJB could be much faster because there is no additional application tier to hop through.*

Summary of Key Approaches

If separation of HTML from Java code is a goal, then neither a pure servlet nor a pure JSP approach is desirable. Although a hybrid approach does allow a clean separation, you may have to create custom JSP tags to take full advantage of this capability. This approach does not support WML output unless you duplicate all of the HTML generation code. Even though the custom JSP tags hide the Java code from the page author, you still end up with Java code somewhere producing HTML programmatically.

Web frameworks typically build on the hybrid approach, including proprietary value-added features and conveniences. Frameworks have the advantage of defining a consistent way to structure the overall application, which is probably more important in terms of software maintenance than any value-added features. The primary disadvantage of frameworks is that you could be locked into a particular approach and vendor.

The XSLT approach achieves the maximum attainable separation of presentation from underlying data. It also supports multiple browsers and even WML targets. XSLT transformation does incur additional processing load on the web tier. This must be carefully weighed against benefits gained from the modular, clean design that XSLT offers.

Table 4-1 summarizes the strengths and weaknesses of different approaches to Web application development.

Table 4-1. Different web technologies

Technology	Strengths	Weaknesses
Pure servlet	Fastest runtime performance.	Changes to HTML require Java code changes. Hard to maintain complex pages. No separation of data, logic, and presentation.
Pure JSP	Best for pages that are mostly display-only, static HTML with small amounts of dynamic content. Fast runtime performance.	Does not enforce separation of Java code and HTML. Not good for validation of incoming requests. Requires deployment to web server for development and testing.

---

* Keep in mind that other benefits of EJB, such as security, will be lost.

Table 4-1. Different web technologies (continued)

Technology	Strengths	Weaknesses
Hybrid servlet/ JSP	Allows greater separation between Java code and HTML than "pure" servlet or JSP approaches. More modular design is easier to maintain for large projects. Fast runtime performance.	Still requires deployment to web server for testing and development. Does not force programmers to keep code out of JSPs. Cannot target multiple client device types as effectively as XSLT.
XSLT	Maximum separation between data, programming logic, and presentation. XML and XSLT can be developed and tested outside of the web server. Maximum modularity improves maintainability. Easy to target multiple client devices and languages via different XSLT stylesheets.	Slowest runtime performance.[a] For pages that are mostly static HTML, XSLT might be harder to write than JSP. Requires an extra step to generate XML.

[a] Once more browsers support XSLT transformation, the server load will be greatly reduced.

5

XSLT Processing with Java

Since many of the XSLT processors are written in Java, they can be directly invoked from a Java application or servlet. Embedding the processor into a Java application is generally a matter of including one or two JAR files on the CLASS-PATH and then invoking the appropriate methods. This chapter shows how to do this, along with a whole host of other programming techniques.

When invoked from the command line, an XSLT processor such as Xalan expects the location of an XML file and an XSLT stylesheet to be passed as parameters. The two files are then parsed into memory using an XML parser such as Xerces or Crimson, and the transformation is performed. But when the XSLT processor is invoked programmatically, you are not limited to using static files. Instead, you can send a precompiled stylesheet and a dynamically generated DOM tree directly to the processor, or even fire SAX events as processor input. A major goal is to eliminate the overhead of parsing, which can dramatically improve performance.

This chapter is devoted to Java and XSLT programming techniques that work for both standalone applications as well as servlets, with a particular emphasis on Sun's Java API for XML Processing (JAXP) API. In Chapter 6, we will apply these techniques to servlets, taking into account issues such as concurrency, deployment, and performance.

A Simple Example

Let's start with perhaps the simplest program that can be written. For this task, we will write a simple Java program that transforms a static XML data file into HTML using an XSLT stylesheet. The key benefit of beginning with a simple program is that it isolates problems with your development environment, particularly CLASS-PATH issues, before you move on to more complex tasks.

Two versions of our Java program will be written, one for Xalan and another for SAXON. A JAXP implementation will follow in the next section, showing how the same code can be utilized for many different processors.

CLASSPATH Problems

CLASSPATH problems are a common culprit when your code is not working, particularly with XML-related APIs. Since so many tools now use XML, it is very likely that a few different DOM and SAX implementations reside on your system. Before trying any of the examples in this chapter, you may want to verify that older parsers are not listed on your CLASSPATH.

More subtle problems can occur if an older library resides in the Java 2 *optional packages* directory. Any JAR file found in the *jre/lib/ext* directory is automatically available to the JVM without being added to the CLASSPATH. You should look for files such as *jaxp.jar* and *parser.jar*, which could contain older, incompatible XML APIs. If you experience problems, remove all JAR files from the optional packages directory.

Unfortunately, you will have to do some detective work to figure out where the JAR files came from. Although Java 2 Version 1.3 introduced enhanced JAR features that included versioning information, most of the JAR files you encounter probably will not utilize this capability.

The Design

The design of this application is pretty simple. A single class contains a `main()` method that performs the transformation. The application requires two arguments: the XML file name followed by the XSLT file name. The results of the transformation are simply written to `System.out`. We will use the following XML data for our example:

```
<?xml version="1.0" encoding="UTF-8"?>
<message>Yep, it worked!</message>
```

The following XSLT stylesheet will be used. It's output method is `text`, and it simply prints out the contents of the `<message>` element. In this case, the text will be `Yep, it worked!`.

```
<?xml version="1.0" encoding="UTF-8"?>
<xsl:stylesheet
    version="1.0"
    xmlns:xsl="http://www.w3.org/1999/XSL/Transform">
  <xsl:output method="text" encoding="UTF-8"/>

  <!-- simply copy the message to the result tree -->
```

```
    <xsl:template match="/">
      <xsl:value-of select="message"/>
    </xsl:template>
  </xsl:stylesheet>
```

Since the filenames are passed as command-line parameters, the application can be used with other XML and XSLT files. You might want to try this out with one of the president examples from Chapters 2 and 3.

Xalan 1 Implementation

The complete code for the Xalan implementation is listed in Example 5-1. As comments in the code indicate, this code was developed and tested using Xalan 1.2.2, which is not the most recent XSLT processor from Apache. Fully qualified Java class names, such as `org.apache.xalan.xslt.XSLTProcessor`, are used for all Xalan-specific code.

TIP   A Xalan 2 example is not shown here because Xalan 2 is compatible with Sun's JAXP. The JAXP version of this program works with Xalan 2, as well as any other JAXP compatible processor.

Example 5-1. SimpleXalan1.java

```
package chap5;

import java.io.*;
import java.net.MalformedURLException;
import java.net.URL;
import org.xml.sax.SAXException;


/**
 * A simple demo of Xalan 1. This code was originally written using
 * Xalan 1.2.2.  It will not work with Xalan 2.
 */
public class SimpleXalan1 {

    /**
     * Accept two command line arguments: the name of an XML file, and
     * the name of an XSLT stylesheet. The result of the transformation
     * is written to stdout.
     */
    public static void main(String[] args)
            throws MalformedURLException, SAXException {
        if (args.length != 2) {
            System.err.println("Usage:");
            System.err.println("  java " + SimpleXalan1.class.getName()
```

Example 5-1. SimpleXalan1.java (continued)

```
                   + " xmlFileName xsltFileName");
        System.exit(1);
    }


    String xmlFileName = args[0];
    String xsltFileName = args[1];


    String xmlSystemId = new File(xmlFileName).toURL().toExternalForm();
    String xsltSystemId = new File(xsltFileName).toURL().toExternalForm();


    org.apache.xalan.xslt.XSLTProcessor processor =
            org.apache.xalan.xslt.XSLTProcessorFactory.getProcessor();


    org.apache.xalan.xslt.XSLTInputSource xmlInputSource =
            new org.apache.xalan.xslt.XSLTInputSource(xmlSystemId);


    org.apache.xalan.xslt.XSLTInputSource xsltInputSource =
            new org.apache.xalan.xslt.XSLTInputSource(xsltSystemId);


    org.apache.xalan.xslt.XSLTResultTarget resultTree =
            new org.apache.xalan.xslt.XSLTResultTarget(System.out);


    processor.process(xmlInputSource, xsltInputSource, resultTree);
    }
}
```

The code begins with the usual list of imports and the class declaration, followed by a simple check to ensure that two command line arguments are provided. If all is OK, then the XML file name and XSLT file name are converted into *system iden-tifier* values:

```
    String xmlSystemId = new File(xmlFileName).toURL().toExternalForm();
    String xsltSystemId = new File(xsltFileName).toURL().toExternalForm();
```

System identifiers are part of the XML specification and really mean the same thing as a Uniform Resource Identifier (URI). A Uniform Resource Locator (URL) is a specific type of URI and can be used for methods that require system identifiers as parameters. From a Java programming perspective, this means that a platform-specific filename such as *C:/data/simple.xml* needs to be converted to *file:/ //C:/data/simple.xml* before it can be used by most XML APIs. The code shown here does the conversion and will work on Unix, Windows, and other platforms supported by Java. Although you could try to manually prepend the filename with the literal string `file:///`, that may not result in portable code. The documentation for `java.io.File` clearly states that its `toURL()` method generates a system-dependent URL, so the results will vary when the same code is executed on a non-Windows platform. In fact, on Windows the code actually produces a nonstandard

URL (with a single slash), although it does work within Java programs: *file:/C:/ data/simple.xml.*

Now that we have system identifiers for our two input files, an instance of the XSLT processor is created:

```
org.apache.xalan.xslt.XSLTProcessor processor =
        org.apache.xalan.xslt.XSLTProcessorFactory.getProcessor();
```

XSLTProcessor is an interface, and XSLTProcessorFactory is a factory for creating new instances of classes that implement it. Because Xalan is open source software, it is easy enough to determine that XSLTEngineImpl is the class that implements the XSLTProcessor interface, although you should try to avoid code that depends on the specific implementation.

The next few lines of code create XSLTInputSource objects, one for the XML file and another for the XSLT file:

```
org.apache.xalan.xslt.XSLTInputSource xmlInputSource =
        new org.apache.xalan.xslt.XSLTInputSource(xmlSystemId);

org.apache.xalan.xslt.XSLTInputSource xsltInputSource =
        new org.apache.xalan.xslt.XSLTInputSource(xsltSystemId);
```

XSLTInputSource is a subclass of org.xml.sax.InputSource, adding the ability to read directly from a DOM Node. XSLTInputSource has the ability to read XML or XSLT data from a system ID, java.io.InputStream, java.io.Reader, org.w3c.dom.Node, or an existing InputSource. As shown in the code, the source of the data is specified in the constructor. XSLTInputSource also has a no-arg constructor, along with get/set methods for each of the supported data source types.

An instance of XSLTResultTarget is created next, sending the result of the transformation to System.out:

```
org.apache.xalan.xslt.XSLTResultTarget resultTree =
        new org.apache.xalan.xslt.XSLTResultTarget(System.out);
```

In a manner similar to XSLTInputSource, the XSLTResultTarget can also be wrapped around an instance of org.w3c.dom.Node, an OutputStream or Writer, a filename (not a system ID!), or an instance of org.xml.sax. DocumentHandler.

The final line of code simply instructs the processor to perform the transformation:

```
processor.process(xmlInputSource, xsltInputSource, resultTree);
```

SAXON Implementation

For comparison, a SAXON 5.5.1 implementation is presented in Example 5-2. As you scan through the code, you will notice the word "trax" appearing in the Java packages. This is an indication that Version 5.5.1 of SAXON was moving towards something called Transformation API for XML (TrAX). More information on TrAX is coming up in the JAXP discussion. In a nutshell, TrAX provides a uniform API that should work with any XSLT processor.

Example 5-2. SimpleSaxon.java

```
package chap5;

import java.io.*;
import java.net.MalformedURLException;
import java.net.URL;
import org.xml.sax.SAXException;

/**
 * A simple demo of SAXON. This code was originally written using
 * SAXON 5.5.1.
 */
public class SimpleSaxon {

    /**
     * Accept two command line arguments: the name of an XML file, and
     * the name of an XSLT stylesheet. The result of the transformation
     * is written to stdout.
     */
    public static void main(String[] args)
            throws MalformedURLException, IOException, SAXException {
        if (args.length != 2) {
            System.err.println("Usage:");
            System.err.println("  java " + SimpleSaxon.class.getName()
                    + " xmlFileName xsltFileName");
            System.exit(1);
        }

        String xmlFileName = args[0];
        String xsltFileName = args[1];

        String xmlSystemId = new File(xmlFileName).toURL().toExternalForm();
        String xsltSystemId = new File(xsltFileName).toURL().toExternalForm();

        com.icl.saxon.trax.Processor processor =
                com.icl.saxon.trax.Processor.newInstance("xslt");

        // unlike Xalan, SAXON uses the SAX InputSource.  Xalan
        // uses its own class, XSLTInputSource
```

Example 5-2. SimpleSaxon.java (continued)

```
        org.xml.sax.InputSource xmlInputSource =
                new org.xml.sax.InputSource(xmlSystemId);
        org.xml.sax.InputSource xsltInputSource =
                new org.xml.sax.InputSource(xsltSystemId);

        com.icl.saxon.trax.Result result =
                new com.icl.saxon.trax.Result(System.out);

        // create a new compiled stylesheet
        com.icl.saxon.trax.Templates templates =
                processor.process(xsltInputSource);

        // create a transformer that can be used for a single transformation
        com.icl.saxon.trax.Transformer trans = templates.newTransformer();
        trans.transform(xmlInputSource, result);
    }
}
```

The SAXON implementation starts exactly as the Xalan implementation does. Following the class declaration, the command-line parameters are validated and then converted to system IDs. The XML and XSLT system IDs are then wrapped in `org.xml.sax.InputSource` objects as follows:

```
    org.xml.sax.InputSource xmlInputSource =
            new org.xml.sax.InputSource(xmlSystemId);
    org.xml.sax.InputSource xsltInputSource =
            new org.xml.sax.InputSource(xsltSystemId);
```

This code is virtually indistinguishable from the Xalan code, except Xalan uses `XSLTInputSource` instead of `InputSource`. As mentioned before, `XSLTInputSource` is merely a subclass of `InputSource` that adds support for reading from a DOM Node. SAXON also has the ability to read from a DOM node, although its approach is slightly different.

Creating a `Result` object sets up the destination for the XSLT result tree, which is directed to `System.out` in this example:

```
    com.icl.saxon.trax.Result result =
            new com.icl.saxon.trax.Result(System.out);
```

The XSLT stylesheet is then compiled, resulting in an object that can be used repeatedly from many concurrent threads:

```
    com.icl.saxon.trax.Templates templates =
            processor.process(xsltInputSource);
```

In a typical XML and XSLT web site, the XML data is generated dynamically, but the same stylesheets are used repeatedly. For instance, stylesheets generating common headers, footers, and navigation bars will be used by many pages. To maximize performance, you will want to process the stylesheets once and reuse the instances for many clients at the same time. For this reason, the thread safety that Templates offers is critical.

An instance of the Transformer class is then created to perform the actual transformation. Unlike the stylesheet itself, the transformer cannot be shared by many clients and is not thread-safe. If this was a servlet implementation, the Transformer instance would have to be created with each invocation of doGet or doPost. In our example, the code is as follows:

```
com.icl.saxon.trax.Transformer trans = templates.newTransformer();
trans.transform(xmlInputSource, result);
```

SAXON, Xalan, or TrAX?

As the previous examples show, SAXON and Xalan have many similarities. While similarities make learning the various APIs easy, they do not result in portable code. If you write code directly against either of these interfaces, you lock yourself into that particular implementation unless you want to rewrite your application.

The other option is to write a facade around both processors, presenting a consistent interface that works with either processor behind the scenes. The only problem with this approach is that as new processors are introduced, you must update the implementation of your facade. It would be very difficult for one individual or organization to keep up with the rapidly changing world of XSLT processors.

But if the facade was an open standard and supported by a large enough user base, the people and organizations that write the XSLT processors would feel pressure to adhere to the common API, rather than the other way around. TrAX was initiated in early 2000 as an effort to define a consistent API to any XSLT processor. Since some of the key people behind TrAX were also responsible for implementing some of the major XSLT processors, it was quickly accepted that TrAX would be a de facto standard, much in the way that SAX is.

Introduction to JAXP 1.1

TrAX was a great idea, and the original work and concepts behind it were absorbed into JAXP Version 1.1. If you search for TrAX on the Web and get the feeling that the effort is waning, this is only because focus has shifted from TrAX to JAXP. Although the name has changed, the concept has not: JAXP provides a standard Java interface to many XSLT processors, allowing you to choose your favorite underlying implementation while retaining portability.

First released in March 2000, Sun's JAXP 1.0 utilized XML 1.0, XML Namespaces 1.0, SAX 1.0, and DOM Level 1. JAXP is a standard extension to Java, meaning that Sun provides a specification through its Java Community Process (JCP) as well as a reference implementation. JAXP 1.1 follows the same basic design philosophies of JAXP 1.0, adding support for DOM Level 2, SAX 2, and XSLT 1.0. A tool like JAXP is necessary because the XSLT specification defines only a transformation language; it says nothing about how to write a Java XSLT processor. Although they all perform the same basic tasks, every processor uses a different API and has its own set of programming conventions.

JAXP is not an XML parser, nor is it an XSLT processor. Instead, it provides a common Java interface that masks differences between various implementations of the supported standards. When using JAXP, your code can avoid dependencies on specific vendor tools, allowing flexibility to upgrade to newer tools when they become available.

The key to JAXP's design is the concept of *plugability layers*. These layers provide consistent Java interfaces to the underlying SAX, DOM, and XSLT implementations. In order to utilize one of these APIs, you must obtain a factory class without hardcoding Xalan or SAXON code into your application. This is accomplished via a lookup mechanism that relies on Java system properties. Since three separate plugability layers are used, you can use a DOM parser from one vendor, a SAX parser from another vendor, and yet another XSLT processor from someone else. In reality, you will probably need to use a DOM parser compatible with your XSLT processor if you try to transform the DOM tree directly. Figure 5-1 illustrates the high-level architecture of JAXP 1.1.

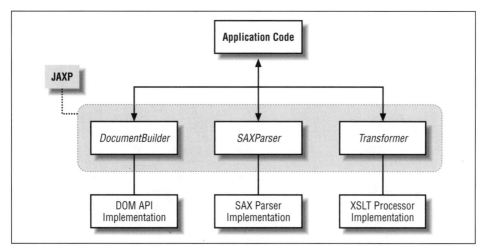

Figure 5-1. JAXP 1.1 architecture

As shown, application code does not deal directly with specific parser or processor implementations, such as SAXON or Xalan. Instead, you write code against abstract classes that JAXP provides. This level of indirection allows you to pick and choose among different implementations without even recompiling your application.

The main drawback to an API such as JAXP is the "least common denominator" effect, which is all too familiar to AWT programmers. In order to maximize portability, JAXP mostly provides functionality that all XSLT processors support. This means, for instance, that Xalan's custom XPath APIs are not included in JAXP. In order to use value-added features of a particular processor, you must revert to nonportable code, negating the benefits of a plugability layer. Fortunately, most common tasks are supported by JAXP, so reverting to implementation-specific code is the exception, not the rule.

Although the JAXP specification does not define an XML parser or XSLT processor, reference implementations do include these tools. These reference implementations are open source Apache XML tools,* so complete source code is available.

JAXP 1.1 Implementation

You guessed it—we will now reimplement the simple example using Sun's JAXP 1.1. Behind the scenes, this could use any JAXP 1.1-compliant XSLT processor; this code was developed and tested using Apache's Xalan 2 processor. Example 5-3 contains the complete source code.

Example 5-3. SimpleJaxp.java

```
package chap5;

import java.io.*;

/**
 * A simple demo of JAXP 1.1
 */
public class SimpleJaxp {

    /**
     * Accept two command line arguments: the name of an XML file, and
     * the name of an XSLT stylesheet. The result of the transformation
     * is written to stdout.
     */
    public static void main(String[] args)
            throws javax.xml.transform.TransformerException {
```

---

* Crimson and Xalan.

Example 5-3. SimpleJaxp.java (continued)

```
    if (args.length != 2) {
        System.err.println("Usage:");
        System.err.println("  java " + SimpleJaxp.class.getName()
                + " xmlFileName xsltFileName");
        System.exit(1);
    }

    File xmlFile = new File(args[0]);
    File xsltFile = new File(args[1]);

    javax.xml.transform.Source xmlSource =
            new javax.xml.transform.stream.StreamSource(xmlFile);
    javax.xml.transform.Source xsltSource =
            new javax.xml.transform.stream.StreamSource(xsltFile);
    javax.xml.transform.Result result =
            new javax.xml.transform.stream.StreamResult(System.out);

    // create an instance of TransformerFactory
    javax.xml.transform.TransformerFactory transFact =
            javax.xml.transform.TransformerFactory.newInstance();

    javax.xml.transform.Transformer trans =
            transFact.newTransformer(xsltSource);

    trans.transform(xmlSource, result);
    }
}
```

As in the earlier examples, explicit package names are used in the code to point out which classes are parts of JAXP. In future examples, import statements will be favored because they result in less typing and more readable code. Our new program begins by declaring that it may throw TransformerException:

```
public static void main(String[] args)
        throws javax.xml.transform.TransformerException {
```

This is a general-purpose exception representing anything that might go wrong during the transformation process. In other processors, SAX-specific exceptions are typically propagated to the caller. In JAXP, TransformerException can be wrapped around any type of Exception object that various XSLT processors may throw.

Next, the command-line arguments are converted into File objects. In the SAXON and Xalan examples, we created a system ID for each of these files. Since

JAXP can read directly from a `File` object, the extra conversion to a URI is not needed:

```
File xmlFile = new File(args[0]);
File xsltFile = new File(args[1]);

javax.xml.transform.Source xmlSource =
        new javax.xml.transform.stream.StreamSource(xmlFile);
javax.xml.transform.Source xsltSource =
        new javax.xml.transform.stream.StreamSource(xsltFile);
```

The `Source` interface is used to read both the XML file and the XSLT file. Unlike the SAX `InputSource` class or Xalan's `XSLTInputSource` class, `Source` is an interface that can have many implementations. In this simple example we are using `StreamSource`, which has the ability to read from a `File` object, an `InputStream`, a `Reader`, or a system ID. Later we will examine additional `Source` implementations that use SAX and DOM as input. Just like `Source`, `Result` is an interface that can have several implementations. In this example, a `StreamResult` sends the output of the transformations to `System.out`:

```
javax.xml.transform.Result result =
        new javax.xml.transform.stream.StreamResult(System.out);
```

Next, an instance of `TransformerFactory` is created:

```
javax.xml.transform.TransformerFactory transFact =
        javax.xml.transform.TransformerFactory.newInstance();
```

The `TransformerFactory` is responsible for creating `Transformer` and `Template` objects. In our simple example, we create a `Transformer` object:

```
javax.xml.transform.Transformer trans =
        transFact.newTransformer(xsltSource);
```

`Transformer` objects are not thread-safe, although they can be used multiple times. For a simple example like this, we will not encounter any problems. In a threaded servlet environment, however, multiple users cannot concurrently access the same `Transformer` instance. JAXP also provides a `Templates` interface, which represents a stylesheet that can be accessed by many concurrent threads.

The transformer instance is then used to perform the actual transformation:

```
trans.transform(xmlSource, result);
```

This applies the XSLT stylesheet to the XML data, sending the result to `System.out`.

XSLT Plugability Layer

JAXP 1.1 defines a specific lookup procedure to locate an appropriate XSLT processor. This must be accomplished without hardcoding vendor-specific code into applications, so Java system properties and JAR file service providers are used. Within your code, first locate an instance of the `TransformerFactory` class as follows:

```
javax.xml.transform.TransformerFactory transFact =
        javax.xml.transform.TransformerFactory.newInstance();
```

Since `TransformerFactory` is abstract, its `newInstance()` factory method is used to instantiate an instance of a specific subclass. The algorithm for locating this subclass begins by looking at the `javax.xml.transform.TransformerFactory` system property. Let us suppose that `com.foobar.AcmeTransformer` is a new XSLT processor compliant with JAXP 1.1. To utilize this processor instead of JAXP's default processor, you can specify the system property on the command line* when you start your Java application:

```
java -Djavax.xml.transform.TransformerFactory=com.foobar.AcmeTransformer MyApp
```

Provided that JAXP is able to instantiate an instance of `AcmeTransformer`, this is the XSLT processor that will be used. Of course, `AcmeTransformer` must be a subclass of `TransformerFactory` for this to work, so it is up to vendors to offer support for JAXP.

If the system property is not specified, JAXP next looks for a property file named *lib/jaxp.properties* in the JRE directory. A property file consists of name=value pairs, and JAXP looks for a line like this:

```
javax.xml.transform.TransformerFactory=com.foobar.AcmeTransformer
```

You can obtain the location of the JRE with the following code:

```
String javaHomeDir = System.getProperty("java.home");
```

TIP   Some popular development tools change the value of *java.home* when they are installed, which could prevent JAXP from locating *jaxp.properties*. JBuilder, for instance, installs its own version of Java 2 that it uses by default.

The advantage of creating *jaxp.properties* in this directory is that you can use your preferred processor for all of your applications that use JAXP without having to specify the system property on the command line. You can still override this file with the **-D** command-line syntax, however.

If *jaxp.properties* is not found, JAXP uses the JAR file *service provider* mechanism to locate an appropriate subclass of `TransformerFactory`. The service provider mechanism is outlined in the JAR file specification from Sun and simply means

---

* System properties can also be specified in Ant build files.

that you must create a file in the *META-INF/services* directory of a JAR file. In JAXP, this file is called *javax.xml.transform.TransformerFactory*. It contains a single line that specifies the implementation of `TransformerFactory`: `com.foobar.AcmeTransformer` in our fictitious example. If you look inside of *xalan.jar* in JAXP 1.1, you will find this file. In order to utilize a different parser that follows the JAXP 1.1 convention, simply make sure its JAR file is located first on your CLASSPATH.

Finally, if JAXP cannot find an implementation class from any of the three locations, it uses its default implementation of `TransformerFactory`. To summarize, here are the steps that JAXP performs when attempting to locate a factory:

1. Use the value of the `javax.xml.transform.TransformerFactory` system property if it exists.

2. If *JRE/lib/jaxp.properties* exists, then look for a `javax.xml.transform.TransformerFactory=ImplementationClass` entry in that file.

3. Use a JAR file service provider to look for a file called *META-INF/services/javax.xml.transform.TransformerFactory* in any JAR file on the CLASSPATH.

4. Use the default `TransformerFactory` instance.

The JAXP 1.1 plugability layers for SAX and DOM follow the exact same process as the XSLT layer, only they use the `javax.xml.parsers.SAXParserFactory` and `javax.xml.parsers.DocumentBuilderFactory` system properties respectively. It should be noted that JAXP 1.0 uses a much simpler algorithm where it checks only for the existence of the system property. If that property is not set, the default implementation is used.

The Transformer Class

As shown in Example 5-3, a `Transformer` object can be obtained from the `TransformerFactory` as follows:

```
javax.xml.transform.TransformerFactory transFact =
        javax.xml.transform.TransformerFactory.newInstance();
javax.xml.transform.Transformer trans =
        transFact.newTransformer(xsltSource);
```

The `Transformer` instance is wrapped around an XSLT stylesheet and allows you to perform as many transformations as you wish. The main caveat is thread safety, because many threads cannot use a single `Transformer` instance concurrently. For each transformation, invoke the `transform` method:

```
abstract void transform(Source xmlSource, Result outputTarget)
    throws TransformerException
```

This method is abstract because the `TransformerFactory` returns a subclass of `Transformer` that does the actual work. The `Source` interface defines where the XML data comes from and the `Result` interface specifies where the transformation result is sent. The `TransformerException` will be thrown if anything goes wrong during the transformation process and may contain the location of the error and a reference to the original exception. The ability to properly report the location of the error is entirely dependent upon the quality of the underlying XSLT transformer implementation's error reporting. We will talk about specific classes that implement the `Source` and `Result` interfaces later in this chapter.

Aside from actually performing the transformation, the `Transformer` implementation allows you to set output properties and stylesheet parameters. In XSLT, a stylesheet parameter is declared and used as follows:

```
<?xml version="1.0" encoding="UTF-8"?>
<xsl:stylesheet version="1.0" xmlns:xsl="http://www.w3.org/1999/XSL/Transform">
  <xsl:output method="html"/>
  <xsl:param name="image_dir" select="'images'"/>

  <xsl:template match="/">
    <html>
      <body>
        <h1>Stylesheet Parameter Example</h1>
        <img src="{$image_dir}/sample.gif"/>
      </body>
    </html>
  </xsl:template>
</xsl:stylesheet>
```

The `<xsl:param>` element declares the parameter name and an optional `select` attribute. This attribute specifies the default value if the stylesheet parameter is not provided. In this case, the string `'images'` is the default value and is enclosed in apostrophes so it is treated as a string instead of an XPath expression. Later, the `image_dir` variable is referred to with the attribute value template syntax: `{$image_dir}`.

Passing a variable for the location of your images is a common technique because your development environment might use a different directory name than your production web server. Another common use for a stylesheet parameter is to pass in data that a servlet generates dynamically, such as a unique ID for session tracking.

From JAXP, pass this parameter via the `Transformer` instance. The code is simple enough:

```
javax.xml.transform.Transformer trans =
        transFact.newTransformer(xsltSource);
trans.setParameter("image_dir", "graphics");
```

You can set as many parameters as you like, and these parameters will be saved and reused for every transformation you make with this `Transformer` instance. If you wish to remove a parameter, you must call `clearParameters()`, which clears all parameters for this `Transformer` instance. Parameters work similarly to a `java.util.Map`; if you set the same parameter twice, the second value overwrites the first value.

Another use for the `Transformer` class is to get and set output properties through one of the following methods:

```
void setOutputProperties(java.util.Properties props)
void setOutputProperty(String name, String value)
java.util.Properties getOutputProperties()
String getOutputProperty(String name)
```

As you can see, properties are specified as name/value pairs of Strings and can be set and retrieved individually or as a group. Unlike stylesheet parameters, you can un-set an individual property by simply passing in `null` for the value. The permitted property names are defined in the `javax.xml.transform.OutputKeys` class and are explained in Table 5-1.

Table 5-1. Constants defined in javax.xml.transform.OutputKeys

Constant	Meaning
CDATA_SECTION_ELEMENTS	Specifies a whitespace-separated list of element names whose content should be output as CDATA sections. See the XSLT specification from the W3C for examples.
DOCTYPE_PUBLIC	Only used if DOCTYPE_SYSTEM is also used, this instructs the processor to output a PUBLIC document type declaration. For example: <!DOCTYPE rootElem PUBLIC "public id" "system id">.
DOCTYPE_SYSTEM	Instructs the processor to output a document-type declaration. For example: <!DOCTYPE rootElem SYSTEM "system id">.
ENCODING	Specifies the character encoding of the result tree, such as UTF-8 or UTF-16.
INDENT	Specifies whether or not whitespace may be added to the result tree, making the output more readable. Acceptable values are yes and no. Although indentation makes the output more readable, it does make the file size larger, thus harming performance.
MEDIA_TYPE	The MIME type of the result tree.
METHOD	The output method, either xml, html, or text. Although other values are possible, such as xhtml, these are implementation-defined and may be rejected by your processor.

Table 5-1. Constants defined in javax.xml.transform.OutputKeys (continued)

Constant	Meaning
OMIT_XML_DECLARATION	Acceptable values are yes and no, specifying whether or not to include the XML declaration on the first line of the result tree.
STANDALONE	Acceptable values are yes and no, specifying whether or not the XML declaration indicates that the document is standalone. For example: <?xml version="1.0" encoding="UTF-8" standalone="yes"?>.
VERSION	Specifies the version of the output method, typically 1.0 for XML output. This shows up in the XML declaration as follows: <?xml version="1.0" encoding="UTF-8"?>.

It is no coincidence that these output properties are the same as the properties you can set on the <xsl:output> element in your stylesheets. For example:

```
<xsl:output method="xml" indent="yes" encoding="UTF-8"/>
```

Using JAXP, you can either specify additional output properties or override those set in the stylesheet. To change the encoding, write this code:

```
// this will take precedence over any encoding specified in the stylesheet
trans.setOutputProperty(OutputKeys.ENCODING, "UTF-16");
```

Keep in mind that this will, in addition to adding encoding="UTF-16" to the XML declaration, actually cause the processor to use that encoding in the result tree. For a value of UTF-16, this means that 16-bit Unicode characters will be generated, so you may have trouble viewing the result tree in many ASCII-only text editors.

JAXP XSLT Design

Now that we have seen some example code and have begun our exploration of the Transformer class, let's step back and look at the overall design of the XSLT plugability layer. JAXP support for XSLT is broken down into the packages listed in Table 5-2.

Table 5-2. JAXP transformation packages

Package	Description
javax.xml.transform	Defines a general-purpose API for XML transformations without any dependencies on SAX or DOM. The Transformer class is obtained from the TransformerFactory class. The Transformer transforms from a Source to a Result.
javax.xml.transform.dom	Defines how transformations can be performed using DOM. Provides implementations of Source and Result: DOMSource and DOMResult.

Table 5-2. JAXP transformation packages (continued)

Package	Description
`javax.xml.transform.sax`	Supports SAX2 transformations. Defines SAX versions of `Source` and `Result`: `SAXSource` and `SAXResult`. Also defines a subclass of `TransformerFactory` that allows SAX2 events to be fed into an XSLT processor.
`javax.xml.transform.stream`	Defines I/O stream implementations of `Source` and `Result`: `StreamSource` and `StreamResult`.

The heart of JAXP XSLT support lies in the `javax.xml.transform` package, which lays out the mechanics and overall process for any transformation that is performed. This package mostly consists of interfaces and abstract classes, except for `OutputKeys` and a few exception and error classes. Figure 5-2 presents a UML class diagram that shows all of the pieces in this important package.

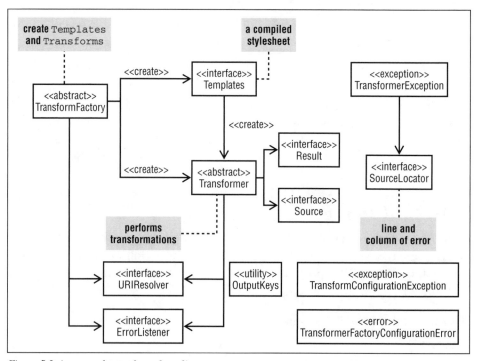

Figure 5-2. javax.xml.transform class diagram

As you can see, this is a small package, indicative of the fact that JAXP is merely a wrapper around the tools that actually perform transformations. The entry point is `TransformerFactory`, which creates instances of `Transformer`, as we have already seen, as well as instances of the `Templates` abstract class. A `Templates` object represents a compiled stylesheet and will be covered in detail later in this chapter.* The advantage of compilation is performance: the same `Templates` object can be used over and over by many threads without reparsing the XSLT file.

The `URIResolver` is responsible for resolving URIs found within stylesheets and is generally something you will not need to deal with directly. It is used when a stylesheet imports or includes another document, and the processor needs to figure out where to look for that document. For example:

```
<xsl:import href="commonFooter.xslt"/>
```

`ErrorListener`, as you may guess, is an interface that allows your code to register as a listener for error conditions. This interface defines the following three methods:

```
void error(TransformerException ex)
void fatalError(TransformerException ex)
void warning(TransformerException ex)
```

The `TransformerException` has the ability to wrap around another `Exception` or `Throwable` object and may return an instance of the `SourceLocator` class. If the underlying XSLT implementation does not provide a `SourceLocator`, `null` is returned. The `SourceLocator` interface defines methods to locate where a `TransformerException` originated. In the case of `error()` and `warning()`, the XSLT processor is required to continue processing the document until the end. For `fatalError()`, on the other hand, the XSLT processor is not required to continue. If you do not register an `ErrorListener` object, then all errors, fatal errors, and warnings are normally written to `System.err`. `TransformerFactoryConfigurationError` and `TransformerConfigurationException` round out the error-handling APIs for JAXP, indicating problems configuring the underlying XSLT processor implementation. The `TransformerFactoryConfigurationError` class is generally used when the implementation class cannot be found on the CLASSPATH or cannot be instantiated at all. `TransformerConfigurationException` simply indicates a "serious configuration error" according to its documentation.

Input and Output

XSLT processors, like other XML tools, can read their input data from many different sources. In the most basic scenario, you will load a static stylesheet and XML document using the `java.io.File` class. More commonly, the XSLT stylesheet will come from a file, but the XML data will be generated dynamically as the result of a database query. In this case, it does not make sense to write the database query

---

* The exact definition of a "compiled" stylesheet is vague. XSLT processors are free to optimize cached stylesheets however they see fit.

results to an XML file and then parse it into the XSLT processor. Instead, it is desirable to pipe the XML data directly into the processor using SAX or DOM. In fact, we will even see how to read nonXML data and transform it using XSLT.

System Identifiers, Files, and URLs

The simple examples presented earlier in this chapter introduced the concept of a system identifier. As mentioned before, system identifiers are nothing more than URIs and are used frequently by XML tools. For example, `javax.xml.transform.Source`, one of the key interfaces in JAXP, has the following API:

```
public interface Source {
    String getSystemId();
    void setSystemId(String systemId);
}
```

The second method, `setSystemId()`, is crucial. By providing a URI to the `Source`, the XSLT processor can resolve URIs encountered in XSLT stylesheets. This allows XSLT code like this to work:

```
<xsl:import href="commonFooter.xslt"/>
```

When it comes to XSLT programming, you will use methods in `java.io.File` and `java.net.URL` to convert platform-specific file names into system IDs. These can then be used as parameters to any methods that expect a system ID as a parameter. For example, you would write the following code to convert a platform-specific filename into a system ID:

```
public static void main(String[] args) {
    // assume that the first command-line arg contains a file name
    // - on Windows, something like "C:\home\index.xml"
    // - on Unix, something like "/usr/home/index.xml"
    String fileName = args[0];
    File fileObject = new File(fileName);
    URL fileURL = fileObject.toURL();
    String systemID = fileURL.toExternalForm();
```

This code was written on several lines for clarity; it can be consolidated as follows:

```
String systemID = new File(fileName).toURL().toExternalForm();
```

Converting from a system identifier back to a filename or a `File` object can be accomplished with this code:

```
URL url = new URL(systemID);
String fileName = url.getFile();
File fileObject = new File(fileName);
```

And once again, this code can be condensed into a single line as follows:

```
File fileObject = new File((new URL(systemID)).getFile());
```

JAXP I/O Design

The Source and Result interfaces in javax.xml.transform provide the basis for all transformation input and output in JAXP 1.1. Regardless of whether a stylesheet is obtained via a URI, filename, or InputStream, its data is fed into JAXP via an implementation of the Source interface. The output is then sent to an implementation of the Result interface. The implementations provided by JAXP are shown in Figure 5-3.

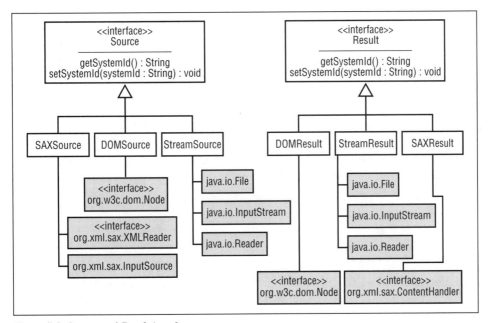

Figure 5-3. Source and Result interfaces

As you can see, JAXP is not particular about where it gets its data or sends its results. Remember that two instances of Source are always specified: one for the XML data and another for the XSLT stylesheet.

JAXP Stream I/O

As shown in Figure 5-3, StreamSource is one of the implementations of the Source interface. In addition to the system identifiers that Source provides, StreamSource allows input to be obtained from a File, an InputStream, or a Reader. The SimpleJaxp class in Example 5-3 showed how to use StreamSource to read from a File object. There are also four constructors that allow you to construct a `StreamSource` from either an `InputStream` or `Reader`. The complete list of constructors is shown here:

```
public StreamSource()
public StreamSource(File f)
public StreamSource(String systemId)
public StreamSource(InputStream byteStream)
public StreamSource(InputStream byteStream, String systemId)
public StreamSource(Reader characterStream)
public StreamSource(Reader characterStream, String systemId)
```

For the constructors that take `InputStream` and `Reader` as arguments, the first argument provides either the XML data or the XSLT stylesheet. The second argument, if present, is used to resolve relative URI references in the document. As mentioned before, your XSLT stylesheet may include the following code:

```
<xsl:import href="commonFooter.xslt"/>
```

By providing a system identifier as a parameter to the `StreamSource`, you are telling the XSLT processor where to look for *commonFooter.xslt*. Without this parameter, you may encounter an error when the processor cannot resolve this URI. The simple fix is to call the `setSystemId()` method as follows:

```
// construct a Source that reads from an InputStream
Source mySrc = new StreamSource(anInputStream);
// specify a system ID (a String) so the Source can resolve relative URLs
// that are encountered in XSLT stylesheets
mySrc.setSystemId(aSystemId);
```

The documentation for `StreamSource` also advises that `InputStream` is preferred to `Reader` because this allows the processor to properly handle the character encoding as specified in the XML declaration.

`StreamResult` is similar in functionality to `StreamSource`, although it is not necessary to resolve relative URIs. The available constructors are as follows:

```
public StreamResult()
public StreamResult(File f)
public StreamResult(String systemId)
public StreamResult(OutputStream byteStream)
public StreamResult(Writer characterStream)
```

Let's look at some of the other options for `StreamSource` and `StreamResult`. Example 5-4 is a modification of the `SimpleJaxp` program that was presented earlier. It downloads the XML specification from the W3C web site and stores it in a temporary file on your local disk. To download the file, construct a `StreamSource` with a system identifier as a parameter. The stylesheet is a simple one that merely performs an identity transformation, copying the unmodified XML data to the result tree. The result is then sent to a `StreamResult` using its `File` constructor.

Example 5-4. Streams.java

```java
package chap5;

import java.io.*;
import javax.xml.transform.*;
import javax.xml.transform.stream.*;

/**
 * A simple demo of JAXP 1.1 StreamSource and StreamResult. This
 * program downloads the XML specification from the W3C and prints
 * it to a temporary file.
 */
public class Streams {

    // an identity copy stylesheet
    private static final String IDENTITY_XSLT =
        "<xsl:stylesheet xmlns:xsl='http://www.w3.org/1999/XSL/Transform'"
        + " version='1.0'>"
        + "<xsl:template match='/'><xsl:copy-of select='.'/>"
        + "</xsl:template></xsl:stylesheet>";

    // the XML spec in XML format
    // (using an HTTP URL rather than a file URL)
    private static String xmlSystemId =
            "http://www.w3.org/TR/2000/REC-xml-20001006.xml";

    public static void main(String[] args) throws IOException,
            TransformerException {

        // show how to read from a system identifier and a Reader
        Source xmlSource = new StreamSource(xmlSystemId);
        Source xsltSource = new StreamSource(
                new StringReader(IDENTITY_XSLT));

        // send the result to a file
        File resultFile = File.createTempFile("Streams", ".xml");
        Result result = new StreamResult(resultFile);

        System.out.println("Results will go to: "
                + resultFile.getAbsolutePath());

        // get the factory
        TransformerFactory transFact = TransformerFactory.newInstance();

        // get a transformer for this particular stylesheet
        Transformer trans = transFact.newTransformer(xsltSource);
```

Example 5-4. Streams.java (continued)

```
    // do the transformation
    trans.transform(xmlSource, result);
  }
}
```

The "identity copy" stylesheet simply matches "/", which is the document itself. It then uses `<xsl:copy-of select='.'/>` to select the document and copy it to the result tree. In this case, we coded our own stylesheet. You can also omit the XSLT stylesheet altogether as follows:

```
// construct a Transformer without any XSLT stylesheet
Transformer trans = transFact.newTransformer();
```

In this case, the processor will provide its own stylesheet and do the same thing that our example does. This is useful when you need to use JAXP to convert a DOM tree to XML text for debugging purposes because the default `Transformer` will simply copy the XML data without any transformation.

JAXP DOM I/O

In many cases, the fastest form of transformation available is to feed an instance of `org.w3c.dom.Document` directly into JAXP. Although the transformation is fast, it does take time to generate the DOM; DOM is also memory intensive, and may not be the best choice for large documents. In most cases, the DOM data will be generated dynamically as the result of a database query or some other operation (see Chapter 1). Once the DOM is generated, simply wrap the `Document` object in a DOMSource as follows:

```
org.w3c.dom.Document domDoc = createDomDocument();
Source xmlSource = new javax.xml.transform.dom.DOMSource(domDoc);
```

The remainder of the transformation looks identical to the file-based transformation shown in Example 5-4. JAXP needs only the alternate input `Source` object shown here to read from DOM.

JAXP SAX I/O

XSLT is designed to transform well-formed XML data into another format, typically HTML. But wouldn't it be nice if we could also use XSLT stylesheets to transform nonXML data into HTML? For example, most spreadsheets have the ability to export their data into Comma Separated Values (CSV) format, as shown here:

```
Burke,Eric,M
Burke,Jennifer,L
Burke,Aidan,G
```

One approach is parsing the file into memory, using DOM to create an XML representation of the data, and then feeding that information into JAXP for transformation. This approach works but requires an intermediate programming step to convert the CSV file into a DOM tree. A better option is to write a custom SAX parser, feeding its output directly into JAXP. This avoids the overhead of constructing the DOM tree, offering better memory utilization and performance.

The approach

It turns out that writing a SAX parser is quite easy.* All a SAX parser does is read an XML file top to bottom and fire event notifications as various elements are encountered. In our custom parser, we will read the CSV file top to bottom, firing SAX events as we read the file. A program listening to those SAX events will not realize that the data file is CSV rather than XML; it sees only the events. Figure 5-4 illustrates the conceptual model.

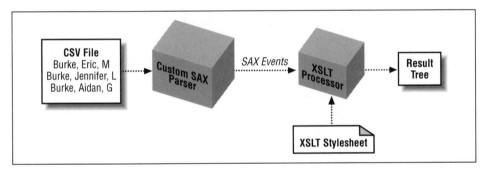

Figure 5-4. Custom SAX parser

In this model, the XSLT processor interprets the SAX events as XML data and uses a normal stylesheet to perform the transformation. The interesting aspect of this model is that we can easily write custom SAX parsers for other file formats, making XSLT a useful transformation language for just about any legacy application data.

In SAX, org.xml.sax.XMLReader is a standard interface that parsers must implement. It works in conjunction with org.xml.sax.ContentHandler, which is the interface that listens to SAX events. For this model to work, your XSLT processor must implement the ContentHandler interface so it can listen to the SAX events that the XMLReader generates. In the case of JAXP, javax.xml.transform.sax.TransformerHandler is used for this purpose.

---

* Our examples use SAX 2.

Obtaining an instance of `TransformerHandler` requires a few extra programming steps. First, create a `TransformerFactory` as usual:

```
TransformerFactory transFact = TransformerFactory.newInstance();
```

As before, the `TransformerFactory` is the JAXP abstraction to some underlying
XSLT processor. This underlying processor may not support SAX features, so you
have to query it to determine if you can proceed:

```
if (transFact.getFeature(SAXTransformerFactory.FEATURE)) {
```

If this returns `false`, you are out of luck. Otherwise, you can safely downcast to a
`SAXTransformerFactory` and construct the `TransformerHandler` instance:

```
SAXTransformerFactory saxTransFact =
            (SAXTransformerFactory) transFact;
  // create a ContentHandler, don't specify a stylesheet.  Without
  // a stylesheet, raw XML is sent to the output.
  TransformerHandler transHand = saxTransFact.newTransformerHandler();
```

In the code shown here, a stylesheet was not specified. JAXP defaults to the identity transformation stylesheet, which means that the SAX events will be "transformed" into raw XML output. To specify a stylesheet that performs an actual
transformation, pass a `Source` to the method as follows:

```
Source xsltSource = new StreamSource(myXsltSystemId);
TransformerHandler transHand = saxTransFact.newTransformerHandler(
        xsltSource);
```

Detailed CSV to SAX design

Before delving into the complete example program, let's step back and look at a
more detailed design diagram. The conceptual model is straightforward, but quite
a few classes and interfaces come into play. Figure 5-5 shows the pieces necessary
for SAX-based transformations.

This diagram certainly appears to be more complex than previous approaches, but
is   similar   in   many   ways.   In   previous   approaches,   we   used   the
`TransformerFactory` to create instances of `Transformer`; in the SAX approach,
we start with a subclass of `TransformerFactory`. Before any work can be done,
you must verify that your particular implementation supports SAX-based transformations. The reference implementation of JAXP does support this, although other
implementations are not required to do so. In the following code fragment, the
`getFeature` method of `TransformerFactory` will return `true` if you can safely
downcast to a `SAXTransformerFactory` instance:

```
TransformerFactory transFact = TransformerFactory.newInstance();
if (transFact.getFeature(SAXTransformerFactory.FEATURE)) {
    // downcast is allowed
    SAXTransformerFactory saxTransFact = (SAXTransformerFactory) transFact;
```

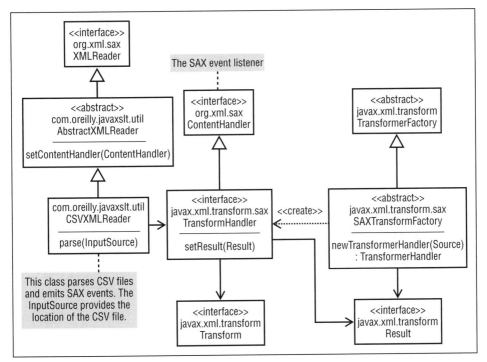

Figure 5-5. SAX and XSLT transformations

If `getFeature` returns `false`, your only option is to look for an implementation that does support SAX-based transformations. Otherwise, you can proceed to create an instance of `TransformerHandler`:

```
TransformerHandler transHand = saxTransFact.newTransformerHandler(myXsltSource);
```

This object now represents your XSLT stylesheet. As Figure 5-5 shows, `TransformerHandler` extends `org.xml.sax.ContentHandler`, so it knows how to listen to events from a SAX parser. The series of SAX events will provide the "fake XML" data, so the only remaining piece of the puzzle is to set the `Result` and tell the SAX parser to begin parsing. The `TransformerHandler` also provides a reference to a `Transformer`, which allows you to set output properties such as the character encoding, whether to indent the output or any other attributes of `<xsl:output>`.

Writing the custom parser

Writing the actual SAX parser sounds harder than it really is. The process basically involves implementing the `org.xml.sax.XMLReader` interface, which provides numerous methods you can safely ignore for most applications. For example, when parsing a CSV file, it is probably not necessary to deal with namespaces or

validation. The code for `AbstractXMLReader.java` is shown in Example 5-5. This
is an abstract class that provides basic implementations of every method in the
`XMLReader` interface except for the `parse()` method. This means that all you
need to do to write a parser is create a subclass and override this single method.

Example 5-5. AbstractXMLReader.java

```
package com.oreilly.javaxslt.util;

import java.io.IOException;
import java.util.*;
import org.xml.sax.*;

/**
 * An abstract class that implements the SAX2 XMLReader interface. The
 * intent of this class is to make it easy for subclasses to act as
 * SAX2 XMLReader implementations. This makes it possible, for example, for
 * them to emit SAX2 events that can be fed into an XSLT processor for
 * transformation.
 */
public abstract class AbstractXMLReader implements org.xml.sax.XMLReader {
    private Map featureMap = new HashMap();
    private Map propertyMap = new HashMap();
    private EntityResolver entityResolver;
    private DTDHandler dtdHandler;
    private ContentHandler contentHandler;
    private ErrorHandler errorHandler;

    /**
     * The only abstract method in this class. Derived classes can parse
     * any source of data and emit SAX2 events to the ContentHandler.
     */
    public abstract void parse(InputSource input) throws IOException,
            SAXException;

    public boolean getFeature(String name)
            throws SAXNotRecognizedException, SAXNotSupportedException {
        Boolean featureValue = (Boolean) this.featureMap.get(name);
        return (featureValue == null) ? false
                : featureValue.booleanValue();
    }

    public void setFeature(String name, boolean value)
            throws SAXNotRecognizedException, SAXNotSupportedException {
        this.featureMap.put(name, new Boolean(value));
    }

    public Object getProperty(String name)
            throws SAXNotRecognizedException, SAXNotSupportedException {
```

Example 5-5. AbstractXMLReader.java (continued)

```
        return this.propertyMap.get(name);
    }

    public void setProperty(String name, Object value)
            throws SAXNotRecognizedException, SAXNotSupportedException {
        this.propertyMap.put(name, value);
    }

    public void setEntityResolver(EntityResolver entityResolver) {
        this.entityResolver = entityResolver;
    }

    public EntityResolver getEntityResolver() {
        return this.entityResolver;
    }

    public void setDTDHandler(DTDHandler dtdHandler) {
        this.dtdHandler = dtdHandler;
    }

    public DTDHandler getDTDHandler() {
        return this.dtdHandler;
    }

    public void setContentHandler(ContentHandler contentHandler) {
        this.contentHandler = contentHandler;
    }

    public ContentHandler getContentHandler() {
        return this.contentHandler;
    }

    public void setErrorHandler(ErrorHandler errorHandler) {
        this.errorHandler = errorHandler;
    }

    public ErrorHandler getErrorHandler() {
        return this.errorHandler;
    }

    public void parse(String systemId) throws IOException, SAXException {
        parse(new InputSource(systemId));
    }
}
```

Creating the subclass, `CSVXMLReader`, involves overriding the `parse()` method and actually scanning through the CSV file, emitting SAX events as elements in the file are encountered. While the SAX portion is very easy, parsing the CSV file is a little more challenging. To make this class as flexible as possible, it was designed to parse through any CSV file that a spreadsheet such as Microsoft Excel can export. For simple data, your CSV file might look like this:

```
Burke,Eric,M
Burke,Jennifer,L
Burke,Aidan,G
```

The XML representation of this file is shown in Example 5-6. The only real drawback here is that CSV files are strictly positional, meaning that names are not assigned to each column of data. This means that the XML output merely contains a sequence of three <value> elements for each line, so your stylesheet will have to select items based on position.

Example 5-6. Example XML output from CSV parser

```xml
<?xml version="1.0" encoding="UTF-8"?>
<csvFile>
  <line>
    <value>Burke</value>
    <value>Eric</value>
    <value>M</value>
  </line>
  <line>
    <value>Burke</value>
    <value>Jennifer</value>
    <value>L</value>
  </line>
  <line>
    <value>Burke</value>
    <value>Aidan</value>
    <value>G</value>
  </line>
</csvFile>
```

One enhancement would be to design the CSV parser so it could accept a list of meaningful column names as parameters, and these could be used in the XML that is generated. Another option would be to write an XSLT stylesheet that transformed this initial output into another form of XML that used meaningful column names. To keep the code example relatively manageable, these features were omitted from this implementation. But there are some complexities to the CSV file format that have to be considered. For example, fields that contain commas must be surrounded with quotes:

```
"Consultant,Author,Teacher",Burke,Eric,M
Teacher,Burke,Jennifer,L
None,Burke,Aidan,G
```

To further complicate matters, fields may also contain quotes ("). In this case, they are doubled up, much in the same way you use double backslash characters (\\) in Java to represent a single backslash. In the following example, the first column contains a single quote, so the entire field is quoted, and the single quote is doubled up:

```
"test""quote",Teacher,Burke,Jennifer,L
```

This would be interpreted as:

```
test"quote,Teacher,Burke,Jennifer,L
```

The code in Example 5-7 shows the complete implementation of the CSV parser.

Example 5-7. CSVXMLReader.java

```java
package com.oreilly.javaxslt.util;

import java.io.*;
import java.net.URL;

import org.xml.sax.*;
import org.xml.sax.helpers.*;

/**
 * A utility class that parses a Comma Separated Values (CSV) file
 * and outputs its contents using SAX2 events. The format of CSV that
 * this class reads is identical to the export format for Microsoft
 * Excel. For simple values, the CSV file may look like this:
 * <pre>
 * a,b,c
 * d,e,f
 * </pre>
 * Quotes are used as delimiters when the values contain commas:
 * <pre>
 * a,"b,c",d
 * e,"f,g","h,i"
 * </pre>
 * And double quotes are used when the values contain quotes. This parser
 * is smart enough to trim spaces around commas, as well.
 *
 * @author Eric M. Burke
 */
public class CSVXMLReader extends AbstractXMLReader {

    // an empty attribute for use with SAX
    private static final Attributes EMPTY_ATTR = new AttributesImpl();

    /**
     * Parse a CSV file. SAX events are delivered to the ContentHandler
```

Example 5-7. CSVXMLReader.java (continued)

```java
         * that was registered via <code>setContentHandler</code>.
         *
         * @param input the comma separated values file to parse.
         */
        public void parse(InputSource input) throws IOException,
                SAXException {
            // if no handler is registered to receive events, don't bother
            // to parse the CSV file
            ContentHandler ch = getContentHandler();
            if (ch == null) {
                return;
            }


            // convert the InputSource into a BufferedReader
            BufferedReader br = null;
            if (input.getCharacterStream() != null) {
                br = new BufferedReader(input.getCharacterStream());
            } else if (input.getByteStream() != null) {
                br = new BufferedReader(new InputStreamReader(
                        input.getByteStream()));
            } else if (input.getSystemId() != null) {
                java.net.URL url = new URL(input.getSystemId());
                br = new BufferedReader(new InputStreamReader(url.openStream()));
            } else {
                throw new SAXException("Invalid InputSource object");
            }

            ch.startDocument();

            // emit <csvFile>
            ch.startElement("","","csvFile",EMPTY_ATTR);

            // read each line of the file until EOF is reached
            String curLine = null;
            while ((curLine = br.readLine()) != null) {
                curLine = curLine.trim();
                if (curLine.length() > 0) {
                    // create the <line> element
                    ch.startElement("","","line",EMPTY_ATTR);
                    // output data from this line
                    parseLine(curLine, ch);
                    // close the </line> element
                    ch.endElement("","","line");
                }
            }

            // emit </csvFile>
            ch.endElement("","","csvFile");
```

Example 5-7. CSVXMLReader.java (continued)

```java
        ch.endDocument();
    }


    // Break an individual line into tokens. This is a recursive function
    // that extracts the first token, then recursively parses the
    // remainder of the line.
    private void parseLine(String curLine, ContentHandler ch)
        throws IOException, SAXException {

        String firstToken = null;
        String remainderOfLine = null;
        int commaIndex = locateFirstDelimiter(curLine);
        if (commaIndex > -1) {
            firstToken = curLine.substring(0, commaIndex).trim();
            remainderOfLine = curLine.substring(commaIndex+1).trim();
        } else {
            // no commas, so the entire line is the token
            firstToken = curLine;
        }

        // remove redundant quotes
        firstToken = cleanupQuotes(firstToken);

        // emit the <value> element
        ch.startElement("","","value",EMPTY_ATTR);
        ch.characters(firstToken.toCharArray(), 0, firstToken.length());
        ch.endElement("","","value");

        // recursively process the remainder of the line
        if (remainderOfLine != null) {
            parseLine(remainderOfLine, ch);
        }
    }


    // locate the position of the comma, taking into account that
    // a quoted token may contain ignorable commas.
    private int locateFirstDelimiter(String curLine) {
        if (curLine.startsWith("\"")) {
            boolean inQuote = true;
            int numChars = curLine.length();
            for (int i=1; i<numChars; i++) {
                char curChar = curLine.charAt(i);
                if (curChar == '"') {
                    inQuote = !inQuote;
                } else if (curChar == ',' && !inQuote) {
                    return i;
                }
            }
        }
```

Example 5-7. CSVXMLReader.java (continued)

```java
        return -1;
    } else {
        return curLine.indexOf(',');
    }
}


// remove quotes around a token, as well as pairs of quotes
// within a token.
private String cleanupQuotes(String token) {
    StringBuffer buf = new StringBuffer();
    int length = token.length();
    int curIndex = 0;

    if (token.startsWith("\"") && token.endsWith("\"")) {
        curIndex = 1;
        length--;
    }

    boolean oneQuoteFound = false;
    boolean twoQuotesFound = false;

    while (curIndex < length) {
        char curChar = token.charAt(curIndex);
        if (curChar == '"') {
            twoQuotesFound = (oneQuoteFound) ? true : false;
            oneQuoteFound = true;
        } else {
            oneQuoteFound = false;
            twoQuotesFound = false;
        }

        if (twoQuotesFound) {
            twoQuotesFound = false;
            oneQuoteFound = false;
            curIndex++;
            continue;
        }

        buf.append(curChar);
        curIndex++;
    }

    return buf.toString();
}
}
```

CSVXMLReader is a subclass of AbstractXMLReader, so it must provide an implementation of the abstract parse method:

```
public void parse(InputSource input) throws IOException,
            SAXException {
        // if no handler is registered to receive events, don't bother
        // to parse the CSV file
        ContentHandler ch = getContentHandler();
        if (ch == null) {
            return;
        }
```

The first thing this method does is check for the existence of a SAX
ContentHandler. The base class, AbstractXMLReader, provides access to this
object, which is responsible for listening to the SAX events. In our example, an
instance of JAXP's TransformerHandler is used as the SAX ContentHandler
implementation. If this handler is not registered, our parse method simply
returns because nobody is registered to listen to the events. In a real SAX parser,
the XML would be parsed anyway, which provides an opportunity to check for
errors in the XML data. Choosing to return immediately was merely a performance optimization selected for this class.

The SAX InputSource parameter allows our custom parser to locate the CSV file.
Since an InputSource has many options for reading its data, parsers must check
each potential source in the order shown here:

```
// convert the InputSource into a BufferedReader
BufferedReader br = null;
if (input.getCharacterStream() != null) {
    br = new BufferedReader(input.getCharacterStream());
} else if (input.getByteStream() != null) {
    br = new BufferedReader(new InputStreamReader(
            input.getByteStream()));
} else if (input.getSystemId() != null) {
    java.net.URL url = new URL(input.getSystemId());
    br = new BufferedReader(new InputStreamReader(url.openStream()));
} else {
    throw new SAXException("Invalid InputSource object");
}
```

Assuming that our InputSource was valid, we can now begin parsing the CSV file
and emitting SAX events. The first step is to notify the ContentHandler that a
new document has begun:

```
ch.startDocument();

// emit <csvFile>
ch.startElement("","","csvFile",EMPTY_ATTR);
```

The XSLT processor interprets this to mean the following:

```
<?xml version="1.0" encoding="UTF-8"?>
<csvFile>
```

Our parser simply ignores many SAX 2 features, particularly XML namespaces. This is why many values passed as parameters to the various ContentHandler methods simply contain empty strings. The EMPTY_ATTR constant indicates that this XML element does not have any attributes.

The CSV file itself is very straightforward, so we merely loop over every line in the file, emitting SAX events as we read each line. The parseLine method is a private helper method that does the actual CSV parsing:

```
// read each line of the file until EOF is reached
String curLine = null;
while ((curLine = br.readLine()) != null) {
    curLine = curLine.trim();
    if (curLine.length() > 0) {
        // create the <line> element
        ch.startElement("","","line",EMPTY_ATTR);
        parseLine(curLine, ch);
        ch.endElement("","","line");
    }
}
```

And finally, we must indicate that the parsing is complete:

```
// emit </csvFile>
ch.endElement("","","csvFile");
ch.endDocument();
```

The remaining methods in CSVXMLReader are not discussed in detail here because they are really just responsible for breaking down each line in the CSV file and checking for commas, quotes, and other mundane parsing tasks. One thing worth noting is the code that emits text, such as the following:

```
<value>Some Text Here</value>
```

SAX parsers use the characters method on ContentHandler to represent text, which has this signature:

```
public void characters(char[] ch, int start, int length)
```

Although this method could have been designed to take a String, using an array allows SAX parsers to preallocate a large character array and then reuse that buffer repeatedly. This is why an implementation of ContentHandler cannot simply assume that the entire ch array contains meaningful data. Instead, it must read only the specified number of characters beginning at the start position.

Our parser uses a relatively straightforward approach, simply converting a `String` to a character array and passing that as a parameter to the `characters` method:

```
// emit the <value>text</value> element
ch.startElement("","","value",EMPTY_ATTR);
ch.characters(firstToken.toCharArray(), 0, firstToken.length());
ch.endElement("","","value");
```

Using the parser

To wrap things up, let's look at how you will actually use this CSV parser with an XSLT stylesheet. The code shown in Example 5-8 is a standalone Java application that allows you to perform XSLT transformations on CSV files. As the comments indicate, it requires the name of a CSV file as its first parameter and can optionally take the name of an XSLT stylesheet as its second parameter. All output is sent to `System.out`.

Example 5-8. SimpleCSVProcessor.java

```
package com.oreilly.javaxslt.util;

import java.io.*;
import javax.xml.transform.*;
import javax.xml.transform.sax.*;
import javax.xml.transform.stream.*;
import org.xml.sax.*;

/**
 * Shows how to use the CSVXMLReader class. This is a command-line
 * utility that takes a CSV file and optionally an XSLT file as
 * command line parameters. A transformation is applied and the
 * output is sent to System.out.
 */
public class SimpleCSVProcessor {

    public static void main(String[] args) throws Exception {
        if (args.length == 0) {
            System.err.println("Usage: java "
                    + SimpleCSVProcessor.class.getName()
                    + " <csvFile> [xsltFile]");
            System.err.println(" - csvFile is required");
            System.err.println(" - xsltFile is optional");
            System.exit(1);
        }

        String csvFileName = args[0];
        String xsltFileName = (args.length > 1) ? args[1] : null;

        TransformerFactory transFact = TransformerFactory.newInstance();
```

Example 5-8. SimpleCSVProcessor.java (continued)

```
            if (transFact.getFeature(SAXTransformerFactory.FEATURE)) {
                SAXTransformerFactory saxTransFact =
                        (SAXTransformerFactory) transFact;
                TransformerHandler transHand = null;
                if (xsltFileName == null) {
                    transHand = saxTransFact.newTransformerHandler();
                } else {
                    transHand = saxTransFact.newTransformerHandler(
                            new StreamSource(new File(xsltFileName)));
                }

                // set the destination for the XSLT transformation
                transHand.setResult(new StreamResult(System.out));

                // hook the CSVXMLReader to the CSV file
                CSVXMLReader csvReader = new CSVXMLReader();
                InputSource csvInputSrc = new InputSource(
                        new FileReader(csvFileName));

                // attach the XSLT processor to the CSVXMLReader
                csvReader.setContentHandler(transHand);
                csvReader.parse(csvInputSrc);
            } else {
                System.err.println("SAXTransformerFactory is not supported.");
                System.exit(1);
            }
        }
    }
}
```

As mentioned earlier in this chapter, the `TransformerHandler` is provided by JAXP and is an implementation of the `org.xml.sax.ContentHandler` interface. It is constructed by the `SAXTransformerFactory` as follows:

```
TransformerHandler transHand = null;
if (xsltFileName == null) {
    transHand = saxTransFact.newTransformerHandler();
} else {
    transHand = saxTransFact.newTransformerHandler(
            new StreamSource(new File(xsltFileName)));
}
```

When the XSLT stylesheet is not specified, the transformer performs an identity transformation. This is useful when you just want to see the raw XML output without applying a stylesheet. You will probably want to do this first to see how your XSLT will need to be written. If a stylesheet is provided, however, it is used for the transformation.

The custom parser is then constructed as follows:

```
CSVXMLReader csvReader = new CSVXMLReader();
```

The location of the CSV file is then converted into a SAX `InputSource`:

```
InputSource csvInputSrc = new InputSource(
        new FileReader(csvFileName));
```

And finally, the XSLT processor is attached to our custom parser. This is accomplished by registering the `TransformerHandler` as the `ContentHandler` on `csvReader`. A single call to the `parse` method causes the parsing and transformation to occur:

```
// attach the XSLT processor to the CSVXMLReader
csvReader.setContentHandler(transHand);
csvReader.parse(csvInputSrc);
```

For a simple test, assume that a list of presidents is available in CSV format:

```
Washington,George,,
Adams,John,,
Jefferson,Thomas,,
Madison,James,,
  etc...
Bush,George,Herbert,Walker
Clinton,William,Jefferson,
Bush,George,W,
```

To see what the XML looks like, invoke the program as follows:

```
java com.oreilly.javaxslt.util.SimpleCSVProcessor presidents.csv
```

This will parse the CSV file and apply the identity transformation stylesheet, sending the following output to the console:

```
<?xml version="1.0" encoding="UTF-8"?>
<csvFile>
  <line>
    <value>Washington</value>
    <value>George</value>
    <value/>
    <value/>
  </line>
  <line>
    etc...
</csvFile>
```

Actually, the output is crammed onto a single long line, but it is broken up here to make it more readable. Any good XML editor application should provide a feature to pretty-print the XML as shown. In order to transform this into something useful, a stylesheet is required. The XSLT stylesheet shown in Example 5-9 takes any output from this program and converts it into an HTML table.

Example 5-9. csvToHTMLTable.xslt

```
<?xml version="1.0" encoding="UTF-8"?>
<xsl:stylesheet
    version="1.0"
    xmlns:xsl="http://www.w3.org/1999/XSL/Transform">
  <xsl:output method="html"/>

  <xsl:template match="/">
    <table border="1">
      <xsl:apply-templates select="csvFile/line"/>
    </table>
  </xsl:template>

  <xsl:template match="line">
    <tr>
      <xsl:apply-templates select="value"/>
    </tr>
  </xsl:template>

  <xsl:template match="value">
    <td>
      <!-- If a value is empty, print a non-breaking space
           so the HTML table looks OK -->
      <xsl:if test=".=''">
        <xsl:text> disable-output-escaping="yes"> </xsl:text>
      </xsl:if>
      <xsl:value-of select="."/>
    </td>
  </xsl:template>
</xsl:stylesheet>
```

In order to apply this stylesheet, type the following command:

```
java com.oreilly.javaxslt.util.SimpleCSVProcessor presidents.csv csvToHTMLTable.
xslt
```

As before, the results are sent to System.out and contain code for an HTML table. This stylesheet will work with any CSV file parsed with SimpleCSVProcessor, not just *presidents.xml*. Now that the concept has been proved, you can add fancy formatting and custom output to the resulting HTML without altering any Java code—just edit the stylesheet or write a new one.

Conclusion

Although writing a SAX parser and connecting it to JAXP does involve quite a few interrelated classes, the resulting application requires only two command-line arguments and will work with any CSV or XSLT file. What makes this example interesting is that the same approach will work with essentially any data source. The steps are broken down as follows:

1. Create a custom SAX parser by implementing `org.xml.sax.XMLReader` or extending `com.oreilly.javaxslt.util.AbstractXMLReader`.

2. In your parser, emit the appropriate SAX events as you read your data.

3. Modify `SimpleCSVProcessor` to utilize your custom parser instead of `CSVXMLReader`.

For example, you might want to write a custom parser that accepts a SQL statement as input rather than a CSV file. Your parser could then connect to a database, issue the query, and fire SAX events for each row in the `ResultSet`. This makes it very easy to extract data from any relational database without writing a lot of custom code. This also eliminates the intermediate step of JDOM or DOM production because the SAX events are fed directly into JAXP for transformation.

Feeding JDOM Output into JAXP

The DOM API is tedious to use, so many Java programmers opt for JDOM instead. The typical usage pattern is to generate XML dynamically using JDOM and then somehow transform that into a web page using XSLT. This presents a problem because JAXP does not provide any direct implementation of the `javax.xml.Source` interface that integrates with JDOM.* There are at least three available options:

• Use `org.jdom.output.SAXOutputter` to pipe SAX 2 events from JDOM to JAXP.

• Use `org.jdom.output.DOMOutputter` to convert the JDOM tree to a DOM tree, and then use `javax.xml.transform.dom.DOMSource` to read the data into JAXP.

• Use `org.jdom.output.XMLOutputter` to serialize the JDOM tree to XML text, and then use `java.xml.transform.stream.StreamSource` to parse the XML back into JAXP.

JDOM to SAX approach

The SAX approach is generally preferable to other approaches. Its primary advantage is that it does not require an intermediate transformation to convert the

---

* As this is being written, members of the JDOM community are writing a JDOM implementation of `javax.xml.Source` that will directly integrate with JAXP.

JDOM tree into a DOM tree or text. This offers the lowest memory utilization and potentially the fastest performance.

In support of SAX, JDOM offers the `org.jdom.output.SAXOutputter` class. The following code fragment demonstrates its usage:

```
TransformerFactory transFact = TransformerFactory.newInstance();
if (transFact.getFeature(SAXTransformerFactory.FEATURE)) {
    SAXTransformerFactory stf = (SAXTransformerFactory) transFact;
    // the 'stylesheet' parameter is an instance of JAXP's
    // javax.xml.transform.Templates interface
    TransformerHandler transHand = stf.newTransformerHandler(stylesheet);

    // result is a Result instance
    transHand.setResult(result);
    SAXOutputter saxOut = new SAXOutputter(transHand);
    // the 'jdomDoc' parameter is an instance of JDOM's
    // org.jdom.Document class. In contains the XML data
    saxOut.output(jdomDoc);
} else {
    System.err.println("SAXTransformerFactory is not supported");
}
```

JDOM to DOM approach

The DOM approach is generally a little slower and will not work if JDOM uses a different DOM implementation than JAXP. JDOM, like JAXP, can utilize different DOM implementations behind the scenes. If JDOM refers to a different version of DOM than JAXP, you will encounter exceptions when you try to perform the transformation. Since JAXP uses Apache's Crimson parser by default, you can configure JDOM to use Crimson with the `org.jdom.adapters.CrimsonDOMAdapter` class. The following code shows how to convert a JDOM Document into a DOM Document:

```
org.jdom.Document jdomDoc = createJDOMDocument();
// add data to the JDOM Document
 ...

// convert the JDOM Document into a DOM Document
org.jdom.output.DOMOutputter domOut = new org.jdom.output.DOMOutputter(
        "org.jdom.adapters.CrimsonDOMAdapter");
org.w3c.dom.Document domDoc = domOut.output(jdomDoc);
```

The second line is highlighted because it is likely to give you the most problems. When JDOM converts its internal object tree into a DOM object tree, it must use some underlying DOM implementation. In many respects, JDOM is similar to

JAXP because it delegates many tasks to underlying implementation classes. The DOMOutputter constructors are overloaded as follows:

```
// use the default adapter class
public DOMOutputter()

// use the specified adapter class
public DOMOutputter(String adapterClass)
```

The first constructor shown here will use JDOM's default DOM parser, which is not necessarily the same DOM parser that JAXP uses. The second method allows you to specify the name of an adapter class, which must implement the org.jdom. adapters.DOMAdapter interface. JDOM includes standard adapters for all of the widely used DOM implementations, or you could write your own adapter class.

JDOM to text approach

In the final approach listed earlier, you can utilize java.io.StringWriter and java.io.StringReader. First create the JDOM data as usual, then use org. jdom.output.XMLOutputter to convert the data into a String of XML:

```
StringWriter sw = new StringWriter();
org.jdom.output.XMLOutputter xmlOut
        = new org.jdom.output.XMLOutputter("", false);
xmlOut.output(jdomDoc, sw);
```

The parameters for XMLOutputter allow you to specify the amount of indentation for the output along with a boolean flag indicating whether or not linefeeds should be included in the output. In the code example, no spaces or linefeeds are specified in order to minimize the size of the XML that is produced. Now that the StringWriter contains your XML, you can use a StringReader along with javax.xml.transform.stream.StreamSource to read the data into JAXP:

```
StringReader sr = new StringReader(sw.toString());
Source xmlSource = new javax.xml.transform.stream.StreamSource(sr);
```

The transformation can then proceed just as it did in Example 5-4. The main drawback to this approach is that the XML, once converted to text form, must then be parsed back in by JAXP before the transformation can be applied.

Stylesheet Compilation

XSLT is a programming language, expressed using XML syntax. This is not for the benefit of the computer, but rather for human interpretation. Before the stylesheet can be processed, it must be converted into some internal machine-readable format. This process should sound familiar, because it is the same process used for every high-level programming language. You, the programmer, work in terms of the high-level language, and an interpreter or compiler converts this language into some machine format that can be executed by the computer.

Interpreters analyze source code and translate it into machine code with each execution. In this case of XSLT, this requires that the stylesheet be read into memory using an XML parser, translated into machine format, and then applied to your XML data. Performance is the obvious problem, particularly when you consider that stylesheets rarely change. Typically, the stylesheets are defined early on in the development process and remain static, while XML data is generated dynamically with each client request.

A better approach is to parse the XSLT stylesheet into memory once, compile it to machine-format, and then preserve that machine representation in memory for repeated use. This is called stylesheet compilation and is no different in concept than the compilation of any programming language.

Templates API

Different XSLT processors implement stylesheet compilation differently, so JAXP includes the `javax.xml.transform.Templates` interface to provide consistency. This is a relatively simple interface with the following API:

```
public interface Templates {
    java.util.Properties getOutputProperties();
    javax.xml.transform.Transformer newTransformer()
            throws TransformerConfigurationException;
}
```

The `getOutputProperties()` method returns a clone of the properties associated with the `<xsl:output>` element, such as `method="xml"`, `indent="yes"`, and `encoding="UTF-8"`. You might recall that `java.util.Properties` (a subclass of `java.util.Hashtable`) provides key/value mappings from property names to property values. Since a clone, or deep copy, is returned, you can safely modify the `Properties` instance and apply it to a future transformation without affecting the compiled stylesheet that the instance of `Templates` represents.

The `newTransformer()` method is more commonly used and allows you to obtain a new instance of a class that implements the `Transformer` interface. It is this `Transformer` object that actually allows you to perform XSLT transformations. Since the implementation of the `Templates` interface is hidden by JAXP, it must be created by the following method on `javax.xml.transform.TransformerFactory`:

```
public Templates newTemplates(Source source)
        throws TransformerConfigurationException
```

As in earlier examples, the Source may obtain the XSLT stylesheet from one of many locations, including a filename, a system identifier, or even a DOM tree. Regardless of the original location, the XSLT processor is supposed to compile the stylesheet into an optimized internal representation.

Whether the stylesheet is actually compiled is up to the implementation, but a safe bet is that performance will continually improve over the next several years as these tools stabilize and vendors have time to apply optimizations.

Figure 5-6 illustrates the relationship between Templates and Transformer instances.

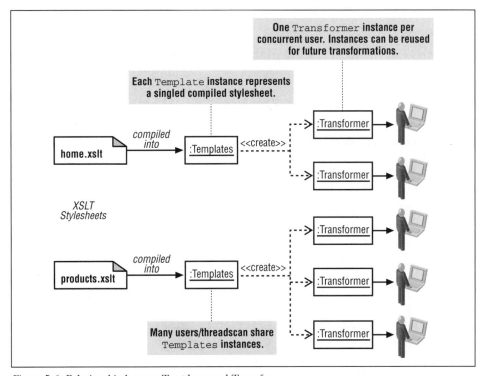

Figure 5-6. Relationship between Templates and Transformer

Thread safety is an important issue in any Java application, particularly in a web context where many users share the same stylesheet. As Figure 5-6 illustrates, an instance of Templates is thread-safe and represents a single stylesheet. During the transformation process, however, the XSLT processor must maintain state information and output properties specific to the current client. For this reason, a separate Transformer instance must be used for each concurrent transformation.

Transformer is an abstract class in JAXP, and implementations should be lightweight. This is an important goal because you will typically create many copies of

Transformer, while the number of Templates is relatively small. Transformer instances are not thread-safe, primarily because they hold state information about the current transformation. Once the transformation is complete, however, these objects can be reused.

A Stylesheet Cache

XSLT transformations commonly occur on a shared web server with a large number of concurrent users, so it makes sense to use Templates whenever possible to optimize performance. Since each instance of Templates is thread-safe, it is desirable to maintain a single copy shared by many clients. This reduces the number of times your stylesheets have to be parsed into memory and compiled, as well as the overall memory footprint of your application.

The code shown in Example 5-10 illustrates a custom XSLT stylesheet cache that automates the mundane tasks associated with creating Templates instances and storing them in memory. This cache has the added benefit of checking the lastModified flag on the underlying file, so it will reload itself whenever the XSLT stylesheet is modified. This is highly useful in a web-application development environment because you can make changes to the stylesheet and simply click on Reload on your web browser to see the results of the latest edits.

Example 5-10. StylesheetCache.java

```
package com.oreilly.javaxslt.util;

import java.io.*;
import java.util.*;
import javax.xml.transform.*;
import javax.xml.transform.stream.*;

/**
 * A utility class that caches XSLT stylesheets in memory.
 *
 */
public class StylesheetCache {
    // map xslt file names to MapEntry instances
    // (MapEntry is defined below)
    private static Map cache = new HashMap();

    /**
     * Flush all cached stylesheets from memory, emptying the cache.
     */
    public static synchronized void flushAll() {
        cache.clear();
    }
```

Example 5-10. StylesheetCache.java (continued)

```java
/**
 * Flush a specific cached stylesheet from memory.
 *
 * @param xsltFileName the file name of the stylesheet to remove.
 */
public static synchronized void flush(String xsltFileName) {
    cache.remove(xsltFileName);
}


/**
 * Obtain a new Transformer instance for the specified XSLT file name.
 * A new entry will be added to the cache if this is the first request
 * for the specified file name.
 *
 * @param xsltFileName the file name of an XSLT stylesheet.
 * @return a transformation context for the given stylesheet.
 */
public static synchronized Transformer newTransformer(String xsltFileName)
        throws TransformerConfigurationException {
    File xsltFile = new File(xsltFileName);

    // determine when the file was last modified on disk
    long xslLastModified = xsltFile.lastModified();
    MapEntry entry = (MapEntry) cache.get(xsltFileName);

    if (entry != null) {
        // if the file has been modified more recently than the
        // cached stylesheet, remove the entry reference
        if (xslLastModified > entry.lastModified) {
            entry = null;
        }
    }

    // create a new entry in the cache if necessary
    if (entry == null) {
        Source xslSource = new StreamSource(xsltFile);

        TransformerFactory transFact = TransformerFactory.newInstance();
        Templates templates = transFact.newTemplates(xslSource);

        entry = new MapEntry(xslLastModified, templates);
        cache.put(xsltFileName, entry);
    }

    return entry.templates.newTransformer();
}


// prevent instantiation of this class
```

Example 5-10. StylesheetCache.java (continued)

```
    private StylesheetCache() {
    }

    /**
     * This class represents a value in the cache Map.
     */
    static class MapEntry {
        long lastModified;  // when the file was modified
        Templates templates;

        MapEntry(long lastModified, Templates templates) {
            this.lastModified = lastModified;
            this.templates = templates;
        }
    }
}
```

Because this class is a singleton, it has a private constructor and uses only static methods. Furthermore, each method is declared as `synchronized` in an effort to avoid potential threading problems.

The heart of this class is the cache itself, which is implemented using `java.util.Map`:

```
    private static Map cache = new HashMap();
```

Although `HashMap` is not thread-safe, the fact that all of our methods are `synchronized` basically eliminates any concurrency issues. Each entry in the map contains a key/value pair, mapping from an XSLT stylesheet filename to an instance of the `MapEntry` class. `MapEntry` is a nested class that keeps track of the compiled stylesheet along with when its file was last modified:

```
    static class MapEntry {
        long lastModified;  // when the file was modified
        Templates templates;

        MapEntry(long lastModified, Templates templates) {
            this.lastModified = lastModified;
            this.templates = templates;
        }
    }
```

Removing entries from the cache is accomplished by one of two methods:

```
    public static synchronized void flushAll() {
        cache.clear();
    }
```

```
public static synchronized void flush(String xsltFileName) {
    cache.remove(xsltFileName);
}
```

The first method merely removes everything from the `Map`, while the second removes a single stylesheet. Whether you use these methods is up to you. The `flushAll` method, for instance, should probably be called from a servlet's `destroy()` method to ensure proper cleanup. If you have many servlets in a web application, each servlet may wish to flush specific stylesheets it uses via the `flush(...)` method. If the `xsltFileName` parameter is not found, the `Map` implementation silently ignores this request.

The majority of interaction with this class occurs via the `newTransformer` method, which has the following signature:

```
public static synchronized Transformer newTransformer(String xsltFileName)
        throws TransformerConfigurationException {
```

The parameter, an XSLT stylesheet filename, was chosen to facilitate the "last accessed" feature. We use the `java.io.File` class to determine when the file was last modified, which allows the cache to automatically reload itself as edits are made to the stylesheets. Had we used a system identifier or `InputStream` instead of a filename, the auto-reload feature could not have been implemented. Next, the `File` object is created and its `lastModified` flag is checked:

```
File xsltFile = new File(xsltFileName);

// determine when the file was last modified on disk
long xslLastModified = xsltFile.lastModified();
```

The compiled stylesheet, represented by an instance of `MapEntry`, is then retrieved from the `Map`. If the entry is found, its timestamp is compared against the current file's timestamp, thus allowing auto-reload:

```
MapEntry entry = (MapEntry) cache.get(xsltFileName);

if (entry != null) {
    // if the file has been modified more recently than the
    // cached stylesheet, remove the entry reference
    if (xslLastModified > entry.lastModified) {
        entry = null;
    }
}
```

Next, we create a new entry in the cache if the entry object reference is still `null`. This is accomplished by wrapping a `StreamSource` around the `File` object, instantiating a `TransformerFactory` instance, and using that factory to create

our `Templates` object. The `Templates` object is then stored in the cache so it can
be reused by the next client of the cache:

```
// create a new entry in the cache if necessary
if (entry == null) {
    Source xslSource = new StreamSource(xsltFile);

    TransformerFactory transFact = TransformerFactory.newInstance();
    Templates templates = transFact.newTemplates(xslSource);

    entry = new MapEntry(xslLastModified, templates);
    cache.put(xsltFileName, entry);
}
```

Finally, a brand new `Transformer` is created and returned to the caller:

```
return entry.templates.newTransformer();
```

Returning a new `Transformer` is critical because, although the `Templates` object
is thread-safe, the `Transformer` implementation is not. Each caller gets its own
copy of `Transformer` so multiple clients do not collide with one another.

One potential improvement on this design could be to add a `lastAccessed`
timestamp to each `MapEntry` object. Another thread could then execute every
couple of hours to flush map entries from memory if they have not been accessed
for a period of time. In most web applications, this will not be an issue, but if you
have a large number of pages and some are seldom accessed, this could be a way
to reduce the memory usage of the cache.

Another potential modification is to allow `javax.xml.transform.Source`
objects to be passed as a parameter to the `newTransformer` method instead of as
a filename. However, this would make the auto-reload feature impossible to implement for all `Source` types.

6

Servlet Basics and XSLT

XSLT and servlets are a natural fit. Java is a cross-platform programming language, XML provides portable data, and XSLT provides a way to transform that data without cluttering up your servlet code with HTML. Because your data can be transformed into many different formats, you can also achieve portability across a variety of browsers and other devices. Best of all, a clean separation between data, presentation, and programming logic allow changes to be made to the look and feel of a web site without digging in to Java code. This makes it possible, for example, to sell highly customizable web applications. You can encourage your customers to modify the XSLT stylesheets to create custom page layouts and corporate logos, while preventing access to your internal Java business logic.

As discussed in previous chapters, an initial challenge faced with XSLT and servlets is the initial configuration. Getting started with a web application is typically harder than client-only applications because there are more pieces to assemble. With a Swing application, for instance, you can start with a single class that has a main() method. But with a web application, you must create an XML deployment descriptor in addition to the servlet, package everything up into a WAR file, and properly deploy to a servlet container. When errors occur, you see something like "HTTP 404—File not found," which is not particularly helpful.

The goal of this chapter is to introduce servlet syntax with particular emphasis on configuration and deployment issues. Once servlet syntax has been covered, integration with XSLT stylesheets and XML is covered, illustrated by the implementation of a basic web application. By the time you have worked through this material, you should have confidence to move on to the more complicated examples found in the remainder of this book.

Servlet Syntax

Servlet architecture was covered in Chapter 4, along with comparisons to many other approaches. The architecture of a system is a mile-high view, ignoring implementation details so you can focus on the big picture. We now need to dig into the low-level syntax issues to proceed with the really interesting examples in later chapters. For a complete discussion of servlets, check out Jason Hunter's *Java Servlet Programming* (O'Reilly). Be sure to look for the second edition because so much has changed in the servlet world since this book was first published.

Splash Screen Servlet Example

Our first servlet example will produce an application splash screen. The servlet will receive a request from a browser and output a simple HTML web page. Figure 6-1 contains the class diagram for `SplashScreenServlet`, which extends from `HttpServlet`.

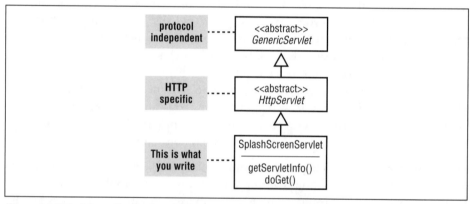

Figure 6-1. SplashScreenServlet class diagram

When writing servlets, you almost always extend from `HttpServlet`. In our example, we override the `doGet()` method, which is called every time the browser issues an HTTP GET request to the server. GET requests occur whenever the user types in a URL, clicks on a hyperlink, or submits an HTML form with GET as the method attribute. The other common type of request is POST, which is used by HTML forms with POST as the method attribute. For example:

```
<form action="someServlet" method="POST">
...form contents
</form>
```

In the case of POST requests, your servlet simply overrides the `doPost()` method instead of `doGet()`. Each of these methods takes two parameters: `HttpServletRequest` and `HttpServletResponse`. The request contains information from the client to the servlet, and the response allows the servlet to send data back to the client. This correlates directly to the request/response nature of HTTP itself. Example 6-1 contains the complete source code for our simple servlet.

Example 6-1. SplashScreenServlet.java

```java
package chap6;

import java.io.*;
import javax.servlet.*;
import javax.servlet.http.*;

/**
 * A simple Servlet example that displays a "Splash Screen"
 * for a web application.
 */
public class SplashScreenServlet extends HttpServlet {
  public String getServletInfo() {
    return "Shows an application splash screen.";
  }

  protected void doGet(HttpServletRequest request,
                    HttpServletResponse response)
      throws IOException, ServletException {

    // demonstrate how to get parameters from the request
    String nextURL = request.getParameter("nextURL");
    if (nextURL == null) {
      nextURL = "/";
    }

    response.setContentType("text/html");
    PrintWriter pw = response.getWriter();
    pw.println("<html>");
    pw.println("<head><title>Splash Screen</title></head>");
    pw.println("<body>");

    pw.println("<div align='center' style='border: 1px navy solid;'>");
    pw.println("<h1>Welcome to Java and XSLT</h1>");
    pw.println("<h3>O'Reilly and Associates</h3>");
    pw.println("<p>First Edition, 2001</p><hr>");
    pw.println("<a href='" + nextURL + "'>Click here to continue...</a>");
    pw.println("</div>");
    pw.println("</body>");
    pw.println("</html>");
  }
}
```

Beginning with the import statements, note that the servlet API is in the javax.
servlet and javax.servlet.http packages. These packages are not part of the
Java 2 Standard Edition; they are considered a required API of the Java 2 Platform
Enterprise Edition. Although many servlet implementations are available,
Apache's Tomcat is the reference implementation officially sanctioned by Sun.
Every example in this book works with Version 4.0 of Tomcat and should also work
on any compliant servlet implementation. You can download Tomcat at *http://
jakarta.apache.org.*

As shown in Figure 6-1, SplashScreenServlet is a subclass of HttpServlet. The
first method we override is getServletInfo(), which simply returns a brief
description of this servlet. Although optional, this text will show up in the administrative console of many servlet containers.

The doGet() method is next, which is designed to handle each client request. It is
important to remember that this method needs to be thread-safe, because many clients could potentially share this servlet instance and call doGet() concurrently. You
may notice that doGet() is a protected method. The call sequence is as follows:

1. The servlet container invokes the service() method on HttpServlet.

2. HttpServlet figures out the type of request (GET, POST, ...).

3. HttpServlet invokes the corresponding method (doGet(), doPost(), ...).

Since the doGet() method is called from its parent class, it can be protected. If
you do not override the doGet() method, the default behavior in HttpServlet is
to return an error page back to the client. If you also want to support POST, you
must override the doPost() method. One common technique is to have the
doGet() method call the doPost() method, or vice-versa. This allows the same
servlet to support both GET and POST without duplicating any code.

The doGet() implementation is very straightforward. The first thing it does is
check for the existence of a parameter called nextURL. This is part of the request
that the browser issues to the servlet. For example, typing the following URL into
your browser will include the next URL parameter:

```
http://localhost:8080/chap6/splash?nextURL=http://www.oreilly.com
```

If the nextURL parameter is not specified, its value will be null. For this reason,
servlets must always check for null when getting parameters from the request:

```
String nextURL = request.getParameter("nextURL");
if (nextURL == null) {
  nextURL = "/";
}
```

In our example, null causes an error, so we replace nextURL with a forward slash
character (/). As you might guess, this is a relative URL that points to the root

directory. In the case of a servlet running on Tomcat, the root directory will point to Tomcat's home page. This is not the same as the root directory on your file system. In Tomcat, the root directory can be found under *TOMCAT_HOME/webapps/ROOT*, where *TOMCAT_HOME* points to the installation directory of Tomcat.

The getParameter() method is also used for retrieving values from an HTML form. When an HTML form is submitted, each component on the form should have a name associated with it, such as firstName, lastName, or ssn. The servlet retrieves the form values simply by calling request.getParameter() for each form element. It is always a good idea to check for null and trim whitespace before accepting any of these parameters. When the form element is missing, the parameter value will be null. This could indicate an error in your HTML or perhaps an intentional attack on your web site.

The HttpServletResponse class provides access to either a PrintWriter or an OutputStream, depending on whether you wish to send text or binary data to the client. For HTML or XML data, use the HttpServletResponse.getWriter() method. For images or other types of binary data, use the HttpServletResponse.getOutputStream() method. You may also note that we set the content type of the response prior to getting the writer:

```
response.setContentType("text/html");
PrintWriter pw = response.getWriter();
```

This is important because the HTTP response consists of a header followed by the actual content. The content type is one of the header values, so it must be sent prior to the actual data. Without going into too many servlet details, it is a good practice to always set the content type before getting the writer. In future examples, we will occasionally use text/xml as the content type, but only when sending raw XML data to the client.

The remainder of SplashScreenServlet simply prints out an HTML response:

```
pw.println("<html>");
pw.println("<head><title>Splash Screen</title></head>");
pw.println("<body>");

pw.println("<div align='center' style='border: 1px navy solid;'>");
pw.println("<h1>Welcome to Java and XSLT</h1>");
pw.println("<h3>O'Reilly and Associates</h3>");
pw.println("<p>First Edition, 2001</p><hr>");
pw.println("<a href='" + nextURL + "'>Click here to continue...</a>");
pw.println("</div>");
pw.println("</body>");
pw.println("</html>");
```

As you can see, the nextURL parameter is used to create a hyperlink to the next page. This is why a value of null is unacceptable for this example.

This approach works fine for simple examples, but quickly gets out of hand for complex pages. This is because all but the most basic web pages require hundreds, if not thousands, of lines of HTML to create fancy tables, colors, and graphics. For reasons discussed in Chapter 5, hardcoding that HTML into the servlet is simply unacceptable in a sophisticated web application.

WAR Files and Deployment

In the servlet model, Web Application Archive (WAR) files are the unit of deployment. WAR files enable portability across a wide range of servlet containers regardless of the vendor. The good news is that WAR files are very easy to create and require only that you carefully follow the guidelines for file and directory names. If you are careful to avoid spelling errors and misplaced files, you should not have any problem with WAR files.

WAR Files

Figure 6-2 shows the standard structure of a WAR file. Since a WAR file is really just a JAR file with a *.war* extension, you can utilize the *jar* command to create your WAR files.

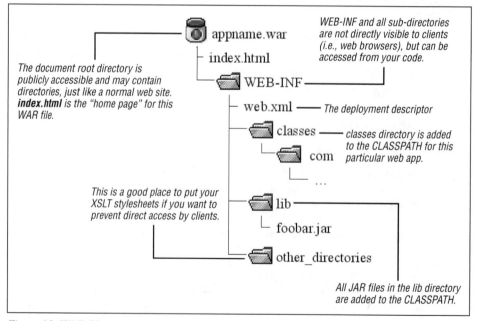

Figure 6-2. WAR file structure

To create a WAR file, simply arrange your files into the directory structure shown in Figure 6-2 and issue the following command from the directory that contains *index.html:**

```
jar -cvfM ../appname.war
```

This command assumes that the WAR file will be placed in the parent of your current working directory; the forward slash (/) works on Windows as well as Unix clients. Once the WAR file has been created, you can view its contents by changing to its directory and issuing the following command:

```
jar -tvf appname.war .
```

This shows the table of contents for the WAR file, which must match the structure shown in Figure 6-2.

The topmost directory in the WAR file is publicly accessible to web browsers and should contain your JSP and HTML files. You can also create subdirectories, which will also be visible to the client. A common practice is to create an *images* directory for storing your graphic files.

The *WEB-INF* directory is always hidden from clients that access your web application. The deployment descriptor, *web.xml*, is located here, as are the *classes* and *lib* directories. As Figure 6-2 indicates, the *classes* directory becomes available to your application's ClassLoader. Any JAR files contained in the *lib* directory are also available to your code, making it very easy to deploy third-party libraries along with a web application. The folder *other_directories* can be anything you want and will also be hidden from clients since it resides under the *WEB-INF* directory. Although clients cannot see any of these directories and files directly, your servlet can access these resources programmatically and then deliver that content.

Deployment Descriptor

The deployment descriptor is always called *web.xml* and must be placed directly in the *WEB-INF* directory of your web application. The job of the deployment descriptor is to provide the servlet container with complete configuration information about a web application. This may include security attributes, aliases for servlets and other resources, *initialization parameters*, and even graphical icons for Integrated Development Environments (IDEs) to utilize. For our needs, a very small subset of this functionality will be sufficient. For SplashScreenServlet, we need to list the Java class of the servlet, an alias for that servlet, and a URL mapping. The complete deployment descriptor for SplashScreenServlet is listed in Example 6-2.

---

* *index.html* is the "home page" for a web application.

Example 6-2. web.xml for SplashScreenServlet.java

```
<?xml version="1.0" encoding="UTF-8"?>
<!DOCTYPE web-app
  PUBLIC "-//Sun Microsystems, Inc.//DTD Web Application 2.2//EN"
  "http://java.sun.com/j2ee/dtds/web-app_2.2.dtd">
<web-app>
  <servlet>
    <!-- define an alias for the Servlet -->
    <servlet-name>splashScreen</servlet-name>
    <servlet-class>chap6.SplashScreenServlet</servlet-class>
  </servlet>

  <servlet-mapping>
    <!-- associate the Servlet with a URL pattern -->
    <servlet-name>splashScreen</servlet-name>
    <url-pattern>/splash/*</url-pattern>
  </servlet-mapping>
</web-app>
```

The DOCTYPE is a required element of a deployment descriptor and must match what is shown in Example 6-2. The only caveat is that newer versions of the servlet specification, such as Version 2.3, use a different version number in the deployment descriptor. Unless you are using 2.3 features, however, you should stick with 2.2 to remain compatible with as many servlet containers as possible.

A servlet definition lists the fully qualified package and class name of the servlet class, as well a name for that servlet. Whenever another section in the deployment descriptor wishes to reference this particular servlet, it uses the name specified here:

```
<servlet>
  <servlet-name>splashScreen</servlet-name>
  <servlet-class>chap6.SplashScreenServlet</servlet-class>
</servlet>
```

As you can see in Example 6-2, the servlet mapping uses this name in order to associate a URL pattern with this particular servlet. This pattern will show up in the address that users type into their web browsers when they access this servlet. In this case, the URL to SplashScreenServlet is:

http://hostname:port/chap6/splash

This is the form that Tomcat defaults to, having the following components:

hostname:port

Typically localhost:8080, although Tomcat can be configured to run on any port number

chap6

    The name of your web application, which is deployed in *chap6.war* for this example

splash

    Part of the URL pattern for the servlet

Wildcards in the URL pattern indicate that any text will match. Since the deployment descriptor listed /splash/* as the pattern, any of the following URLs also invoke SplashScreenServlet:

- *http://localhost:8080/chap6/splash/*

- *http://localhost:8080/chap6/splash/whatever.html*

- *http://localhost:8080/chap6/splash/a/b/c*

Deploying SplashScreenServlet to Tomcat

The simple steps for getting SplashScreenServlet up and running are to compile the code, create the deployment descriptor listed in Example 6-2, and create the WAR file using the *jar* utility. The WAR file contents for this servlet are shown in Figure 6-3.

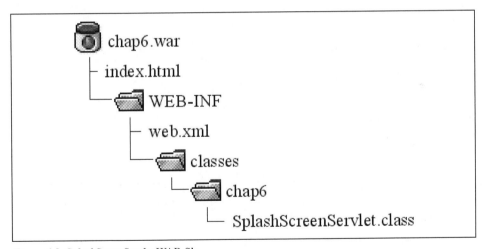

Figure 6-3. SplashScreenServlet WAR file

Once you have created *chap6.war*, be sure to execute **jar -tvf chap6.war** to confirm that the contents are structured properly. The final step is to simply copy the entire JAR file to Tomcat's *webapps* directory.

TIP   If a WAR file is copied into the *webapps* directory while Tomcat is
               running, it will not be recognized. Simply restart Tomcat to begin
               using the web application.

Once the WAR file has been copied, you can execute *startup.bat* or *startup.sh* in
Tomcat's *bin* directory and then enter *http://localhost:8080/chap6/splash* into your
favorite web browser. If you see error messages, check to see that the JAVA_HOME
and TOMCAT_HOME environment variables are properly set. You can also look
in Tomcat's *webapps* directory to see if the WAR file is properly expanded. When a
web application is first invoked, Tomcat expands the WAR file into its actual directory structure. When you look in the *webapps* directory, you should see *chap6.war* as
well as the *chap6* directory.

If all else fails, check the documentation for Tomcat, double check your deployment descriptor, and try the example servlets that come with Tomcat. To see the
Tomcat home page, start Tomcat and visit *http://localhost:8080*. If this does not
work, then something more fundamental is wrong with your Tomcat installation.

Servlet API Highlights

We will see more complex servlets throughout this book, but a recurring theme is
to minimize dependence on obscure servlet tricks and focus instead on using XML
and XSLT to generate a majority of the content in your web application. To make
this happen, it is necessary to look at a few of the commonly used classes that are
part of the servlet package.

The `javax.servlet.ServletConfig` class provides initialization parameters to a
servlet at startup time. Each servlet has the following method, which is called once
when the servlet is first initialized:

```
public void init(ServletConfig config) throws ServletException
```

The `ServletConfig` object provides name/value `String` pairs used to configure
servlets without hardcoding values into the application code. For example, you
might write code that looks like this:

```
String xmlLocation = config.getInitParameter("xmlLocation");
```

Since `xmlLocation` is an initialization parameter that is part of the XML deployment descriptor, its value does not have to be hardcoded into your application.
For additional examples, see "Locating Stylesheets with Initialization Parameters"
later in this chapter.

Another important class is `javax.servlet.ServletContext`. This class does a lot more than `ServletConfig`, and its instance is shared among a group of servlets. Use `ServletConfig` to obtain a reference to the `ServletContext`:

```
// config is an instance of ServletConfig
ServletContext ctx = config.getServletContext();
```

Later in this book, we will focus on `ServletContext`'s ability to locate *resources* in a portable way. You may be familiar with the `getResource()` and `getResourceAsStream()` methods on `java.lang.Class`. These methods allow you to locate files and directories based on the system CLASSPATH.

`ServletContext` provides its own `getResource()` and `getResourceAsStream()` methods, but they are not based on CLASSPATH. Instead, the directory locations are based on the location of the current web application. For example, you can write something such as:

```
context.getResource("/WEB-INF/stylesheets/home.xslt")
```

to load a stylesheet from the current WAR file. Regardless of where Tomcat was installed, this approach will always locate the stylesheet without hardcoding a path name such as *C:\path*....

Another Servlet Example

In our next example, the servlet will utilize DOM and XSLT to create its web pages. This achieves our goal of separation between data and presentation, making it possible to fully customize the HTML output without making any changes to the Java code. Although an XML approach makes the code more complex for a small example program such as this, the benefits quickly outweigh the costs as web applications get more sophisticated. The same is true for an Enterprise JavaBeans approach. For a trivial program, the configuration requirements seem very complex; but as the application complexity increases, the benefits of a sophisticated architecture become obvious.

Our program will consist of two web pages, allowing visitors to enter personal information. The first page will prompt for their name, phone, and email, and the second page will display a summary of the data that was entered. The first page does validation, forcing the user to enter all of the required fields.

Design

The primary goal of this small application is to demonstrate how to use XSLT from a servlet. Specifically, JAXP will be used with DOM to create some dynamic

XML data, then XSLT stylesheets will be used to transform that data into HTML. The design is presented in Figure 6-4.

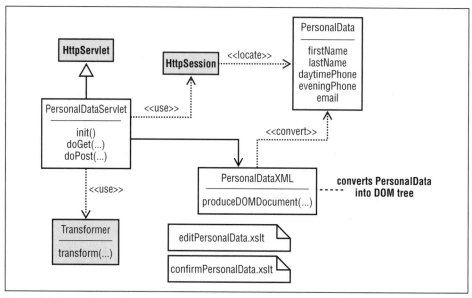

Figure 6-4. Personal data design

As Figure 6-4 shows, `PersonalDataServlet` is a subclass of `HttpServlet`. This servlet overrides both `doGet()` and `doPost()`. When the visitor first visits this web site, an HTTP GET request causes the `doGet()` method to be called, which shows a form that allows the user to enter his or her information. When they hit the submit button on the web page, the `doPost()` method validates all form fields and shows the confirmation page if everything is valid. If one or more fields are missing, the form is redisplayed with an error message.

The `PersonalData` class simply holds data that the user has entered, and is located via the `HttpSession`. Each visitor gets his or her own copy of `HttpSession`, therefore they get their own copy of `PersonalData`. In order to convert this data to XML, a separate helper class called `PersonalDataXML` was created.

The decision to use a separate helper class for XML generation was not arbitrary. Many people like to put code directly into classes like `PersonalData`, such as a `getXML()` method, that performs this task. By placing the XML generation logic into a totally separate class, however, it will be easier to migrate to a technology like JDOM without breaking current clients in any way. A new class called `PersonalDataJDOM` could be added to the system while preserving all of the existing code. This approach also keeps the `PersonalData` class smaller, since all it has to do is hang on to the data.

The first web page is shown in Figure 6-5. As you can see, required fields are marked with an asterisk (*). This screen is rendered using *editPersonalData.xslt*.

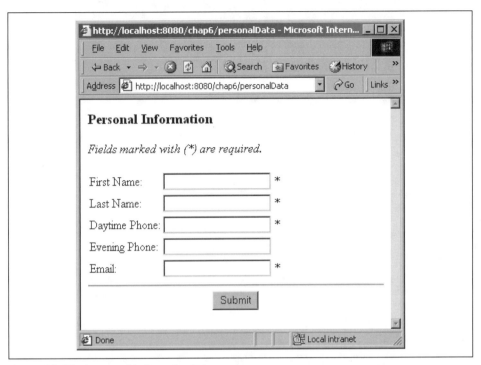

Figure 6-5. Blank personal information form

Figure 6-6 shows how this same screen looks after the user clicks on the Submit button. If data is missing, an error message is displayed in red and required fields are marked in bold. Any other error messages are also displayed in red. This view is also rendered using `editPersonalData.xslt`.

Once all of the data has been entered properly, the screen shown in Figure 6-7 is displayed. Unlike the previous examples, this screen is rendered using *confirmPersonalData.xslt*. To make changes to any of these screens, one needs to edit only the appropriate stylesheet.

XML and Stylesheets

Deciding how to structure your XML can have significant impact on your ability to customize the output of a web application. In our current example, the same XML file is used for all web pages. This XML is shown in Example 6-3.

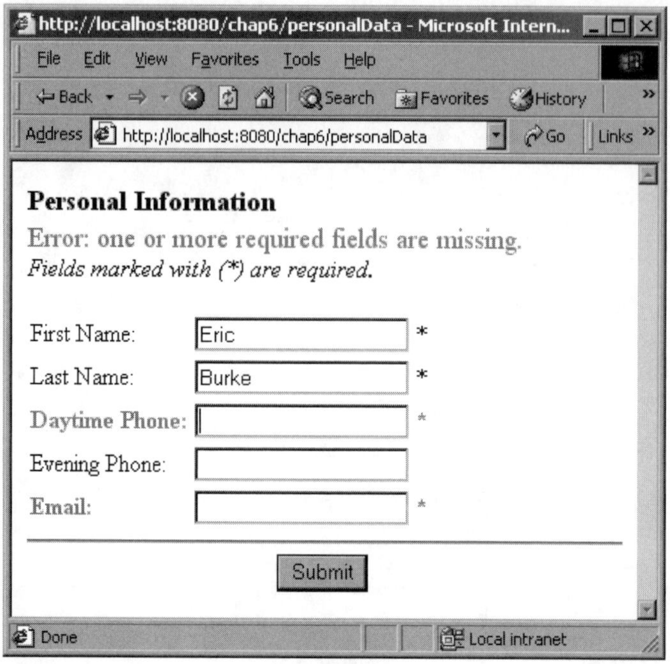

Figure 6-6. Personal information form with errors

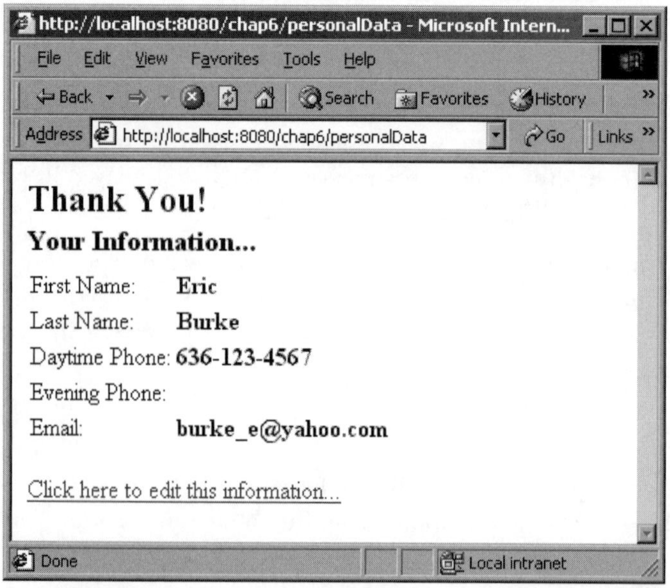

Figure 6-7. Confirmation page

Example 6-3. Example XML output

```
<?xml version="1.0" encoding="UTF-8"?>
<page>
  <!-- the next element is optional: -->
  <!-- <requiredFieldsMissing/> -->
  <personalData>
    <firstName required="true">Eric</firstName>
    <lastName required="true">Burke</lastName>
    <daytimePhone required="true">636-123-4567</daytimePhone>
    <eveningPhone/>
    <email required="true">burke_e@yahoo.com</email>
  </personalData>
</page>
```

As you can see, the XML is very minimal. None of the captions, such as `"First Name:"`, are included, because they are all specified in the XSLT stylesheets. Even the asterisk character (*) is omitted, giving the XSLT author complete control over how things are rendered. The XML is used only for data, so you can use the stylesheets to include graphics, render the output in a foreign language, or combine page fragments from other sources, such as headers and footers, into your web pages.

The `<requiredFieldsMissing/>` element is optional. If omitted, the XSLT stylesheet will not display error messages about missing fields. This is useful when the data is generated the first time because all fields will be blank, and you probably don't want to show a bunch of error messages. In our servlet, the `doGet()` method is called when the user first requests this web page, so it is here where we disable this element.

It is important to mention that this XML is used only for documentation purposes and for testing the XSLT stylesheets. Once you move into a production environment, the XML will be generated dynamically using the `PersonalData` and `PersonalDataXML` classes, so this static file will not be required. You will probably want to hang on to your static XML, however, as this will make it easier to experiment with changes to the XSLT.

The XSLT stylesheet that creates the HTML form is shown in Example 6-4. The stylesheets are substantially longer than the XML data, which is typical. In a more simplistic approach to servlet development, all of this logic would be hardcoded into the source code as a series of `println()` statements, making the servlet much larger and less flexible.

Example 6-4. editPersonalData.xslt

```
<?xml version="1.0" encoding="UTF-8"?>
<xsl:stylesheet version="1.0"
    xmlns:xsl="http://www.w3.org/1999/XSL/Transform"
    xmlns="http://www.w3.org/1999/xhtml">
```

Example 6-4. editPersonalData.xslt (continued)

```
<xsl:output method="xml" indent="yes" encoding="UTF-8"
    doctype-public="-//W3C//DTD XHTML 1.0 Transitional//EN"
    doctype-system="http://www.w3.org/TR/xhtml1/DTD/xhtml1-transitional.dtd"/>
<!--

****************************************************************
** Top level template. Creates the framework for the XHTML page
****************************************************************-->
<xsl:template match="/">
  <html>
    <head><title>Edit Personal Information</title></head>
    <body>
      <xsl:apply-templates select="page/personalData"/>
    </body>
  </html>
</xsl:template>
<!--

****************************************************************
** Match the <personalData> element.
****************************************************************-->
<xsl:template match="personalData">
  <h3>Personal Information</h3>
  <xsl:if test="../requiredFieldsMissing">
    <div style="color: red; font-size: larger;">
      Error: one or more required fields are missing.
    </div>
  </xsl:if>
  <i>Fields marked with (*) are required.</i>
  <form action="/chap6/personalData" method="post">
    <table border="0" cellpadding="2" cellspacing="0">
      <!-- Select all immediate children, such as firstName,
           lastName, daytimePhone, etc... -->
      <xsl:apply-templates/>
    </table>
    <div align="center">
      <hr/>
      <input type="submit" name="submitBtn" value="Submit"/>
    </div>
  </form>
</xsl:template>
<!--

****************************************************************
** Output a new row in the table for each field.
****************************************************************-->
<xsl:template
    match="firstName|lastName|daytimePhone|eveningPhone|email">
```

Example 6-4. editPersonalData.xslt (continued)

```
    <tr>
      <xsl:if test="@required='true'
                    and ../../requiredFieldsMissing
                    and .=''">
        <xsl:attribute name="style">
          <xsl:text>color:red; font-weight:bold;</xsl:text>
        </xsl:attribute>
      </xsl:if>
      <td>
        <xsl:choose>
          <xsl:when test="name()='firstName'">
            First Name:</xsl:when>
          <xsl:when test="name()='lastName'">
            Last Name:</xsl:when>
          <xsl:when test="name()='daytimePhone'">
            Daytime Phone:</xsl:when>
          <xsl:when test="name()='eveningPhone'">
            Evening Phone:</xsl:when>
          <xsl:when test="name()='email'">
            Email:</xsl:when>
        </xsl:choose>
      </td>
      <td>
        <input type="text" name="{name()}" value="{.}"/>
      </td>
      <td>
        <xsl:if test="@required='true'">*</xsl:if>
      </td>
    </tr>
  </xsl:template>
</xsl:stylesheet>
```

The first seven lines of *editPersonalData.xslt* contain boilerplate code that configures the XSLT processor to produce XHTML 1.0 using the transitional DTD. In particular, our result tree uses the `<i>...</i>` tag, so we cannot use the XHTML strict DTD. The top level template matches the `"/"` pattern as usual, outputting the framework for the XHTML document.

The next template matches the `<personalData>` element, producing a heading followed by an optional error message. The error message is displayed if the XML data contains the `<requiredFieldsMissing/>` element, which is easily determined via the `<xsl:if>` element:

```
<xsl:template match="personalData">
  <h3>Personal Information</h3>
  <xsl:if test="../requiredFieldsMissing">
    <div style="color: red; font-size: larger;">
      Error: one or more required fields are missing.
```

```
    </div>
  </xsl:if>
```

This template then produces the `<form>` element, which specifies that HTTP POST should be used to submit the information. The `action` attribute indicates that this form will send its data to our servlet. As you will see, the form action[*] matches the URL pattern that we will set up in the deployment descriptor later in this chapter:

```
<i>Fields marked with (*) are required.</i>
<form action="/chap6/personalData" method="post">
```

The template finally produces a table so that all of the headings and text fields are properly aligned. As in earlier stylesheet examples, this template creates the table, while another template creates each row in the table:

```
<table border="0" cellpadding="2" cellspacing="0">
  <!-- Select all immediate children, such as firstName,
       lastName, daytimePhone, etc... -->
  <xsl:apply-templates/>
</table>
<div align="center">
  <hr/>
  <input type="submit" name="submitBtn" value="Submit"/>
</div>
</form>
</xsl:template>
```

Since this particular instance of `<xsl:apply-templates/>` does not utilize the `select` attribute, all child elements will be selected. The next template is designed to match each of the possible types of elements that can appear and will be instantiated once for each occurrence of `<firstName>`, `<lastName>`, etc.:

```
<xsl:template
    match="firstName|lastName|daytimePhone|eveningPhone|email">
```

This template first produces a `<tr>` element. If this particular element has a `required="true"` attribute, the XML data contains `<requiredFieldsMissing/>`. The value of this element is an empty string, the font is changed to bold and red. This indicates to the user that a required field was missing. The font weight and color are inserted as the `style` attribute on the `<tr>` element as follows:

```
<tr>
  <xsl:if test="@required='true'
                and ../../requiredFieldsMissing
                and .=''">
    <xsl:attribute name="style">
      <xsl:text>color:red; font-weight:bold;</xsl:text>
```

---

* To avoid hardcoding the form action in the XSLT stylesheet, pass it as a stylesheet parameter.

```
    </xsl:attribute>
  </xsl:if>
```

The template then produces its first `<td>` tag, which contains the caption for the current field. It would be nice if XSLT offered a lookup table mechanism for situations such as this, but `<xsl:choose>` does get the job done:

```
<td>
  <xsl:choose>
    <xsl:when test="name()='firstName'">
      First Name:</xsl:when>
    <xsl:when test="name()='lastName'">
      Last Name:</xsl:when>
    <xsl:when test="name()='daytimePhone'">
      Daytime Phone:</xsl:when>
    <xsl:when test="name()='eveningPhone'">
      Evening Phone:</xsl:when>
    <xsl:when test="name()='email'">
      Email:</xsl:when>
  </xsl:choose>
</td>
```

This is still better than hardcoding the captions into the XML or servlet because we can make changes to the stylesheet without recompiling anything. You can even change the captions to a foreign language without affecting any of the Java code, offering remarkable flexibility to web page designers.

The next column in the table contains the input field:

```
<td>
  <input type="text" name="{name()}" value="{.}"/>
</td>
```

In the XHTML output, this yields a cell containing `<input  type="text" name="firstName"  value="Eric"/>`. Finally, the last column in the table contains an asterisk if the field has the `required="true"` attribute:

```
<td>
  <xsl:if test="@required='true'">*</xsl:if>
</td>
</tr>
</xsl:template>
```

The next stylesheet, *confirmPersonalData.xslt*, is listed in Example 6-5. This stylesheet is shorter because it shows only a summary of what the user entered on the previous page. It does not have to display any error messages or show an HTML form. The overall structure of the stylesheet is identical to *editPersonalData. xslt*, however, so a line-by-line description is not necessary.

Design Choices

The two stylesheets, *editPersonalData.xslt* and *confirmPersonalData.xslt*, had a lot in common. To keep things simple, they were written as two independent stylesheets. This is not the only way to implement this code, however. For instance, we could have searched for common functionality and included that functionality from both stylesheets using <xsl:import> or <xsl:include>. This approach did not work here because, although the stylesheets were structured similarly, each template produced different output. As the web site gets more sophisticated, however, you will begin to encounter common page elements such as navigation bars that should not be duplicated in multiple places.

Another approach would be to combine both stylesheets into a single stylesheet and pass a top-level parameter indicating whether to use "edit" mode or "confirm" mode. In this approach, the servlet would pass the parameter to the stylesheet via JAXP's Transformer class and the <xsl:param> element. Inside of the stylesheet, we would write lots of <xsl:choose> or <xsl: if> elements to control the output based on the value of the parameter. The JAXP code would look something like this:

```
javax.xml.transform.Transformer trans = ...
trans.setParameter("personalDataMode", "edit");
```

While this approach has its place, it did not make sense for this particular example because every template produced different output. It would have resulted in a more complex solution than simply writing two separate stylesheets. On the other hand, if you encounter a situation where several web pages are almost identical except for a small section that changes, passing a stylesheet parameter is probably the way to go, because you only have to write the conditional logic around the section that changes.

Example 6-5. confirmPersonalData.xslt

```
<?xml version="1.0" encoding="UTF-8"?>
<xsl:stylesheet version="1.0"
  xmlns:xsl="http://www.w3.org/1999/XSL/Transform"
  xmlns="http://www.w3.org/1999/xhtml">
 <xsl:output method="xml" indent="yes" encoding="UTF-8"
    doctype-public="-//W3C//DTD XHTML 1.0 Strict//EN"
    doctype-system="http://www.w3.org/TR/xhtml1/DTD/xhtml1-strict.dtd"/>
 <!--

 ****************************************************************
 ** Top level template. Creates the framework for the XHTML page
 ****************************************************************-->
 <xsl:template match="/">
```

Example 6-5. confirmPersonalData.xslt (continued)

```
    <html>
      <head>
        <title>Personal Data Summary</title>
      </head>
      <body>
        <xsl:apply-templates select="page/personalData"/>
      </body>
    </html>
</xsl:template>
<!--

****************************************************************
** Match the <personalData> element.
****************************************************************-->
<xsl:template match="personalData">
  <h2>Thank You!</h2>
  <h3>Your Information...</h3>

  <table border="0" cellpadding="2" cellspacing="0">
    <!-- Select all immediate children, such as firstName,
         lastName, daytimePhone, etc... -->
    <xsl:apply-templates/>
  </table>

  <p><a href="/chap6/personalData">Click here
        to edit this information...</a></p>

</xsl:template>
<!--

****************************************************************
** Output a new row in the table for each field.
****************************************************************-->
<xsl:template
  match="firstName|lastName|daytimePhone|eveningPhone|email">

  <tr>
    <td>
      <xsl:choose>
        <xsl:when test="name()='firstName'">
          First Name:</xsl:when>
        <xsl:when test="name()='lastName'">
          Last Name:</xsl:when>
        <xsl:when test="name()='daytimePhone'">
          Daytime Phone:</xsl:when>
        <xsl:when test="name()='eveningPhone'">
          Evening Phone:</xsl:when>
        <xsl:when test="name()='email'">
```

Example 6-5. confirmPersonalData.xslt (continued)

```
            Email:</xsl:when>
        </xsl:choose>
      </td>
      <td>
        <b><xsl:value-of select="."/></b>
      </td>
    </tr>
  </xsl:template>
</xsl:stylesheet>
```

Source Code

The first piece of source code to examine is shown in Example 6-6. The
PersonalData class is simply a data holder and does not contain any XML code
or database code. By keeping classes like this simple, you can easily write standalone unit tests that verify if your code is written properly. If this code were written as part of the servlet instead of a standalone class, it would be very difficult to
test outside of the web browser environment.

Example 6-6. PersonalData.java

```java
package chap6;

/**
 * A helper class that stores personal information. XML generation
 * is intentionally left out of this class. This class ensures
 * that its data cannot be null, nor can it contain extra
 * whitespace.
 */
public class PersonalData {
    private String firstName;
    private String lastName;
    private String daytimePhone;
    private String eveningPhone;
    private String email;

    public PersonalData() {
        this("", "", "", "", "");
    }

    public PersonalData(String firstName, String lastName,
            String daytimePhone, String eveningPhone, String email) {
        this.firstName = cleanup(firstName);
        this.lastName = cleanup(lastName);
        this.daytimePhone = cleanup(daytimePhone);
        this.eveningPhone = cleanup(eveningPhone);
        this.email = cleanup(email);
    }
```

Example 6-6. PersonalData.java (continued)

```java
    /**
     * <code>eveningPhone</code> is the only optional field.
     *
     * @return true if all required fields are present.
     */
    public boolean isValid() {
        return this.firstName.length() > 0
                && this.lastName.length() > 0
                && this.daytimePhone.length() > 0
                && this.email.length() > 0;
    }

    public void setFirstName(String firstName) {
        this.firstName = cleanup(firstName);
    }

    public void setLastName(String lastName) {
        this.lastName = cleanup(lastName);
    }

    public void setDaytimePhone(String daytimePhone) {
        this.daytimePhone = cleanup(daytimePhone);
    }

    public void setEveningPhone(String eveningPhone) {
        this.eveningPhone = cleanup(eveningPhone);
    }

    public void setEmail(String email) {
        this.email = cleanup(email);
    }

    public String getFirstName() { return this.firstName; }
    public String getLastName() { return this.lastName; }
    public String getDaytimePhone() { return this.daytimePhone; }
    public String getEveningPhone() { return this.eveningPhone; }
    public String getEmail() { return this.email; }

    /**
     * Cleanup the String parameter by replacing null with an
     * empty String, and by trimming whitespace from non-null Strings.
     */
    private static String cleanup(String str) {
        return (str != null) ? str.trim() : "";
    }
}
```

Although the `PersonalData` class is merely a data holder, it can include simple validation logic. For example, the default constructor initializes all fields to non-null values:

```
public PersonalData() {
    this("", "", "", "", "");
    }
```

Additionally, all of the set methods make use of the private `cleanup()` method:

```
private static String cleanup(String str) {
    return (str != null) ? str.trim() : "";
}
```

As a result, instances of this class will avoid null references and whitespace, eliminating the need to perform constant error checking in the servlet and XML generation classes. Trimming whitespace is particularly helpful because a user may simply press the spacebar in one of the required fields, potentially bypassing your validation rules. The `PersonalData` class also contains an explicit validation method that checks for all required fields:

```
public boolean isValid() {
    return this.firstName.length() > 0
            && this.lastName.length() > 0
            && this.daytimePhone.length() > 0
            && this.email.length() > 0;
}
```

The only field that is not required is `eveningPhone`, so it is not checked here. By putting this method into this class, we further reduce the work required of the servlet.

The next class, `PersonalDataXML`, is presented in Example 6-7. It is responsible for converting `PersonalData` objects into DOM `Document` objects. By converting to DOM instead of a text XML file, we avoid having to parse the XML as it is fed into an XSLT processor. Instead, we will use the `javax.xml.transform. DOMSource` class to pass the DOM tree directly.

Example 6-7. PersonalDataXML.java

```
package chap6;

import javax.xml.parsers.*;
import org.w3c.dom.*;

/**
 * Responsible for converting a PersonalData object into an XML
 * representation using DOM.
```

Example 6-7. PersonalDataXML.java (continued)

```java
 */
public class PersonalDataXML {

    /**
     * @param personalData the data to convert to XML.
     * @param includeErrors if true, an extra field will be included in
     * the XML, indicating that the browser should warn the user about
     * required fields that are missing.
     * @return a DOM Document that contains the web page.
     */
    public Document produceDOMDocument(PersonalData personalData,
            boolean includeErrors) throws ParserConfigurationException {

        // use Sun's JAXP to create the DOM Document
        DocumentBuilderFactory dbf = DocumentBuilderFactory.newInstance();
        DocumentBuilder docBuilder = dbf.newDocumentBuilder();
        Document doc =  docBuilder.newDocument();

        // create <page>, the root of the document
        Element pageElem = doc.createElement("page");
        doc.appendChild(pageElem);

        // if needed, append <requiredFieldsMissing/>
        if (includeErrors && !personalData.isValid()) {
            pageElem.appendChild(doc.createElement(
                    "requiredFieldsMissing"));
        }

        Element personalDataElem = doc.createElement("personalData");
        pageElem.appendChild(personalDataElem);

        // use a private helper function to avoid some of DOM's
        // tedious code
        addElem(doc, personalDataElem, "firstName",
                personalData.getFirstName(), true);
        addElem(doc, personalDataElem, "lastName",
                personalData.getLastName(), true);
        addElem(doc, personalDataElem, "daytimePhone",
                personalData.getDaytimePhone(), true);
        addElem(doc, personalDataElem, "eveningPhone",
                personalData.getEveningPhone(), false);
        addElem(doc, personalDataElem, "email",
                personalData.getEmail(), true);

        return doc;
    }
```

Example 6-7. PersonalDataXML.java (continued)

```
/**
 * A helper method that simplifies this class.
 *
 * @param doc the DOM Document, used as a factory for
 *            creating Elements.
 * @param parent the DOM Element to add the child to.
 * @param elemName the name of the XML element to create.
 * @param elemValue the text content of the new XML element.
 * @param required if true, insert 'required="true"' attribute.
 */
private void addElem(Document doc, Element parent, String elemName,
        String elemValue, boolean required) {
    Element elem = doc.createElement(elemName);
    elem.appendChild(doc.createTextNode(elemValue));
    if (required) {
        elem.setAttribute("required", "true");
    }
    parent.appendChild(elem);
}
}
```

The following code begins with its two `import` statements. The `javax.xml.parsers` package contains the JAXP interfaces, and the `org.w3c.dom` package contains the standard DOM interfaces and classes:

```
import javax.xml.parsers.*;
import org.w3c.dom.*;
```

The key to this class is its public API, which allows a `PersonalData` object to be converted into a DOM Document object:

```
public Document produceDOMDocument(PersonalData personalData,
        boolean includeErrors) throws ParserConfigurationException {
```

The `includeErrors` parameter indicates whether or not to include the `<requiredFieldsMissing/>` element in the result. If this method throws a `ParserConfigurationException`, the most likely cause is a CLASSPATH problem. This frequently occurs when an older version of JAXP is present.

When using JAXP, it takes a few lines of code to obtain the appropriate implementation of the `DocumentBuilder` abstract class. By using the factory pattern, our code is safely insulated from vendor-specific DOM implementations:

```
// use Sun's JAXP to create the DOM Document
DocumentBuilderFactory dbf = DocumentBuilderFactory.newInstance();
DocumentBuilder docBuilder = dbf.newDocumentBuilder();
Document doc = docBuilder.newDocument();
```

Once the doc object has been created, we use it to create all remaining elements in the XML data. For example, the <page> element is created first:

```
// create <page>, the root of the document
Element pageElem = doc.createElement("page");
doc.appendChild(pageElem);
```

Since <page> is the root element, it is the only thing added directly to our document. All remaining elements will be added as children or descendents of <page>. Even though we are not adding anything else directly to the doc object, we must continue using it as the factory for creating the remaining elements:

```
// if needed, append <requiredFieldsMissing/>
if (includeErrors && !personalData.isValid()) {
    pageElem.appendChild(doc.createElement(
            "requiredFieldsMissing"));
}
```

Since DOM can be tedious, the children of <personalData> are created in a helper method called addElem():

```
Element personalDataElem = doc.createElement("personalData");
pageElem.appendChild(personalDataElem);

// use a private helper function to avoid some of DOM's
// tedious code
addElem(doc, personalDataElem, "firstName",
        personalData.getFirstName(), true);
...
```

You can refer back to Example 6-7 for the complete implementation of the addElem() method. A sample of its output is:

```
<firstName required="true">Eric</firstName>
```

The final piece of code, *PersonalDataServlet.java*, is presented in Example 6-8. This is a basic approach to servlet development that works for smaller programs such as this, but has a few scalability problems that we will discuss later in this chapter. Although we have removed all of the HTML and XML generation from this servlet, it is still responsible for handling incoming requests from the browser. As your web application grows to more and more screens, the code gets correspondingly larger.

Example 6-8. PersonalDataServlet.java

```
package chap6;

import java.io.*;
import java.net.*;
import javax.servlet.*;
import javax.servlet.http.*;
```

Example 6-8. PersonalDataServlet.java (continued)

```java
import javax.xml.transform.*;
import javax.xml.transform.dom.*;
import javax.xml.transform.stream.*;

/**
 * A demonstration servlet that produces two pages. In the first page,
 * the user is prompted to enter "personal information", including
 * name, phone number, and Email. In the second page, a summary of this
 * information is displayed. XSLT is used for all HTML rendering,
 * so this servlet does not enforce any particular look and feel.
 */
public class PersonalDataServlet extends HttpServlet {
    private PersonalDataXML personalDataXML = new PersonalDataXML();
    private Templates editTemplates;
    private Templates thanksTemplates;

    /**
     * One-time initialization of this Servlet.
     */
    public void init() throws UnavailableException {
        TransformerFactory transFact = TransformerFactory.newInstance();
        String curName = null;
        try {
            curName = "/WEB-INF/xslt/editPersonalData.xslt";
            URL xsltURL = getServletContext().getResource(curName);
            String xsltSystemID = xsltURL.toExternalForm();
            this.editTemplates = transFact.newTemplates(
                    new StreamSource(xsltSystemID));

            curName = "/WEB-INF/xslt/confirmPersonalData.xslt";
            xsltURL = getServletContext().getResource(curName);
            xsltSystemID = xsltURL.toExternalForm();
            this.thanksTemplates = transFact.newTemplates(
                    new StreamSource(xsltSystemID));
        } catch (TransformerConfigurationException tce) {
            log("Unable to compile stylesheet", tce);
            throw new UnavailableException("Unable to compile stylesheet");
        } catch (MalformedURLException mue) {
            log("Unable to locate XSLT file: " + curName);
            throw new UnavailableException(
                    "Unable to locate XSLT file: " + curName);
        }
    }

    /**
     * Handles HTTP GET requests, such as when the user types in
     * a URL into his or her browser or clicks on a hyperlink.
     */
```

Example 6-8. PersonalDataServlet.java (continued)

```java
protected void doGet(HttpServletRequest request,
        HttpServletResponse response) throws IOException,
        ServletException {
    PersonalData personalData = getPersonalData(request);
    // the third parameter, 'false', indicates that error
    // messages should not be displayed when showing the page.
    showPage(response, personalData, false, this.editTemplates);
}


/**
 * Handles HTTP POST requests, such as when the user clicks on
 * a Submit button to update his or her personal data.
 */
protected void doPost(HttpServletRequest request,
        HttpServletResponse response) throws IOException,
        ServletException {

    // locate the personal data object and update it with
    // the information the user just submitted.
    PersonalData pd = getPersonalData(request);
    pd.setFirstName(request.getParameter("firstName"));
    pd.setLastName(request.getParameter("lastName"));
    pd.setDaytimePhone(request.getParameter("daytimePhone"));
    pd.setEveningPhone(request.getParameter("eveningPhone"));
    pd.setEmail(request.getParameter("email"));

    if (!pd.isValid()) {
        // show the 'Edit' page with an error message
        showPage(response, pd, true, this.editTemplates);
    } else {
        // show a confirmation page
        showPage(response, pd, false, this.thanksTemplates);
    }
}


/**
 * A helper method that sends the personal data to the client
 * browser as HTML. It does this by applying an XSLT stylesheet
 * to the DOM tree.
 */
private void showPage(HttpServletResponse response,
        PersonalData personalData, boolean includeErrors,
        Templates stylesheet) throws IOException, ServletException {
    try {
        org.w3c.dom.Document domDoc =
                this.personalDataXML.produceDOMDocument(
                personalData, includeErrors);
```

Example 6-8. PersonalDataServlet.java (continued)

```
            Transformer trans = stylesheet.newTransformer();

            response.setContentType("text/html");
            PrintWriter writer = response.getWriter();

            trans.transform(new DOMSource(domDoc), new StreamResult(writer));
        } catch (Exception ex) {
            showErrorPage(response, ex);
        }
    }


    /**
     * If any exceptions occur, this method can be called to display
     * the stack trace in the browser window.
     */
    private void showErrorPage(HttpServletResponse response,
            Throwable throwable) throws IOException {
        PrintWriter pw = response.getWriter();
        pw.println("<html><body><h1>An Error Has Occurred</h1><pre>");
        throwable.printStackTrace(pw);
        pw.println("</pre></body></html>");
    }


    /**
     * A helper method that retrieves the PersonalData object from
     * the HttpSession.
     */
    private PersonalData getPersonalData(HttpServletRequest request) {
        HttpSession session = request.getSession(true);
        PersonalData pd = (PersonalData) session.getAttribute(
                "chap6.PersonalData");
        if (pd == null) {
            pd = new PersonalData();
            session.setAttribute("chap6.PersonalData", pd);
        }
        return pd;
    }
}
```

Our servlet begins with a long list of `import` statements, indicating dependencies on the servlet API as well as the JAXP package. The servlet itself is a subclass of `HttpServlet`, as usual, and has three private fields:

```
public class PersonalDataServlet extends HttpServlet {
    private PersonalDataXML personalDataXML = new PersonalDataXML();
    private Templates editTemplates;
    private Templates thanksTemplates;
```

It is important to ensure that each of these fields is thread-safe. Because many clients share the same servlet instance, it is highly probable that these fields will be accessed concurrently. Instances of `PersonalDataXML` are thread-safe because they are stateless, meaning they contain no data that can be concurrently modified. The `Templates` instances are compiled representations of the two stylesheets this servlet uses and are also designed to be thread-safe.

As the comments indicate, the `init()` method performs a one-time initialization of the servlet. A servlet container will invoke this method before this servlet is asked to handle any client requests. The `init()` method is further guaranteed to execute to completion before any other threads can access this servlet, so concurrency is not an issue at this point. If anything fails during initialization, an instance of `UnavailableException` is thrown:

```
public void init() throws UnavailableException {
    TransformerFactory transFact = TransformerFactory.newInstance();
    String curName = null;
    ...
```

This exception is provided in the `javax.servlet` package and indicates that the servlet could not be loaded successfully. In our case, the most common cause of this error is a configuration problem. For example, your XSLT stylesheets may be installed in the wrong directory, or some JAR file was not found.

The next thing the `init()` method does is load the two stylesheets into memory. The XSLT stylesheets are stored on the file system, so `StreamSource` will be used to read them into JAXP. But you definitely do not want to hardcode the absolute pathname of the stylesheets. If you do this, your code will probably work on your personal machine but will fail once it is deployed onto a production web server. For example, *C:/java/tomcat/webapps/chap6/WEB-INF* is a Windows-specific absolute pathname. Using something so specific would cause the servlet to fail on all non-Windows platforms, as well as other Windows machines that have Tomcat installed in a different directory. The best approach is to use a relative pathname such as */WEB-INF*, so the stylesheets can be located regardless of where your web application is deployed.

A relative pathname has to be relative to some starting location, so we use the `ServletContext` class. `ServletContext` has the ability to locate resources relative to the deployed directory of the current web application, so you can avoid absolute pathnames in your code. The details of mapping the relative pathname to the absolute pathname are taken care of by the servlet container, thus making your code more portable.

In this example, *chap6.war* is deployed to Tomcat's *webapps* directory. Tomcat will expand it into the *webapps/chap6* directory, which contain subdirectories that match the directory structure of the WAR file. We start by assigning the current XSLT filename to the `curName` variable, using the following pathname:

```
try {
    curName = "/WEB-INF/xslt/editPersonalData.xslt";
```

Two options are available at this point. The `ServletContext` can provide either an `InputStream` or a `URL`, both of which represent the XSLT stylesheet. If you use an `InputStream`, however, the XSLT processor sees your stylesheet as a stream of bytes. It will not know where this datastream originated, so it will not automatically know how to resolve URI references. This becomes a problem if your stylesheet imports or includes another stylesheet because this other stylesheet will not be located. To resolve this problem when using `InputStream`, the `javax.xml.transform.Source` interface provides the `setSystemId()` method. This allows the XSLT processor to resolve URI references in the stylesheet (see Chapter 5).

For this servlet, we avoid this issue by using a `URL` instead of an `InputStream`. The `URL` is converted into a system identifier, which makes it possible to create a `StreamSource` instance. That is, in turn, used to create a `Templates` instance for this stylesheet:

```
URL xsltURL = getServletContext().getResource(curName);
String xsltSystemID = xsltURL.toExternalForm();
this.editTemplates = transFact.newTemplates(
        new StreamSource(xsltSystemID));
```

The same process is repeated for the second stylesheet, followed by basic exception handling:

```
    curName = "/WEB-INF/xslt/confirmPersonalData.xslt";
    xsltURL = getServletContext().getResource(curName);
    xsltSystemID = xsltURL.toExternalForm();
    this.thanksTemplates = transFact.newTemplates(
            new StreamSource(xsltSystemID));
    } catch (TransformerConfigurationException tce) {
    log("Unable to compile stylesheet", tce);
        throw new UnavailableException("Unable to compile stylesheet");
} catch (MalformedURLException mue) {
    log("Unable to locate XSLT file: " + curName);
    throw new UnavailableException(
            "Unable to locate XSLT file: " + curName);
}
}
```

The `log()` method causes messages to be written to one of Tomcat's log files, found in the *TOMCAT_HOME/logs* directory. The `UnavailableException` simply indicates that this servlet is unavailable, so it will not be loaded into memory. The user will see an error page in their browser at this point.

If the init() method completes successfully, the servlet will be available to handle requests from clients. In this servlet, the doGet() and doPost() methods have been implemented; therefore, both HTTP GET and POST protocols are supported. When the user first enters the application, they will click on a hyperlink, type a URL into their browser, or visit a saved bookmark. In all of these cases, the browser issues an HTTP GET request that ultimately causes the doGet() method to be invoked:

```
protected void doGet(HttpServletRequest request,
        HttpServletResponse response) throws IOException,
        ServletException {
    PersonalData personalData = getPersonalData(request);
    // the third parameter, 'false', indicates that error
    // messages should not be displayed when showing the page.
    showPage(response, personalData, false, this.editTemplates);
}
```

The first thing the doGet() method does is retrieve the instance of PersonalData associated with this particular user. The appropriate code has been factored out into the getPersonalData() helper method, since this same functionality is required by the doPost() method as well. You can refer back to Example 6-8 to see how getPersonalData() is implemented. It basically uses HttpSession to locate the appropriate instance of PersonalData. If the object is not found in the session, a new instance is created and stored.

The doGet() method then calls the showPage() method, which does the actual work of sending the web page to the browser. The parameters to showPage() include:

- The HttpServletResponse, which provides access to the PrintWriter. The result of the transformation will be sent to this writer.

- The instance of PersonalData, so the showPage() method knows what data to display.

- A false parameter, indicating that error messages should not be shown. That makes sense because doGet() is called when the page is first displayed, and users should not be warned about invalid data before they type something.

- A reference to the appropriate stylesheet. In this case, the stylesheet will show the HTML form so the user can fill out his or her information.

Once the user fills out the form and submits it to the servlet, the doPost() method is invoked. The code for doPost() is similar to doGet() (see Example 6-8). The only difference here is that all incoming data is validated via the PersonalData class. If the request is valid, the "Thank You" page is displayed.

Otherwise, the current page is redisplayed with error messages enabled. As you can see in the code, the only distinction between these two pages is that they use different stylesheets.

The final piece to this puzzle resides in the showPage() method. This method begins by creating a DOM Document instance by delegating to the PersonalDataXML helper class. As you can see in the following code, the servlet stays quite small because the DOM generation is factored out into the helper class:

```
private void showPage(HttpServletResponse response,
        PersonalData personalData, boolean includeErrors,
        Templates stylesheet) throws IOException, ServletException {
    try {
        org.w3c.dom.Document domDoc =
                this.personalDataXML.produceDOMDocument(
                personalData, includeErrors);
```

This method then proceeds to create a new instance of Transformer. You may recall from Chapter 5 that Transformer instances are very lightweight and merely hold state information for the current transformation. Since Transformer instances are not thread-safe, the instance is a local variable in this method. With local variables, each thread gets its own copy:

```
Transformer trans = stylesheet.newTransformer();
```

Next, the content type is configured for the HttpServletResponse, a PrintWriter is obtained, and the transformation is performed. The result tree is sent directly to the response's PrintWriter:

```
        response.setContentType("text/html");
        PrintWriter writer = response.getWriter();

        trans.transform(new DOMSource(domDoc), new StreamResult(writer));
    } catch (Exception ex) {
        showErrorPage(response, ex);
    }
}
```

If any exception occurs, the showErrorPage() method is invoked. Since an exception can indicate that some XML library is unavailable, the showErrorPage() does not attempt to use XML or XSLT for its output. If it does, another similar exception would almost certainly occur. Instead, it uses hard-coded println() statements to generate its HTML (see Example 6-8).

Deployment

Figure 6-8 shows the complete contents of the WAR file used in this example. You may notice that *SplashScreenServlet.class* is still listed in this WAR file. This example is merely an extension of the example created earlier in this chapter. As in the earlier example, placing the `.class` files under the classes directory made them available to the `ClassLoader` used by this web application.

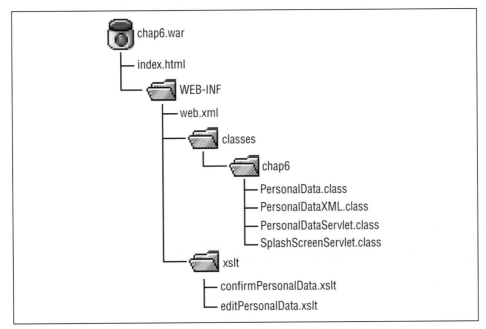

Figure 6-8. WAR file for PersonalDataServlet

The XSLT stylesheets are placed under the *WEB-INF/xslt* directory. Since anything under the *WEB-INF* directory is hidden from clients, the XSLT stylesheets are not directly visible to anyone visiting your web site. If you want to make these stylesheets publicly visible, move them out of the *WEB-INF* directory. The *index. html* file, for example, is the publicly visible "home page" for this web application. It merely contains a link that the user can click on to view the servlet. Although the stylesheets are hidden from clients, they are accessible from your Java code. Referring back to the code in Example 6-8, the `init()` method used the following to locate the stylesheets:

```
curName = "/WEB-INF/xslt/editPersonalData.xslt";
URL xsltURL = getServletContext().getResource(curName);
```

As this code illustrates, the locations of the stylesheets are entirely relative to their position in the WAR file. Therefore, your servlet will still work as the web application is moved onto a production web server.

The deployment descriptor, listed in Example 6-9, has been expanded to include the new `PersonalDataServlet` class. The lines that have changed from our first iteration are emphasized.

Example 6-9. Expanded deployment descriptor

```xml
<?xml version="1.0" encoding="UTF-8"?>
<!DOCTYPE web-app
    PUBLIC "-//Sun Microsystems, Inc.//DTD Web Application 2.2//EN"
    "http://java.sun.com/j2ee/dtds/web-app_2.2.dtd">
<web-app>
  <servlet>
    <servlet-name>personalDataServlet</servlet-name>
    <servlet-class>chap6.PersonalDataServlet</servlet-class>
  </servlet>
  <servlet>
    <servlet-name>splashScreen</servlet-name>
    <servlet-class>chap6.SplashScreenServlet</servlet-class>
  </servlet>
  <servlet-mapping>
    <servlet-name>personalDataServlet</servlet-name>
    <url-pattern>/personalData/*</url-pattern>
  </servlet-mapping>
  <servlet-mapping>
    <servlet-name>splashScreen</servlet-name>
    <url-pattern>/splash/*</url-pattern>
  </servlet-mapping>
</web-app>
```

How to Compile, Deploy, and Run

In Java, it often seems that half of the battle is devoted to figuring out CLASS-PATH issues. In order to compile this example, the following JAR files must be listed on the CLASSPATH:

jaxp.jar
    Java API for XML Processing (JAXP) 1.1

xalan.jar
    Xalan XSLT processor (use the one included with JAXP)

crimson.jar
    Crimson XML parser (use the one included with JAXP)

servlet.jar
    Included with the Tomcat servlet container

Of course, the directory containing your own source code must also be listed on the CLASSPATH. Once everything is set up, you can compile *PersonalData.java*,

PersonalDataXML.java, and *PersonalDataServlet.java* by typing **javac   *.java**. Whether you also wish to include *SplashScreenServlet.java* is entirely up to you.

As mentioned earlier in this chapter, use the *jar* command to create the WAR file. To create *chap6.war,* simply arrange your files into the directory structure shown in Figure 6-8 and issue the following command from the directory that contains *index.html*:

```
jar -cvfM ../chap6.war .
```

This command places *chap6.war* in the parent of your current working directory; the forward slash (/) works on Windows as well as Unix clients. Once the WAR file has been created, you can view its contents by changing to its directory and issuing the following command:

```
jar -tvf chap6.war
```

This shows the table of contents for the WAR file, which must match the structure shown in Figure 6-8.

Deployment to Tomcat is easy: just copy *chap6.war* to the *TOMCAT_HOME/webapps* directory while Tomcat is not running. You can attempt to execute the servlet now, but it will probably not work because *jaxp.jar, xalan.jar,* and *crimson.jar* must be installed in the *TOMCAT_HOME/lib* directory before they can be available for your web application.

The most difficult aspect of this step is installing the correct versions of these JAR files. Depending on which version of Tomcat you are running, older versions of *jaxp. jar* and *crimson.jar* may already be found in the *TOMCAT_HOME/lib* directory. The safest approach is to download JAXP 1.1, which includes all three of these JAR files, and copy them from the JAXP distribution to the *TOMCAT_HOME/lib* directory.

Once these steps are complete, start Tomcat and access the following URL:

http://localhost:8080/chap6/personalData

This should bring up the personal information page with a blank form, ready for input.

Locating Stylesheets with Initialization Parameters

As you just saw, an easy way to locate stylesheets is simply to place them somewhere underneath the *WEB-INF* directory of a WAR file. While this is an ideal solution for solitary web applications, there are situations where the same stylesheets are shared across a whole group of web apps. In this case, embedding the stylesheets into various WAR files is not viable.

Ideally, the stylesheets will be located in a shared directory somewhere, but that directory location will not be hardcoded into any servlets. The simple way to accomplish this is via initialization parameters. These are name/value pairs of strings specified in the deployment descriptor and retrieved via the `Servlet` or `ServletContext`.

Servlet initialization parameters are tied to specific servlets, and context initialization parameters are tied to an entire web application. For the purposes of specifying the XSLT stylesheet location, it makes sense to use context parameters. These can be specified in the deployment descriptor as follows:

```
<web-app>
  <context-param>
    <param-name>xslt_directory</param-name>
    <param-value>C:/dev/xslt</param-value>
  </context-param>
  <servlet>
    ...
  </servlet>
</web-app>
```

And the values of these parameters can be retrieved using the following methods on the `javax.servlet.ServletContext` interface:

```
public interface ServletContext {
    // if the parameter name does not exist, return null
    String getInitParameter(String name);
    Enumeration getInitParameterNames();
    ...remaining methods omitted
}
```

So in order to locate the stylesheet, one might write the following code in a servlet's `init()` method:

```
public class MyServlet extends HttpServlet {
    private String xsltDirectory;

    public void init(ServletConfig config) throws ServletException {
        super.init(config);
        this.xsltDirectory = config.getServletContext().getInitParameter(
                "xslt_directory");
        if (this.xsltDirectory == null) {
            throw new UnavailableException(
                    "xslt_directory is a required context-param");
        }
    }

    ...remainder of code omitted
}
```

Now that the actual location of the stylesheets has been moved into the deployment descriptor, changes can be made without any edits to the servlet.

Stylesheet Caching Revisited

We have seen two approaches that eliminate the need to hardcode the absolute pathname of XSLT stylesheets in your servlet code. In the first approach, the ServletContext was used to load resources from the web application using a relative pathname. In the second approach, the location was specified as a context initialization parameter.

This takes care of compilation changes, but now we have the issue of dynamic loading. In the PersonalDataServlet class, the two XSLT stylesheets are located and "compiled" into instances of the javax.xml.transform.Templates interface. Although this offers high performance for transformations, the two stylesheets are never flushed from memory. If changes are made to the XSLT stylesheets on disk, the servlet must be stopped and started again.

Integration with the Stylesheet Cache

In Chapter 5, a stylesheet cache was implemented. In this next example, PersonalDataServlet is modified to use the cache instead of Templates directly. This will offer virtually the same runtime performance. However, you will be able to modify the stylesheets and immediately see those changes in your web browser. Each time a stylesheet is requested, the cache will check its timestamp on the file system. If the file has been modified, a new Templates instance is instantiated without bringing down the servlet.

Fortunately, integration with the cache actually makes the PersonalDataServlet simpler to implement. Example 6-10 contains the modified listing, and all modified lines are emphasized.

Example 6-10. Modified PersonalDataServlet.java with stylesheet cache

```
package chap6;

import com.oreilly.javaxslt.util.StylesheetCache;
import java.io.*;
import java.net.*;
import javax.servlet.*;
import javax.servlet.http.*;
import javax.xml.transform.*;
import javax.xml.transform.dom.*;
import javax.xml.transform.stream.*;

/**
 * A modification of PersonalDataServlet that uses the
 * com.oreilly.javaxslt.util.StylesheetCache class.
 */
public class PersonalDataServlet extends HttpServlet {
    private PersonalDataXML personalDataXML = new PersonalDataXML();
```

Example 6-10. Modified PersonalDataServlet.java with stylesheet cache (continued)

```java
private String editXSLTFileName;
private String thanksXSLTFileName;

/**
 * One-time initialization of this Servlet.
 */
public void init() throws UnavailableException {
    this.editXSLTFileName = getServletContext().getRealPath(
            "/WEB-INF/xslt/editPersonalData.xslt");
    this.thanksXSLTFileName = getServletContext().getRealPath(
            "/WEB-INF/xslt/confirmPersonalData.xslt");
}


/**
 * Handles HTTP GET requests, such as when the user types in
 * a URL into his or her browser or clicks on a hyperlink.
 */
protected void doGet(HttpServletRequest request,
        HttpServletResponse response) throws IOException,
        ServletException {
    PersonalData personalData = getPersonalData(request);
    // the third parameter, 'false', indicates that error
    // messages should not be displayed when showing the page.
    showPage(response, personalData, false, this.editXSLTFileName);
}


/**
 * Handles HTTP POST requests, such as when the user clicks on
 * a Submit button to update his or her personal data.
 */
protected void doPost(HttpServletRequest request,
        HttpServletResponse response) throws IOException,
        ServletException {

    // locate the personal data object and update it with
    // the information the user just submitted.
    PersonalData pd = getPersonalData(request);
    pd.setFirstName(request.getParameter("firstName"));
    pd.setLastName(request.getParameter("lastName"));
    pd.setDaytimePhone(request.getParameter("daytimePhone"));
    pd.setEveningPhone(request.getParameter("eveningPhone"));
    pd.setEmail(request.getParameter("email"));

    if (!pd.isValid()) {
        // show the 'Edit' page with an error message
        showPage(response, pd, true, this.editXSLTFileName);
    } else {
        // show a confirmation page
```

Example 6-10. Modified PersonalDataServlet.java with stylesheet cache (continued)

```
            showPage(response, pd, false, this.thanksXSLTFileName);
        }
    }

    /**
     * A helper method that sends the personal data to the client
     * browser as HTML. It does this by applying an XSLT stylesheet
     * to the DOM tree.
     */
    private void showPage(HttpServletResponse response,
            PersonalData personalData, boolean includeErrors,
            String xsltFileName) throws IOException, ServletException {
        try {
            org.w3c.dom.Document domDoc =
                    this.personalDataXML.produceDOMDocument(
                    personalData, includeErrors);

            Transformer trans =
                    StylesheetCache.newTransformer(xsltFileName);

            response.setContentType("text/html");
            PrintWriter writer = response.getWriter();

            trans.transform(new DOMSource(domDoc), new StreamResult(writer));
        } catch (Exception ex) {
            showErrorPage(response, ex);
        }
    }

    /**
     * If any exceptions occur, this method can be showed to display
     * the stack trace in the browser window.
     */
    private void showErrorPage(HttpServletResponse response,
            Throwable throwable) throws IOException {
        PrintWriter pw = response.getWriter();
        pw.println("<html><body><h1>An Error Has Occurred</h1><pre>");
        throwable.printStackTrace(pw);
        pw.println("</pre></body></html>");
    }

    /**
     * A helper method that retrieves the PersonalData object from
     * the HttpSession.
     */
    private PersonalData getPersonalData(HttpServletRequest request) {
        HttpSession session = request.getSession(true);
        PersonalData pd = (PersonalData) session.getAttribute(
```

Example 6-10. Modified PersonalDataServlet.java with stylesheet cache (continued)

```
            "chap6.PersonalData");
    if (pd == null) {
        pd = new PersonalData();
        session.setAttribute("chap6.PersonalData", pd);
    }
    return pd;
    }
}
```

One key difference in this example is its reliance on the `com.oreilly.`
`javaxslt.util.StylesheetCache` class. This will, of course, require that you
add *StylesheetCache.class* to your WAR file in the appropriate directory. Another
option is to place the stylesheet cache into a JAR file, and place that JAR file into
the *TOMCAT_HOME/lib* directory. This approach is taken when you download the
example code for this book.

The biggest code savings occur in the `init()` method because the filenames for
the stylesheets are stored instead of `Templates` instances. This is because the
stylesheet cache requires filenames as inputs and will create its own instances of
`Templates`, which accounts for a majority of the simple changes throughout the
servlet.

Once you get this example up and running, testing the stylesheet reloading capability is a snap. As before, *chap6.war* is copied to the *TOMCAT_HOME/webapps*
directory. After you run the servlet the first time, you will notice that the WAR file
is expanded into the *TOMCAT_HOME/webapps/chap6* directory. Simply go into the
TOMCAT_HOME/webapps/chap6/WEB-INF/xslt directory and edit one of the
stylesheets. Then click on the Refresh button on your web browser, and you
should see the results of the edits that were just made.

If you don't see the changes, there might be some leftover files from earlier examples in this chapter. Be sure to shut down Tomcat and remove both *chap6.war* and
the *chap6* directory from Tomcat's *webapps* directory. Then re-deploy and try again.

Servlet Threading Issues

Like it or not, a servlet must be capable of serving more than one client at a time.
Built-in threading capability is one of the key reasons why Java is so well-suited to
server applications, particularly when compared to a traditional CGI model. As
usual, however, tradeoffs are involved. In particular, writing code that can handle
many concurrent tasks without corrupting data can be quite challenging at times.
Ideally, this material can alert you to the most common causes of threading problems found in a servlet environment.

Servlet Threading Model

In the standard servlet model, a client makes a request via the servlet's `service()` method. In the `HttpServlet` class, the `service()` method determines the type of HTTP request and delegates to methods such as `doGet()` or `doPost()`. If several clients issue requests at the same time, these methods will serve each client in a different thread. Since most servlets are subclasses of `HttpServlet`, your main concern is insuring that `service()`, `doGet()`, and `doPost()` can handle many concurrent clients.

Before handling any requests, a servlet's `init()` method is invoked. According to the servlet API specification, this method must be invoked by only a single thread and must complete successfully before subsequent threads are allowed to enter the `service()` method. For this reason, you do not have to worry about threading problems inside of the `init()` method. From there, however, all bets are off.

One simplistic approach to thread safety is to declare a method as synchronized. In this approach, your `doGet()` method would be declared as follows:

```
protected synchronized void doGet(HttpServletRequest request,
        HttpServletResponse response) throws IOException, ServletException {
    ...
}
```

The `synchronized` keyword will require that any thread wishing to invoke this method first obtain a lock on the servlet object. Once the first client obtains the lock and begins to execute the method, all others must wait their turn. If the `doGet()` method takes 0.5 seconds to execute, then a load of a mere 100 users will result in nearly a minute-long wait for many visitors to your site, since each waits in a queue for access to the lock.

This is almost never a viable option, so another choice is to declare that your servlet implements the `javax.servlet.SingleThreadModel` interface as follows:

```
public class MyServlet extends HttpServlet implements SingleThreadModel {
    ...
}
```

The `SingleThreadModel` interface is a marker interface, meaning that it does not declare any methods. It merely indicates to the servlet container that your servlet is not thread-safe, and can handle only one request at a time in its `service()` method. A typical servlet container will maintain a pool of servlet instances in this case, allowing each instance to handle a single request at a time.

This is somewhat better than merely synchronizing the `doGet()` or `doPost()` method. However, it does mean that multiple copies of the servlet will be instantiated. This results in higher memory overhead and still does not ensure that all threading issues will be resolved. For example, concurrent modifications to a shared resource such as a file or a static field are not prevented in any way.

Thread Safety Tips

Most servlet threading problems occur when two or more threads make changes to the same resource. This might mean that two threads try to modify a file, or perhaps several threads all update the value of a shared variable at the same instant. This causes unpredictable behavior and can be very hard to diagnose. Another type of thread problem is deadlock, where two threads are in contention for the same resource, each holding a lock that the other thread needs. Yet another problem is performance. As mentioned earlier, synchronizing access to a method can introduce significant performance penalties.

The best overall approach to servlet thread safety is to avoid the `SingleThreadModel` interface and synchronizing access to the `service()` method. This way, your servlet can handle multiple client requests at the same time. This also means that you must avoid situations where more than one thread can modify a shared resource concurrently. The following tips should offer some guidance.

Tip 1: Local variables are thread-safe

Object fields in a servlet are often bad news. Consider the following code:

```
public class HomeServlet extends HttpServlet {
    private Customer currentCust;

    protected void doGet(HttpServletRequest request,
            HttpServletResponse response) throws IOException,
            ServletException {
        HttpSession session = request.getSession(true);
        currentCust = (Customer) session.getAttribute("cust");
        currentCust.setLastAccessedTime(new Date());
        ...
    }
}
```

In this code, the `currentCust` field is obtained from the `HttpSession` whenever a client enters the `doGet()` method. Unfortunately, if another thread invokes this method an instant later, the `currentCust` field will be overwritten before the first thread is complete. In fact, dozens of threads could enter the `doGet()` method at roughly the same time, repeatedly replacing the `currentCust` reference. This would lead to complete failure of this servlet.

The easy fix is to make `currentCust` a local variable as follows:

```
public class HomeServlet extends HttpServlet {
    protected void doGet(HttpServletRequest request,
            HttpServletResponse response) throws IOException,
            ServletException {
        HttpSession session = request.getSession(true);
        Customer currentCust = (Customer) session.getAttribute("cust");
        currentCust.setLastAccessedTime(new Date());

        ...

    }
}
```

This fixes our problem because each thread gets its own copy of local variables in Java. By simply removing the object field and replacing it with a local variable, this particular threading problem is resolved.

Tip 2: Immutable objects are thread-safe

Whenever two or more threads make changes to the same object at the same time, a race condition can occur. Consider the following code:

```
public class Person {
    private String firstName;
    private String lastName;

    public void setName(String firstName, String lastName) {
        this.firstName = firstName;
        this.lastName = lastName;
    }

    ...getter methods omitted
}
```

If two threads invoke the `setName()` method at roughly the same time, the following scenario can occur:

1. Thread "A" sets the first name to "Bill," but is interrupted by thread "B".

2. Thread "B" sets the first and last names to "George" and "Bush."

3. Thread "A" regains control, and sets the last name to "Clinton."

At this point, the person's name is George Clinton, which is clearly not what was intended. Although you could make the `setName()` method `synchronized`, you would also have to make any get methods `synchronized` as well.

Another option is to make this an *immutable* object. An immutable object cannot be modified, so multiple threads cannot concurrently alter it. The `Person` class can be modified as follows:

```
public class Person {
    private String firstName;
    private String lastName;

    public Person(String firstName, String lastName) {
        this.firstName = firstName;
        this.lastName = lastName;
    }

    public String getFirstName() { return this.firstName; }
    public String getLastName() { return this.lastName; }
}
```

Since instances of the `Person` class cannot be modified, its methods do not have to be `synchronized`. This makes the objects fast and allows them to be read by many threads concurrently. The only drawback is that you cannot make changes to these objects once they are constructed. The simple fix is to create a brand new `Person` object whenever a change needs to be made. This is essentially the approach that `java.lang.String` takes.

Immutable objects are not always an option but can be a useful technique for many smaller "data helper" classes that seem to pop up in every application.

Tip 3: Provide a single point of entry

When dealing with a single instance of a shared resource, such as a file that needs to be modified, you should consider creating a facade around that resource. This is a single class that provides controlled access to that resource, thus providing a single point in your code for proper synchronization. The following code snippet illustrates how you can essentially create a facade around a data source that holds `Customer` objects. It is assumed that the `Customer` class is immutable, making it impossible to change a `Customer` instance without going through this well-defined API:

```
public class CustomerSource {
    public static synchronized Customer getCustomer(String id) {
        // read the customer from a file, or perhaps
        // from a database...
    }

    public static synchronized Customer createCustomer() {
        // create a new customer in the file or database
        // and return it...
    }
```

```
        public static synchronized void deleteCustomer(String id) {
            // ...
        }
    }
```

This is just one simple approach that works best on smaller applications. A servlet's doGet() or doPost() method should utilize the CustomerSource class without any data corruption. If the methods in CustomerSource are slow, however, they will hinder scalability as more and more clients wait for their turn to access the underlying data source.

Tip 4: *Understand the Templates interface*

Multiple threads can share implementations of javax.xml.transform. Templates. Therefore, instances can be stored as object fields on a servlet:

```
    public class MyServlet extends HttpServlet {
        private Templates homePageStylesheet;


        ...
    }
```

But instances of javax.xml.transform.Transformer are not thread-safe; they should be declared as local variables within the doGet() or doPost() method:

```
    public class MyServlet extends HttpServlet {
        private Templates homePageStylesheet;

        public void init() throws UnavailableException {
            ... create the Templates instance
        }

        protected void doGet() {
            Transformer trans = homePageStylesheet.newTransformer();
            ... use this Transformer instance, a local variable
        }
    }
```

7

Discussion Forum

Up until now, the examples in this book have been short and to the point. The goal of this chapter is to show how a much more sophisticated web application is designed and implemented from the ground up. This is the culmination of everything covered so far, combining XML, servlets, XSLT, JDBC, JAXP, and JDOM into a fully functioning web-based discussion forum. As with the other examples in this book, the full source code is available from the companion web site.

Walking the line between "textbook quality" and "real-world" examples is difficult. First and foremost, the goal of this chapter is to demonstrate how to design and implement a nontrivial web application using XSLT and Java. The second goal is to produce a decent application that can actually be used in the real world. Hopefully this has been achieved. Although making an example of this size fit into a single chapter involves a few tradeoffs, the design is flexible enough to allow new features, such as user authentication, to be implemented without too much additional effort.

The discussion forum requires the following Java packages:

*   Java 2 Standard Edition v1.2 or later
*   JDOM beta 6
*   Any JAXP 1.1 compatible XML parser and XSLT processor
*   Any servlet container that supports Version 2.2 or later of the servlet specification
*   Either MySQL or Microsoft Access

Overall Process

Developing a web application using Java and XSLT can be broken down into several key steps. As in any software development project, a modular approach that can be dispatched to several developers simultaneously is highly desirable. This speeds the overall process and allows developers of different skill levels to participate.

Our process consists of the following high-level steps:

- Define the requirements.
- Create prototype XHTML web pages.
- Create prototype XML datafiles.
- Create XSLT stylesheets.
- Design and implement the Java domain classes.
- Design and implement the database and related code.
- Create "XML producer" objects.
- Implement the servlets and related code.

Although the list shown here approximates the order in which these steps will be performed, in larger applications it is typical to implement a vertical slice of the system first. This slice will implement one or two key screens and will require the development team to follow all of the previous steps. As more screens are added to the system, the process is followed again for each piece of functionality that is added. This is very typical of most lightweight software development processes in which the system is developed in iterative steps rather than trying to implement the entire system in one pass.

The remainder of this chapter will present the implementation of the discussion forum. The requirements, design, and code will be presented in roughly the same order as the list shown in this section.

Requirements

An online discussion forum will be developed using Java and XSLT. For the reference implementation, all features will be accessible via a web browser using XHTML, and no client-side Java or JavaScript will be required. The target for deployment is a web-hosting provider that supports Java 2, servlet 2.2, and access to a relational database such as MySQL. It is assumed that any additional Java JAR files, such as those required for JAXP and JDOM, can be installed along with the web application.

The discussion forum will be divided into message boards, each of which covers a different topic such as "Dog Lovers" or "Cat Lovers." Each message belongs to one of these boards and may be a response to a previous message. This is known as a *threaded* discussion forum. Each message will also contain a subject, create date, author email, and the actual message text.

When visiting the web site, users can read existing messages, post new messages, or reply to existing messages. Only administrators can create new message boards. Although XHTML is specified for the reference implementation, every effort will be made to facilitate alternatives, such as XHTML Basic or WML. Other than practical limitations such as bandwidth and database capacity, no artificial constraints shall be placed on the number of boards or messages.

A few features will be omitted to keep this example reasonably sized. These include a web-based administrative interface, user authentication and security, and the ability to search the archive. Suggestions for implementing these features are mentioned at the end of this chapter.

Screen Flow

The forum user interface consists of four primary screens, as shown in Figure 7-1. Each box represents a different web page that visitors encounter, and lines indicate screen-to-screen flow as the user clicks on links.

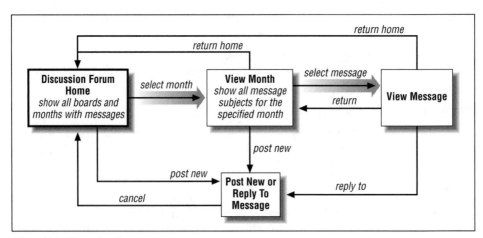

Figure 7-1. Discussion forum screens

Creating a graphical layout of the web pages as shown here is sometimes called *storyboarding*, a common user interface design technique that has its roots in the animation, television, and motion picture industries. Such high-level diagrams typically start as hand-drawn sketches on paper, with the intent of capturing the overall application flow. This is a good place to start because it shows how everything fits together without delving too deeply into technical design details.

The "Discussion Forum Home" page is the starting point and displays the list of all message boards. For each message board, a list of months with messages is displayed. From this screen, the user can either click on a month to view a list of message subjects, or click on a link to post a new message. The user can always return to the home page from any other page in the application.

The "View Month" page shows message subjects for a particular month in a given board. These messages are displayed in a tree that shows the message subject, author, and create date. The structure of the tree represents threads of discussion, with replies indented underneath the original messages. From this page, the user can either select a message to view or click on a link to visit the "Post New Message" page.

The "View Message" screen shows details for an individual message. From this page, visitors can either return to the month view or click on a link to reply to this message.

The final page allows users to either post a new message or reply to an existing message. Since posting and replying are quite similar, much of the Java and XSLT stylesheet code is reused. Although using the same code for multiple web pages reduces the size of the application, it can add complexity because the code must be capable of two modes of operation.

Prototyping the XML

Once the requirements and screen flow are well understood, it is possible to move on to a more rigorous design process. Web sites based on XSLT are highly modular, facilitating a design and implementation process that can be farmed out to several members of a development team. Each piece can be developed and tested independently before finally bringing everything together into the completed web application.

XHTML Prototypes

Creating user interface prototypes is an early task that can be handed off to less experienced programmers or perhaps to a dedicated web page designer. At this stage in the game, an overly complex and graphical web interface is not required. The bells and whistles can be added later by merely updating XSLT stylesheets. In fact, too much effort at this early stage can make it more difficult to figure out what the XML and XSLT should look like.

Since the front end will be created using *XHTML Strict*, a separate cascading style sheet (CSS) will be required to make the pages look presentable.* The strict variant of XHTML does not allow most of the HTML 4.0 formatting tags, but instead encourages the use of CSS. Example 7-1 contains the complete CSS file used by the discussion forum.

Example 7-1. forum.css

```
body {
  font-family : Verdana, Geneva, Arial, Helvetica, sans-serif;
}

.box1 {
  border: 3px solid Navy;
  text-align: center;
  padding: 4px;
  margin : 2px;
  background-color: #c0c0c0;
}

.box2 {
  border: 1px solid Navy;
  padding: 4px;
  margin: 2px;
  background-color: #FFFFCC;
}

h1 {
  font-size: 22pt;
  font-weight: normal;
  margin: 0px 0px 0px 0px;
}

h2 {
  font-size: 18pt;
  font-weight: normal;
  margin: 0px 0px 0px 0px;
}

h3 {
  font-size: 14pt;
  font-weight: normal;
  margin: 0px 0px 0px 0px;
}

ul {
```

* See *http://www.w3.org/TR/xhtml1* for more information on XHTML Strict.

Example 7-1. forum.css (continued)

```
  margin-top: 0px;
}

.msgSummaryLine {
  font-size: smaller;
  font-weight: normal;
}

a:hover {
  background-color:yellow;
}

.error {
  font-weight: bold;
  color: red;
}
```

Each of the XHTML web pages refers to this CSS file using the following syntax:

```
<link type="text/css" rel="stylesheet" href="/forum/forum.css" />
```

This is a great technique because it keeps the size of the XSLT stylesheets and each XHTML page much smaller. Changes to fonts and colors can be made in the single CSS file and are immediately reflected throughout the web application. The primary obstacle at this time is noncompliant web browsers. Although support for CSS is gradually improving, web pages must be tested on a variety of browsers to identify formatting problems.

TIP   A common theme presented throughout this book is the separation
               of data and presentation that XSLT supports. CSS expands upon this
               theme by separating XHTML content from many aspects of its visual
               presentation. CSS and XSLT are very different technologies that
               complement one another nicely.

Most of the code in a CSS file is fairly self-explanatory. For example, the h2 style applies to <h2> elements in the XHTML. One style element that many programmers may not be familiar with is:

```
  .box2 {
    border: 1px solid Navy;
    padding: 4px;
    margin: 2px;
    background-color: #FFFFCC;
  }
```

The dot in `.box2` indicates a *style class* definition. Here is how the `box2` style class is used in the XHTML:

```
<div class="box2">Messages for March, 2001</div>
```

The advantage of a style class is that it can be applied to any element in the XHTML. In this case, a thin border and yellow background are applied to any element that has the `box2` class.

The web page designers should create basic representations of every page in the application at this point. The home page is shown in Figure 7-2.

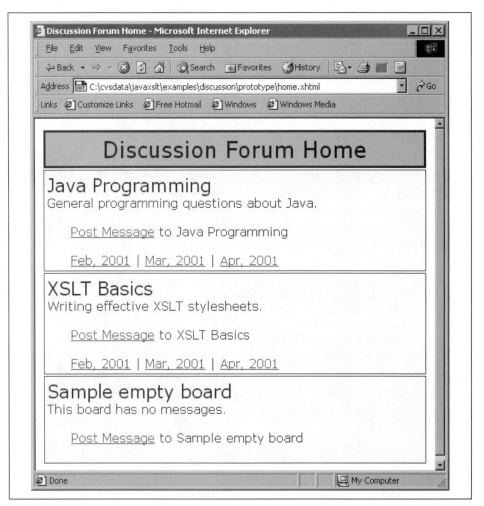

Figure 7-2. Home page prototype

The complete XHTML source code for the home page is shown in Example 7-2. As shown, the actual hyperlinks are not valid because the design for the servlets has not been completed, and the final URLs are probably unknown at this point. At any rate, this is only prototype code, because the actual XHTML web pages are dynamic and will be produced as the result of an XSLT transformation from XML data.

Example 7-2. Home page XHTML source

```
<?xml version="1.0" encoding="UTF-8"?>
<!DOCTYPE html PUBLIC "-//W3C//DTD XHTML 1.0 Strict//EN"
    "http://www.w3.org/TR/xhtml1/DTD/xhtml1-strict.dtd">
<html xmlns="http://www.w3.org/1999/xhtml">
  <head>
    <title>Discussion Forum Home</title>
    <link href="../docroot/forum.css" rel="stylesheet" type="text/css" />
  </head>
  <body>
    <div class="box1">
      <h1>Discussion Forum Home</h1>
    </div>
    <div class="box2">
      <h2>Java Programming</h2>
      <div>General programming questions about Java.</div>
      <div style="margin-left: 2em;">
        <p>
          <a href="link_to_post_message">Post Message</a>
          to Java Programming</p>
          <a href="link_to_feb_messages">Feb, 2001</a> |
          <a href="link_to_mar_messages">Mar, 2001</a> |
          <a href="link_to_apr_messages">Apr, 2001</a>
      </div>
    </div>
    <div class="box2">
      <h2>XSLT Basics</h2>
      <div>Writing effective XSLT stylesheets.</div>
      <div style="margin-left: 2em;">
        <p>
        <a href="link_to_post_message">Post Message</a> to XSLT Basics</p>
        <a href="link_to_feb_messages">Feb, 2001</a> |
        <a href="link_to_mar_messages">Mar, 2001</a> |
        <a href="link_to_apr_messages">Apr, 2001</a>
      </div>
    </div>
    <div class="box2">
      <h2>Sample empty board</h2>
      <div>This board has no messages.</div>
      <div style="margin-left: 2em;">
        <p>
          <a href="link_to_post_msg">Post Message</a>
          to Sample empty board</p>
```

Example 7-2. Home page XHTML source (continued)

```
      </div>
    </div>
  </body>
</html>
```

`<div>` and `<span>` tags may be unfamiliar because they were ignored by many HTML authors until CSS became more prevalent. Basically, a `<div>` tag is wrapped around any number of other elements, turning them into a block-level element group. The `<span>` tag is similar, but it is an inline element. This means that `<span>` tags will be embedded into the current line, while `<div>` tags will wrap to a new line much like `<p>` or `<h1>` tags do. The ability to define style classes make `<div>` and `<span>` particularly useful for XHTML Strict, which disallows deprecated HTML 4.0 elements such as `<font>`. Although `<span>` is not used in this particular example, `<div>` is used frequently to introduce line breaks and to apply styles using CSS.

The next prototype, shown in Figure 7-3, shows what a message board looks like. XHTML source code for the remaining screens is not listed here.

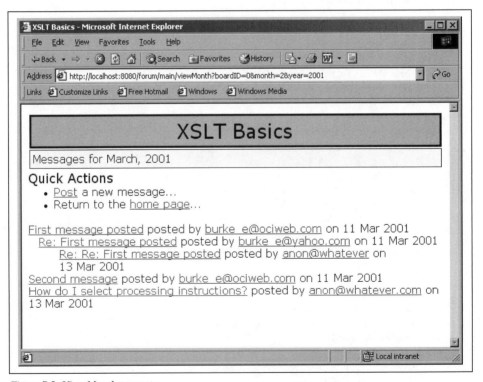

Figure 7-3. View Month prototype

Messages that are replies to other messages are indented a few spaces. Later, a simple change to the XSLT stylesheet can be employed to show graphical folders or other icons in front of each message. The next screen, shown in Figure 7-4, shows how users can post new messages to the discussion forum.

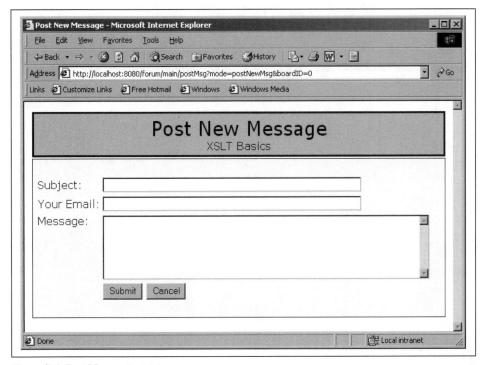

Figure 7-4. Post Message prototype

This page is also used to reply to an existing message. Although not shown here, the title changes to "Reply to Message," and the subject and message text are prefilled with text from the original message. If the user submits this form without filling in all values, the web page is redisplayed with an error message.

The final screen prototype is shown in Figure 7-5. This screen allows users to view existing messages.

XML Samples

While page designers are hard at work on the XHTML prototype screens, someone else can be working on sample XML data for each web page. Although different people may work on these tasks, a certain degree of coordination is critical at this point. The prototype XHTML pages may look great, but the XML must provide the data to enable those pages to be created. The XML designer will also have

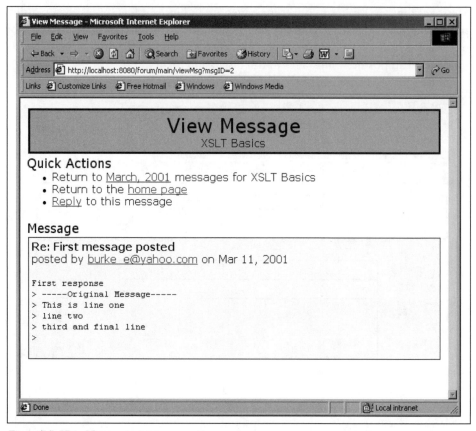

Figure 7-5. View Message prototype

to work with the people who are designing the back-end data sources to determine if the desired data is even available.

When designing XML, the focus should be on data rather than presentation. All
of the fonts and colors that are part of the CSS should have absolutely zero impact
on the design of the XML. The XML will contain additional data that is not displayed, however. For example, creating hyperlinks requires some sort of identifier
for each object. This allows the servlet to figure out which message the user
clicked on. The XML data contains the identifier for the message, but the actual
XHTML markup for the hyperlink comes from an XSLT stylesheet.

The XML data for the home page is shown in Example 7-3. Because the XML does
not contain presentation information, it is smaller than the XHTML markup.

Example 7-3. home.xml

```
<?xml version="1.0" encoding="UTF-8"?>
<?xml-stylesheet type="text/xsl" href="../xslt/home.xslt"?>
<home>
  <board id="0">
    <name>Java Programming</name>
    <description>General programming questions about Java.</description>
    <messages month="1" year="2001"/>
    <messages month="2" year="2001"/>
    <messages month="3" year="2001"/>
  </board>
  <board id="1">
    <name>XSLT Basics</name>
    <description>Writing effective XSLT stylesheets</description>
    <messages month="1" year="2001"/>
    <messages month="2" year="2001"/>
    <messages month="3" year="2001"/>
  </board>
  <board id="3">
    <name>Sample empty board</name>
    <description>This board has no messages.</description>
  </board>
</home>
```

Do not forget that this is still just a prototype XML file. The actual XML data will be dynamically generated by JDOM once the application is finished; this XML prototype code is used only for testing and development purposes.

In this XML data, each message board is represented by a <board> element that has an id attribute. When the user clicks on the "Post Message" web page hyperlink, this id is used to figure out which message board he or she wants to post to. The list of <messages> elements indicates months that have messages in them. These do not need id attributes because the month and year are used in the hyperlink.

The second line of the XML links to the XSLT stylesheet:

```
<?xml-stylesheet type="text/xsl" href="../xslt/home.xslt"?>
```

This is not used in the final application but is very useful during the prototyping and development process. By linking to the stylesheet, the transformation can be quickly viewed in an XSLT-compatible web browser by simply loading the XML page.

The next XML file, shown in Example 7-4, contains data for the "View Month" page.

Iterative Design

The examples shown in this chapter are the result of several attempts to get the design "right." As in other areas of software design, figuring out what to place in the XHTML, XML, and XSLT is an iterative process that requires several attempts before the design can be finalized.

In a nutshell, the process works something like this:

- Prototype the web pages using HTML or XHTML.

- Create the XML datafile prototypes and optionally create DTDs.

- Create XSLT stylesheets that transform the XML into XHTML.

- Design and create back-end data sources and classes that know how to produce the required XML data.

- Create servlets that tie everything together.

As each piece of the application is implemented, missing or redundant features will manifest themselves in other areas. This is where the iterative process comes into effect. If some features are not right the first time, simply refine the prototypes and repeat various steps in the process until all the pieces fit together.

Example 7-4. viewMonth.xml

```
<?xml version="1.0" encoding="UTF-8"?>
<?xml-stylesheet type="text/xsl" href="../xslt/viewMonth.xslt"?>
<viewMonth month="1" year="2001">
  <board id="1">
    <name>Java Programming</name>
    <description>General programming questions about Java.</description>
  </board>
  <message id="1" day="1">
    <subject>First test message</subject>
    <authorEmail>burke_e@yahoo.com</authorEmail>
    <message id="2" day="2">
      <subject>Re: First test message</subject>
      <authorEmail>aidan@nowhere.com</authorEmail>
    </message>
  </message>
  <message id="3" day="4">
    <subject>Another test message</subject>
    <authorEmail>burke_e@yahoo.com</authorEmail>
  </message>
</viewMonth>
```

Moving on to Example 7-5, we have the XML for the "Post/Reply Message" page.

Example 7-5. postMsg.xml

```xml
<?xml version="1.0" encoding="UTF-8"?>
<?xml-stylesheet type="text/xsl" href="../xslt/postMsg.xslt"?>
<postMsg>
  <board id="1">
    <name>Java Programming</name>
    <description>The board description...</description>
  </board>
  <inResponseTo id="4">
    <subject>Test Subject</subject>
  </inResponseTo>
  <error code="ALL_FIELDS_REQUIRED"/>
  <prefill>
    <subject>Test Subject</subject>
    <authorEmail></authorEmail>
    <message>My Message</message>
  </prefill>
</postMsg>
```

This XML is used for both posting new messages and replying to existing messages because the web pages are virtually identical, and the data is the same in both cases. The <error> and <prefill> elements were not part of the original prototype, but it was quickly determined that these were needed if the user did not provide information for all required fields. When the "Post New Message" page is first displayed, these XML elements are not present. After the user clicks on the Submit button, however, these elements are inserted into the XML if a field is missing and the page needs to be redisplayed.

And finally, the XML for the "View Message" page is shown in Example 7-6.

Example 7-6. viewMsg.xml

```xml
<?xml version="1.0" encoding="UTF-8"?>
<?xml-stylesheet type="text/xsl" href="../xslt/viewMsg.xslt"?>
<message id="5" month="1" day="4" year="2001">
  <board id="1">
    <name>Java Programming</name>
  </board>
  <inResponseTo id="4">
    <subject>Test Subject</subject>
  </inResponseTo>
  <subject>Re: Test Subject</subject>
  <authorEmail>burke_e@yahoo.com</authorEmail>
  <text>This is a test of the message
    text.</text>
</message>
```

A quick study of this data reveals that *postMsg.xml* and *viewMsg.xml* have many similarities. A few modifications to either XML file will enable us to reuse the same

JDOM code later when producing these pages. The alternative is to keep these pages separate, which results in at least one additional Java class later on. The advantage of keeping these files separate is so that the XML generation code does not have to be cluttered up with a lot of if/else statements to figure out the mode of operation it is in.

XSLT Stylesheets

Yet another member of the development team can be assigned to the task of creating XSLT stylesheets, although he or she will have to wait until the XML and XHTML prototypes are complete. More often than not, the person designing the XML will be the one creating the initial XSLT stylesheets.

At this point in the process, a tool such as XML Spy can be invaluable.* The ability to edit the XSLT stylesheet and click on the Refresh button in an IDE makes development a snap. Alternately, an XSLT-compatible web browser can quickly display changes as stylesheets are edited. As explained in Chapter 1, Microsoft's Internet Explorer 5.x supports XSLT, provided that the updated *msxml* parser is installed using the *xmlinst* utility.†

Example 7-7 shows the XSLT for the discussion forum home page.

Example 7-7. XSLT for the home page

```
<?xml version="1.0" encoding="UTF-8"?>
<!--
*************************************************************
** home.xslt
**
** Transforms the home page into XHTML
*************************************************************
-->
<xsl:stylesheet version="1.0"
  xmlns:xsl="http://www.w3.org/1999/XSL/Transform">
  <xsl:import href="utils.xslt"/>
  <xsl:param name="rootDir" select="'../docroot/'"/>
  <xsl:output method="xml" version="1.0" encoding="UTF-8"
    indent="yes"
    doctype-public="-//W3C//DTD XHTML 1.0 Strict//EN"
    doctype-system="http://www.w3.org/TR/xhtml1/DTD/xhtml1-strict.dtd"/>

  <!--
*************************************************************
```

---

* XML Spy is a commercial XML editor that works nicely for XSLT development. It is available at *http://www.xmlspy.com*.

† As this is written, IE 6.0 is in beta testing. It supports the latest XSLT specification. The Mozilla browser will also support XSLT at some point.

Example 7-7. XSLT for the home page (continued)

```
** Create the XHTML web page
********************************************************-->
<xsl:template match="/">
  <html xmlns="http://www.w3.org/1999/xhtml">
    <head>
      <title>Discussion Forum Home</title>
      <link href="{$rootDir}forum.css"
          rel="stylesheet" type="text/css"/>
    </head>
    <body>
      <div class="box1">
        <h1>Discussion Forum Home</h1>
      </div>
      <xsl:apply-templates select="home/board"/>
    </body>
  </html>
</xsl:template>


<!--
*********************************************************
** Output a box for each board in the discussion forum
*********************************************************
-->
<xsl:template match="board">
  <xsl:variable name="boardID" select="@id"/>

  <div class="box2">
    <h2><xsl:value-of select="name"/></h2>
    <div><xsl:value-of select="description"/></div>
    <div style="margin-left: 2em;">
      <!-- create a link so the user can post a new message
           to this board -->
      <p>
      <a href="/forum/main/postMsg?mode=postNewMsg&amp;boardID={@id}">Post Message</a>
      to <xsl:value-of select="name"/>
      </p>

      <!-- For each month that has messages, show the
           month name and year number as a link -->
      <xsl:for-each select="messages">
        <ahref="forum/main/viewMonth?boardID={$boardID}&amp;month={@month}&amp;year={@year}">
          <xsl:call-template name="utils.printShortMonthName">
            <xsl:with-param name="monthNumber" select="@month"/>
          </xsl:call-template>
          <xsl:text>, </xsl:text>
          <xsl:value-of select="@year"/>
        </a>
        <!-- put a pipe character after
```

Example 7-7. XSLT for the home page (continued)

```
              all but the last month -->
        <xsl:if test="position() != last()">
          <xsl:text> | </xsl:text>
        </xsl:if>
      </xsl:for-each>
    </div>
  </div>
  </xsl:template>
</xsl:stylesheet>
```

This stylesheet opens with the usual `<xsl:stylesheet>` tag and then proceeds to import *utils.xslt*. This is a stylesheet that contains common templates for formatting dates. Since these utilities are needed on just about every page, they are defined a common file that is imported, as shown here. This stylesheet also takes a parameter named `rootDir`, allowing the web application to specify the location of the document root directory:

```
<xsl:param name="rootDir" select="'../docroot/'"/>
```

The `select` attribute defines a default value for this parameter if none was specified. During the stylesheet development process, the XSLT is tested using a static XML file. This is done outside of a web application, so the parameter is not specified and the root directory defaults to `../docroot/`. This makes it possible to locate the CSS file during development, when developers are working from a static directory structure on their file systems. Later, when the XSLT stylesheet is deployed to a web application and the servlet is running, the servlet can specify a different value for this parameter that indicates a directory relative to the web application context. This is a useful technique whenever a stylesheet has to reference external resources such as CSS files, JavaScript files, or images.

Next, the `<xsl:output>` element is used to set up XHTML output. The *XHTML 1.0 Strict* DTD is used, which eliminates many deprecated HTML 4.0 features. Because the strict DTD does away with many formatting tags, a CSS file is required to make the pages look presentable. All the XSLT needs to do is produce HTML code that references the external stylesheet, as shown here:

```
<html xmlns="http://www.w3.org/1999/xhtml">
  <head>
    <title>Discussion Forum Home</title>
    <link href="{$rootDir}forum.css"
        rel="stylesheet" type="text/css"/>
  </head>
```

The XSLT processor does not actually deal with the CSS file. From the perspective of XSLT, the `<link>` tag is just text that is copied to the result tree during the transformation process. Later, when the web browser displays the XHTML page, the actual CSS file is loaded. This technique is great because styles can be shared across all web pages without complicating the XSLT stylesheets.

The remainder of the stylesheet is pretty basic—just matching patterns in the XML and producing XHTML content to the result tree. One important thing to point out here is the way that hyperlinks are created:

```
<a href="/forum/main/postMsg?mode=postNewMsg&amp;boardID={@id}">Post Message</a>
```

Since the ampersand character (&) is not allowed in an XML attribute value, it must be written using the `&amp;` built-in entity. As it turns out, browsers deal with this just fine, and the hyperlink works anyway.*

What Is the URL?

You may be wondering how you are supposed to know what each hyperlink is actually supposed to be. At this stage of the game, you probably will not know, and your links will actually look something like this:

```
<a href="TODO: link to post a new message">Post Message</a>
```

This is fine for now, because you really won't know what to put there until the servlets are fully designed. Part of the servlet design process involves figuring out what parameters are required and what the legal values are. Until this work has been completed, however, an educated guess or "TODO" comment is fine.

Another key piece of this stylesheet shows how to call a utility template:

```
<xsl:call-template name="utils.printShortMonthName">
  <xsl:with-param name="monthNumber" select="@month"/>
</xsl:call-template>
```

The `utils.printShortMonthName` template is part of *utils.xslt* and is invoked just like a local template. The only difference is that the current stylesheet must import *utils.xslt* or the code will fail. Prefixing the template name with `utils.` has nothing to do with the actual filename; it is a convention adopted only for this application that makes the code a little easier to read, reducing the chances for naming conflicts.

The reusable XSLT stylesheet, *utils.xslt*, is shown next in Example 7-8.

---

* We will see this again when dealing with WML in Chapter 10.

Example 7-8. Reusable XSLT code

```xml
<?xml version="1.0" encoding="UTF-8"?>
<xsl:stylesheet version="1.0" xmlns:xsl="http://www.w3.org/1999/XSL/Transform">

  <xsl:template name="utils.printShortMonthName">
    <xsl:param name="monthNumber"/>
    <xsl:choose>
      <xsl:when test="$monthNumber='0'">Jan</xsl:when>
      <xsl:when test="$monthNumber='1'">Feb</xsl:when>
      <xsl:when test="$monthNumber='2'">Mar</xsl:when>
      <xsl:when test="$monthNumber='3'">Apr</xsl:when>
      <xsl:when test="$monthNumber='4'">May</xsl:when>
      <xsl:when test="$monthNumber='5'">Jun</xsl:when>
      <xsl:when test="$monthNumber='6'">Jul</xsl:when>
      <xsl:when test="$monthNumber='7'">Aug</xsl:when>
      <xsl:when test="$monthNumber='8'">Sep</xsl:when>
      <xsl:when test="$monthNumber='9'">Oct</xsl:when>
      <xsl:when test="$monthNumber='10'">Nov</xsl:when>
      <xsl:when test="$monthNumber='11'">Dec</xsl:when>
    </xsl:choose>
  </xsl:template>

  <xsl:template name="utils.printLongMonthName">
    <xsl:param name="monthNumber"/>
    <xsl:choose>
      <xsl:when test="$monthNumber='0'">January</xsl:when>
      <xsl:when test="$monthNumber='1'">February</xsl:when>
      <xsl:when test="$monthNumber='2'">March</xsl:when>
      <xsl:when test="$monthNumber='3'">April</xsl:when>
      <xsl:when test="$monthNumber='4'">May</xsl:when>
      <xsl:when test="$monthNumber='5'">June</xsl:when>
      <xsl:when test="$monthNumber='6'">July</xsl:when>
      <xsl:when test="$monthNumber='7'">August</xsl:when>
      <xsl:when test="$monthNumber='8'">September</xsl:when>
      <xsl:when test="$monthNumber='9'">October</xsl:when>
      <xsl:when test="$monthNumber='10'">November</xsl:when>
      <xsl:when test="$monthNumber='11'">December</xsl:when>
    </xsl:choose>
  </xsl:template>
</xsl:stylesheet>
```

Month numbers are indexed from position 0 to be consistent with the `java.util.Calendar` class, which also uses 0 to represent January. The templates convert the month number into an English month name.

viewMonth.xslt is shown in Example 7-9. It generates an XHTML page that shows all messages in a month for a particular board.

Example 7-9. XSLT for the View Month page

```
<?xml version="1.0" encoding="UTF-8"?>
<!--
*************************************************************
** viewMonth.xslt
**
** Shows a month-view of messages in a given board.
*************************************************************
-->
<xsl:stylesheet version="1.0"
  xmlns:xsl="http://www.w3.org/1999/XSL/Transform">
  <xsl:import href="utils.xslt"/>
  <xsl:param name="rootDir" select="'../docroot/'"/>
  <xsl:output method="xml" version="1.0" encoding="UTF-8"
    indent="yes"
    doctype-public="-//W3C//DTD XHTML 1.0 Strict//EN"
    doctype-system="http://www.w3.org/TR/xhtml1/DTD/xhtml1-strict.dtd"/>
  <!-- ================= Global Variables ================= -->
  <xsl:variable name="global.boardName" select="/viewMonth/board/name"/>
  <xsl:variable name="global.boardID" select="/viewMonth/board/@id"/>
  <xsl:variable name="global.monthNum" select="/viewMonth/@month"/>
  <xsl:variable name="global.yearNum" select="/viewMonth/@year"/>

  <!--
  *************************************************************
  ** Create the XHTML web page
  *************************************************************-->
  <xsl:template match="/">
    <html xmlns="http://www.w3.org/1999/xhtml">
      <head>
        <title>
          <xsl:value-of select="$global.boardName"/>
        </title>
        <!-- reference an external CSS file to keep this
             XSLT stylesheet smaller -->
        <link href="{$rootDir}forum.css"
            rel="stylesheet" type="text/css"/>
      </head>
      <body>
        <div class="box1">
          <h1>
            <xsl:value-of select="$global.boardName"/>
          </h1>
        </div>
        <div class="box2">
          <xsl:text>Messages for </xsl:text>
          <xsl:call-template name="utils.printLongMonthName">
            <xsl:with-param name="monthNumber" select="$global.monthNum"/>
          </xsl:call-template>
```

Example 7-9. XSLT for the View Month page (continued)

```
          <xsl:text>, </xsl:text>
          <xsl:value-of select="$global.yearNum"/>
      </div>
      <!-- ===== Quick Actions ====== -->
      <h3>Quick Actions</h3>
      <ul>
        <li>
          <a href="postMsg?mode=postNewMsg&amp;boardID={$global.boardID}">
          Post</a> a new message...</li>
          <li>Return to the <a href="home">home page</a>...</li>
      </ul>
      <!-- ===== Recursively show the message tree ===== -->
      <xsl:apply-templates select="viewMonth/message"/>
    </body>
  </html>
</xsl:template>


<!--
**********************************************************
** Display a one-line summary for each message.
**********************************************************-->
<xsl:template match="message">
  <xsl:param name="indent" select="0"/>

  <!-- indent according to the 'indent' parameter -->
  <div style="margin-left: {$indent}em;">
    <a href="viewMsg?msgID={@id}">
      <xsl:value-of select="subject"/>
    </a>
    <xsl:text> posted by </xsl:text>
    <xsl:apply-templates select="authorEmail"/>
    <xsl:text> on </xsl:text>
    <xsl:value-of select="@day"/>
    <xsl:text disable-output-escaping="yes"> 
    <xsl:call-template name="utils.printShortMonthName">
      <xsl:with-param name="monthNumber" select="$global.monthNum"/>
    </xsl:call-template>
        <xsl:text disable-output-escaping="yes"> 
    <xsl:value-of select="$global.yearNum"/>

    <!-- recursively select all messages that are
         responses to this one. Increment the indentation
         with each call -->
    <xsl:apply-templates select="message">
      <xsl:with-param name="indent" select="$indent + 1"/>
    </xsl:apply-templates>
  </div>
</xsl:template>
```

Example 7-9. XSLT for the View Month page (continued)

```
<!--
*************************************************************
** Show the author's email address.
*************************************************************-->
<xsl:template match="authorEmail">
  <a href="mailto:{.}">
    <xsl:value-of select="."/>
  </a>
</xsl:template>
</xsl:stylesheet>
```

Because *viewMonth.xslt* shows a summary view of a large number of messages, the actual text content for each message is not included in the output. Instead, the message subject, author, and create date are displayed. These lines are grouped and indented according to replies, making threads of discussion immediately visible.

This stylesheet declares a series of global variables. These can be referenced throughout the stylesheet and are designed to make the code more maintainable. Since each variable is prefixed with `global.`, the code is easy to understand when using the variables:

```
<xsl:value-of select="$global.boardName"/>
```

TIP The `global.` naming convention is not a standard part of XSLT. It is just a convention used here to make the XSLT more self-documenting.

The interesting part of this stylesheet involves construction of the tree of messages. Since messages in the XML are hierarchical, the XSLT must recursively process the data to properly show threads of discussion. Here is another look at a portion of the *viewMonth.xml* file presented earlier in this chapter:

```
<viewMonth month="1" year="2001">
  <board id="1">
    <name>Java Programming</name>
    <description>General programming questions about Java.</description>
  </board>
  <message id="1" day="1">
    <subject>First test message</subject>
    <authorEmail>burke_e@yahoo.com</authorEmail>
    <message id="2" day="2">
      <subject>Re: First test message</subject>
      <authorEmail>aidan@nowhere.com</authorEmail>
    </message>
  </message>
  <message id="3" day="4">
    <subject>Another test message</subject>
```

```
    <authorEmail>burke_e@yahoo.com</authorEmail>
  </message>
</viewMonth>
```

In the XSLT stylesheet, the first part of the recursive process selects all <message> elements occurring immediately below the <viewMonth> element:

```
<xsl:apply-templates select="viewMonth/message"/>
```

This selects messages with ids 1 and 3, causing the following template to be instantiated:

```
<xsl:template match="message">
  <xsl:param name="indent" select="0"/>
```

This template takes a parameter for the level of indentation. If the parameter is not specified, as in this first usage, it defaults to 0. This code is followed by very basic XSLT code to produce a one-line summary of the current message, and then the template recursively instantiates itself:

```
<xsl:apply-templates select="message">
  <xsl:with-param name="indent" select="$indent + 1"/>
</xsl:apply-templates>
```

This efficiently selects all <message> elements that occur immediately within the current message and increments the indentation by 1. This allows the stylesheet to indent replies appropriately. The recursive process continues until no messages remain.

Another stylesheet, *viewMsg.xslt*, is responsible for displaying a single message. This is a simple XSLT stylesheet and can be found in Appendix A. The only remaining stylesheet, *postMsg.xslt*, is shown in Example 7-10. This stylesheet supports two modes of operation. Therefore, it is more complicated than the previous examples.

Example 7-10. XSLT for the Post/Reply message page

```
<?xml version="1.0" encoding="UTF-8"?>
<!--
**********************************************************
** postMsg.xslt
**
** Creates the "Post New Message" XHTML page and the
** "Reply to Message" XHTML page.
**********************************************************
-->
<xsl:stylesheet version="1.0"
  xmlns:xsl="http://www.w3.org/1999/XSL/Transform">
  <xsl:import href="utils.xslt"/>

  <!-- pass the root directory as a parameter, thus
       allowing this stylesheet to refer to the CSS file -->
```

Example 7-10. XSLT for the Post/Reply message page (continued)

```
<xsl:param name="rootDir" select="'../docroot/'"/>

<xsl:output method="xml" version="1.0" encoding="UTF-8"
  indent="yes"
  doctype-public="-//W3C//DTD XHTML 1.0 Strict//EN"
  doctype-system="http://www.w3.org/TR/xhtml1/DTD/xhtml1-strict.dtd"/>

<!-- ===== Global Variables ===== -->
<xsl:variable name="global.subject" select="/postMsg/prefill/subject"/>
<xsl:variable name="global.email" select="/postMsg/prefill/authorEmail"/>
<xsl:variable name="global.message" select="/postMsg/prefill/message"/>

<xsl:variable name="global.title">
  <xsl:choose>
    <xsl:when test="/postMsg/inResponseTo">
      <xsl:text>Reply to Message</xsl:text>
    </xsl:when>
    <xsl:otherwise>
      <xsl:text>Post New Message</xsl:text>
    </xsl:otherwise>
  </xsl:choose>
</xsl:variable>

<!--
**********************************************************
** Create the XHTML web page
**********************************************************-->
<xsl:template match="/">
  <html xmlns="http://www.w3.org/1999/xhtml">
    <head>
      <title><xsl:value-of select="$global.title"/></title>
      <link href="{$rootDir}forum.css"
          rel="stylesheet" type="text/css"/>
    </head>
    <body>
      <!-- show the page title and board name -->
      <div class="box1">
        <h1><xsl:value-of select="$global.title"/></h1>
        <div>
          <xsl:value-of select="postMsg/board/name"/>
        </div>
      </div>
      <xsl:apply-templates select="postMsg/inResponseTo"/>

      <div class="box2">
        <!-- optionally display error message -->
        <xsl:if test="postMsg/error/@code='ALL_FIELDS_REQUIRED'">
          <p class="error">All fields are required...</p>
```

Example 7-10. XSLT for the Post/Reply message page (continued)

```
        </xsl:if>

        <!-- Create an XHTML form. The user will provide
             the subject, and Email address, and
             the message text -->
    <form method="post" action="postMsg">
      <div>
        <input type="hidden" name="boardID"
           value="{postMsg/board/@id}"/>

        <!-- Determine the mode of operation -->
        <xsl:choose>
          <xsl:when test="/postMsg/inResponseTo">
            <input type="hidden" name="origMsgID"
                    value="{postMsg/inResponseTo/@id}"/>
            <input type="hidden" name="mode" value="replyToMsg"/>
          </xsl:when>
          <xsl:otherwise>
            <input type="hidden" name="mode" value="postNewMsg"/>
          </xsl:otherwise>
        </xsl:choose>
      </div>

        <!-- Show the input fields in a table to
             keep things aligned properly -->
      <table>
        <tr>
          <td>Subject:</td>
          <td>
            <input type="text" name="msgSubject"
                value="{$global.subject}" size="60" maxlength="70"/>
          </td>
        </tr>
        <tr>
          <td nowrap="nowrap">Your Email:</td>
          <td>
            <input type="text" name="authorEmail"
                value="{$global.email}" size="60" maxlength="70"/>
          </td>
        </tr>
        <tr valign="top">
          <td>Message:</td>
          <td>
            <!-- xsl:text prevents the XSLT processor from collapsing to
                  <textarea/>, which caused problems with many browsers. -->
            <textarea name="msgText" wrap="hard" rows="12"
                cols="60"><xsl:value-of
                select="$global.message"/><xsl:text> </xsl:text></textarea>
```

Example 7-10. XSLT for the Post/Reply message page (continued)

```
              </td>
            </tr>
            <!-- The last table row contains a submit
                 and cancel button -->
            <tr>
              <td> </td>
              <td>
                <input type="submit" name="submitBtn" value="Submit"/>
                <input type="submit" name="cancelBtn" value="Cancel"/>
              </td>
            </tr>
          </table>
        </form>
      </div>
    </body>
  </html>
</xsl:template>


<!--
*********************************************************
** Show the text: 'In Response to: Msg Subject'
*********************************************************-->
<xsl:template match="inResponseTo">
  <div>
    In Response to:
    <span style="font-weight: bold;">
    <xsl:value-of select="subject"/>
    </span>
  </div>
</xsl:template>
</xsl:stylesheet>
```

Since this stylesheet must work for posting new messages as well as for replying to messages, it must determine the appropriate mode of operation. This can be accomplished by checking for the existence of elements that occur only in one mode or the other. For example, the `<inResponseTo>` XML element occurs only when the user replies to an existing message. Therefore, the XSLT stylesheet can define a variable for the page title as follows:

```
<xsl:variable name="global.title">
  <xsl:choose>
    <xsl:when test="/postMsg/inResponseTo">
      <xsl:text>Reply to Message</xsl:text>
    </xsl:when>
    <xsl:otherwise>
      <xsl:text>Post New Message</xsl:text>
    </xsl:otherwise>
```

```
    </xsl:choose>
  </xsl:variable>
```

`<xsl:when    test="/postMsg/inResponseTo">` returns true when the `<inResponseTo>` element exists in the original XML data. In this case, the `global.title` variable is set to "Reply to Message." Otherwise, the title defaults to "Post New Message."

This stylesheet optionally displays an error message when the user partially fills out the XHTML form and submits the data. The servlet redisplays the page with an error message, allowing the user to fix the problem. It does this by inserting the following XML element into the data:

```
<error code="ALL_FIELDS_REQUIRED"/>
```

The XSLT stylesheet tests for the existence of this element as follows:

```
<xsl:if test="postMsg/error/@code='ALL_FIELDS_REQUIRED'">
  <p class="error">All fields are required...</p>
</xsl:if>
```

An additional trick used in this stylesheet involves its interaction with a servlet. When the user submits the XHTML form data, the servlet must determine which mode of operation the user was in. For this task, the servlet looks for a request parameter called `mode`. Legal values for this parameter are `replyToMsg` and `postNewMsg`. Since the user is submitting an XHTML form, the easiest way to pass this data is via a hidden form field named `mode`. Here is the code that does the work:

```
<xsl:choose>
  <xsl:when test="/postMsg/inResponseTo">
    <input type="hidden" name="origMsgID"
          value="{postMsg/inResponseTo/@id}"/>
    <input type="hidden" name="mode" value="replyToMsg"/>
  </xsl:when>
  <xsl:otherwise>
    <input type="hidden" name="mode" value="postNewMsg"/>
  </xsl:otherwise>
</xsl:choose>
```

The stylesheet also inserts a hidden form field that contains the original message ID whenever the mode is `replyToMsg`. On the servlet side, the code looks something like this:

```
public void doGet(HttpServletRequest request, HttpServletResponse response) ... {
    String mode = request.getParameter("mode");
    if ("replyToMsg".equals(mode)) {
        String origMsgID = request.getParameter("origMsgID");
        ....
```

Making the XML Dynamic

At this point in the process, we have specified what each web page looks like, the XML data for each page, and the XSLT stylesheets to perform the necessary transformations. The next step is to figure out where the XML actually comes from. During the design and prototyping process, all XML data is created as a collection of static text files. This makes development of the XSLT stylesheets much easier, because the stylesheet authors can see results immediately without waiting for the back-end business logic and database access code to be created.

In the real system, static XML will not meet our requirements. We need the ability to extract data from a relational database and convert it into XML on the fly, as each page is requested. This makes the application "live," making updates to the database immediately visible to users. To the XSLT stylesheet developer, this is a moot point. The XSLT transformations work the same, regardless of whether the XML data came from a flat file, a relational database, or any other source.

Domain Classes

A *domain class* is a Java class that represents something in the problem domain. That's a fancy way to describe a class that represents the underlying problem you are trying to solve. In this example, we need to model the discussion forum as a series of Java classes to provide a buffer between the XML and the underlying relational database. In addition to representing data about the discussion forum, these Java classes can contain business logic.

Figure 7-6 contains a UML diagram of the classes found in the `com.oreilly.forum.domain` package. These classes do not contain any database access code, nor do they have any XML capability. Instead, they are simply data structures with a few key pieces of functionality. This makes it possible, for example, to rip out the relational database and replace it with some other back-end data source without changing to the XML generation logic.

`BoardSummary`, `MessageSummary`, and `Message` are the key interfaces that describe the basic discussion forum capabilities. For each interface, an associated `Impl` class provides a basic implementation that contains get and set methods, which are not shown here. The `MonthYear`, `DayMonthYear`, and `DateUtil` classes are designed to represent and manipulate dates in an easy way and are listed in Appendix B. Finally, the `MessageTree` class encapsulates some business logic to sort a collection of messages into a hierarchical tree based on message replies and creation dates.

The `BoardSummary` interface, shown in Example 7-11, contains data that will eventually be used to build the discussion forum home page.

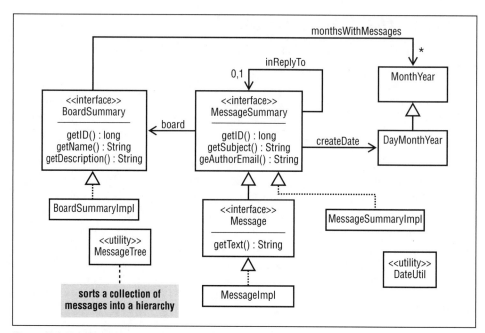

Figure 7-6. Key domain classes

Example 7-11. BoardSummary.java

```
package com.oreilly.forum.domain;

import java.util.Iterator;

/**
 * Information about a message board.
 */
public interface BoardSummary {
    /**
     * @return a unique ID for this board.
     */
    long getID();

    /**
     * @return a name for this board.
     */
    String getName();

    /**
     * @return a description for this board.
     */
    String getDescription();

    /**
```

Example 7-11. BoardSummary.java (continued)

```
    * @return an iterator of <code>MonthYear</code> objects.
    */
   Iterator getMonthsWithMessages();
}
```

By design, the `BoardSummary` interface is read-only. This is an important feature because it means that once an instance of this class is extracted from the back-end data source, a programmer cannot accidentally call a set method only to discover later that the updates were not saved in the database. Technically, the client of this class could retrieve an `Iterator` of months with messages and then call the `remove()` method on the `Iterator` instance. Although we could take steps to make instances of this interface truly immutable, such efforts are probably overkill.

An early decision made in the design of the discussion forum was to assign a unique `long` identifier to each domain object. These identifiers have absolutely no meaning other than to identify objects uniquely, which will make the SQL queries much simpler later on.* This technique also makes it easy to reference objects from hyperlinks in the XHTML, because a simple identifier can be easily converted to and from a string representation.

The next interface, shown in Example 7-12, provides a summary for an individual message.

Example 7-12. MessageSummary.java

```
package com.oreilly.forum.domain;

import java.util.*;

/**
 * Basic information about a message, not including the message text.
 */
public interface MessageSummary extends Comparable {

    /**
     * @return the ID of the message that this one is a reply to, or
     *           -1 if none.
     */
    long getInReplyTo();

    /**
     * @return the unique ID of this message.
     */
    long getID();
```

---

* The code to actually generate these unique IDs is found in the `DBUtil` class, shown in Example 7-18.

Example 7-12. MessageSummary.java (continued)

```
    /**
     * @return when this message was created.
     */
    DayMonthYear getCreateDate();

    /**
     * @return the board that this message belongs to.
     */
    BoardSummary getBoard();

    /**
     * @return the subject of this message.
     */
    String getSubject();

    /**
     * The author Email can be 80 characters.
     */
    String getAuthorEmail();
}
```

The only thing missing from the MessageSummary interface is the actual message text. The Message interface, which extends from MessageSummary, adds the getText() method. This interface is shown in Example 7-13.

Example 7-13. Message.java

```
package com.oreilly.forum.domain;

/**
 * Represent a message, including the text.
 */
public interface Message extends MessageSummary {
    /**
     * @return the text of this message.
     */
    String getText();
}
```

The decision to keep the message text in a separate interface was driven by a prediction that performance could be dramatically improved. Consider a web page that shows a hierarchical view of all messages for a given month. This page may contain hundreds of messages, displaying key information found in the MessageSummary interface. But the text of each message could contain thousands of words, so it was decided that the text should be retrieved later when a message is displayed in its entirety. For this page, an instance of a class that implements Message can be created.

These are the sorts of design decisions that cannot be made in complete isolation. Regardless of how cleanly XSLT and XML separate the presentation from the underlying data model, heavily used web pages should have some influence on design decisions made on the back end. The trick is to avoid falling into the trap of focusing too hard on early optimization at the expense of a clean design. In this case, the potential for large numbers of very long messages was significant enough to warrant a separate interface for `Message`.

The three reference implementation classes are `MessageImpl`, `Message-SummaryImpl`, and `BoardSummaryImpl`. These are basic Java classes that hold data and are listed in Appendix B. The JDBC data adapter layer (see the section "Data Adapter Layer") will create and return new instances of these classes, which implement the interfaces in this package. If creating a new back-end data source in the future, it is possible to reuse these classes or write brand new classes that implement the appropriate interfaces.

The final class in this package, `MessageTree`, is listed in Example 7-14.

Example 7-14. MessageTree.java

```
package com.oreilly.forum.domain;

import java.util.*;

/**
 * Arranges a collection of MessageSummary objects into a tree.
 */
public class MessageTree {
    private List topLevelMsgs = new ArrayList();

    // map ids to MessageSummary objects
    private Map idToMsgMap = new HashMap();

    // map reply-to ids to lists of MessageSummary objects
    private Map replyIDToMsgListMap = new HashMap();

    /**
     * Construct a new message tree from an iterator of MessageSummary
     * objects.
     */
    public MessageTree(Iterator messages) {
        while (messages.hasNext()) {
            // store each message in a map for fast retrieval by ID
            MessageSummary curMsg = (MessageSummary) messages.next();
            this.idToMsgMap.put(new Long(curMsg.getID()), curMsg);

            // build the inverted map that maps reply-to IDs to
            // lists of messages
```

Example 7-14. MessageTree.java (continued)

```java
        Long curReplyID = new Long(curMsg.getInReplyTo());
        List replyToList =
                (List) this.replyIDToMsgListMap.get(curReplyID);
        if (replyToList == null) {
            replyToList = new ArrayList();
            this.replyIDToMsgListMap.put(curReplyID, replyToList);
        }
        replyToList.add(curMsg);
    }


    // build the list of top-level messages. A top-level message
    // fits one of the following two criteria:
    //  - its reply-to ID is -1
    //  - its reply-to ID was not found in the list of messages. This
    //    occurs when a message is a reply to a previous month's message
    Iterator iter = this.replyIDToMsgListMap.keySet().iterator();
    while (iter.hasNext()) {
        Long curReplyToID = (Long) iter.next();
        if (curReplyToID.longValue() == -1
                || !this.idToMsgMap.containsKey(curReplyToID)) {
            List msgsToAdd =
                    (List) this.replyIDToMsgListMap.get(curReplyToID);
            this.topLevelMsgs.addAll(msgsToAdd);
        }
    }
    Collections.sort(this.topLevelMsgs);
}

public Iterator getTopLevelMessages() {
    return this.topLevelMsgs.iterator();
}


/**
 * @return an iterator of MessageSummary objects that are replies
 *         to the specified message.
 */
public Iterator getReplies(MessageSummary msg) {
    List replies = (List) this.replyIDToMsgListMap.get(
            new Long(msg.getID()));
    if (replies != null) {
        Collections.sort(replies);
        return replies.iterator();
    } else {
        return Collections.EMPTY_LIST.iterator();
    }
}
}
```

The `MessageTree` class helps organize a list of messages according to threads of discussion. If you look back at the code for `MessageSummary`, you will see that each message keeps track of the message that it is in reply to:

```
public interface MessageSummary extends Comparable {
    ...
    long getInReplyTo();
    ...
}
```

If the message is a top-level message, then the reply-to id is –1. Otherwise, it always refers to some other message. Since a message does not have a corresponding method to retrieve a list of replies, the `MessageTree` class must build this list for each message. This leads to the three data structures found in the `MessageTree` class:

```
private List topLevelMsgs = new ArrayList();
private Map idToMsgMap = new HashMap();
private Map replyIDToMsgListMap = new HashMap();
```

When the `MessageTree` is constructed, it is given an `Iterator` of all messages in a month. From this `Iterator`, the `idToMsgMap` data structure is built. All messages are stored in `idToMsgMap`, which is used for rapid retrieval based on message ids. While building the `idToMsgMap`, the constructor also builds the `replyIDToMsgListMap`. The keys in this map are reply-to ids, and the values are lists of message ids. In other words, each key maps to a list of replies.

After the first two data structures are built, the list of top-level messages is built. This is accomplished by looping over all keys in the `idToMsgMap` and then looking for messages that have a reply-to id of –1. In addition, messages whose reply-to id could not be located are also considered to be top-level messages. This occurs when a message is in reply to a previous month's message. All of this code can be seen in the `MessageTree` constructor.

Data Adapter Layer

Bridging the gap between an object-oriented class library and a physical database is often quite difficult. Enterprise JavaBeans (EJB) can be used for this purpose. However, this makes it extremely hard to deploy the discussion forum at a typical web hosting service. By limiting the application to servlets and a relational database, it is possible to choose from several ISPs that support both servlets and JDBC access to databases such as MySQL.

In addition to the software constraints found at most web hosting providers, design flexibility is another consideration. Today, direct access to a MySQL database may be the preferred approach. In the future, a full EJB solution with some other database may be desired. Or, we may choose to store messages in flat files instead of any database at all. All of these capabilities are achieved by using an abstract class called `DataAdapter`. This class is shown in Figure 7-7 along with several related classes.

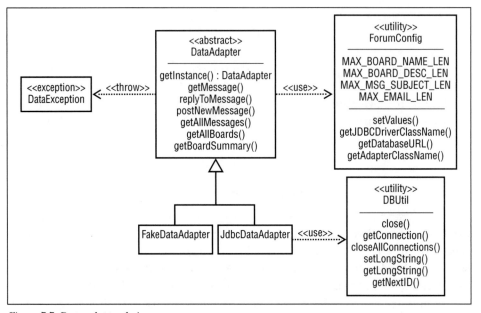

Figure 7-7. Data adapter design

The `DataAdapter` class defines an interface to some back-end data source. As shown in the class diagram, `FakeDataAdapter` and `JdbcDataAdapter` are subclasses. These implement the data tier using flat files and relational databases, respectively. It is easy to imagine someone creating an `EJBDataAdapter` at some point in the future. `ForumConfig` is used to determine which subclass of `DataAdapter` to instantiate, and the `DBUtil` class encapsulates a few commonly used JDBC functions.

The source code for `ForumConfig` is shown in Example 7-15. This is a simple class that places configurable application settings in a single place. As shown later in this chapter, all configurable settings are stored in the servlet's deployment descriptor, so they do not have to be hardcoded. The first thing the servlet does is read the values and store them in `ForumConfig`.*

---

* JNDI could also be used for this purpose. However, JNDI requires more configuration and may make it harder to deploy to some ISPs.

Example 7-15. ForumConfig.java

```java
package com.oreilly.forum;

/**
 * Define application-wide configuration information. The Servlet
 * must call the setValues() method before any of the get
 * methods in this class can be used.
 */
public class ForumConfig {
    // maximum sizes of various fields in the database
    public static final int MAX_BOARD_NAME_LEN = 80;
    public static final int MAX_BOARD_DESC_LEN = 255;
    public static final int MAX_MSG_SUBJECT_LEN = 80;
    public static final int MAX_EMAIL_LEN = 80;

    private static String jdbcDriverClassName;
    private static String databaseURL;
    private static String adapterClassName;

    public static void setValues(
            String jdbcDriverClassName,
            String databaseURL,
            String adapterClassName) {
        ForumConfig.jdbcDriverClassName = jdbcDriverClassName;
        ForumConfig.databaseURL = databaseURL;
        ForumConfig.adapterClassName = adapterClassName;
    }

    /**
     * @return the JDBC driver class name.
     */
    public static String getJDBCDriverClassName() {
        return ForumConfig.jdbcDriverClassName;
    }

    /**
     * @return the JDBC database URL.
     */
    public static String getDatabaseURL() {
        return ForumConfig.databaseURL;
    }

    /**
     * @return the data adapter implementation class name.
     */
    public static String getAdapterClassName() {
        return ForumConfig.adapterClassName;
```

Example 7-15. ForumConfig.java (continued)

```
    }

    private ForumConfig() {
    }
}
```

The `DataException` class is a very basic exception that indicates a problem with
the back-end data source. It hides database-specific exceptions from the client,
leaving the door open for nondatabase implementations in the future. For example, an EJB tier could be added, but the EJBs would throw `RemoteException` and
`EJBException` instead of `SQLException`. Therefore, whenever a specific exception is thrown, it is wrapped in an instance of `DataException` before being propo-
gated to the caller. The source code for `DataException` is found in Appendix B.

The code for `DataAdapter`, shown in Example 7-16, demonstrates how each
method throws `DataException`. This class is the centerpiece of the "data
abstraction" layer, insulating the domain classes from the underlying database
implementation.

Example 7-16. DataAdapter.java

```
package com.oreilly.forum.adapter;

import com.oreilly.forum.*;
import com.oreilly.forum.domain.*;
import java.util.*;

/**
 * Defines an interface to a data source.
 */
public abstract class DataAdapter {
    private static DataAdapter instance;

    /**
     * @return the singleton instance of this class.
     */
    public static synchronized DataAdapter getInstance()
            throws DataException {
        if (instance == null) {
            String adapterClassName = ForumConfig.getAdapterClassName();
            try {
                Class adapterClass = Class.forName(adapterClassName);
                instance = (DataAdapter) adapterClass.newInstance();
            } catch (Exception ex) {
                throw new DataException("Unable to instantiate "
                        + adapterClassName);
```

Example 7-16. DataAdapter.java (continued)

```
            }
        }
        return instance;
    }


    /**
     * @param msgID must be a valid message identifier.
     * @return the message with the specified id.
     * @throws DataException if msgID does not exist or a database
     * error occurs.
     */
    public abstract Message getMessage(long msgID) throws DataException;


    /**
     * Add a reply to an existing message.
     *
     * @throws DataException if a database error occurs, or if any
     * parameter is illegal.
     */
    public abstract Message replyToMessage(long origMsgID, String msgSubject,
            String authorEmail, String msgText) throws DataException;


    /**
     * Post a new message.
     *
     * @return the newly created message.
     * @throws DataException if a database error occurs, or if any
     * parameter is illegal.
     */
    public abstract Message postNewMessage(long boardID, String msgSubject,
            String authorEmail, String msgText) throws DataException;


    /**
     * If no messages exist for the specified board and month, return
     * an empty iterator.
     * @return an iterator of <code>MessageSummary</code> objects.
     * @throws DataException if the boardID is illegal or a database
     * error occurs.
     */
    public abstract Iterator getAllMessages(long boardID, MonthYear month)
            throws DataException;


    /**
     * @return an iterator of all <code>BoardSummary</code> objects.
     */
    public abstract Iterator getAllBoards() throws DataException;


    /**
```

Example 7-16. DataAdapter.java (continued)

```
    * @return a board summary for the given id.
    * @throws DataException if boardID is illegal or a database
    *                         error occurs.
    */
   public abstract BoardSummary getBoardSummary(long boardID)
          throws DataException;
}
```

`DataAdapter` consists of abstract methods and one static method called `getInstance()`. This implements a singleton design pattern, returning an instance of a `DataAdapter` subclass.* The actual return type is specified in the `ForumConfig` class, and Java reflection APIs are used to instantiate the object:

```
   String adapterClassName = ForumConfig.getAdapterClassName();
   try {
       Class adapterClass = Class.forName(adapterClassName);
       instance = (DataAdapter) adapterClass.newInstance();
   } catch (Exception ex) {
       throw new DataException("Unable to instantiate "
               + adapterClassName);
   }
```

All remaining methods are abstract and are written in terms of interfaces defined in the `com.oreilly.forum.domain` package. For example, a message can be retrieved by its ID:

```
   public abstract Message getMessage(long msgID) throws DataException;
```

By writing this code in terms of the `Message` interface, a future programmer could easily write a new class that implements `Message` in a different way. Throughout the `DataAdapter` class, a `DataException` occurs when an id is invalid, or when the underlying database fails.

The downloadable discussion forum implementation comes with a "fake" implementation of `DataAdapter` as well as a JDBC-based implementation. The fake implementation is listed in Appendix B. The database implementation has been tested on Microsoft Access as well as MySQL and should work on just about any relational database that includes a JDBC driver. Figure 7-8 shows the physical database design that the `JdbcDataAdapter` class uses.

The database is quite simple. Each table has an `id` column that defines a unique identifier and primary key for each row of data. `Message.inReplyToID` contains a reference to another message that this one is in reply to, or –1 if this is a top-level message. The create date for each message is broken down into month, day, and

---

* See Gamma et al., *Design Patterns: Elements of Reusable Object-Oriented Software* (Addison-Wesley, 1994).

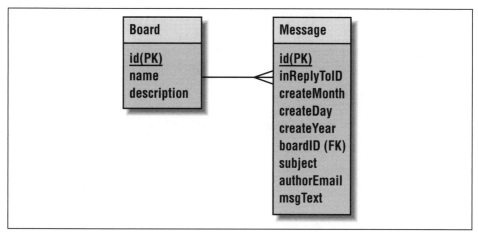

Figure 7-8. Database design

year. Although the application could store the date and time in some other for-mat, this approach makes it really easy to issue queries such as:

```
SELECT subject
FROM Message
WHERE createMonth=3 AND createYear=2001
```

The `Message.boardID` column is a foreign key that identifies which board a mes-sage belongs to. The `Message.msgText` column can contain an unlimited amount of text, while the remaining fields all contain fixed-length text.

If you are using MySQL, Example 7-17 shows a "dump" file that can be used to eas-ily recreate the database using the import utility that comes with the database.

Example 7-17. MySQL dump

```
# MySQL dump 8.8
#
# Host: localhost    Database: forum
#--------------------------------------------------------
# Server version3.23.23-beta

#
# Table structure for table 'board'
#

CREATE TABLE board (
  id bigint(20) DEFAULT '0' NOT NULL,
  name char(80) DEFAULT '' NOT NULL,
  description char(255) DEFAULT '' NOT NULL,
  PRIMARY KEY (id)
);
```

Example 7-17. MySQL dump (continued)

```
#
# Dumping data for table 'board'
#

INSERT INTO board VALUES (0,'XSLT Basics',
    'How to create and use XSLT stylesheets and processors');
INSERT INTO board VALUES (1,'JAXP Programming Techniques','How to use JAXP 1.1');


#
# Table structure for table 'message'
#

CREATE TABLE message (
   id bigint(20) DEFAULT '0' NOT NULL,
   inReplyToID bigint(20) DEFAULT '0' NOT NULL,
   createMonth int(11) DEFAULT '0' NOT NULL,
   createDay int(11) DEFAULT '0' NOT NULL,
   createYear int(11) DEFAULT '0' NOT NULL,
   boardID bigint(20) DEFAULT '0' NOT NULL,
   subject varchar(80) DEFAULT '' NOT NULL,
   authorEmail varchar(80) DEFAULT '' NOT NULL,
   msgText text DEFAULT '' NOT NULL,
   PRIMARY KEY (id),
   KEY inReplyToID (inReplyToID),
   KEY createMonth (createMonth),
   KEY createDay (createDay),
   KEY boardID (boardID)
);
```

The DBUtil class, shown in Example 7-18, consists of utility functions that make it a little easier to work with relational databases from Java code.

Example 7-18. DBUtil.java

```
package com.oreilly.forum.jdbcimpl;

import java.io.*;
import java.sql.*;
import java.util.*;

/**
 * Helper methods for relational database access using JDBC.
 */
public class DBUtil {

    // a map of table names to maximum ID numbers
    private static Map tableToMaxIDMap = new HashMap();
```

Example 7-18. DBUtil.java (continued)

```java
/**
 * Close a statement and connection.
 */
public static void close(Statement stmt, Connection con) {
    if (stmt != null) {
        try {
            stmt.close();
        } catch (Exception ignored1) {
        }
    }
    if (con != null) {
        try {
            con.close();
        } catch (Exception ignored2) {
        }
    }
}

/**
 * @return a new Connection to the database.
 */
public static Connection getConnection(String dbURL)
        throws SQLException {
    // NOTE: implementing a connection pool would be a worthy
    //        enhancement
    return DriverManager.getConnection(dbURL);
}

/**
 * Close any connections that are still open. The Servlet will
 * call this method from its destroy() method.
 */
public static void closeAllConnections() {
    // NOTE: if connection pooling is ever implemented, close
    //        the connections here.
}

/**
 * Store a long text field in the database. For example, a message's
 * text will be quite long and cannot be stored using JDBC's
 * setString() method.
 */
public static void setLongString(PreparedStatement stmt,
        int columnIndex, String data) throws SQLException {
    if (data.length() > 0) {
        stmt.setAsciiStream(columnIndex,
                new ByteArrayInputStream(data.getBytes()),
                data.length());
```

Example 7-18. DBUtil.java (continued)

```java
        } else {
            // this 'else' condition was introduced as a bug fix.  It was
            // discovered that the 'setAsciiStream' code shown above
            // caused MS Access throws a "function sequence error"
            // when the string was zero length.  This code now works.
            stmt.setString(columnIndex, "");
        }
    }


/**
 * @return a long text field from the database.
 */
public static String getLongString(ResultSet rs, int columnIndex)
        throws SQLException {
    try {
        InputStream in = rs.getAsciiStream(columnIndex);
        if (in == null) {
            return "";
        }

        byte[] arr = new byte[250];
        StringBuffer buf = new StringBuffer();
        int numRead = in.read(arr);
        while (numRead != -1) {
            buf.append(new String(arr, 0, numRead));
            numRead = in.read(arr);
        }
        return buf.toString();
    } catch (IOException ioe) {
        ioe.printStackTrace();
        throw new SQLException(ioe.getMessage());
    }
}


/**
 * Compute a new unique ID. It is assumed that the specified table
 * has a column named 'id' of type 'long'. It is assumed that
 * that all parts of the program will use this method to compute
 * new IDs.
 * @return the next available unique ID for a table.
 */
public static synchronized long getNextID(String tableName,
        Connection con) throws SQLException {
    Statement stmt = null;

    try {
        // if a max has already been retrieved from this table,
        // compute the next id without hitting the database
```

Example 7-18. DBUtil.java (continued)

```
            if (tableToMaxIDMap.containsKey(tableName)) {
                Long curMax = (Long) tableToMaxIDMap.get(tableName);
                Long newMax = new Long(curMax.longValue() + 1L);
                tableToMaxIDMap.put(tableName, newMax);
                return newMax.longValue();
            }

            stmt = con.createStatement();
            ResultSet rs = stmt.executeQuery(
                    "SELECT MAX(id) FROM " + tableName);
            long max = 0;
            if (rs.next()) {
                max = rs.getLong(1);
            }
            max++;
            tableToMaxIDMap.put(tableName, new Long(max));
            return max;
        } finally {
            // just close the statement
            close(stmt, null);
        }
    }
}
```

DBUtil has a private class field called `tableToMaxIDMap` that keeps track of the largest unique id found in each table. This works in conjunction with the `getNextID()` method, which returns the next available unique id for a given table name. By keeping the unique ids cached in the `Map`, the application reduces the required database hits. It should be noted that this approach is likely to fail if anyone manually adds a new id to the database without consulting this method.

The `close()` method is useful because nearly everything done with JDBC requires the programmer to close a `Statement` and `Connection`. This method should always be called from a `finally` block, which is guaranteed to be called regardless of whether or not an exception was thrown. For example:

```
Connection con = null;
Statement stmt = null;
try {
    // code to create the Connection and Statement
    ...
    // code to access the database
    ...
} finally {
    DBUtil.close(stmt, con);
}
```

If JDBC resources are not released inside of a `finally` block, it is possible to accidentally leave `Connections` open for long periods of time. This is problematic because database performance can suffer, and some databases limit the number of concurrent connections.

Although connection pooling is not supported in this version of the application, `DBUtil` does include the following method:

```
public static Connection getConnection(String dbURL)
```

In a future version of the class, it will be very easy to have this method return a `Connection` instance from pool, rather than creating a new instance with each call. Additionally, the `DBUtil.close()` method could return the `Connection` back to the pool instead of actually closing it. These are left as future considerations to keep things reasonably sized for the book.

The `setLongString()` and `getLongString()` methods are used for setting and retrieving text for messages. Since this text may be extremely long, it cannot be stored in the same way that shorter strings are stored. In some databases, these are referred to as CLOB columns. MS Access uses the MEMO type, while MySQL uses the TEXT data type. Since this is an area where databases can be implemented differently, the code is placed into the `DBUtil` class for consistency. If a special concession has to be made for a particular database, it can be made in one place rather than in every SQL statement throughout the application.

Finally, the `JdbcDataAdapter` class is presented in Example 7-19. This is the relational database implementation of the `DataAdapter` class and should work with just about any relational database.

Example 7-19. JdbcDataAdapter.java

```
package com.oreilly.forum.jdbcimpl;

import com.oreilly.forum.*;
import com.oreilly.forum.adapter.*;
import com.oreilly.forum.domain.*;
import java.sql.*;
import java.util.*;

/**
 * An implementation of the DataAdapter that uses JDBC.
 */
public class JdbcDataAdapter extends DataAdapter {

    private static String dbURL = ForumConfig.getDatabaseURL();

    /**
     * Construct the data adapter and load the JDBC driver.
     */
```

Example 7-19. JdbcDataAdapter.java (continued)

```java
public JdbcDataAdapter() throws DataException {
    try {
        Class.forName(ForumConfig.getJDBCDriverClassName());
    } catch (Exception ex) {
        ex.printStackTrace();
        throw new DataException("Unable to load JDBC driver: "
                + ForumConfig.getJDBCDriverClassName());
    }
}

/**
 * @param msgID must be a valid message identifier.
 * @return the message with the specified id.
 * @throws DataException if msgID does not exist or a database
 * error occurs.
 */
public Message getMessage(long msgID) throws DataException {
    Connection con = null;
    Statement stmt = null;
    try {
        con = DBUtil.getConnection(dbURL);
        stmt = con.createStatement();
        ResultSet rs = stmt.executeQuery(
                "SELECT inReplyToID, createDay, createMonth, createYear, "
                + "boardID, subject, authorEmail, msgText "
                + "FROM Message WHERE id="
                + msgID);
        if (rs.next()) {
            long inReplyToID = rs.getLong(1);
            int createDay = rs.getInt(2);
            int createMonth = rs.getInt(3);
            int createYear = rs.getInt(4);
            long boardID = rs.getLong(5);
            String subject = rs.getString(6);
            String authorEmail = rs.getString(7);
            String msgText = DBUtil.getLongString(rs, 8);

            BoardSummary boardSummary = this.getBoardSummary(boardID, stmt);

            return new MessageImpl(msgID,
                    new DayMonthYear(createDay, createMonth, createYear),
                    boardSummary, subject, authorEmail, msgText,
                    inReplyToID);
        } else {
            throw new DataException("Illegal msgID");
        }
    } catch (SQLException sqe) {
        sqe.printStackTrace();
```

Example 7-19. JdbcDataAdapter.java (continued)

```
            throw new DataException(sqe.getMessage());
        } finally {
            DBUtil.close(stmt, con);
        }
    }


    /**
     * Add a reply to an existing message.
     *
     * @throws DataException if a database error occurs, or if any
     * parameter is illegal.
     */
    public Message replyToMessage(long origMsgID,
            String msgSubject, String authorEmail, String msgText)
            throws DataException {
        Message inReplyToMsg = this.getMessage(origMsgID);
        return insertMessage(inReplyToMsg.getBoard(), origMsgID,
                msgSubject, authorEmail, msgText);


    }


    /**
     * Post a new message.
     *
     * @return the newly created message.
     * @throws DataException if a database error occurs, or if any
     * parameter is illegal.
     */
    public Message postNewMessage(long boardID, String msgSubject,
            String authorEmail, String msgText) throws DataException {

        BoardSummary board = this.getBoardSummary(boardID);
        return insertMessage(board, -1, msgSubject, authorEmail, msgText);
    }


    /**
     * If no messages exist for the specified board and month, return
     * an empty iterator.
     * @return an iterator of <code>MessageSummary</code> objects.
     * @throws DataException if the boardID is illegal or a database
     * error occurs.
     */
    public Iterator getAllMessages(long boardID, MonthYear month)
            throws DataException {
        List allMsgs = new ArrayList();

        Connection con = null;
        Statement stmt = null;
```

Example 7-19. JdbcDataAdapter.java (continued)

```java
        try {
            con = DBUtil.getConnection(dbURL);
            stmt = con.createStatement();

            BoardSummary boardSum = this.getBoardSummary(boardID, stmt);

            ResultSet rs = stmt.executeQuery(
                    "SELECT id, inReplyToID, createDay, "
                    + "subject, authorEmail "
                    + "FROM Message WHERE createMonth="
                    + month.getMonth()
                    + " AND createYear="
                    + month.getYear()
                    + " AND boardID="
                    + boardID);

            while (rs.next()) {
                long msgID = rs.getLong(1);
                long inReplyTo = rs.getLong(2);
                int createDay = rs.getInt(3);
                String subject = rs.getString(4);
                String authorEmail = rs.getString(5);

                DayMonthYear createDMY = new DayMonthYear(
                        createDay, month.getMonth(), month.getYear());

                allMsgs.add(new MessageSummaryImpl(msgID, createDMY,
                        boardSum,
                        subject, authorEmail, inReplyTo));
            }
            return allMsgs.iterator();
        } catch (SQLException sqe) {
            sqe.printStackTrace();
            throw new DataException(sqe);
        } finally {
            DBUtil.close(stmt, con);
        }
    }

    /**
     * @return an iterator of all <code>BoardSummary</code> objects.
     */
    public Iterator getAllBoards() throws DataException {
        List allBoards = new ArrayList();

        Connection con = null;
        Statement stmt = null;
        Statement stmt2 = null;
```

Example 7-19. JdbcDataAdapter.java (continued)

```java
        try {
            con = DBUtil.getConnection(dbURL);
            stmt = con.createStatement();
            stmt2 = con.createStatement();
            ResultSet rs = stmt.executeQuery(
                    "SELECT id, name, description FROM Board "
                    + "ORDER BY name");

            while (rs.next()) {
                long id = rs.getLong(1);
                String name = rs.getString(2);
                String description = rs.getString(3);

                // get the months with messages. Use a different
                // Statement object because we are in the middle of
                // traversing a ResultSet that was created with the
                // first Statement.
                List monthsWithMessages =
                        this.getMonthsWithMessages(id, stmt2);

                allBoards.add(new BoardSummaryImpl(id, name, description,
                        monthsWithMessages));
            }
            return allBoards.iterator();
        } catch (SQLException sqe) {
            sqe.printStackTrace();
            throw new DataException(sqe);
        } finally {
            if (stmt2 != null) {
                try {
                    stmt2.close();
                } catch (SQLException ignored) {
                }
            }
            DBUtil.close(stmt, con);
        }
    }


    /**
     * @return a board summary for the given id.
     * @throws DataException if boardID is illegal or a database
     *                       error occurs.
     */
    public BoardSummary getBoardSummary(long boardID)
            throws DataException {
        Connection con = null;
        Statement stmt = null;
        try {
```

Example 7-19. JdbcDataAdapter.java (continued)

```java
            con = DBUtil.getConnection(dbURL);
            stmt = con.createStatement();
            return getBoardSummary(boardID, stmt);
        } catch (SQLException sqe) {
            sqe.printStackTrace();
            throw new DataException(sqe);
        } finally {
            DBUtil.close(stmt, con);
        }
    }

    private BoardSummary getBoardSummary(long boardID, Statement stmt)
            throws DataException, SQLException {
        ResultSet rs = stmt.executeQuery(
                "SELECT name, description FROM Board WHERE id=" + boardID);

        if (rs.next()) {
            String name = rs.getString(1);
            String description = rs.getString(2);

            List monthsWithMessages = getMonthsWithMessages(boardID, stmt);

            return new BoardSummaryImpl(boardID, name, description,
                    monthsWithMessages);
        } else {
            throw new DataException("Unknown boardID");
        }
    }

    /**
     * @return a list of MonthYear objects
     */
    private List getMonthsWithMessages(long boardID, Statement stmt)
            throws SQLException {

        List monthsWithMessages = new ArrayList();
        ResultSet rs = stmt.executeQuery(
                "SELECT DISTINCT createMonth, createYear "
                + "FROM Message "
                + "WHERE boardID=" + boardID);
        while (rs.next()) {
            monthsWithMessages.add(new MonthYear(
                    rs.getInt(1), rs.getInt(2)));
        }
        return monthsWithMessages;
    }

    private Message insertMessage(BoardSummary board, long inReplyToID,
```

Example 7-19. JdbcDataAdapter.java (continued)

```
        String msgSubject, String authorEmail,
        String msgText) throws DataException {
    // avoid overflowing the max database column lengths
    if (msgSubject.length() > ForumConfig.MAX_MSG_SUBJECT_LEN) {
        msgSubject = msgSubject.substring(0,
                ForumConfig.MAX_MSG_SUBJECT_LEN);
    }
    if (authorEmail.length() > ForumConfig.MAX_EMAIL_LEN) {
        authorEmail = authorEmail.substring(0,
                ForumConfig.MAX_EMAIL_LEN);
    }

    DayMonthYear createDate = new DayMonthYear();

    Connection con = null;
    PreparedStatement stmt = null;
    try {
        con = DBUtil.getConnection(dbURL);
        long newMsgID = DBUtil.getNextID("Message", con);
        stmt = con.prepareStatement("INSERT INTO Message "
                + "(id, inReplyToID, createMonth, createDay, createYear, "
                + "boardID, subject, authorEmail, msgText) "
                + "VALUES (?,?,?,?,?,?,?,?,?)");
        stmt.setString(1, Long.toString(newMsgID));
        stmt.setString(2, Long.toString(inReplyToID));
        stmt.setInt(3, createDate.getMonth());
        stmt.setInt(4, createDate.getDay());
        stmt.setInt(5, createDate.getYear());
        stmt.setString(6, Long.toString(board.getID()));
        stmt.setString(7, msgSubject);
        stmt.setString(8, authorEmail);
        DBUtil.setLongString(stmt, 9, msgText);

        stmt.executeUpdate();

        return new MessageImpl(newMsgID, createDate,
                board, msgSubject, authorEmail,
                msgText, inReplyToID);

    } catch (SQLException sqe) {
        sqe.printStackTrace();
        throw new DataException(sqe);
    } finally {
        DBUtil.close(stmt, con);
    }
}
}
```

Since this is not a book about relational database access using Java, we will not focus on the low-level JDBC details found in this class. The SQL code is intentionally simple to make this class portable to several different relational databases. The database URL and JDBC driver class name are retrieved from the `ForumConfig` class instead of hardcoded into the class:

```
private static String dbURL = ForumConfig.getDatabaseURL();


/**
 * Construct the data adapter and load the JDBC driver.
 */
public JdbcDataAdapter() throws DataException {
    try {
       Class.forName(ForumConfig.getJDBCDriverClassName());
    } catch (Exception ex) {
        ex.printStackTrace();
        throw new DataException("Unable to load JDBC driver: "
                + ForumConfig.getJDBCDriverClassName());
    }
}
```

Creating connections with the `DBUtil` class is another common pattern:

```
Connection con = null;
try {
    con = DBUtil.getConnection(dbURL);
```

As mentioned earlier, this approach leaves the door open for connection pooling in a future implementation. When the pool is written, it only needs to be added to the `DBUtil` class in a single place. When connections and statements are no longer needed, they should always be closed in a `finally` block:

```
} finally {
    DBUtil.close(stmt, con);
}
```

As mentioned earlier, this ensures that they will be closed because `finally` blocks are executed regardless of whether an exception occurs.

JDOM XML Production

The discussion forum code presented up to this point can extract data from a relational database and create instances of Java domain classes. The next step is to convert the domain objects into XML that can be transformed using XSLT. For this task, we use the JDOM class library. As mentioned in earlier chapters, JDOM is available at *http://www.jdom.org* and is open source software. Although the DOM

API can also be used, JDOM is somewhat easier to work with, which results in cleaner code.*

The basic pattern relies on various JDOM "producer" classes, each of which knows how to convert one or more domain objects into XML. This approach capitalizes on the recursive nature of XML by having each class produce a JDOM `Element` instance. Some of these `Element` instances represent entire documents, while others represent a small fragment of XML. These fragments can be recursively embedded into other `Element` instances to build up more complex structures.

Keeping XML production outside of domain objects is useful for several reasons:

- JDOM producer classes can be replaced with DOM producers or some other technology.

- Additional producers can be written to generate new forms of XML without modifying the domain objects or existing XML producers.

- Domain objects may be represented as Java interfaces with several different implementation classes. By keeping XML production separate, the same producer works with all implementations of the domain interfaces.

The `HomeJDOM` class, shown in Example 7-20, is quite simple. It merely produces a `<home>` element containing a list of `<board>` elements. Since a separate JDOM producer class creates the `<board>` elements, the `HomeJDOM` class merely assembles those XML fragments into a larger structure.

Example 7-20. HomeJDOM.java

```
package com.oreilly.forum.xml;

import com.oreilly.forum.domain.*;
import java.util.*;
import org.jdom.*;

/**
 * Produce JDOM data for the home page.
 */
public class HomeJDOM {

    /**
     * @param boards an iterator of <code>BoardSummary</code> objects.
     */
    public static Element produceElement(Iterator boards) {
        Element homeElem = new Element("home");
        while (boards.hasNext()) {
```

---

* For a DOM example, see the `LibraryDOMCreator` class shown in Example 1-4.

Example 7-20. HomeJDOM.java (continued)

```
            BoardSummary curBoard = (BoardSummary) boards.next();
            homeElem.addContent(BoardSummaryJDOM.produceElement(curBoard));
        }

        return homeElem;
    }

    private HomeJDOM() {
    }
}
```

As shown in the HomeJDOM class, the constructor is private. This prevents instantiation of the class, another decision made in the name of efficiency. Since each of the JDOM producer classes for the discussion forum are stateless and thread-safe, the produceElement() method can be static. This means that there is no reason to create instances of the JDOM producers, because the same method is shared by many concurrent threads. Additionally, there is no common base class because each of the produceElement() methods accept different types of objects as parameters.

Other JDOM Options

The static-method technique shown in this chapter is certainly not the only way to produce JDOM data. You may prefer to create custom subclasses of JDOM's Element class. In your subclass, the constructor can take a domain object as a parameter. So instead of calling a static method to produce XML, you end up writing something like:

```
Iterator boards = ...
Element homeElem = new HomeElement(boards);
```

Yet another option is to embed the JDOM production code into the domain objects. In this approach, your code would resemble this:

```
BoardSummary board = ...
Element elem = board.convertToJDOM();
```

This approach is probably not the best, because it tightly couples the JDOM code with the domain classes. It also will not work for cases where the XML data is produced from a group of domain objects instead of from a single object.

Regardless of the technique followed, consistency is the most important goal. If every class follows the same basic pattern, then the development team only has to understand one example to be familiar with the entire system.

The code for `ViewMonthJDOM` is shown in Example 7-21. This class creates XML data for an entire month's worth of messages.

Example 7-21. ViewMonthJDOM.java

```java
package com.oreilly.forum.xml;

import java.util.*;
import com.oreilly.forum.*;
import com.oreilly.forum.adapter.*;
import com.oreilly.forum.domain.*;
import org.jdom.*;

/**
 * Creates the JDOM for the month view of a board.
 */
public class ViewMonthJDOM {

    /**
     * @param board the message board to generate JDOM for.
     * @param month the month and year to view.
     */
    public static Element produceElement(BoardSummary board,
            MonthYear month) throws DataException {
        Element viewMonthElem = new Element("viewMonth");
        viewMonthElem.addAttribute("month",
                Integer.toString(month.getMonth()));
        viewMonthElem.addAttribute("year",
                Integer.toString(month.getYear()));

        // create the <board> element...
        Element boardElem = BoardSummaryJDOM.produceNameIDElement(board);
        viewMonthElem.addContent(boardElem);

        DataAdapter adapter = DataAdapter.getInstance();

        MessageTree msgTree = new MessageTree(adapter.getAllMessages(
                board.getID(), month));

        // get an iterator of MessageSummary objects
        Iterator msgs = msgTree.getTopLevelMessages();

        while (msgs.hasNext()) {
            MessageSummary curMsg = (MessageSummary) msgs.next();
            Element elem = produceMessageElement(curMsg, msgTree);
            viewMonthElem.addContent(elem);
        }

        return viewMonthElem;
    }
```

Example 7-21. ViewMonthJDOM.java (continued)

```
    /**
     * Produce a fragment of XML for an individual message. This
     * is a recursive function.
     */
    private static Element produceMessageElement(MessageSummary msg,
            MessageTree msgTree) {
        Element msgElem = new Element("message");
        msgElem.addAttribute("id", Long.toString(msg.getID()));
        msgElem.addAttribute("day",
                Integer.toString(msg.getCreateDate().getDay()));

        msgElem.addContent(new Element("subject")
                .setText(msg.getSubject()));
        msgElem.addContent(new Element("authorEmail")
                .setText(msg.getAuthorEmail()));

        Iterator iter = msgTree.getReplies(msg);
        while (iter.hasNext()) {
            MessageSummary curReply = (MessageSummary) iter.next();

            // recursively build the XML for all replies
            msgElem.addContent(produceMessageElement(curReply, msgTree));
        }
        return msgElem;
    }


    private ViewMonthJDOM() {
    }
}
```

The recursive method that produces <message> elements is the only difficult code in ViewMonthJDOM. Since <message> elements are nested according to replies, the XML forms a recursive tree structure that could be arbitrarily deep. JDOM supports this nicely, because a JDOM Element can contain other nested Elements. The produceMessageElement() method is designed to create the required XML data.

The next JDOM producer class, shown in Example 7-22, is quite simple. It merely creates an XML view of an individual message.

Example 7-22. ViewMessageJDOM.java

```
package com.oreilly.forum.xml;

import com.oreilly.forum.domain.*;
import java.util.Date;
import org.jdom.*;
```

Example 7-22. ViewMessageJDOM.java (continued)

```java
import org.jdom.output.*;

/**
 * Generate JDOM for the View Message page.
 */
public class ViewMessageJDOM {

    /**
     * @param message the message to view.
     * @param inResponseTo the message this one is in response to, or
     * perhaps null.
     */
    public static Element produceElement(Message message,
            MessageSummary inResponseTo) {
        Element messageElem = new Element("message");
        messageElem.addAttribute("id", Long.toString(message.getID()));
        DayMonthYear d = message.getCreateDate();
        messageElem.addAttribute("month",
                Integer.toString(d.getMonth()));
        messageElem.addAttribute("day",
                Integer.toString(d.getDay()));
        messageElem.addAttribute("year",
                Integer.toString(d.getYear()));

        Element boardElem = BoardSummaryJDOM.produceNameIDElement(
                message.getBoard());
        messageElem.addContent(boardElem);


        if (inResponseTo != null) {
            Element inRespToElem = new Element("inResponseTo")
                    .addAttribute("id", Long.toString(inResponseTo.getID()));
            inRespToElem.addContent(new Element("subject")
                    .setText(inResponseTo.getSubject()));
            messageElem.addContent(inRespToElem);
        }

        messageElem.addContent(new Element("subject")
                .setText(message.getSubject()));
        messageElem.addContent(new Element("authorEmail")
                .setText(message.getAuthorEmail()));
        messageElem.addContent(new Element("text")
                .setText(message.getText()));
        return messageElem;
```

Example 7-22. ViewMessageJDOM.java (continued)

```
    }

    private ViewMessageJDOM() {
    }
}
```

The JDOM producer shown in Example 7-23 is also quite simple. Its job is to create XML for a `BoardSummary` object. This class is unique because it is not designed to create an entire XML document. Instead, the elements produced by `BoardSummaryJDOM` are embedded into other XML pages in the application. For example, the home page shows a list of all `<board>` elements found in the system, each of which is generated by `BoardSummaryJDOM`. As you design your own systems, you will certainly find common fragments of XML that are reused by several pages. When this occurs, write a common helper class rather than duplicate code.

Example 7-23. BoardSummaryJDOM.java

```
package com.oreilly.forum.xml;

import com.oreilly.forum.domain.*;
import java.util.*;
import org.jdom.*;

/**
 * Produces JDOM for a BoardSummary object.
 */
public class BoardSummaryJDOM {
    public static Element produceNameIDElement(BoardSummary board) {
        // produce the following:
        // <board id="123">
        //    <name>the board name</name>
        //    <description>board description</description>
        // </board>
        Element boardElem = new Element("board");
        boardElem.addAttribute("id", Long.toString(board.getID()));
        boardElem.addContent(new Element("name")
                .setText(board.getName()));
        boardElem.addContent(new Element("description")
                .setText(board.getDescription()));
        return boardElem;
    }

    public static Element produceElement(BoardSummary board) {
        Element boardElem = produceNameIDElement(board);

        // add the list of messages
        Iterator iter = board.getMonthsWithMessages();
        while (iter.hasNext()) {
```

Example 7-23. BoardSummaryJDOM.java (continued)

```java
            MonthYear curMonth = (MonthYear) iter.next();
            Element elem = new Element("messages");
            elem.addAttribute("month", Integer.toString(curMonth.getMonth()));
            elem.addAttribute("year", Integer.toString(curMonth.getYear()));
            boardElem.addContent(elem);
        }


        return boardElem;
    }


    private BoardSummaryJDOM() {
    }
}
```

The final JDOM producer, `PostMessageJDOM`, is shown in Example 7-24. The `produceElement()` method takes numerous arguments that allow the method to produce XML for posting a new message or replying to an existing message. Also, values for the message subject, author email, and message text may be pre-filled in the XML. The application takes advantage of this capability whenever it must redisplay an HTML form to a user with its values filled in.

Example 7-24. PostMessageJDOM.java

```java
package com.oreilly.forum.xml;

import com.oreilly.forum.domain.*;
import org.jdom.*;

/**
 * Produce JDOM for the "Post Message" page.
 */
public class PostMessageJDOM {

    public static Element produceElement(
            BoardSummary board,
            MessageSummary inResponseToMsg,
            boolean showError,
            String subject,
            String authorEmail,
            String msgText) {
        Element messageElem = new Element("postMsg");

        // reuse the BoardSummaryJDOM class to produce a
        // fragment of the XML
        messageElem.addContent(BoardSummaryJDOM.produceNameIDElement(board));

        if (inResponseToMsg != null) {
            Element inRespTo = new Element("inResponseTo")
```

Example 7-24. PostMessageJDOM.java (continued)

```
                .addAttribute("id", Long.toString(inResponseToMsg.getID()));
        inRespTo.addContent(new Element("subject")
                .setText(inResponseToMsg.getSubject()));
        messageElem.addContent(inRespTo);
    }

    if (showError) {
        messageElem.addContent(new Element("error")
                .addAttribute("code", "ALL_FIELDS_REQUIRED"));
    }

    Element prefill = new Element("prefill");
    prefill.addContent(new Element("subject")
            .setText(subject));
    prefill.addContent(new Element("authorEmail")
            .setText(authorEmail));
    prefill.addContent(new Element("message")
            .setText(msgText));
    messageElem.addContent(prefill);

    return messageElem;
    }


    private PostMessageJDOM() {
    }
}
```

Servlet Implementation

We are almost finished! The remaining piece of the puzzle is to coordinate activity between the web browser, database, domain objects, JDOM producers, and XSLT stylesheets. This task lies in the servlet implementation and related classes. In an XSLT-driven web application, the servlet itself really does not do all that much. Instead, it acts as a mediator between all of the other actions taking place in the application.

Figure 7-9 shows the UML class diagram for the com.oreilly.forum.servlet package. This design consists of a few key classes along with numerous subclasses of Renderer and ReqHandler. These subclasses are very repetitive in nature, which is indicative of the highly structured application design that XML and XSLT facilitate.

A single-servlet design has been adopted for this application. In this approach, the ForumServlet intercepts all inbound requests from clients. The requests are then delegated to subclasses of ReqHandler, which handle requests for individual

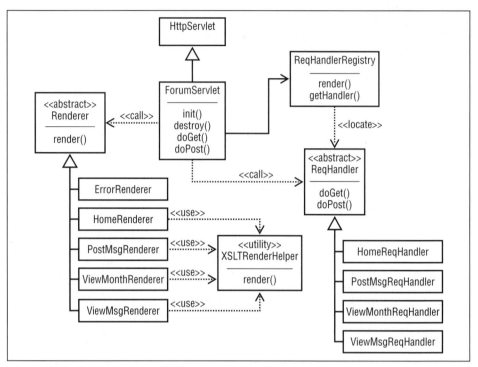

Figure 7-9. Servlet design

pages. Once the request has been processed, a subclass of Renderer selects the XML and XSLT stylesheet. XSLTRenderHelper does the actual XSLT transformation, sending the resulting XHTML back to the browser.

This is not designed to be a heavyweight web application framework. Instead, it is just a simple set of coding conventions and patterns that help keep the application highly modular. It is easy to eliminate the ReqHandler classes and use several servlets instead. The main advantage of explicit request handlers and renderers is that the design is clearly modularized, which may promote more consistency across a team of developers.

The overall flow of control may be the hardest part to understand. Once this flow is clear, the implementation is a matter of creating additional request handlers and renderers. Figure 7-10 is a UML sequence diagram that shows how a single web browser request is intercepted and processed.

When a browser issues a request, it is always directed to the single servlet. This servlet then locates the appropriate request handler based on information found in the requested URL. The request handler is responsible for interacting with the data adapter layer to create and update domain objects and for creating the appropriate renderer.

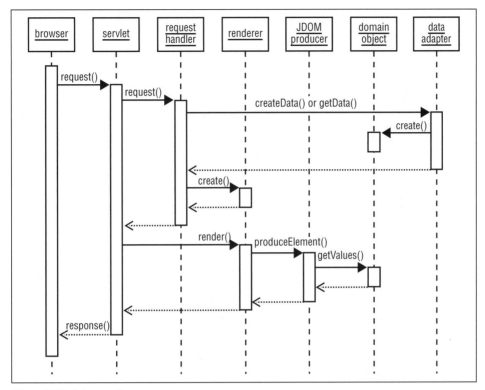

Figure 7-10. Sequence diagram

Once the renderer is created, the servlet asks it to `render()` its content. The renderer then asks the appropriate JDOM producer to create the XML data and performs the transformation using an XSLT stylesheet. The result of the transformation is sent back to the client browser.

One request handler might map to several renderers. For example, suppose the user is trying to post a new message and submits this information to the `PostMsgReqHandler` class. If the request handler determines that some required fields are missing, it can return an instance of the `PostMsgRenderer` class. This allows the user to fill in the remaining fields. On the other hand, if a database error occurs, an instance of `ErrorRenderer` can be returned. Otherwise, `ViewMsgRenderer` is returned when the message is successfully posted. Because request handlers and renderers are cleanly separated, renderers can be invoked from any request handler.

The code for `ForumServlet` is shown in Example 7-25. As already mentioned, this is the only servlet in the application.

Example 7-25. ForumServlet.java

```java
package com.oreilly.forum.servlet;

import com.oreilly.forum.ForumConfig;
import com.oreilly.forum.jdbcimpl.DBUtil;
import java.io.*;
import java.util.*;
import javax.servlet.*;
import javax.servlet.http.*;

/**
 * The single servlet in the discussion forum.
 */
public class ForumServlet extends HttpServlet {
    private ReqHandlerRegistry registry;

    /**
     * Registers all request handlers and sets up the
     * ForumConfig object.
     */
    public void init(ServletConfig sc) throws ServletException {
        super.init(sc);

        // get initialization parameters from the deployment
        // descriptor (web.xml)
        String jdbcDriverClassName = sc.getInitParameter(
                "jdbcDriverClassName");
        String databaseURL = sc.getInitParameter(
                "databaseURL");
        String adapterClassName = sc.getInitParameter(
                "adapterClassName");
        ForumConfig.setValues(jdbcDriverClassName,
                databaseURL, adapterClassName);

        try {
            // load all request handlers
            this.registry = new ReqHandlerRegistry(new HomeReqHandler());
            this.registry.register(new PostMsgReqHandler());
            this.registry.register(new ViewMonthReqHandler());
            this.registry.register(new ViewMsgReqHandler());
        } catch (Exception ex) {
            log(ex.getMessage(), ex);
            throw new UnavailableException(ex.getMessage(), 10);
        }
    }

    /**
     * Closes all database connections. This method is invoked
```

Example 7-25. ForumServlet.java (continued)

```
    * when the Servlet is unloaded.
    */
   public void destroy() {
       super.destroy();
       DBUtil.closeAllConnections();
   }

   protected void doPost(HttpServletRequest request,
           HttpServletResponse response) throws IOException,
           ServletException {
       ReqHandler rh = this.registry.getHandler(request);
       Renderer rend = rh.doPost(this, request, response);
       rend.render(this, request, response);
   }

   protected void doGet(HttpServletRequest request,
           HttpServletResponse response) throws IOException,
           ServletException {
       ReqHandler rh = this.registry.getHandler(request);
       Renderer rend = rh.doGet(this, request, response);
       rend.render(this, request, response);
   }
}
```

`ForumServlet` overrides the `init()` method to perform one-time initialization before any client requests are handled. This is where context initialization parameters are read from the deployment descriptor and stored in the `ForumConfig` instance:

```
String jdbcDriverClassName = sc.getInitParameter("jdbcDriverClassName");
String databaseURL = sc.getInitParameter("databaseURL");
String adapterClassName = sc.getInitParameter("adapterClassName");
ForumConfig.setValues(jdbcDriverClassName, databaseURL, adapterClassName);
```

The `init()` method then sets up instances of each type of request handler. These are registered with the `ReqHandlerRegistry` class, which has the ability to locate request handlers later on.

In the `destroy()` method, which is called when the servlet is unloaded, any outstanding database connections are closed:

```
public void destroy() {
    super.destroy();
    DBUtil.closeAllConnections();
}
```

While this currently has no real effect, the code was put in place because a future version of the software may use database connection pooling. This allows the application to close all connections in the pool just before exiting.

The only remaining methods in the servlet are `doGet()` and `doPost()`, which are virtually identical. All these methods do is locate the appropriate request handler instance, ask the handler to perform a GET or POST, and then use the renderer to send a response to the client.

The code for *ReqHandler.java* is shown in Example 7-26. This is an abstract class that provides `doGet()` and `doPost()` methods. By default, each method returns an error message back to the client, so a derived class must override one or both methods to enable HTTP GET and/or POST. Once the method is complete, the derived class must return an instance of `Renderer`, which produces the next page to display.

Example 7-26. ReqHandler.java

```
package com.oreilly.forum.servlet;

import java.io.*;
import javax.servlet.*;
import javax.servlet.http.*;

/**
 * All request handlers must extend from this class.
 */
public abstract class ReqHandler {
    protected abstract String getPathInfo();

    protected Renderer doGet(HttpServlet servlet, HttpServletRequest request,
            HttpServletResponse response)
            throws IOException, ServletException {
        return new ErrorRenderer("GET not allowed");
    }

    protected Renderer doPost(HttpServlet servlet, HttpServletRequest request,
            HttpServletResponse response)
            throws IOException, ServletException {
        return new ErrorRenderer("POST not allowed");
    }
}
```

The `Renderer` class is shown in Example 7-27. This class, like `ReqHandler`, is abstract. Derived classes are responsible for nothing more than producing content to the `HttpServletResponse`. Basically, each page in the discussion forum application is created using a subclass of `Renderer`.

Example 7-27. Renderer.java

```
package com.oreilly.forum.servlet;

import java.io.*;
import javax.servlet.*;
import javax.servlet.http.*;

/**
 * All page renderers must extend from this class.
 */
public abstract class Renderer {
    public abstract void render(HttpServlet servlet,
            HttpServletRequest request, HttpServletResponse response)
            throws IOException, ServletException;
}
```

The most basic renderer is `ErrorRenderer`, which is shown in Example 7-28. This class displays an error message in a web browser using simple `println()` statements that generate HTML. Unlike all other parts of this application, the `ErrorRenderer` class does not use XML and XSLT. The reason for this is that a large percentage of errors occurs because an XML parser is not properly configured on the CLASSPATH.* If this sort of error occurs, this renderer will not be affected.

TIP   `ErrorRenderer` can be written to use XML and XSLT, provided
             that a `try/catch` block catches any transformation errors and
             reverts to `println()` statements for error reporting.

Example 7-28. ErrorRenderer.java

```
package com.oreilly.forum.servlet;

import java.io.*;
import javax.servlet.*;
import javax.servlet.http.*;

/**
 * Shows an error page. Since errors are frequently caused by improperly
 * configured JAR files, XML And XSLT are not used by this class.
 * If XML and XSLT were used, then the same CLASSPATH issue that caused
 * the original exception to occur would probably cause this page
 * to fail as well.
 */
public class ErrorRenderer extends Renderer {
```

---

* CLASSPATH issues are discussed in great detail in Chapter 9.

Example 7-28. ErrorRenderer.java (continued)

```java
    private String message;
    private Throwable throwable;

    public ErrorRenderer(Throwable throwable) {
        this(throwable, throwable.getMessage());
    }

    public ErrorRenderer(String message) {
        this(null, message);
    }

    public ErrorRenderer(Throwable throwable, String message) {
        this.throwable = throwable;
        this.message = message;
    }

    public void render(HttpServlet servlet, HttpServletRequest request,
            HttpServletResponse response)
            throws IOException, ServletException {
        response.setContentType("text/html");
        PrintWriter pw = response.getWriter();
        // just show a simple error page for now.
        pw.println("<html>");
        pw.println("<body>");
        pw.println("<p>");
        pw.println(this.message);
        pw.println("</p>");
        if (this.throwable != null) {
            pw.println("<pre>");
            this.throwable.printStackTrace(pw);
            pw.println("</pre>");
        }
        pw.println("</body></html>");
    }
}
```

XSLTRenderHelper, shown in Example 7-29, is a utility class used by all remaining renderers. This class does the low-level XSLT transformations, eliminating a lot of duplicated code in each of the renderers. XSLTRenderHelper also maintains a cache of stylesheet filenames so they do not have to be repeatedly located using the ServletContext.getRealPath() method.

Example 7-29. XSLTRenderHelper.java

```java
package com.oreilly.forum.servlet;

import com.oreilly.javaxslt.util.StylesheetCache;
import java.io.*;
```

Example 7-29. XSLTRenderHelper.java (continued)

```
import java.net.URL;
import java.util.*;
import javax.servlet.*;
import javax.servlet.http.*;
import javax.xml.transform.*;
import javax.xml.transform.stream.*;
import org.jdom.*;
import org.jdom.output.*;


/**
 * A helper class that makes rendering of XSLT easier. This
 * eliminates the need to duplicate a lot of code for each
 * of the web pages in this app.
 */
public class XSLTRenderHelper {
    private static Map filenameCache = new HashMap();

    /**
     * Perform an XSLT transformation.
     *
     * @param servlet provides access to the ServletContext so
     *                the XSLT directory can be determined.
     * @param xmlJDOMData JDOM data for the XML Document.
     * @param xsltBaseName the name of the stylesheet without a directory.
     * @param response the Servlet response to write output to.
     */
    public static void render(HttpServlet servlet, Document xmlJDOMData,
            String xsltBaseName, HttpServletResponse response)
            throws ServletException, IOException {

        String xsltFileName = null;
        try {
            // figure out the complete XSLT stylesheet file name
            synchronized (filenameCache) {
                xsltFileName = (String) filenameCache.get(xsltBaseName);
                if (xsltFileName == null) {
                    ServletContext ctx = servlet.getServletContext();
                    xsltFileName = ctx.getRealPath(
                            "/WEB-INF/xslt/" + xsltBaseName);
                    filenameCache.put(xsltBaseName, xsltFileName);
                }
            }

            // write the JDOM data to a StringWriter
            StringWriter sw = new StringWriter();
            XMLOutputter xmlOut = new XMLOutputter("", false, "UTF-8");
            xmlOut.output(xmlJDOMData, sw);
```

Example 7-29. XSLTRenderHelper.java (continued)

```
            response.setContentType("text/html");
            Transformer trans = StylesheetCache.newTransformer(xsltFileName);

            // pass a parameter to the XSLT stylesheet
            trans.setParameter("rootDir", "/forum/");

            trans.transform(new StreamSource(new StringReader(sw.toString())),
                            new StreamResult(response.getWriter()));
        } catch (IOException ioe) {
            throw ioe;
        } catch (Exception ex) {
            throw new ServletException(ex);
        }
    }

    private XSLTRenderHelper() {
    }
}
```

XSLTRenderHelper performs the XSLT transformation by first converting the JDOM Document into a String of XML and then reading that String back into a JAXP-compliant XSLT processor. This is not necessarily the most efficient way to integrate JDOM with JAXP, but it works reliably with some beta versions of JDOM. By the time you read this, JDOM will have more standardized APIs for integrating with JAXP.

Another utility class, ReqHandlerRegistry, is shown in Example 7-30. This class is responsible for locating instances of ReqHandler based on *path information* found in the request URL. Basically, path information is any text that occurs after a slash character (/) following the servlet mapping. HttpServletRequest includes a method called getPathInfo() that returns any path information that is present.

Example 7-30. ReqHandlerRegistry.java

```
package com.oreilly.forum.servlet;

import java.util.*;
import javax.servlet.http.*;

/**
 * A utility class that locates request handler instances based
 * on extra path information.
 */
public class ReqHandlerRegistry {
    private ReqHandler defaultHandler;
    private Map handlerMap = new HashMap();
```

Example 7-30. ReqHandlerRegistry.java (continued)

```java
public ReqHandlerRegistry(ReqHandler defaultHandler) {
    this.defaultHandler = defaultHandler;
}

public void register(ReqHandler handler) {
    this.handlerMap.put(handler.getPathInfo(), handler);
}

public ReqHandler getHandler(HttpServletRequest request) {
    ReqHandler rh = null;
    String pathInfo = request.getPathInfo();
    if (pathInfo != null) {
        int firstSlashPos = pathInfo.indexOf('/');
        int secondSlashPos = (firstSlashPos > -1) ?
                pathInfo.indexOf('/', firstSlashPos+1) : -1;

        String key = null;
        if (firstSlashPos > -1) {
            if (secondSlashPos > -1) {
                key = pathInfo.substring(firstSlashPos+1, secondSlashPos);
            } else {
                key = pathInfo.substring(firstSlashPos+1);
            }
        } else {
            key = pathInfo;
        }
        if (key != null && key.length() > 0) {
            rh = (ReqHandler) this.handlerMap.get(key);
        }
    }
    return (rh != null) ? rh : this.defaultHandler;
}
}
```

Throughout the discussion forum application, URLs take on the following form:

```
http://hostname:port/forum/main/home
```

In this URL, forum represents the web application and is the name of the WAR file. The next part of the URL, main, is a mapping to ForumServlet. Since the WAR file and servlet will not change, this part of the URL remains constant. The remaining data, /home, is path information. This is the portion of the URL that ReqHandlerRegistry uses to locate instances of ReqHandler. If the path information is null or does not map to any request handlers, the default request handler is returned. This simply returns the user to the home page.

The first real request handler, HomeReqHandler, is shown in Example 7-31. This class is quite simple and merely returns an instance of HomeRenderer. The code is

simple because the home page does not have any modes of operation other than
to display all message boards. Other request handlers are more complex because
they must process HttpServletRequest parameters.

Example 7-31. HomeReqHandler.java

```
package com.oreilly.forum.servlet;

import java.io.*;
import javax.servlet.*;
import javax.servlet.http.*;

/**
 * This is the 'default' request handler in the app. The
 * first inbound request generally goes to an instance
 * of this class, which returns the home page renderer.
 */
public class HomeReqHandler extends ReqHandler {

    protected String getPathInfo() {
        return "home";
    }

    protected Renderer doGet(HttpServlet servlet, HttpServletRequest request,
            HttpServletResponse response)
            throws IOException, ServletException {
        return new HomeRenderer();
    }

}
```

All of the request handlers must override the getPathInfo() method. This determines the path info portion of the URL, so each request handler must return a
unique string.

The renderer for the home page, shown in Example 7-32, is also quite simple. As
with the home request handler, this renderer is simple because it has only one
mode of operation. Like other renderers, this class gets some data from the database using the DataAdapter class, asks a JDOM producer to convert the data into
XML, and then tells XSLTRenderHelper which XSLT stylesheet to use when performing the transformation.

Example 7-32. HomeRenderer.java

```
package com.oreilly.forum.servlet;

import com.oreilly.forum.*;
import com.oreilly.forum.adapter.*;
import com.oreilly.forum.domain.*;
```

Example 7-32. HomeRenderer.java (continued)

```java
import com.oreilly.forum.xml.*;
import java.io.*;
import java.util.*;
import javax.servlet.*;
import javax.servlet.http.*;
import org.jdom.*;

/**
 * Shows the home page.
 */
public class HomeRenderer extends Renderer {

    public void render(HttpServlet servlet, HttpServletRequest request,
            HttpServletResponse response)
            throws IOException, ServletException {
        try {
            // get the data for the home page
            DataAdapter adapter = DataAdapter.getInstance();

            // an iterator of BoardSummary objects
            Iterator boards = adapter.getAllBoards();

            // convert the data into XML (a JDOM Document)
            Document doc = new Document(HomeJDOM.produceElement(boards));

            // apply the appropriate stylesheet
            XSLTRenderHelper.render(servlet, doc, "home.xslt", response);
        } catch (DataException de) {
            new ErrorRenderer(de).render(servlet, request, response);
        }
    }
}
```

`ViewMonthReqHandler`, shown in Example 7-33, is slightly more complex than the home page request handler. Since this request handler requires the board id, month number, and year number as parameters, it must perform validation before it can handle the request properly.

Example 7-33. ViewMonthReqHandler.java

```java
package com.oreilly.forum.servlet;

import com.oreilly.forum.*;
import com.oreilly.forum.adapter.*;
import com.oreilly.forum.domain.*;
import java.io.*;
import javax.servlet.*;
import javax.servlet.http.*;
```

Example 7-33. ViewMonthReqHandler.java (continued)

```java
/**
 * Handle a request to view a month for a message board.
 */
public class ViewMonthReqHandler extends ReqHandler {

    protected String getPathInfo() {
        return "viewMonth";
    }

    protected Renderer doGet(HttpServlet servlet, HttpServletRequest request,
            HttpServletResponse response)
            throws IOException, ServletException {
        try {
            DataAdapter adapter = DataAdapter.getInstance();

            // these are all required parameters
            long boardID = 0L;
            int month = 0;
            int year = 0;
            try {
                boardID = Long.parseLong(request.getParameter("boardID"));
                month = Integer.parseInt(request.getParameter("month"));
                year = Integer.parseInt(request.getParameter("year"));
            } catch (Exception ex) {
                return new ErrorRenderer("Invalid request");
            }
            BoardSummary board = adapter.getBoardSummary(boardID);
            if (board == null) {
                return new ErrorRenderer("Invalid request");
            }

            return new ViewMonthRenderer(board, new MonthYear(month, year));
        } catch (DataException de) {
            return new ErrorRenderer(de);
        }
    }
}
```

Throughout this application, a seemingly harsh approach to error handling is followed. If any "impossible" requests are detected, the user is presented with a terse error message:

```java
    try {
        boardID = Long.parseLong(request.getParameter("boardID"));
        month = Integer.parseInt(request.getParameter("month"));
        year = Integer.parseInt(request.getParameter("year"));
    } catch (Exception ex) {
        return new ErrorRenderer("Invalid request");
    }
```

When considering error-handling approaches, the primary concern should be break-in attempts by hackers. It is far too easy for a user to determine which parameters are passed to a web application and then try to wreak havoc by manually keying in various permutations of those parameters. By checking for illegal parameters and simply rejecting them as invalid, a web application gains a big security advantage.

Web Application Security

In the `ViewMonthRegHandler` class, a `NumberFormatException` is thrown if any of these parameters are nonnumeric or `null`. Basically, there are only two possible causes for this sort of error. First, one of the XSLT stylesheets may have a bug, making it forget to pass one of these required parameters. If this is the case, a developer should theoretically catch this error during development and testing. The second possibility is that someone is manually keying in parameters without using the standard XHTML user interface. This could be a hacker attacking the site by probing for an application error, so we simply deny the request.

Standalone GUI applications do not have to contend with such issues because the user interface can prevent illegal user input. But web applications are essentially wide open for the entire world to see, so developers must adopt a highly defensive style of programming. If suppressing hack attempts is not a priority, the code could simply redirect the user to the home page when an illegal request occurs. It might be a good idea to write a log file entry that contains the requesting user's IP address and any other relevant information when errors occur. Log entries can be very useful when diagnosing application bugs as well.

`ViewMonthRenderer` is shown in Example 7-34. This is another simple class that displays an entire month's worth of messages in a given board. Although the XHTML display can be quite complex for this page, the JDOM producer and XSLT stylesheet handle the real work, keeping the Java code to a minimum.

Example 7-34. ViewMonthRenderer.java

```
package com.oreilly.forum.servlet;

import com.oreilly.forum.*;
import com.oreilly.forum.adapter.*;
import com.oreilly.forum.domain.*;
import com.oreilly.forum.xml.*;
```

Example 7-34. ViewMonthRenderer.java (continued)

```java
import java.io.*;
import javax.servlet.*;
import javax.servlet.http.*;
import org.jdom.*;

/**
 * Renders a page that shows all messages in a given month.
 */
public class ViewMonthRenderer extends Renderer {

    private BoardSummary board;
    private MonthYear month;

    public ViewMonthRenderer(BoardSummary board, MonthYear month) {
        this.board = board;
        this.month = month;
    }

    public void render(HttpServlet servlet, HttpServletRequest request,
            HttpServletResponse response)
            throws IOException, ServletException {
        try {
            // convert the data into XML (a JDOM Document)
            Document doc = new Document(ViewMonthJDOM.produceElement(
                    this.board, this.month));

            // apply the appropriate stylesheet
            XSLTRenderHelper.render(servlet, doc,
                    "viewMonth.xslt", response);
        } catch (DataException de) {
            throw new ServletException(de);
        }
    }
}
```

ViewMsgReqHandler, shown in Example 7-35, requires a parameter named msgID. As before, if this parameter is invalid, an error page is displayed to the user. Otherwise, an instance of ViewMsgRenderer is returned to the servlet.

Example 7-35. ViewMsgReqHandler.java

```java
package com.oreilly.forum.servlet;

import com.oreilly.forum.*;
import com.oreilly.forum.adapter.*;
import com.oreilly.forum.domain.*;
import java.io.*;
```

Example 7-35. ViewMsgReqHandler.java (continued)

```java
import javax.servlet.*;
import javax.servlet.http.*;

/**
 * Handle a request to view a message.
 */
public class ViewMsgReqHandler extends ReqHandler {

    protected String getPathInfo() {
        return "viewMsg";
    }

    protected Renderer doGet(HttpServlet servlet, HttpServletRequest request,
            HttpServletResponse response)
            throws IOException, ServletException {
        try {
            DataAdapter adapter = DataAdapter.getInstance();

            // msgID is a required parameter and must be valid
            String msgIDStr = request.getParameter("msgID");

            if (msgIDStr == null) {
                servlet.log("Required parameter 'msgID' was missing");
                return new ErrorRenderer("Invalid request");
            }

            Message msg = adapter.getMessage(Long.parseLong(msgIDStr));
            MessageSummary inResponseTo = null;
            if (msg.getInReplyTo() > -1) {
                inResponseTo = adapter.getMessage(msg.getInReplyTo());
            }
            return new ViewMsgRenderer(msg, inResponseTo);
        } catch (NumberFormatException nfe) {
            servlet.log("'msgID' parameter was not a number");
            return new ErrorRenderer("Invalid request");
        } catch (DataException de) {
            return new ErrorRenderer(de);
        }
    }
}
```

The corresponding renderer, ViewMsgRenderer, is shown in Example 7-36. This class follows the same basic approach as other renderers: it produces a JDOM Document and uses XSLTRenderHelper to perform the XSLT transformation.

Example 7-36. ViewMsgRenderer.java

```java
package com.oreilly.forum.servlet;

import com.oreilly.forum.*;
import com.oreilly.forum.domain.*;
import com.oreilly.forum.xml.*;
import java.io.*;
import javax.servlet.*;
import javax.servlet.http.*;
import org.jdom.*;

/**
 * Show the "view message" page.
 */
public class ViewMsgRenderer extends Renderer {

    private Message message;
    private MessageSummary inResponseTo;

    public ViewMsgRenderer(Message message, MessageSummary inResponseTo) {
        this.message = message;
        this.inResponseTo = inResponseTo;
    }

    public void render(HttpServlet servlet, HttpServletRequest request,
            HttpServletResponse response)
            throws IOException, ServletException {

        // convert the data into XML (a JDOM Document)
        Document doc = new Document(ViewMessageJDOM.produceElement(
                this.message, this.inResponseTo));

        // apply the appropriate stylesheet
        XSLTRenderHelper.render(servlet, doc, "viewMsg.xslt", response);
    }
}
```

The next class, `PostMsgReqHandler`, is shown in Example 7-37. In the `doGet()` method, the `mode` parameter indicates whether the user is trying to post a new message or reply to an existing message. The `doGet()` method is invoked as a result of an HTTP GET request, such as the user clicking on a hyperlink or typing in a URL.

Example 7-37. PostMsgReqHandler.java

```java
package com.oreilly.forum.servlet;

import com.oreilly.forum.*;
import com.oreilly.forum.adapter.*;
```

Example 7-37. PostMsgReqHandler.java (continued)

```java
import com.oreilly.forum.domain.*;
import java.io.*;
import javax.servlet.*;
import javax.servlet.http.*;

/**
 * Handles GET and POST requests for the page that allows users
 * to post or reply to a message.
 */
public class PostMsgReqHandler extends ReqHandler {

    protected String getPathInfo() {
        return "postMsg";
    }

    /**
     * When an HTTP GET is issued, show the web page for the
     * first time.
     */
    protected Renderer doGet(HttpServlet servlet, HttpServletRequest request,
            HttpServletResponse response)
            throws IOException, ServletException {
        try {
            // mode must be "postNewMsg" or "replyToMsg"
            String mode = request.getParameter("mode");

            DataAdapter adapter = DataAdapter.getInstance();
            if ("replyToMsg".equals(mode)) {
                long origMsgID = Long.parseLong(
                        request.getParameter("origMsgID"));
                Message inResponseToMsg = adapter.getMessage(origMsgID);
                if (inResponseToMsg != null) {
                    return new PostMsgRenderer(inResponseToMsg);
                }
            } else if ("postNewMsg".equals(mode)) {
                long boardID = Long.parseLong(
                        request.getParameter("boardID"));
                BoardSummary board = adapter.getBoardSummary(boardID);
                if (board != null) {
                    return new PostMsgRenderer(board);
                }
            }

            return new ErrorRenderer("Invalid request");
        } catch (NumberFormatException nfe) {
            return new ErrorRenderer(nfe);
        } catch (DataException de) {
            return new ErrorRenderer(de);
```

Example 7-37. PostMsgReqHandler.java (continued)

```
        }
    }


    /**
     * Handles HTTP POST requests, indicating that the user has
     * filled in the form and pressed the Submit button.
     */
    protected Renderer doPost(HttpServlet servlet, HttpServletRequest request,
            HttpServletResponse response)
            throws IOException, ServletException {

        // if the user hit the Cancel button, return to the home page
        if (request.getParameter("cancelBtn") != null) {
            return new HomeRenderer();
        }


        // lots of error checking follows...
        if (request.getParameter("submitBtn") == null) {
            servlet.log("Expected 'submitBtn' parameter to be present");
            return new ErrorRenderer("Invalid request");
        }


        // a null parameter indicates either a hack attempt, or a
        // syntax error in the HTML
        String mode = request.getParameter("mode");
        String msgSubject = request.getParameter("msgSubject");
        String authorEmail = request.getParameter("authorEmail");
        String msgText = request.getParameter("msgText");
        if (mode == null || msgSubject == null || authorEmail == null
                || msgText == null) {
            return new ErrorRenderer("Invalid request");
        }
        // one of these may be null
        String origMsgIDStr = request.getParameter("origMsgID");
        String boardIDStr = request.getParameter("boardID");
        if (origMsgIDStr == null && boardIDStr == null) {
            return new ErrorRenderer("Invalid request");
        }

        long origMsgID = 0;
        long boardID = 0;
        try {
            origMsgID = (origMsgIDStr != null) ? Long.parseLong(origMsgIDStr) : 0;
            boardID = (boardIDStr != null) ? Long.parseLong(boardIDStr) : 0;
        } catch (NumberFormatException nfe) {
            return new ErrorRenderer("Invalid request");
        }
```

Example 7-37. PostMsgReqHandler.java (continued)

```
        // remove extra whitespace then verify that the user filled
        // in all required fields
        msgSubject = msgSubject.trim();
        authorEmail = authorEmail.trim();
        msgText = msgText.trim();

        try {
            DataAdapter adapter = DataAdapter.getInstance();
            if (msgSubject.length() == 0
                    || authorEmail.length() == 0
                    || msgText.length() == 0) {
                BoardSummary board = (boardIDStr == null) ? null
                        : adapter.getBoardSummary(boardID);
                MessageSummary inResponseToMsg = (origMsgIDStr == null) ? null
                        : adapter.getMessage(origMsgID);

                return new PostMsgRenderer(board, inResponseToMsg,
                        true, msgSubject, authorEmail, msgText);
            }

            //
            // If this point is reached, no errors were detected so the
            // new message can be posted, or a response can be created
            //
            Message msg = null;
            if ("replyToMsg".equals(mode)) {
                msg = adapter.replyToMessage(origMsgID, msgSubject,
                        authorEmail, msgText);
            } else if ("postNewMsg".equals(mode)) {
                msg = adapter.postNewMessage(boardID, msgSubject,
                        authorEmail, msgText);
            }


            if (msg != null) {
                MessageSummary inResponseTo = null;
                if (msg.getInReplyTo() > -1) {
                    inResponseTo = adapter.getMessage(msg.getInReplyTo());
                }
                return new ViewMsgRenderer(msg, inResponseTo);
            }
            return new ErrorRenderer("Invalid request");
        } catch (DataException dex) {
            return new ErrorRenderer(dex);
        }
    }
}
```

Unlike other request handlers in this application, `PostMsgReqHandler` also has a `doPost()` method. The `doGet()` method is responsible for returning a renderer that displays the XHTML form, while the `doPost()` method is responsible for processing the form submission. Because the XHTML form contains several required fields and buttons, the `doPost()` method is far more complex than `doGet()`. As the code reveals, almost all of this complexity is introduced because of error checking and validation logic.

The `doPost()` method checks for illegal/impossible parameters first, returning an error page if any problems occur. Next, it checks to see what the user typed in. If the user left a required field blank, the parameter value will be an empty string rather than `null`. Of course, leading and trailing spaces must be trimmed in case the user hit the space bar:

```
msgSubject = msgSubject.trim();
authorEmail = authorEmail.trim();
msgText = msgText.trim();
```

If any of these fields are empty, the `PostMsgRenderer` is returned with form field values pre-filled:

```
return new PostMsgRenderer(board, inResponseToMsg,
        true, msgSubject, authorEmail, msgText);
```

This gives the user an opportunity to fill in missing values and try to submit the form again. If all is well, an instance of `ViewMsgRenderer` is returned. This allows the user to view the message that was just submitted.

The source code for `PostMsgRenderer` is shown in Example 7-38.

Example 7-38. PostMsgRenderer.java

```
package com.oreilly.forum.servlet;

import com.oreilly.forum.*;
import com.oreilly.forum.domain.*;
import com.oreilly.forum.xml.*;
import java.io.*;
import java.util.*;
import javax.servlet.*;
import javax.servlet.http.*;
import org.jdom.*;

/**
 * Show the web page that allows a user to post or reply to
 * a message.
 */
public class PostMsgRenderer extends Renderer {
    private MessageSummary inResponseToMsg;
    private BoardSummary board;
```

Example 7-38. PostMsgRenderer.java (continued)

```java
private String msgSubject;
private String authorEmail;
private String msgText;
private boolean showError;

/**
 * This constructor indicates that the user is replying to an
 * existing message.
 */
public PostMsgRenderer(Message inResponseToMsg) {
    this.board = inResponseToMsg.getBoard();
    this.inResponseToMsg = inResponseToMsg;
    this.showError = false;
    this.msgSubject = "Re: " + inResponseToMsg.getSubject();
    this.authorEmail = "";

    StringTokenizer st = new StringTokenizer(
            inResponseToMsg.getText(), "\n");
    StringBuffer buf = new StringBuffer();
    buf.append("\n");
    buf.append("\n> -----Original Message-----");
    buf.append("\n>    Posted by ");
    buf.append(inResponseToMsg.getAuthorEmail());
    buf.append(" on ");
    buf.append(inResponseToMsg.getCreateDate().toString());
    buf.append("\n");
    while (st.hasMoreTokens()) {
        String curLine = st.nextToken();
        buf.append("> ");
        buf.append(curLine);
        buf.append("\n");
    }
    buf.append("> ");
    this.msgText = buf.toString();
}

/**
 * This constructor indicates that the user is posting
 * a new message.
 */
public PostMsgRenderer(BoardSummary board) {
    this(board, null, false, "", "", "");
}

/**
 * This constructor is used when the user submitted a form
 * but did not fill out all required fields.
 */
```

Example 7-38. PostMsgRenderer.java (continued)

```
    public PostMsgRenderer(BoardSummary board,
            MessageSummary inResponseToMsg,
            boolean showError,
            String msgSubject,
            String authorEmail,
            String msgText) {
        this.board = board;
        this.inResponseToMsg = inResponseToMsg;
        this.showError = showError;
        this.msgSubject = msgSubject;
        this.authorEmail = authorEmail;
        this.msgText = msgText;
    }


    public void render(HttpServlet servlet, HttpServletRequest request,
            HttpServletResponse response)
            throws IOException, ServletException {

        // convert the data into XML (a JDOM Document)
        Document doc = new Document(PostMessageJDOM.produceElement(
                this.board,
                this.inResponseToMsg,
                this.showError,
                this.msgSubject,
                this.authorEmail,
                this.msgText));

        // apply the appropriate stylesheet
        XSLTRenderHelper.render(servlet, doc, "postMsg.xslt", response);
    }
}
```

As the code shows, this class has several constructors that support different modes of operation. The first constructor does the most work, prefixing the original message with > characters as many email clients do when creating replies to existing messages. Other than having several constructors, however, the renderer works just like other renderers in the application. The JDOM producer and XSLT stylesheet actually do most of the work, distinguishing between the various modes of operation.

Finishing Touches

That about does it for the code walkthrough. Since this is a moderately large application, downloading the code from this book's web site is much easier than typing everything in by hand. Do not forget that several additional classes are listed in Appendix B.

Deployment

A deployment descriptor and WAR file are required to deploy and test the application. The deployment descriptor, *web.xml*, is shown in Example 7-39.

Example 7-39. Deployment descriptor

```
<?xml version="1.0" encoding="ISO-8859-1"?>
<!DOCTYPE web-app PUBLIC "-//Sun Microsystems, Inc.//DTD Web Application 2.2//EN"
  "http://java.sun.com/j2ee/dtds/web-app_2.2.dtd">
<web-app>
  <servlet>
    <servlet-name>forumServlet</servlet-name>
    <servlet-class>com.oreilly.forum.servlet.ForumServlet</servlet-class>
    <init-param>
      <param-name>jdbcDriverClassName</param-name>
      <!-- MySQL version is commented out:
      <param-value>org.gjt.mm.mysql.Driver</param-value>
      -->
      <param-value>sun.jdbc.odbc.JdbcOdbcDriver</param-value>
    </init-param>
    <init-param>
      <param-name>databaseURL</param-name>
      <!-- MySQL version is commented out:
      <param-value>jdbc:mysql://localhost:3306/forum</param-value>
      -->
      <param-value>jdbc:odbc:forum</param-value>
    </init-param>
    <init-param>
      <param-name>adapterClassName</param-name>
      <!-- Relational database version is commented out:
      <param-value>com.oreilly.forum.jdbcimpl.JdbcDataAdapter</param-value>
      -->
      <param-value>com.oreilly.forum.fakeimpl.FakeDataAdapter</param-value>
    </init-param>
  </servlet>
  <servlet-mapping>
    <servlet-name>forumServlet</servlet-name>
    <url-pattern>/main/*</url-pattern>
  </servlet-mapping>
</web-app>
```

The deployment descriptor contains context initialization parameters for the data adapter layer. The default settings utilize a "fake" data adapter, allowing the discussion forum to function without creating any sort of database. Once this is up and running, you will want to create a relational database and configure the appropriate parameter values as shown in *web.xml*.

Ideas for Enhancements

A few key features were omitted to keep this chapter reasonably sized (as you can see, this is already far longer than any other chapter in the book). Some ideas for enhancements include:

- Database connection pooling
- Web-based administration tools
- Authentication of users
- The ability to search the entire archive
- Alternate client user interfaces, such as XHTML Basic or WML

Any one of these features can be added without fundamentally changing the existing architecture. User authentication is probably the biggest change, because new database tables may be required to associate messages with users. For web-based administration tools, additional request handlers and renderers need to be written. These tools also need to be integrated with the security and authentication mechanism; otherwise, any user can run the administrative tools.

Searching is beyond the abilities of XML and XSLT and is best handled by a dedicated search engine technology. This could be as simple as embedding a few lines of HTML into each page that links to a search engine such as Google.* Another approach is to write custom search code that integrates more directly with the underlying database. Finally, the whole issue of supporting alternate client user interfaces will be discussed in the next chapter. In a nutshell, this will involve detecting the client browser type and selecting an appropriate XSLT stylesheet.

---

* Even though all pages are generated dynamically, many web crawlers such as Google index every page in the application.

8

Additional Techniques

This chapter presents solutions to a few commonly encountered problems that were not covered in previous chapters, such as implementing session tracking without browser cookies, detecting the browser type, and using XSLT as a rudimentary code generator. None of these techniques are remarkably difficult to implement or use. However, they all build upon the technologies presented throughout this book and are important for programmers to understand. The chapter concludes with advice for internationalization using XSLT and Java.

XSLT Page Layout Templates

In many cases, dynamically generated, highly interactive web applications are overkill. A small company may need only a static web site that displays job openings, new product announcements, and other basic information. Corporate intranets present another common scenario. In a typical intranet, a large number of departments and individual project teams may be responsible for various web sites within the corporation. Many of these groups are composed of nonprogrammers who can create basic XHTML pages but are not technical enough to write XML, XSLT, and servlets. In either scenario, consistent look and feel are essential.

XSLT is very effective for defining consistent page layout. In the approach outlined here, web page authors create XHTML pages using whatever tools they are familiar with. These pages should not use frames or include navigation areas. As Figure 8-1 shows, an XSLT stylesheet is used to insert navigation areas on the top and left sides of input XHTML pages. This is why individual pages should not attempt to insert their own navigation areas.

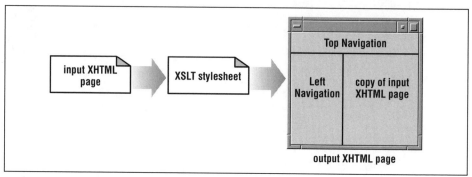

Figure 8-1. XSLT template layout

Since the top navigation area is dynamic, page authors must also include a `<meta>` tag in every XHTML page that is published:

```
<meta name="navigationCategory" content="home"/>
```

This tag allows the top navigation area to visually highlight the category that the current page belongs to.* The XSLT stylesheet selects this tag and generates the appropriate XHTML for the navigation area. As shown in Figure 8-2, the sample stylesheet uses hyperlinks for each of the navigation categories. This same approach also works for fancy graphical navigation areas.

Since a single stylesheet controls page layout, changes to this stylesheet are visible across the entire web site. The code for the home page is listed in Example 8-1. The required elements are emphasized.

Example 8-1. home.xml

```
<?xml version="1.0" encoding="UTF-8"?>
<html>
  <head>
    <title>Home Page</title>
    <meta name="navigationCategory" content="home"/>
  </head>
  <body>
    <h1>Welcome to the Home Page!</h1>
    <div>
      This is a normal XHTML page that authors
      create. The guidelines are as follows:
      <ul>
        <li>Each page must be valid XHTML</li>
        <li>Each page must have a meta tag that
            indicates the navigation category.</li>
        <li>The templatePage.xslt stylesheet will add
```

---

* You can extend this technique by adding a second `<meta>` tag for subcategories.

Example 8-1. home.xml (continued)

```
            the top and side navigation bars.</li>
    </ul>
    Pages are published to the WEB-INF/xml directory
    of a web app. This forces clients to access pages
    through a Servlet, because the Servlet container
    prevents direct access to anything under WEB-INF.
    </div>
  </body>
</html>
```

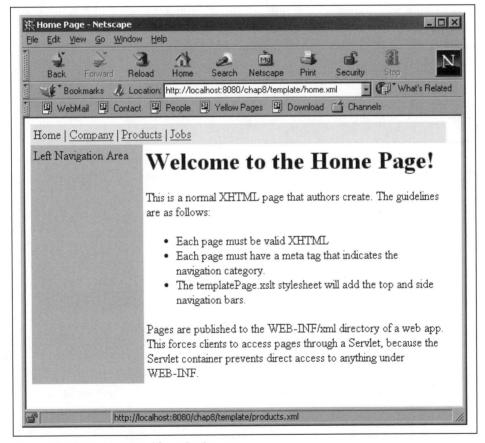

Figure 8-2. XHTML output with navigation areas

Since XSLT is used to insert the appropriate navigation areas, all pages must be well-formed XML. This is a good practice, and anyone who knows HTML should be able to make the transition to XHTML.* Programmers can provide scripts for

---

* HTML TIDY is a free tool that converts HTML to XHTML. It is available at *http://www.w3.org/People/ Raggett/tidy*.

page authors to run that validate the XML against one of the XHTML DTDs, reporting errors before pages are published to the web site.

TIP   Strictly adhering to XHTML DTDs makes it much easier for pro-
               grammers to write all sorts of programs that manage web site con-
               tent because page content is consistently structured and can be easily
               parsed.

The XSLT stylesheet searches for the <meta> tag; therefore, <html>, <head>, and <meta> are required elements. If the <meta> tag is not found, the navigation category defaults to "unknown," and none of the navigation links are highlighted. Any content found inside of <head> and <body> is simply copied to the appropriate location within the result tree document. Example 8-2 lists the XSLT stylesheet that inserts the navigation areas.

Example 8-2. templatePage.xslt

```
<?xml version="1.0" encoding="UTF-8"?>
<!--
*********************************************************************
** A stylesheet used by every page on a web site. This stylesheet
** defines where the page header and navigation bar are placed.
*********************************************************************-->
<xsl:stylesheet version="1.0"
   xmlns:xsl="http://www.w3.org/1999/XSL/Transform">

  <!--
  *********************************************************************
  ** The result tree is XHTML
  *********************************************************************-->
  <xsl:output method="xml"
     doctype-public="-//W3C//DTD XHTML 1.0 Transitional//EN"
     doctype-system="http://www.w3.org/TR/xhtml1/DTD/xhtml1-transitional.dtd"
     encoding="UTF-8"/>

  <!--
  *********************************************************************
  ** The navigation category is determined by the <meta> tag in the
  ** source XHTML document. The top navigation bar uses this variable.
  *********************************************************************-->
  <xsl:variable name="global.nav.category">
    <xsl:choose>
      <xsl:when test="/html/head/meta[@name='navigationCategory']">
        <xsl:value-of select="/html/head/meta
               [@name='navigationCategory']/@content"/>
      </xsl:when>
      <xsl:otherwise>
        <xsl:text>unknown</xsl:text>
```

Example 8-2. templatePage.xslt (continued)

```
      </xsl:otherwise>
    </xsl:choose>
  </xsl:variable>

  <!--
  ******************************************************************
  ** This template produces the XHTML document.
  ****************************************************************-->
  <xsl:template match="/">
    <html xmlns="http://www.w3.org/1999/xhtml">
      <!-- copy the <head> from the source document -->
      <xsl:copy-of select="html/head"/>

      <body>
        <!-- this table defines the overall layout of the page -->
        <table width="100%" cellpadding="4"
               cellspacing="0" border="0">
          <tr bgcolor="#f0f0f0">
            <td colspan="2">
              <xsl:call-template name="createTopNavbar"/>
            </td>
          </tr>
          <tr valign="top">
            <td bgcolor="#cccccc" width="150px">
              <xsl:call-template name="createLeftNavbar"/>
            </td>
            <td bgcolor="white">
              <!--
              ******************************************************
              ** Copy all contents of the <body> from the source
              ** XHTML document to the result tree XHTML document.
              ****************************************************-->
              <xsl:copy-of select="html/body/* | html/body/text()"/>
            </td>
          </tr>
        </table>
      </body>
    </html>
  </xsl:template>

  <!--
  ******************************************************************
  ** This template produces the top navigation bar.
  ****************************************************************-->
  <xsl:template name="createTopNavbar">
    <xsl:call-template name="navButton">
      <xsl:with-param name="category" select="'home'"/>
      <xsl:with-param name="displayName" select="'Home'"/>
```

Example 8-2. templatePage.xslt (continued)

```
        <xsl:with-param name="url" select="'home.xml'"/>
    </xsl:call-template>
    |
    <xsl:call-template name="navButton">
      <xsl:with-param name="category" select="'company'"/>
      <xsl:with-param name="displayName" select="'Company'"/>
      <xsl:with-param name="url" select="'company.xml'"/>
    </xsl:call-template>
    |
    <xsl:call-template name="navButton">
      <xsl:with-param name="category" select="'products'"/>
      <xsl:with-param name="displayName" select="'Products'"/>
      <xsl:with-param name="url" select="'products.xml'"/>
    </xsl:call-template>
    |
    <xsl:call-template name="navButton">
      <xsl:with-param name="category" select="'jobs'"/>
      <xsl:with-param name="displayName" select="'Jobs'"/>
      <xsl:with-param name="url" select="'jobs.xml'"/>
    </xsl:call-template>
</xsl:template>

<!--
********************************************************************
** This template produces a "button" in the top navigation bar.
********************************************************************-->
<xsl:template name="navButton">
  <xsl:param name="category"/>
  <xsl:param name="displayName"/>
  <xsl:param name="url"/>
  <xsl:choose>
    <!-- The current category is displayed as text -->
    <xsl:when test="$category = $global.nav.category">
      <xsl:value-of select="$displayName"/>
    </xsl:when>

    <!-- All other categories are displayed as hyperlinks -->
    <xsl:otherwise>
      <a href="{$url}">
        <xsl:value-of select="$displayName"/>
      </a>
    </xsl:otherwise>
  </xsl:choose>
</xsl:template>

<!--
********************************************************************
** This template creates the left navigation area.
```

Example 8-2. templatePage.xslt (continued)

```
*******************************************************************-->
<xsl:template name="createLeftNavbar">
  Left Navigation Area
</xsl:template>
</xsl:stylesheet>
```

This stylesheet is quite simple in concept. First, it sets up the global.nav. category variable. The stylesheet uses XPath to check for the existence of a <meta> tag that contains a navigationCategory attribute:

```
<xsl:variable name="global.nav.category">
  <xsl:choose>
    <xsl:when test="/html/head/meta[@name='navigationCategory']">
      <xsl:value-of select="/html/head/meta
              [@name='navigationCategory']/@content"/>
    </xsl:when>
    <xsl:otherwise>
      <xsl:text>unknown</xsl:text>
    </xsl:otherwise>
  </xsl:choose>
</xsl:variable>
```

The first part of the XPath expression used by <xsl:when> locates any <meta> tags:

```
/html/head/meta
```

Next, a predicate is used to narrow down the list to the one <meta> tag that contains a navigationCategory attribute:

```
[@name='navigationCategory']
```

If this is found, the value of the content attribute is assigned to the global.nav. category variable. Otherwise, the value is unknown.

The XSLT stylesheet then contains a template that matches the / pattern. This template defines the overall XHTML page layout by creating a <table>. The document <head>, however, is simply copied from the input XHTML document:

```
<xsl:copy-of select="html/head"/>
```

Because the original <head> is merely copied to the result tree, any styles or scripts that page authors include in their own documents are preserved. The only drawback occurs when people define CSS styles that change the look and feel of the navigation areas, such as changing the fonts and colors used in a page. If this is a concern, you might want to include logic in the XSLT stylesheet that ignores all <style> tags and style attributes in the original XHTML document.

Once the <head> is copied, the XSLT stylesheet creates the <body> for the result tree. An XHTML <table> controls the overall page layout, and named XSLT templates are used to create the navigation areas:

```
<xsl:call-template name="createTopNavbar"/>
...
<xsl:call-template name="createLeftNavbar"/>
```

The createTopNavbar template is somewhat more complicated because it contains logic to display the current category differently. The createLeftNavbar template, on the other hand, simply copies some static content to the result. Finally, the contents of the <body> tag are copied from the original document to the result tree:

```
<xsl:copy-of select="html/body/* | html/body/text()"/>
```

Unlike the <head>, the <body> is not copied directly. Instead, all elements and text within the <body> are copied. This prevents the following invalid XHTML from being produced:

```
<tr><td><body>...</body></td></tr>
```

The createTopNavbar named template is used to create the row of links in the top navigation area. For each navigation category, it calls the navButton template:

```
<xsl:call-template name="navButton">
  <xsl:with-param name="category" select="'home'"/>
  <xsl:with-param name="displayName" select="'Home'"/>
  <xsl:with-param name="url" select="'home.xml'"/>
</xsl:call-template>
```

The category parameter allows the navButton template to determine if the displayName parameter should be displayed as a hyperlink or text. The code to do this is emphasized in the navButton template (in Example 8-2) and is not repeated here.

None of this works without a servlet driving the process. In this example, all XHTML pages are stored in the web application's *WEB-INF* directory and saved with *.xml* filename extensions. Remember that these are the original web pages and do not contain any navigation areas. They are stored in the *WEB-INF* directory to ensure that clients cannot access them directly. Instead, clients must use a servlet called TemplateServlet to request all pages. This servlet locates the XML file, performs the XSLT transformation using *templatePage.xslt*, and sends the result tree back to the client browser. The entire process is transparent to clients because they see only the results of the transformation.

Table 8-1 shows the complete structure of the WAR file that supports this example.

Table 8-1. WAR file contents

File	Description
WEB-INF/web.xml	The deployment descriptor (see Example 8-3)
WEB-INF/classes/chap8/ TemplateServlet.class	The servlet that drives the XSLT transformation (see Example 8-4)
WEB-INF/lib/javaxslt.jar	Contains the `StylesheetCache` class
WEB-INF/xml/company.xml	An example web page
WEB-INF/xml/home.xml	An example web page (see Example 8-1)
WEB-INF/xml/jobs.xml	An example web page
WEB-INF/xml/products.xml	An example web page
WEB-INF/xslt/templatePage.xslt	The XSLT stylesheet (see Example 8-2)

The deployment descriptor, *web.xml*, is shown in Example 8-3.

Example 8-3. Deployment descriptor

```
<?xml version="1.0" encoding="ISO-8859-1"?>
<!DOCTYPE web-app PUBLIC "-//Sun Microsystems, Inc.//DTD Web Application 2.2//EN"
  "http://java.sun.com/j2ee/dtds/web-app_2.2.dtd">
<web-app>
  <servlet>
    <servlet-name>template</servlet-name>
    <servlet-class>chap8.TemplateServlet</servlet-class>
  </servlet>
  <servlet-mapping>
    <servlet-name>template</servlet-name>
    <url-pattern>/template/*</url-pattern>
  </servlet-mapping>
</web-app>
```

Since all files are protected under the *WEB-INF* directory, the `/template/*` URL pattern specified in the deployment descriptor is the only way for clients to access this application. The URL users type into their browser is: *http://localhost:8080/ chap8/template/home.xml.*

This displays the page shown earlier in Figure 8-2. In this URL, the word `template` maps to the servlet, and `/home.xml` is the *path information*. This is retrieved by the servlet using the `getPathInfo()` method of `HttpServletRequest`. The source code for `TemplateServlet` is shown in Example 8-4.

Example 8-4. TemplateServlet.java

```java
package chap8;

import com.oreilly.javaxslt.util.StylesheetCache;
import java.io.*;
import java.net.*;
import javax.servlet.*;
import javax.servlet.http.*;
import javax.xml.transform.*;
import javax.xml.transform.stream.*;

/**
 * Applies a standard stylesheet to every XML page on a site.
 */
public class TemplateServlet extends HttpServlet {
    private String xsltFileName;

    /**
     * Locate the template stylesheet during servlet initialization.
     */
    public void init() throws UnavailableException {
        ServletContext ctx = getServletContext();
        this.xsltFileName = ctx.getRealPath(
                "/WEB-INF/xslt/templatePage.xslt");
        File f = new File(this.xsltFileName);

        if (!f.exists()) {
            throw new UnavailableException(
                    "Unable to locate XSLT stylesheet: "
                    + this.xsltFileName, 30);
        }
    }

    public void doGet(HttpServletRequest req, HttpServletResponse res)
            throws ServletException, IOException {
        try {
            // use the ServletContext to locate the XML file
            ServletContext ctx = getServletContext();
            String xmlFileName = ctx.getRealPath("/WEB-INF/xml"
                    + req.getPathInfo());

            // verify that the file exists
            if (!new File(xmlFileName).exists()) {
                res.sendError(HttpServletResponse.SC_NOT_FOUND, xmlFileName);
            } else {
                res.setContentType("text/html");

                // load the XML file
                Source xmlSource = new StreamSource(new BufferedReader(
```

Example 8-4. TemplateServlet.java (continued)

```
                        new FileReader(xmlFileName)));

                // use a cached version of the XSLT
                Transformer trans =
                        StylesheetCache.newTransformer(xsltFileName);
                trans.transform(xmlSource, new StreamResult(res.getWriter()));
            }
        } catch (TransformerConfigurationException tce) {
            throw new ServletException(tce);
        } catch (TransformerException te) {
            throw new ServletException(te);
        }
    }
}
```

This is a fairly basic servlet whose sole purpose is to locate XML files and perform XSLT transformations. The `init()` method is used to locate *templatePage.xslt* from the *WEB-INF/xslt* directory:

```
ServletContext ctx = getServletContext();
this.xsltFileName = ctx.getRealPath(
            "/WEB-INF/xslt/templatePage.xslt");
```

As discussed in earlier chapters, the `getRealPath()` method converts the path into a system-specific pathname. This allows the `StylesheetCache` class to locate the XSLT stylesheet properly. Later, in the `doGet()` method of the servlet, the same method is used to locate the requested XML file:

```
ServletContext ctx = getServletContext();
String xmlFileName = ctx.getRealPath("/WEB-INF/xml"
        + req.getPathInfo());
```

As shown back in the source for `TemplateServlet`, it then checks for the existence of this file and sends an error if necessary. Otherwise, it uses JAXP to perform the XSLT transformation. This is where the navigation areas get added to the document.

More on Caching

In the `TemplateServlet` class, the XSLT stylesheets are cached using the `com.oreilly.javaxslt.util.StylesheetCache` class. In this particular example, however, the XML data and XSLT stylesheets are all static files. Because these files are not dynamically generated, it becomes possible to cache the transformation *result*, yielding the highest possible performance. The next chapter discusses a class called `ResultCache` that makes this possible.

Using XSLT stylesheets for page layout templates is a useful technique because individual page authors do not have to duplicate headers, footers, and navigation areas into every page they create. By centralizing page layout in one or more standard XSLT stylesheets, fewer changes are required to update the look of an entire web site.

Session Tracking Without Cookies

Session tracking is an essential part of most web applications. By nature, the HTTP protocol is connectionless. This means that each time users click on a hyperlink or submit an XHTML form, the browser establishes a new connection to the web server. Once the request is sent and the response is received, the connection between browser and server is broken.

This presents a problem for servlet authors. Although the browser and web server do not maintain a persistent connection between page views, applications must maintain state information for each user. Stateful applications make technologies like shopping carts possible, for instance. With each request from the browser, the servlet must reestablish the identity of the user and locate his session information.

Servlet Session-Tracking API

The traditional servlet approach to session tracking utilizes the `javax.servlet.http.HttpSession` interface. This interface allows a web application to store information about a user that persists across page requests. The interface is easy to use, mapping attribute names to attribute values. The code shown here is part of a servlet that uses `HttpSession`:

```
public void doGet(HttpServletRequest req, HttpServletResponse res)
        throws ServletException, IOException {
    // retrieve an instance of HttpSession for this user. The "true" parameter
    // indicates that the object should be created if it does not exist.
    HttpSession session = req.getSession(true);

    // retrieve the cart for this user
    Cart cart = (Cart) session.getAttribute("shoppingCart");

    if (cart == null) {
        cart = new Cart();
        session.setAttribute("shoppingCart", cart);
    }

    ...
}
```

The first line of the doGet() method locates the HttpSession instance associated with the current user. The true parameter indicates that a new session should be created if one does not already exist. Once the session is created, a Cart object can be retrieved using HttpSession's getAttribute() method.

Browser cookies provide the standard method of implementing HttpSession. A cookie is a small piece of information stored on the client machine and generally contains a randomly generated sequence of characters that uniquely identifies a user. When the browser issues a request to the servlet, the servlet looks for a cookie named jsessionid and uses its value to locate an instance of HttpSession. Figure 8-3 illustrates the normal session-tracking model.

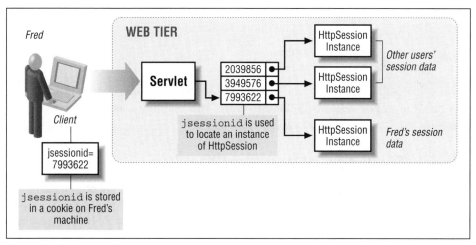

Figure 8-3. Session tracking

Cookies are a mixed blessing. Although they make session tracking very easy to implement, this leads to security concerns because people do not want their browsing habits monitored. Therefore, quite a few people set their browsers to disable all cookies. When users disable cookies, servlets must use another technique to enable session tracking.

The standard servlet API has a fallback mechanism when cookies are disabled. It reverts to a technique called URL rewriting. If cookies are disabled, the session identifier is appended to the URL. This way, whenever a user clicks on a hyperlink or submits an XHTML form, the session identifier is transmitted along with the request. This cannot happen without some level of programmer intervention, however. Imagine a scenario where a servlet is requested, and it returns an XHTML page with the following content:

```
Click on the link to move next:
<a href="/shopping/moveNext"/>Move Next</a>
```

This causes session tracking to fail, because the session identifier is lost whenever the user clicks on the hyperlink. We really want the HTML to look like this:

```
Click on the link to move next:
<a href="/shopping/moveNext;jsessionid=0e394s8a576f67b38s7"/>Move Next</a>
```

Now, when the user clicks on the hyperlink, the session identifier (jsessionid) is transmitted to the servlet as part of the requested URL.

The value for jsessionid cannot be hardcoded. It must be dynamically generated for each instance of HttpSession, making it much harder for hackers to obtain session identifiers to impersonate users.* This means that the XHTML cannot be entirely static; the session identifier must be dynamically inserted into the XHTML whenever a link or form action is required. HttpServletResponse has a method called encodeURL() that makes this possible:

```
String originalURL = "/shopping/moveNext";
String encodedURL = response.encodeURL(originalURL);
```

Now, encodedURL will be encoded with the session id if the jsessionid cookie was not found. For session tracking to work, this technique must be used consistently for every hyperlink and form action on a web site.

Session Tracking with Java and XSLT

With XSLT, session tracking is a little harder because the stylesheet generates the URL rather than the servlet. For instance, a stylesheet might contain the following code:

```
<xsl:template match="cart">
  Click on the link to move next:
  <a href="/shopping/moveNext"/>Move Next</a>
  ...
</xsl:template>
```

Like before, the jsessionid needs to be concatenated to the URL. To make this happen, the following steps must be performed:

1. In the servlet, determine if cookies are enabled or disabled.

2. If cookies are disabled, get the value of jsessionid.

3. Pass ;jsessionid=XXXX as a parameter to the XSLT stylesheet, where XXXX is the session identifier.

4. In the stylesheet, append the session id parameter to all URLs in hyperlinks and form actions.

---

* Sessions and their associated identifiers typically expire after 30 minutes of inactivity and must be regenerated.

If cookies are enabled, there is no reason to manually implement session tracking. This is easy to check because the `javax.servlet.http.HttpServletRequest` interface provides the `isRequestedSessionIdFromCookie()` method. When this method returns `true`, cookies are enabled, and the remaining steps can be ignored. The code in Example 8-5 shows what a servlet's `doGet()` method looks like when implementing session tracking.

Example 8-5. Session-tracking code

```
public void doGet(HttpServletRequest req, HttpServletResponse res)
        throws ServletException, IOException {
    try {
        // retrieve current settings from the session
        HttpSession session = req.getSession(true);
        Cart cart = (Cart) session.getAttribute("shoppingCart");

        if (cart == null) {
            cart = new Cart();
            session.setAttribute("shoppingCart", cart);
        }

        // produce the DOM tree
        Document doc = CartDOMProducer.createDocument(cart);

        // prepare the XSLT transformation
        Transformer trans = StylesheetCache.newTransformer(
                this.xsltFileName);

        // allow cookieless session tracking
        if (!req.isRequestedSessionIdFromCookie()) {
            String sessionID = session.getId();
            trans.setParameter("global.sessionID",
                ";jsessionid=" + sessionID);
        }

        // send the web page back to the user
        res.setContentType("text/html");
        trans.transform(new javax.xml.transform.dom.DOMSource(doc),
                new StreamResult(res.getWriter()));

    } catch (ParserConfigurationException pce) {
        throw new ServletException(pce);
    } catch (TransformerConfigurationException tce) {
        throw new ServletException(tce);
    } catch (TransformerException te) {
        throw new ServletException(te);
    }
}
```

The critical lines of code are emphasized. The first of these checks to see if the session was not obtained using a cookie:

```
if (!req.isRequestedSessionIdFromCookie()) {
```

For the very first request, the cookie will not be present because the servlet has not had a chance to create it. For all subsequent requests, the cookie will be missing if the user has disabled cookies in the browser. Under either scenario, the session identifier is obtained from the `HttpSession` instance:

```
String sessionID = session.getId();
```

The servlet API takes care of generating a random session identifier; you are responsible for preserving this identifier by passing it as a parameter to the stylesheet. This is done as follows:

```
trans.setParameter("global.sessionID",
        ";jsessionid=" + sessionID);
```

This servlet also takes the liberty of prefixing the session identifier with `";jessionid="`. This makes the XSLT stylesheet simpler, because it does not have to check if the session ID is an empty string or not. As implemented here, the value of `global.sessionID` can be appended to all URLs:

```
<a href="/whatever{$global.sessionID}">click here</a>
```

The end result is that if cookies are enabled, the URL will be unaffected. Otherwise, it will be properly encoded to use session tracking. A larger XSLT example follows in Example 8-6.

Example 8-6. Session-tracking XSLT stylesheet

```
<?xml version="1.0" encoding="UTF-8"?>

<xsl:stylesheet version="1.0"
    xmlns:xsl="http://www.w3.org/1999/XSL/Transform">

  <!--
  **********************************************************************
  ** global.sessionID : Used for URL-rewriting to implement
  **                     session tracking without cookies.
  **********************************************************-->
  <xsl:param name="global.sessionID"/>

  <!-- This stylesheet produces XHTML -->
  <xsl:output method="xml" indent="yes" encoding="UTF-8"
  doctype-public="-//W3C//DTD XHTML 1.0 Transitional//EN"
  doctype-system="http://www.w3.org/TR/xhtml1/DTD/xhtml1-transitional.dtd"/>

  <!--
  **********************************************************************
```

Example 8-6. Session-tracking XSLT stylesheet (continued)

```
** This template produces the skeletal XHTML document.
********************************************************************-->
<xsl:template match="/">
  <html xmlns="http://www.w3.org/1999/xhtml">
    <head>
      <title>Shopping Example</title>
    </head>
    <body>
      <!-- Create a form for this page -->
      <form method="post" action="/chap8/shopping{$global.sessionID}">
      <h1>Shopping Example</h1>
        ...remainder of page omitted
      </form>
    </body>
  </html>
</xsl:template>

<xsl:template match="cart">
  Click on the link to move next:
  <a href="/shopping/moveNext{$global.sessionID}?param=value"/>Move Next</a>
  ...
</xsl:template>

</xsl:stylesheet>
```

This stylesheet fully illustrates the three key components that make session tracking with XSLT possible. First, the session identifier is passed to the stylesheet as a parameter:

```
<xsl:param name="global.sessionID"/>
```

Next, this session identifier is used for the form action:

```
<form method="post" action="/chap8/shopping{$global.sessionID}">
```

And finally, it is used for all hyperlinks:

```
<a href="/shopping/moveNext{$global.sessionID}?param=value"/>Move Next</a>
```

The `?param=value` string was added here to illustrate that request parameters are appended after the session identifier. Therefore, the full URL will look similar to the following when the user clicks on the hyperlink:

```
http://localhost:8080/shopping/moveNext;jsessionid=298ulkj2348734jkj43?param=value
```

Tracking sessions is essential, and the technique shown in this section works when browser cookies are disabled. You should always test your web applications by disabling all browser cookies to see if every URL is properly encoded with the session identifier.

Identifying the Browser

A strength of XSLT is its ability to help keep data and presentation separate. As you know, supporting different transformations is a matter of writing different XSLT stylesheets. Figuring out which stylesheet to apply is the only missing piece. For web applications, the `User-Agent` HTTP header offers the solution.

HTTP requests consist of a header followed by content; the header contains name/value pairs of data, allowing the client and server to exchange additional information with each other. The text shown in Example 8-7 contains the complete HTTP request issued by Netscape 6.0 when running on Windows 2000.

Example 8-7. Netscape 6 HTTP request

```
GET / HTTP/1.1
Host: localhost:80
User-Agent: Mozilla/5.0 (Windows; U; Windows NT 5.0; en-US; m18) Gecko/20001108
Netscape6/6.0
Accept: */*
Accept-Language: en
Accept-Encoding: gzip,deflate,compress,identity
Keep-Alive: 300
Connection: keep-alive
```

For the purposes of browser detection, the value of `User-Agent` must be parsed to determine what kind of browser is requesting information from the servlet. Based on this information, the servlet can select an appropriate XSLT stylesheet that supports the particular strengths and weaknesses of the browser in question.

Unfortunately, there are hundreds of variations of `User-Agent`, and browser vendors do not rigorously adhere to any standard format. The common browsers can be identified, however, with a small amount of parsing logic. Table 8-2 lists some of the more common browsers you might encounter.

Table 8-2. Common User-Agent values

User-Agent	**Browser**
Lynx/2.8rel.3 libwww-FM/2.14	Lynx 2.8rel3
Mozilla/4.0 (compatible; MSIE 4.0; Windows NT)	Internet Explorer 4.0
Mozilla/4.0 (compatible; MSIE 5.5; Windows NT 5.0)	Internet Explorer 5.5
Mozilla/4.08 [en] (WinNT; U ;Nav)	Netscape 4.08
Mozilla/5.0 (Windows; U; Windows NT 5.0; en-US; m18) Gecko/20001108 Netscape 6/6.0	Netscape 6
Mozilla/3.0 (compatible; Opera/3.0; Windows 95/ NT4) v3.1	Opera 3.0

The first browser, Lynx, is listed because it is the most common text-only browser. Whenever the User-Agent begins with Lynx, your web application can select an XSLT stylesheet that omits all graphics from the web page.

The three most popular browsers are clearly Microsoft Internet Explorer, Netscape Navigator, and Opera Software's Opera. Of these three browsers, Navigator was available first, and its User-Agent always begins with Mozilla. In the early days of web development, many sites checked for this and only provided fancy versions of their web sites to Netscape browsers.

When Microsoft Internet Explorer became available, it had to begin its User-Agent string with Mozilla to maintain compatibility with many existing web sites. Therefore, you cannot simply check for Mozilla to determine the browser type. As you can see in Table 8-2, Microsoft browsers include the text MSIE followed by the version number, making them easily identifiable.

A more recent entry, Opera, also begins with Mozilla. The User-Agent for Opera browsers always contains Opera/[version];, where [version] is something like 2.0 or 3.0. With these rules in mind, the algorithm for detecting a browser might look something like this:

```
if (begins-with "Lynx") {
  browser is only capable of displaying text
}
else if (contains "MSIE") {
  browser is Internet Explorer
}
else if (contains "Opera") {
  browser is Opera
}
else if (begins-with "Mozilla") {
  browser is Netscape-compatible
}
else {
  browser is unknown
}
```

In a servlet, the following code is used to obtain the value of User-Agent:

```
protected void doGet(HttpServletRequest req, HttpServletResponse res)
        throws IOException, ServletException {
    String userAgent = req.getHeader("User-Agent");
    String xslt = null;
    if (userAgent.startsWith("Lynx")) {
        xslt = "textHomePage.xslt";
    } else {
        xslt = "htmlHomePage.xslt";
    }
    ...
```

For more sophisticated applications, it is desirable to use a utility class that can identify the browser, its version number, and possibly even its platform. Although you can certainly write your own class using basic `java.lang.String` operations, a better option is to use an existing API that someone else has written. The screen capture shown in Figure 8-4 illustrates the output from a simple servlet that identifies various pieces of information about the browser.

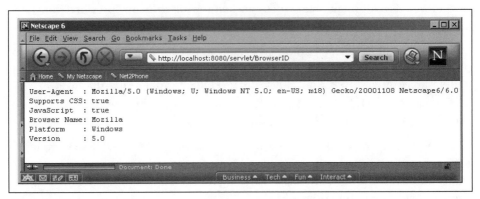

Figure 8-4. Browser detection

This servlet utilizes the `org.apache.turbine.util.BrowserDetector` class, which is part of Apache's Turbine web application framework.* This class actually has only one dependency on anything else in Turbine, so you can either comment out its reference to Turbine's `RunData` class or simply include the Turbine JAR files in your CLASSPATH.† Turbine can be obtained from *http://jakarta.apache.org*. The code for the servlet is shown in Example 8-8.

Example 8-8. BrowserID.java

```
import java.io.*;
import javax.servlet.*;
import javax.servlet.http.*;

import org.apache.turbine.util.BrowserDetector;

public class BrowserID extends HttpServlet {

    protected void doGet(HttpServletRequest req, HttpServletResponse res)
            throws IOException, ServletException {
        BrowserDetector bd = new BrowserDetector(req.getHeader(
            "User-Agent"));
```

---

* This example is based on Version 2.1 of Turbine.

† Be sure to read and follow the Apache licensing agreement if you extract this class from Turbine.

Example 8-8. BrowserID.java (continued)

```
        res.setContentType("text/plain");

        PrintWriter pw = res.getWriter();
        pw.println("User-Agent  : " + bd.getUserAgentString());
        pw.println("Supports CSS: " + bd.isCssOK());
        pw.println("JavaScript  : " + bd.isJavascriptOK());
        pw.println("Browser Name: " + bd.getBrowserName());
        pw.println("Platform    : " + bd.getBrowserPlatform());
        pw.println("Version     : " + bd.getBrowserVersion());
    }
}
```

Servlet Filters

Version 2.3 of the Java servlet specification adds a new feature called *filters*. A filter is an object that intercepts requests to a servlet, JSP, or static file in a web application. The filter has the opportunity to modify the request before passing it along to the underlying resource and can capture and modify the response before sending it back to the client. Since filters can be specified declaratively using the web application deployment descriptor, they can be inserted into existing web applications without altering any of the existing code.

Filter Overview

Servlet filters are useful for many purposes, including logging, user authentication, data compression, encryption, and XSLT transformation. Many filters can be chained together, each performing one specific task. For the purposes of this book, XSLT transformations are the most interesting use of filters. Figure 8-5 illustrates the general filter architecture.

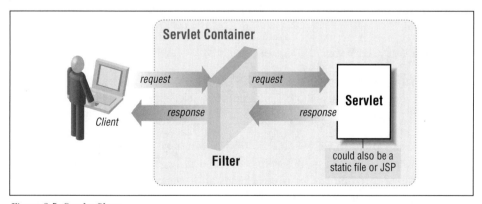

Figure 8-5. Servlet filters

`javax.servlet.Filter` is an interface that all custom filters must implement. It defines the following three methods:

```
void init(FilterConfig config)
void destroy()
void doFilter(ServletRequest req, ServletResponse res, FilterChain chain)
```

The `init()` and `destroy()` methods are virtually identical to the `init()` and `destroy()` methods found in any servlet. `init()` is called when the filter is first loaded, and the `FilterConfig` parameter provides access to the `ServletContext` and to a list of initialization parameters. The code in Example 8-11 demonstrates each of these features. `destroy()`, as expected, is called once when the filter is unloaded. This gives the filter a chance to release resources.

The `doFilter()` method is called whenever a client request is received. The filter participates in a `FilterChain` set up by the servlet container, which allows multiple filters to be attached to one another. If this filter wishes to block the request, it can simply do nothing. Otherwise, it must pass control to the next resource in the chain:

```
chain.doFilter(req, res);
```

Although the next entry in the chain might be another filter, it is probably a servlet or a JSP. Either way, the filter does not have to know this.

Simply calling `doFilter(req, res)` merely passes control to the next entry in the chain. To modify the request or response, the filter must modify the `ServletRequest` and/or `ServletResponse` object. Unfortunately, these are both interfaces, and their implementation classes are specific to each servlet container. Furthermore, the interfaces do not allow values to be modified.

To facilitate this capability, Version 2.3 of the servlet API also adds wrapper classes that allow the request and response to be modified. The following new classes are now available:

- `javax.servlet.ServletRequestWrapper`

- `javax.servlet.ServletResponseWrapper`

- `javax.servlet.http.HttpServletRequestWrapper`

- `javax.servlet.http.HttpServletResponseWrapper`

Each of these classes merely wraps around another request or response, and all methods merely delegate to the wrapped object. To modify behavior, programmers must extend from one of these classes and override one or more methods. Here is how a custom filter might look:

```
public class MyFilter implements Filter {
    public void doFilter (ServletRequest req, ServletResponse res,
```

```
                    FilterChain chain) throws IOException, ServletException {
            // wrap around the original request and response
            MyRequestWrapper reqWrap = new MyRequestWrapper(req);
            MyResponseWrapper resWrap = new MyResponseWrapper(res);

            // pass the wrappers on to the next entry
            chain.doFilter(reqWrap, resWrap);
        }
    }
```

In this case, `MyRequestWrapper` and `MyResponseWrapper` are doing the actual work of modifying the request and response. This works fine for many types of simple filters but is more complex when modifying the response content. To illustrate this point, consider the `getOutputStream()` method in `javax.servlet.ServletResponse`:

```
public interface ServletResponse {
    ServletOutputStream getOutputStream() throws IOException;
    ...additional methods
}
```

Here is how `javax.servlet.ServletResponseWrapper` defines the same method:

```
public class ServletResponseWrapper implements ServletResponse {
    private ServletResponse response;

    public ServletResponseWrapper(ServletResponse response) {
        this.response = response;
    }

    // default implementation delegates to the wrapped response
    public ServletOutputStream getOutputStream() throws IOException {
        return this.response.getOutputStream();
    }

    ...additional methods behave the same way
}
```

To modify the response sent to the client browser, the custom wrapper subclass must override the `getOutputStream()` method as follows:

```
public class MyResponseWrapper extends ServletResponseWrapper {

    public ServletOutputStream getOutputStream() throws IOException {
        // cannot return the ServletOutputStream from the superclass, because
        // that object does not allow us to capture its output. Therefore,
        // return a custom subclass of ServletOutputStream:
        return new MyServletOutputStream();
    }
}
```

`ServletOutputStream` is an abstract class and does not provide methods that allow it to be modified. Instead, programmers must create custom subclasses of `ServletOutputStream` that allow them to capture the output and make any necessary modifications. This is what makes modification of the servlet response so difficult.

XSLT Transformation Filter

The previous discussion introduced a lot of concepts about servlet filters without a lot of details. Next, a complete example for performing XSLT transformations using a filter is presented. Hopefully this will illustrate some of the issues mentioned so far.

The basic goal is to create a servlet filter that performs XSLT transformations. A servlet, JSP, or static XML file will provide the raw XML data. The filter will intercept this XML before it is sent to the client browser and apply an XSLT transformation. The result tree is then sent back to the browser.

Example 8-9 is the first of three classes that comprise this example. This is a custom subclass of `ServletOutputStream` that captures its output in a byte array buffer. The XML data is queued up in this buffer as a first step before it is transformed.

Example 8-9. BufferedServletOutputStream.java

```
package com.oreilly.javaxslt.util;

import java.io.*;
import javax.servlet.*;

/**
 * A custom servlet output stream that stores its data in a buffer,
 * rather than sending it directly to the client.
 *
 * @author Eric M. Burke
 */
public class BufferedServletOutputStream extends ServletOutputStream {
    // the actual buffer
    private ByteArrayOutputStream bos = new ByteArrayOutputStream();

    /**
     * @return the contents of the buffer.
     */
    public byte[] getBuffer() {
        return this.bos.toByteArray();
    }

    /**
     * This method must be defined for custom servlet output streams.
```

Example 8-9. BufferedServletOutputStream.java (continued)

```
    */
   public void write(int data) {
       this.bos.write(data);
   }

   // BufferedHttpResponseWrapper calls this method
   public void reset() {
       this.bos.reset();
   }

   // BufferedHttpResponseWrapper calls this method
   public void setBufferSize(int size) {
       // no way to resize an existing ByteArrayOutputStream
       this.bos = new ByteArrayOutputStream(size);
   }
}
```

The `BufferedServletOutputStream` class extends directly from `Servlet-OutputStream`. The only abstract method in `ServletOutputStream` is `write()`; therefore, our class must define that method. Instead of writing the data to the client, however, our class writes the data to a `ByteArrayOutput-Stream`. The remaining methods, `reset()` and `setBufferSize()`, are required by the class shown in Example 8-10.

Example 8-10. BufferedHttpResponseWrapper.java

```
package com.oreilly.javaxslt.util;

import java.io.*;
import javax.servlet.*;
import javax.servlet.http.*;

/**
 * A custom response wrapper that captures all output in a buffer.
 */
public class BufferedHttpResponseWrapper extends HttpServletResponseWrapper {
    private BufferedServletOutputStream bufferedServletOut
            = new BufferedServletOutputStream();

    private PrintWriter printWriter = null;
    private ServletOutputStream outputStream = null;

    public BufferedHttpResponseWrapper(HttpServletResponse origResponse) {
        super(origResponse);
    }

    public byte[] getBuffer() {
```

Example 8-10. BufferedHttpResponseWrapper.java (continued)

```
        return this.bufferedServletOut.getBuffer();
    }

    public PrintWriter getWriter() throws IOException {
        if (this.outputStream != null) {
            throw new IllegalStateException(
                    "The Servlet API forbids calling getWriter() after"
                    + " getOutputStream() has been called");
        }

        if (this.printWriter == null) {
            this.printWriter = new PrintWriter(this.bufferedServletOut);
        }
        return this.printWriter;
    }

    public ServletOutputStream getOutputStream() throws IOException {
        if (this.printWriter != null) {
            throw new IllegalStateException(
                "The Servlet API forbids calling getOutputStream() after"
                + " getWriter() has been called");
        }

        if (this.outputStream == null) {
            this.outputStream = this.bufferedServletOut;
        }
        return this.outputStream;
    }

    // override methods that deal with the response buffer

    public void flushBuffer() throws IOException {
        if (this.outputStream != null) {
            this.outputStream.flush();
        } else if (this.printWriter != null) {
            this.printWriter.flush();
        }
    }

    public int getBufferSize() {
        return this.bufferedServletOut.getBuffer().length;
    }

    public void reset() {
        this.bufferedServletOut.reset();
    }

    public void resetBuffer() {
```

Example 8-10. BufferedHttpResponseWrapper.java (continued)

```
        this.bufferedServletOut.reset();
    }

    public void setBufferSize(int size) {
        this.bufferedServletOut.setBufferSize(size);
    }
}
```

`BufferedHttpResponseWrapper` is an extension of `HttpServlet-ResponseWrapper` and overrides all methods that affect the `Writer` or `OutputStream` back to the client. This allows us to fully capture and control the response before anything is sent back to the client browser.

According to the servlet API, either `getWriter()` or `getOutputStream()` can be called, but not both. This custom response wrapper class cannot know which is needed, so it must support both. This is definitely an area where the servlet filtering API can make things a lot easier for programmers.

WARNING   Very little of this is currently documented in the servlet specification. Perhaps this will improve by the time this book is published. However, there are currently very few examples that show how to capture and modify the response. Hopefully this will improve as more containers are upgraded to support the servlet 2.3 specification.

The primary class in this example is shown in Example 8-11. This is the actual filter that performs XSLT transformations.

Example 8-11. Servlet filter for XSLT transformations

```
package com.oreilly.javaxslt.util;

import java.io.*;
import javax.servlet.*;
import javax.servlet.http.*;
import javax.xml.transform.*;
import javax.xml.transform.stream.*;

/**
 * A utility class that uses the Servlet 2.3 Filtering API to apply
 * an XSLT stylesheet to a servlet response.
 *
 * @author Eric M. Burke
 */
public class StylesheetFilter implements Filter {
    private FilterConfig filterConfig;
    private String xsltFileName;
```

Example 8-11. Servlet filter for XSLT transformations (continued)

```
    /**
     * This method is called once when the filter is first loaded.
     */
    public void init(FilterConfig filterConfig) throws ServletException {
        this.filterConfig = filterConfig;

        // xsltPath should be something like "/WEB-INF/xslt/a.xslt"
        String xsltPath = filterConfig.getInitParameter("xsltPath");
        if (xsltPath == null) {
            throw new UnavailableException(
                    "xsltPath is a required parameter. Please "
                    + "check the deployment descriptor.");
        }

        // convert the context-relative path to a physical path name
        this.xsltFileName = filterConfig.getServletContext()
                .getRealPath(xsltPath);

        // verify that the file exists
        if (this.xsltFileName == null ||
                !new File(this.xsltFileName).exists()) {
            throw new UnavailableException(
                    "Unable to locate stylesheet: " + this.xsltFileName, 30);
        }
    }


    public void doFilter (ServletRequest req, ServletResponse res,
            FilterChain chain) throws IOException, ServletException {

        if (!(res instanceof HttpServletResponse)) {
            throw new ServletException("This filter only supports HTTP");
        }


        BufferedHttpResponseWrapper responseWrapper =
                new BufferedHttpResponseWrapper((HttpServletResponse) res);
        chain.doFilter(req, responseWrapper);

        // Tomcat 4.0 reuses instances of its HttpServletResponse
        // implementation class in some scenarios. For instance, hitting
        // reload() repeatedly on a web browser will cause this to happen.
        // Unfortunately, when this occurs, output is never written to the
        // BufferedHttpResponseWrapper's OutputStream. This means that the
        // XML output array is empty when this happens. The following
        // code is a workaround:
        byte[] origXML = responseWrapper.getBuffer();
        if (origXML == null || origXML.length == 0) {
            // just let Tomcat deliver its cached data back to the client
            chain.doFilter(req, res);
```

Example 8-11. Servlet filter for XSLT transformations (continued)

```
            return;
        }

        try {
            // do the XSLT transformation
            Transformer trans = StylesheetCache.newTransformer(
                    this.xsltFileName);

            ByteArrayInputStream origXMLIn = new ByteArrayInputStream(origXML);
            Source xmlSource = new StreamSource(origXMLIn);

            ByteArrayOutputStream resultBuf = new ByteArrayOutputStream();
            trans.transform(xmlSource, new StreamResult(resultBuf));

            res.setContentLength(resultBuf.size());
            res.setContentType("text/html");
            res.getOutputStream().write(resultBuf.toByteArray());
            res.flushBuffer();
        } catch (TransformerException te) {
            throw new ServletException(te);
        }
    }

    /**
     * The counterpart to the init() method.
     */
    public void destroy() {
        this.filterConfig = null;
    }
}
```

This filter requires the deployment descriptor to provide the name of the XSLT stylesheet as an initialization parameter. The following line of code retrieves the parameter:

```
String xsltPath = filterConfig.getInitParameter("xsltPath");
```

By passing the stylesheet as a parameter, the filter can be configured to work with any XSLT. Since the filter can be applied to a servlet, JSP, or static file, the XML data is also completely configurable.

The doFilter() method illustrates another weakness of the current filtering API:

```
if (!(res instanceof HttpServletResponse)) {
    throw new ServletException("This filter only supports HTTP");
}
```

Since there is no HTTP-specific filter interface, custom filters must use instanceof and downcasts to ensure that only HTTP requests are filtered.

Next, the filter creates the buffered response wrapper and delegates to the next entry in the chain:

```
BufferedHttpResponseWrapper responseWrapper =
        new BufferedHttpResponseWrapper((HttpServletResponse) res);
chain.doFilter(req, responseWrapper);
```

This effectively captures the XML output from the chain, making the XSLT transformation possible. Before doing the transformation, however, one "hack" is required to work with Tomcat 4.0:

```
byte[] origXML = responseWrapper.getBuffer();
if (origXML == null || origXML.length == 0) {
    // just let Tomcat deliver its cached data back to the client
    chain.doFilter(req, res);
    return;
}
```

The complete explanation is captured in the source code comments in Example 8-11. Basically, Tomcat seems to cache its response when the user tries to reload the same static file consecutive times. Without this check, the code fails because the `origXML` byte array is empty.*

Finally, the filter uses JAXP to perform the XSLT transformation, sending the result tree to the original servlet response.

The deployment descriptor is listed in Example 8-12.

Example 8-12. Filter deployment descriptor

```
<?xml version="1.0" encoding="ISO-8859-1"?>
<!DOCTYPE web-app PUBLIC
   "-//Sun Microsystems, Inc.//DTD Web Application 2.3//EN"
   "http://java.sun.com/j2ee/dtds/web-app_2.3.dtd">

<web-app>
  <filter>
    <filter-name>xsltFilter</filter-name>
    <filter-class>com.oreilly.javaxslt.util.StylesheetFilter</filter-class>
    <init-param>
      <param-name>xsltPath</param-name>
      <param-value>/WEB-INF/xslt/templatePage.xslt</param-value>
    </init-param>
  </filter>

  <filter-mapping>
    <filter-name>xsltFilter</filter-name>
    <url-pattern>/home.xml</url-pattern>
```

---

* This was quite difficult to figure out. Because the servlet specification is not specific on this topic, different servlet containers may behave slightly differently.

Example 8-12. Filter deployment descriptor (continued)

```
    </filter-mapping>
    <filter-mapping>
      <filter-name>xsltFilter</filter-name>
      <url-pattern>/company.xml</url-pattern>
    </filter-mapping>
    <filter-mapping>
      <filter-name>xsltFilter</filter-name>
      <url-pattern>/jobs.xml</url-pattern>
    </filter-mapping>
    <filter-mapping>
      <filter-name>xsltFilter</filter-name>
      <url-pattern>/products.xml</url-pattern>
    </filter-mapping>

</web-app>
```

As the first few lines of the deployment descriptor indicate, filters require Version 2.3 of the web application DTD.

The filter initialization parameter is specified next, inside of the `<filter>` element. This provides the name of the XSLT stylesheet for this particular filter instance. It is also possible to specify multiple `<filter>` elements using the same filter class but different filter names. This allows the same web application to utilize a single filter with many different configurations.

Finally, the deployment descriptor lists several explicit mappings for this filter. In the examples shown, the filter is applied to static XML files. It can just as easily be applied to a servlet or JSP, however.

Closing Thoughts on Filters

Using filters for XSLT transformations is an interesting concept, primarily because it allows different stylesheets to be applied to XML from many different sources using the web application deployment descriptor. To use a different stylesheet, merely change the deployment descriptor. One interesting approach is using JSP to generate pure XML, then applying a filter to transform that XML into XHTML for the client.

Filters do suffer drawbacks and probably are not the best solution for most applications. First and foremost, the filter API is available only in Version 2.3 of the servlet specification; many existing servlet containers do not support filters at all. In the case of XSLT transformations, a custom `ServletOutputStream` must be written to capture the response output, and downcasts are required because there is no HTTP-specific filter class. Because some servlet containers may cache the response for performance reasons, workarounds must be implemented to function reliably.

Finally, this approach is slower than others. The XML must be converted into text and buffered in memory before the XSLT transformation can be performed, which is generally slower than sending SAX events or a DOM tree directly to the XSLT processor. Generating XML and performing the XSLT transformation in a servlet can avoid the extra conversions to and from text that filters require.

XSLT as a Code Generator

For performance reasons, EJB components typically return *dependent objects* rather than many individual fields. These are implemented as read-only classes that encapsulate a group of related fields. Borrowing an example from *Enterprise JavaBeans* by Richard Monson-Haefel (O'Reilly), Example 8-13 shows a typical dependent object.

Example 8-13. Address.java

```java
public class Address implements java.io.Serializable {

    private String street;
    private String city;
    private String state;
    private String zip;

    /**
     * Construct a new dependent object instance.
     */
    public Address(String street, String city, String state, String zip) {
        this.street = street;
        this.city = city;
        this.state = state;
        this.zip = zip;

    }

    public String getStreet() {
        return this.street;
    }

    public String getCity() {
        return this.city;
    }

    public String getState() {
        return this.state;
```

Example 8-13. Address.java (continued)

```
    }

    public String getZip() {
        return this.zip;
    }
}
```

Now, rather than containing numerous fine-grained methods, an entity bean can provide a single method to retrieve an instance of `Address`. This reduces load on the network and database and makes the code somewhat easier to understand. As you can see, the `Address` class is very straightforward. It has a constructor that initializes all fields and a series of get methods.

Although `Address` is small, some dependent objects may have dozens of fields. These are tedious to write at best, resulting in a typing exercise rather than programming creativity. XSLT can help by acting as a simple code generator, minimizing the tedious part of the programmer's job. *AddressDO.xml*, shown in Example 8-14, contains the data that will feed into our code generator.

Example 8-14. AddressDO.xml

```
<?xml version="1.0" encoding="UTF-8"?>
<dependentObject class="Address">
    <property name="street" type="String" getter="getStreet"/>
    <property name="city" type="String" getter="getCity"/>
    <property name="state" type="String" getter="getState"/>
    <property name="zip" type="String" getter="getZip"/>
</dependentObject>
```

The XML data is obviously much shorter than the generated code, and the difference is magnified for larger dependent objects with many fields. The `<dependentObject>` element contains a list of `<property>` elements, each of which defines the field name, datatype, and get method name. Now that the data is captured in a well-defined XML format, a DTD or Schema can be used to perform validation. A really ambitious programmer might want to create a simple GUI front-end that allows graphical editing of the `<dependentObject>` structure.

An XSLT stylesheet performs the actual code generation. The output method should be set to `text`, and particular attention must be given to whitespace. With HTML or XHTML output, whitespace is largely irrelevant. Since browsers collapse multiple spaces and linefeeds into a single space, the XSLT stylesheet can be indented and spaced however you like. But with a code generator, formatting is a much higher priority. This can lead to stylesheets that are much harder to read, which is the main drawback of using XSLT as a code generator. Example 8-15 shows the dependent object code generator stylesheet.

Example 8-15. dependentObject.xslt

```
<?xml version="1.0" encoding="UTF-8"?>

<xsl:stylesheet version="1.0"
        xmlns:xsl="http://www.w3.org/1999/XSL/Transform">
    <xsl:output method="text"/>
    <xsl:variable name="className" select="/dependentObject/@class"/>
    <!--
    **********************************************************************
    ** Generate the class skeleton. Other templates will generate
    ** portions of the class.
    ********************************************************************-->
    <xsl:template match="/dependentObject">public class <xsl:value-of
            select="$className"/>
        <xsl:text> implements java.io.Serializable {
</xsl:text>
    <xsl:apply-templates select="property" mode="generateField"/>
    <xsl:text>

    /**
     * Construct a new dependent object instance.
     */
    public </xsl:text>
            <xsl:value-of select="$className"/>(<xsl:apply-templates
                select="property" mode="generateConstructorParam"/>
            <xsl:text>) {
</xsl:text>
            <xsl:apply-templates select="property"
                mode="generateInitializers"/>
    }


    <xsl:apply-templates select="property" mode="generateGetter"/>
}
    </xsl:template>

    <!--
    **********************************************************************
    ** Generate a private field declaration.
    ********************************************************************-->
    <xsl:template match="property" mode="generateField">
    private <xsl:value-of select="@type"/>
    <xsl:text> </xsl:text>
    <xsl:value-of select="@name"/>;</xsl:template>

    <!--
    **********************************************************************
    ** Generate a "get" method for a property.
    ********************************************************************-->
    <xsl:template match="property" mode="generateGetter">
```

Example 8-15. dependentObject.xslt (continued)

```
    public <xsl:value-of select="@type"/>
    <xsl:text> </xsl:text>
    <xsl:value-of select="@getter"/>() {
        return this.<xsl:value-of select="@name"/>;
    }
    </xsl:template>


    <!--
    ******************************************************************
    ** Generate one of the constructor parameters.
    ******************************************************************-->
    <xsl:template match="property" mode="generateConstructorParam">
        <xsl:text xml:space="preserve"/>
        <xsl:value-of select="@type"/>
        <xsl:text> </xsl:text>
        <xsl:value-of select="@name"/>
        <xsl:if test="position() != last()">, </xsl:if>
    </xsl:template>


    <!--
    ******************************************************************
    ** Generate the initialization code inside of the constructor.
    ******************************************************************-->
    <xsl:template match="property" mode="generateInitializers">
        <xsl:text xml:space="preserve">        this.</xsl:text>
        <xsl:value-of select="@name"/>
        <xsl:text> = </xsl:text>
        <xsl:value-of select="@name"/>;
    </xsl:template>
</xsl:stylesheet>
```

This stylesheet produces the code for `Address.java`. It starts by setting the output method to `text` and creating a variable for the class name. The variable allows us to avoid typing `<xsl:value-of  select="/dependentObject/@class"/>` whenever the class name is needed.

The `<xsl:text>` element is used frequently in code-generator stylesheets because it allows for more control over whitespace. In several places, this element is used to introduce linefeeds in the output. For instance:

```
        <xsl:text> implements java.io.Serializable {
    </xsl:text>
```

Because the closing tag is on the next line, the linefeed character will be preserved faithfully. `<xsl:text>` is also used to introduce individual spaces:

```
    private <xsl:value-of select="@type"/>
    <xsl:text> </xsl:text>
    <xsl:value-of select="@name"/>;</xsl:template>
```

By default, XSLT processors ignore whitespace between two XSLT elements unless some nonwhitespace characters are also present. The `private` text shown just before `<xsl:value-of  select="@type"/>`, for example, contains non-whitespace text followed by a space. In this case, the space after the word `private` will be preserved. But the space between the two `<xsl:value-of>` elements will be ignored unless it is explicitly preserved with `<xsl:text> </xsl:text>`.

Getting everything to indent and line up is challenging but is not an insurmountable problem. It usually boils down to a lot of XSLT tweaking until everything looks just right. Using a code beautifier is another option. Products such as JIndent (*http://www.jindent.com*) can automatically clean up Java code by wrapping long lines, inserting spaces, and putting braces at the correct locations. If you are fortunate enough to have access to a tool like this, you can ignore most whitespace issues in the XSLT and rely on JIndent to fix formatting problems later on.

Internationalization with XSLT

In this section, we explore the key techniques for internationalization (i18n) using XSLT. Although both Java and XSLT offer excellent support for i18n, pulling everything together into a working application is quite challenging. Hopefully this material will help to minimize some of the common obstacles.

XSLT Stylesheet Design

In its simplest form, i18n is accomplished by providing a separate XSLT stylesheet for each supported language. While this is easy to visualize, it results in far too much duplication of effort. This is because XSLT stylesheets typically contain some degree of programming logic in addition to pure display information. To illustrate this point, *directory.xml* is presented in Example 8-16. This is a very basic XML datafile that will be transformed using either English or Spanish XSLT stylesheets.

Example 8-16. directory.xml

```
<?xml version="1.0" encoding="UTF-8"?>
<directory>
  <employee category="manager">
    <name>Joe Smith</name>
    <phone>4-0192</phone>
  </employee>
  <employee category="programmer">
    <name>Sally Jones</name>
    <phone>4-2831</phone>
  </employee>
  <employee category="programmer">
```

Example 8-16. directory.xml (continued)

```
    <name>Roger Clark</name>
    <phone>4-3345</phone>
  </employee>
</directory>
```

The screen shot shown in Figure 8-6 shows how an XSLT stylesheet transforms this XML into HTML.

And finally, Example 8-17 lists the XSLT stylesheet that produces this output.

Figure 8-6. English XSLT output

Example 8-17. directory_basic.xslt

```
<?xml version="1.0" encoding="UTF-8"?>
<xsl:stylesheet version="1.0" xmlns:xsl="http://www.w3.org/1999/XSL/Transform">
  <xsl:output method="html" encoding="UTF-8"/>
  <xsl:template match="/">
    <html>
      <head>
        <title>Employee Directory</title>
      </head>
      <body>
        <h1>Employee Directory</h1>
        <table cellpadding="4" cellspacing="0" border="1">
          <tr>
            <th>Name</th>
            <th>Category</th>
            <th>Phone</th>
```

Example 8-17. directory_basic.xslt (continued)

```
            </tr>
            <xsl:for-each select="directory/employee">
              <tr>
                <td>
                  <xsl:value-of select="name"/>
                </td>
                <td>
                  <xsl:choose>
                    <xsl:when test="@category='manager'">
                      <xsl:text>Manager</xsl:text>
                    </xsl:when>
                    <xsl:when test="@category='programmer'">
                      <xsl:text>Programmer</xsl:text>
                    </xsl:when>
                    <xsl:otherwise>
                      <xsl:text>Other</xsl:text>
                    </xsl:otherwise>
                  </xsl:choose>
                </td>
                <td>
                  <xsl:value-of select="phone"/>
                </td>
              </tr>
            </xsl:for-each>
          </table>
        </body>
      </html>
    </xsl:template>
</xsl:stylesheet>
```

In this stylesheet, all *locale-specific* content is highlighted. This is information that must be changed to support a different language. As you can see, only a small portion of the XSLT is specific to the English language and is embedded directly within the stylesheet logic. The entire stylesheet must be rewritten to support another language.

Fortunately, there is an easy solution to this problem. XSLT stylesheets can import other stylesheets; templates and variables in the importing stylesheet take precedence over conflicting items in the imported stylesheet. By isolating locale-specific content, we can use `<xsl:import>` to support multiple languages while reusing all of the stylesheet logic. Example 8-18 shows a revised version of our XSLT stylesheet.

Example 8-18. directory_en.xslt

```
<?xml version="1.0" encoding="UTF-8"?>
<xsl:stylesheet version="1.0" xmlns:xsl="http://www.w3.org/1999/XSL/Transform">
  <xsl:output method="html" encoding="UTF-8"/>

  <!-- Isolate locale-specific content -->
  <xsl:variable name="lang.pageTitle" select="'Employee Directory'"/>
  <xsl:variable name="lang.nameHeading" select="'Name'"/>
  <xsl:variable name="lang.categoryHeading" select="'Category'"/>
  <xsl:variable name="lang.phoneHeading" select="'Phone'"/>
  <xsl:variable name="lang.manager" select="'Manager'"/>
  <xsl:variable name="lang.programmer" select="'Programmer'"/>
  <xsl:variable name="lang.other" select="'Other'"/>

  <xsl:template match="/">
    <html>
      <head>
        <title><xsl:value-of select="$lang.pageTitle"/></title>
      </head>
      <body>
        <h1><xsl:value-of select="$lang.pageTitle"/></h1>
        <table cellpadding="4" cellspacing="0" border="1">
          <tr>
            <th><xsl:value-of select="$lang.nameHeading"/></th>
            <th><xsl:value-of select="$lang.categoryHeading"/></th>
            <th><xsl:value-of select="$lang.phoneHeading"/></th>
          </tr>
          <xsl:for-each select="directory/employee">
            <tr>
              <td>
                <xsl:value-of select="name"/>
              </td>
              <td>
                <xsl:choose>
                  <xsl:when test="@category='manager'">
                    <xsl:value-of select="$lang.manager"/>
                  </xsl:when>
                  <xsl:when test="@category='programmer'">
                    <xsl:value-of select="$lang.programmer"/>
                  </xsl:when>
                  <xsl:otherwise>
                    <xsl:value-of select="$lang.other"/>
                  </xsl:otherwise>
                </xsl:choose>
              </td>
              <td>
                <xsl:value-of select="phone"/>
              </td>
            </tr>
```

Example 8-18. directory_en.xslt (continued)

```
        </xsl:for-each>
      </table>
    </body>
  </html>
  </xsl:template>
</xsl:stylesheet>
```

The XSLT stylesheet is now much more amenable to i18n. All locale-specific content is declared as a series of variables. Therefore, importing stylesheets can override them. The `lang.` naming convention makes the stylesheet more maintainable; it is not a requirement or part of the XSLT specification. Other than isolating this content, the remainder of the stylesheet is exactly the same as it was before.

The Spanish version of the stylesheet is shown in Example 8-19.

Example 8-19. directory_es.xslt

```
<?xml version="1.0" encoding="UTF-8"?>
<xsl:stylesheet version="1.0" xmlns:xsl="http://www.w3.org/1999/XSL/Transform">
  <xsl:import href="directory_en.xslt"/>
  <xsl:output method="html" encoding="UTF-8"/>

  <!-- Isolate locale-specific content -->
  <xsl:variable name="lang.pageTitle" select="'Empleado guía telefónica'"/>
  <xsl:variable name="lang.nameHeading" select="'Nombre'"/>
  <xsl:variable name="lang.categoryHeading" select="'Categoría'"/>
  <xsl:variable name="lang.phoneHeading" select="'Teléfono'"/>
  <xsl:variable name="lang.manager" select="'Gerente'"/>
  <xsl:variable name="lang.programmer" select="'Programador'"/>
  <xsl:variable name="lang.other" select="'Otro'"/>

</xsl:stylesheet>
```

The Spanish stylesheet is much shorter because it merely overrides each of the locale-specific variables. The `<xsl:import>` is key:

```
<xsl:import href="directory_en.xslt"/>
```

Because of XSLT conflict-resolution rules, the variables defined in *directory_es.xslt* take precedence over those defined in *directory_en.xslt*. The same logic can be applied to templates, as well. This is useful in scenarios where the importing stylesheet needs to change behavior in addition to simply defining text translations.

The following line is optional:

```
<xsl:output method="html" encoding="UTF-8"/>
```

In this example, the output method and encoding are identical to the English version of the stylesheet, so this line has no effect. However, the importing stylesheet may specify a different output method and encoding if desired.

To perform the Spanish transformation using Xalan, issue the following command:

```
$ java org.apache.xalan.xslt.Process -IN directory.xml -XSL directory_es.xslt
```

Figure 8-7 shows the result of this transformation when displayed in a web browser.

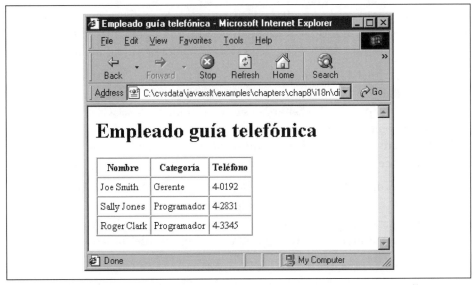

Figure 8-7. Spanish output

TIP	In the i18n example stylesheets presented in this chapter, common functionality is placed into one stylesheet. Importing stylesheets then replace locale-specific text. This same technique can be applied to any stylesheet and is particularly important when writing custom XSLT for a specific browser. Most of your code should be portable across a variety of browsers and should be placed into reusable stylesheets. The parts that change should be placed into browser-specific stylesheets that import the common stylesheets.

Encodings

A *character encoding* is a numeric representation of a particular character.* The US-ASCII encoding for the A character, for example, is 65. When computers read

---

* Refer to *Java Internationalization* by Andy Deitsch and David Czarnecki (O'Reilly) for more detailed information on character encodings.

and write files using US-ASCII encoding, each character is stored as one byte of data. Of this byte, only seven bits are actually used to represent characters. The first (most significant) bit must always be 0. Therefore, US-ASCII can represent only 128 different characters. Of course, this presents a problem for languages that require more than 128 characters. For these languages, another character encoding must be used.

The most comprehensive character encoding is called ISO/IEC 10646. This is also known as the Universal Character Set (UCS) and allocates a 32-bit number for each character. Although this allows UCS to uniquely identify every character in every language, it is not directly compatible with most computer software. Also, using 32 bits to represent each character results in a lot of wasted memory.

Unicode is the official implementation of ISO/IEC 10646 and currently uses 16-bit characters. You can learn more about Unicode at *http://www.unicode.org*. UCS Transformation Formats (UTFs) are designed to support the UCS encoding while maintaining compatibility with existing computer software and encodings. UTF-8 and UTF-16 are the most common transformation formats, and all XML parsers and XSLT processors are required to support both.

If you deal mostly with English text, UTF-8 is the most efficient and easiest to use. Because the first 128 UTF-8 characters are the same as the US-ASCII characters, existing applications can utilize many UTF-8 files transparently. When additional characters are required, however, UTF-8 encoding will use up to three bytes per character.

UTF-16 is more efficient than UTF-8 for Chinese, Japanese, and Korean (CJK) ideographs. When using UTF-16, each character requires two bytes, while many will require three bytes under UTF-8 encoding. Either UTF-8 or UTF-16 should work. However, it is wise to test actual transformations with both encodings to determine which results in the smallest file for your particular data. On a pragmatic note, many applications and operating systems, particularly Unix and Linux variants, offer better support for UTF-8 encoding.

As nearly every XSLT example in this book has shown, the <xsl:output> element determines the encoding of the XSLT result tree:

```
<xsl:output method="html" encoding="UTF-16"/>
```

If this element is missing from the stylesheet, the XSLT processor is supposed to default to either UTF-8 or UTF-16 encoding.*

---

* The XSLT specification does not say how the processor is supposed to select between UTF-8 and UTF-16.

Creating the XML and XSLT

The XML input data, XSLT stylesheet, and result tree do not have to use the same character encodings or language. For example, an XSLT stylesheet may be encoded in UTF-16, but may specify UTF-8 as its output method:

```
<?xml version="1.0" encoding="UTF-16"?>
<xsl:stylesheet version="1.0" xmlns:xsl="http://www.w3.org/1999/XSL/Transform">
  <xsl:output method="html" encoding="UTF-8"/>
  ...
```

Even though the first line specifies UTF-16, it is important that the text editor used to create this stylesheet actually uses UTF-16 encoding when saving the file. Otherwise, tools such as XML Spy (*http://www.xmlspy.com*) may report errors as shown in Figure 8-8.

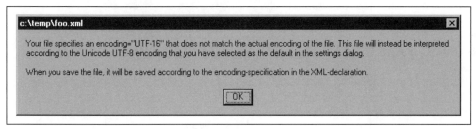

Figure 8-8. Error dialog

To further complicate matters, there are actually two variants of UTF-16. In UTF-16 Little Endian (UTF-16LE) encoding, the low byte of each two-byte character precedes the high byte. As expected, the high byte precedes the low byte in UTF-16 Big Endian (UTF-16BE) encoding. Fortunately, XML parsers can determine the encoding of a file by looking for a byte order mark. In UTF-16LE, the first byte of the file should start with 0xFFFE. In UTF-16BE files, the byte order mark is 0xFEFF.

For the upcoming Chinese example, the NJStar Chinese word processor (*http://www.njstar.com*) was used to input the Chinese characters. This is an example of an editor that has the ability to input ideographs and store files in various encodings. The Windows NT version of Notepad can save files in Unicode (UTF-16LE) format, and the Windows 2000 version of Notepad adds support for UTF-8 and UTF-16BE.

If all else fails, encoded text files can be created with Java using the `java.io.OutputStreamWriter` class as follows:

```
FileOutputStream fos = new FileOutputStream("myFile.xml");
// the OutputStreamWriter specifies the encoding of the file
PrintWriter pw = new PrintWriter(new OutputStreamWriter(fos, "UTF-16"));
```

```
...write to pw just like any other PrintWriter
pw.close();
```

Putting It All Together

Getting all of the pieces to work together is often the trickiest aspect of i18n. To demonstrate the concepts, we will now look at XML datafiles, XSLT stylesheets, and a servlet that work together to support any combination of English, Chinese, and Spanish. A basic HTML form makes it possible for users to select which XML file and XSLT stylesheet will be used to perform a transformation. The screen shot in Figure 8-9 shows what this web page looks like.

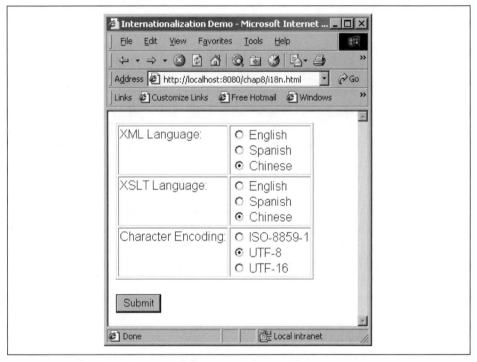

Figure 8-9. XML and XSLT language selection

As you can see, there are three versions of the XML data, one for each language. Other than the language, the three files are identical. There are also three versions of the XSLT stylesheet, and the user can select any combination of XML and XSLT language. The character encoding for the resulting transformation is also configurable. UTF-8 and UTF-16 are compatible with Unicode and can display the Spanish and Chinese characters directly. ISO-8859-1, however, can display only extended character sets using entities such as 文.

In this example, users explicitly specify their language preference. It is also possible to write a servlet that uses the `Accept-Language` HTTP header, which may contain a list of preferred languages:

    en, es, ja

From this list, the application can attempt to select the appropriate language and character encoding without prompting the user. Chapter 13 of *Java Servlet Programming, Second Edition* by Jason Hunter (O'Reilly) presents a detailed discussion of this technique along with a class called `LocaleNegotiator` that maps more than 30 language codes to their appropriate character encodings.

In Figure 8-10, the results of three different transformations are displayed. In the first window, a Chinese XSLT stylesheet is applied to a Chinese XML datafile. In the second window, the English version of the XSLT stylesheet is applied to the Spanish XML data. Finally, the Spanish XSLT stylesheet is applied to the Chinese XML data.

Figure 8-10. Several language combinations

The character encoding is generally transparent to the user. Switching to a different encoding makes no difference to the output displayed in Figure 8-10. However, it does make a difference when the page source is viewed. For example, when the output is UTF-8, the actual Chinese or Spanish characters are displayed in the source of the HTML page. When using ISO-8859-A, however, the source code looks something like this:

```
<html>
<head>
<META http-equiv="Content-Type" content="text/html; charset=ISO-8859-1">
<title>&#20013;&#25991;XSLT</title>
</head>
<body>
<h1>&#20013;&#25991;XSLT</h1>
...remainder of page omitted
```

As you can see, the Chinese characters are replaced by their corresponding character entities, such as `&#20013;`. The XSLT processor creates these entities automatically when the output encoding type cannot display the characters directly.

Browser Fonts

Recent versions of any major web browser can display UTF-8 and UTF-16 encoded characters without problems. Font configuration is the primary concern. If you are using Internet Explorer, be sure to select the View → Encoding → Auto Select menu option. Under Netscape 6, the View → Character Coding → Auto Detect menu option is comparable. If you run the examples and see question marks and garbled text, this is a good indication that the proper fonts are not installed on your system.

For the Chinese examples shown in this chapter, the Windows 2000 SimHei and SimSun fonts were installed. These and many other fonts are included with Windows 2000 but are not automatically installed unless the appropriate language settings are selected under the regional options window. This window can be found in the Windows 2000 Control Panel. A good source for font information on other versions of Windows is Fontboard at *http://www.geocities. com/fontboard.*

Sun Solaris users should start at the Sun Global Application Developer Corner web site at *http://www.sun.com/developer/gadc.* This offers information on internationalization support in the latest versions of the Solaris operating system. For other versions of Unix or Linux, a good starting point is the Netscape 6 Help menu. The International Users option brings up a web page that provides numerous sources of fonts for various versions of Unix and Linux on which Netscape runs.

XML data

Each of the three XML datafiles used by this example follows the format shown in Example 8-20. As you can see, the XML data merely lists translations from English to another language. All three files follow the same naming convention: *numbers_english.xml, numbers_spanish.xml,* and *numbers_chinese.xml.*

Example 8-20. numbers_spanish.xml

```
<?xml version="1.0" encoding="UTF-8"?>
<numbers>
  <language>Español (Spanish)</language>
  <number english="one">uno</number>
  <number english="two">dos</number>
  <number english="three">tres</number>
  <number english="four">cuatro</number>
  <number english="five">cinco</number>
  <number english="six">seis</number>
  <number english="seven">siete</number>
  <number english="eight">ocho</number>
  <number english="nine">nueve</number>
  <number english="ten">diez</number>
</numbers>
```

XSLT stylesheets

The *numbers_english.xslt* stylesheet is shown in Example 8-21 and follows the same pattern that was introduced earlier in this chapter. Specifically, it isolates locale-specific data as a series of variables.

Example 8-21. numbers_english.xslt

```
<?xml version="1.0" encoding="UTF-8"?>
<xsl:stylesheet version="1.0" xmlns:xsl="http://www.w3.org/1999/XSL/Transform">
  <xsl:output method="html" encoding="UTF-8"/>

  <xsl:variable name="lang.pageTitle">XSLT in English</xsl:variable>
  <xsl:variable name="lang.tableCaption">
    Here is a table of numbers:
  </xsl:variable>
  <xsl:variable name="lang.englishHeading">English</xsl:variable>

  <xsl:template match="/">
    <html>
      <head>
        <title><xsl:value-of select="$lang.pageTitle"/></title>
      </head>
      <body>
        <xsl:apply-templates select="numbers"/>
      </body>
    </html>
  </xsl:template>
  <xsl:template match="numbers">
```

Example 8-21. numbers_english.xslt (continued)

```
    <h1><xsl:value-of select="$lang.pageTitle"/></h1>
    <xsl:value-of select="$lang.tableCaption"/>
    <table border="1">
      <tr>
        <th><xsl:value-of select="$lang.englishHeading"/></th>
        <th>
          <xsl:value-of select="language"/>
        </th>
      </tr>
      <xsl:apply-templates select="number"/>
    </table>
  </xsl:template>
  <xsl:template match="number">
    <tr>
      <td>
        <xsl:value-of select="@english"/>
      </td>
      <td>
        <xsl:value-of select="."/>
      </td>
    </tr>
  </xsl:template>
</xsl:stylesheet>
```

As you can see, the default output encoding of this stylesheet is UTF-8. This can (and will) be overridden by the servlet, however. The Spanish stylesheet, *numbers_spanish.xslt*, is shown in Example 8-22.

Example 8-22. numbers_spanish.xslt

```
<?xml version="1.0" encoding="UTF-8"?>
<xsl:stylesheet version="1.0" xmlns:xsl="http://www.w3.org/1999/XSL/Transform">
  <xsl:import href="numbers_english.xslt"/>

  <xsl:variable name="lang.pageTitle">XSLT en Español</xsl:variable>
  <xsl:variable name="lang.tableCaption">
    Aquí está un vector de números:
  </xsl:variable>
  <xsl:variable name="lang.englishHeading">Inglés</xsl:variable>

</xsl:stylesheet>
```

The Chinese stylesheet, *numbers_chinese.xslt*, is not listed here because it is structured exactly like the Spanish stylesheet. In both cases, *numbers_english.xslt* is imported, and the three variables are overridden with language-specific text.

Web page and servlet

The user begins with the web page that was shown in Figure 8-9. The HTML source for this page is listed in Example 8-23. The language and encoding selections are posted to a servlet when the user clicks on the Submit button.

Example 8-23. i18n.html

```html
<html>
<head>
<title>Internationalization Demo</title>
</head>
<body>
<form method="post" action="/chap8/languageDemo">
  <table border="1">
    <tr valign="top">
    <td>XML Language:</td>
    <td>
      <input type="radio" name="xmlLanguage"
             checked="checked" value="english"> English<br />
      <input type="radio" name="xmlLanguage" value="spanish"> Spanish<br />
      <input type="radio" name="xmlLanguage" value="chinese"> Chinese
    </td>
  </tr>

  <tr valign="top">
    <td>XSLT Language:</td>
    <td>
      <input type="radio" name="xsltLanguage"
             checked="checked" value="english"> English<br />
      <input type="radio" name="xsltLanguage" value="spanish"> Spanish<br />
      <input type="radio" name="xsltLanguage" value="chinese"> Chinese
    </td>
  </tr>

  <tr valign="top">
    <td>Character Encoding:</td>
    <td>
      <input type="radio" name="charEnc" value="ISO-8859-1"> ISO-8859-1<br />
      <input type="radio" name="charEnc" value="UTF-8"
             checked="checked"> UTF-8<br />
      <input type="radio" name="charEnc" value="UTF-16"> UTF-16<br />
    </td>
  </tr>
  </table>

  <p>
  <input type="submit" name="submitBtn" value="Submit">
```

Example 8-23. i18n.html (continued)

```
  </p>
</form>
</body>
</html>
```

The servlet, *LanguageDemo.java*, is shown in Example 8-24. This servlet accepts input from the *i18n.html* web page and then applies the XSLT transformation.

Example 8-24. LanguageDemo.java servlet

```java
package chap8;

import java.io.*;
import javax.servlet.*;
import javax.servlet.http.*;
import javax.xml.transform.*;
import javax.xml.transform.stream.*;

/**
 * Allows any combination of English, Spanish, and Chinese XML
 * and XSLT.
 */
public class LanguageDemo extends HttpServlet {

    public void doPost(HttpServletRequest req, HttpServletResponse res)
            throws ServletException, IOException {
        ServletContext ctx = getServletContext();

        // these are all required parameters from the HTML form
        String xmlLang = req.getParameter("xmlLanguage");
        String xsltLang = req.getParameter("xsltLanguage");
        String charEnc = req.getParameter("charEnc");

        // convert to system-dependent path names
        String xmlFileName = ctx.getRealPath(
                "/WEB-INF/xml/numbers_" + xmlLang + ".xml");
        String xsltFileName = ctx.getRealPath(
                "/WEB-INF/xslt/numbers_" + xsltLang + ".xslt");

        // do this BEFORE calling HttpServletResponse.getWriter()
        res.setContentType("text/html; charset=" + charEnc);

        try {
            Source xmlSource = new StreamSource(new File(xmlFileName));
            Source xsltSource = new StreamSource(new File(xsltFileName));

            TransformerFactory transFact = TransformerFactory.newInstance();
```

Example 8-24. LanguageDemo.java servlet (continued)

```
        Transformer trans = transFact.newTransformer(xsltSource);

        trans.setOutputProperty(OutputKeys.ENCODING, charEnc);

        // note: res.getWriter() will use the encoding type that was
        //        specified earlier in the call to res.setContentType()
        trans.transform(xmlSource, new StreamResult(res.getWriter()));

    } catch (TransformerConfigurationException tce) {
        throw new ServletException(tce);
    } catch (TransformerException te) {
        throw new ServletException(te);
    }
  }
}
```

After getting the three request parameters for XML, XSLT, and encoding, the servlet converts the XML and XSLT names to actual filenames:

```
String xmlFileName = ctx.getRealPath(
        "/WEB-INF/xml/numbers_" + xmlLang + ".xml");
String xsltFileName = ctx.getRealPath(
        "/WEB-INF/xslt/numbers_" + xsltLang + ".xslt");
```

Because the XML files and XSLT stylesheets are named consistently, it is easy to determine the filenames. The next step is to set the content type of the response:

```
// do this BEFORE calling HttpServletResponse.getWriter()
res.setContentType("text/html; charset=" + charEnc);
```

This is a critical step that instructs the servlet container to send the response to the client using the specified encoding type. This gets inserted into the Content-Type HTTP response header, allowing the browser to determine which encoding to expect. In our example, the three possible character encodings result in the following possible content types:

```
Content-Type: text/html; charset=ISO-8869-1
Content-Type: text/html; charset=UTF-8
Content-Type: text/html; charset=UTF-16
```

Next, the servlet uses the `javax.xml.transform.Source` interface and the `javax.xml.transform.stream.StreamSource` class to read from the XML and XSLT files:

```
Source xmlSource = new StreamSource(new File(xmlFileName));
Source xsltSource = new StreamSource(new File(xsltFileName));
```

By using `java.io.File`, the `StreamSource` will correctly determine the encoding of the XML and XSLT files by looking at the XML declaration within each of the files. The `StreamSource` constructor also accepts `InputStream` or `Reader` as parameters. Special precautions must be taken with the `Reader` constructors, because Java `Reader` implementations use the default Java character encoding, which is determined when the VM starts up. The `InputStreamReader` is used to explicitly specify an encoding as follows:

```
Source xmlSource = new StreamSource(new InputStreamReader(
        new FileInputStream(xmlFileName), "UTF-8"));
```

For more information on how Java uses encodings, see the JavaDoc package description for the `java.lang` package.

Our servlet then overrides the XSLT stylesheet's output encoding as follows:

```
trans.setOutputProperty(OutputKeys.ENCODING, charEnc);
```

This takes precedence over the encoding that was specified in the `<xsl:output>` element shown earlier in Example 8-21.

Finally, the servlet performs the transformation, sending the result tree to a `Writer` obtained from `HttpServletResponse`:

```
// note: res.getWriter() will use the encoding type that was
//       specified earlier in the call to res.setContentType()
trans.transform(xmlSource, new StreamResult(res.getWriter()));
```

As the comment indicates, the servlet container should set up the `Writer` to use the correct character encoding, as specified by the `Content-Type` HTTP header.[*]

I18n Troubleshooting Checklist

Here are a few things to consider when problems occur. First, rule out obvious problems:

*   Visit a web site that uses the language you are trying to produce. For example, *http://www.chinadaily.com.cn/* has an option to view the site in Chinese. This will confirm that your browser loads the correct fonts.

*   Test your application with English XML data and XSLT stylesheets to verify that the transformations are performed correctly.

*   Perform the XSLT transformation on the command line. Save the result to a file and view with a Unicode-compatible text editor. If all else fails, view with a binary editor to see how the characters are being encoded.

---

[*] UTF-16 works under Tomcat 3.2.x but fails under Tomcat 4.0 beta 5. Hopefully this will be addressed in later versions of Tomcat.

- Verify that your XML parser supports the encodings you are trying to parse.*

If these tests do not uncover the problem, try the following:

- Stick with UTF-8 encoding until problems are resolved. This is the most compatible encoding.

- Verify that the servlet sets the `Content-Type` header to:

      Content-Type: text/html; charset=UTF-8

- Verify that the XSLT stylesheet sets the appropriate encoding on the `<xsl:output>` element or override the encoding programmatically:

      transformer.setOutputProperty(OutputKeys.ENCODING, "UTF-8");

- Insert some code into the servlet that performs the transformation but sends the result to a file instead of the `HttpServletResponse`'s `Writer`. Inspect this file with a Unicode-compatible text editor.

- Use `java.io.File` or `java.io.InputStream` instead of `java.io.Reader` when reading XML and XSLT files.

---

* Encoding supported by Apache's Xerces parser are documented at *http://xml.apache.org/xerces-j/faq-general.html.*

9

Development
Environment, Testing,
and Performance

This chapter provides an overview of many different technologies that comprise a typical Java and XSLT software development environment. Once the most commonly used tools are introduced, strategies for testing XSLT and tuning performance are presented. Instead of presenting specific performance benchmarks for various XSLT processors, this chapter's focus is on effective programming techniques that should be applicable to a wide range of tools. XSLT is a very young technology, and tools are improving all the time.

Development Environment

Specialized, lightweight development tools have never been more important to Java developers. Commercial integrated development environments (IDEs) are now only one small piece of a larger suite of essential tools used by a majority of Java development projects. These build tools such as Ant, testing tools such as JUnit, and various XML parsers and XSLT processors. Figure 9-1 illustrates some of the tools found in a typical Java and XSLT development environment.

Although this is a typical development environment, it can be a large number of tools to keep track of. Table 9-1 summarizes how each of these tools is used.

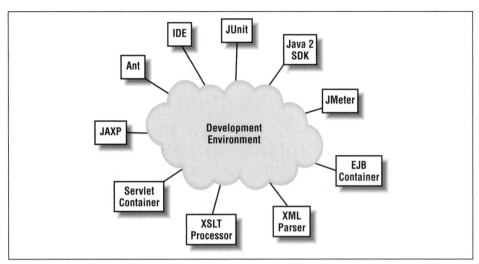

Figure 9-1. Common Java, XML, and XSLT tools

Table 9-1. Tool overview

Tool	Description
Java 2 SDK	The Java 2 software development kit, i.e., the JDK.
Apache's JMeter	A stress-testing tool, primarily used to test scalability and performance of servlets and web sites.
EJB Container	Enterprise JavaBeans server, such as JBoss, Enhydra, WebLogic, or WebSphere.
XML Parser	Xerces, Crimson, or another SAX and/or DOM parser.
XSLT Processor	Xalan, SAXON, or any other XSLT processor.
Servlet Container	Apache's Tomcat or any other servlet host. Many application servers include both servlet containers and EJB containers.
JAXP	Provides a common API to XML parsers and XSLT processors.
Apache's Ant	A Java replacement for *make*. Ant build files provide a consistent way for every member of the development team to compile and test code.
IDE	An integrated development environment, such as Borland's JBuilder.
JUnit	An open source unit testing framework.

Some individual tools are much more powerful when used in the context of an overall development environment. JUnit is much more effective when used in combination with Ant, because Ant ensures that every developer on the team is compiling and testing with the same settings. This means that unit tests executed by one developer should work the same way for everyone else. Without Ant, unit tests that succeed for one developer may fail for others, since they may be using different versions of some tools.

CLASSPATH Issues

The migration from first generation XML parsers and XSLT processors has been a somewhat painful experience for Java developers. Although the newer APIs are great, older JAR files linger throughout many applications and directories, causing more than their fair share of configuration difficulties. This section describes some of the most common problems and offers advice for configuring several popular tools.

JAR hell?

A common complaint against Microsoft Windows systems is known as "DLL Hell." This refers to problems that occur when two applications require different versions of the same DLL file. Installing a new application may overwrite an older version of a DLL file that existing applications depend on, causing erratic behavior or outright system crashes.*

More frequently than ever before, Java developers must contend with incompatible JAR file versions. For instance, JAXP 1.0 and JAXP 1.1 both ship with a JAR file named *jaxp.jar*. Applications that require JAXP 1.1 functionality will fail if the 1.0 version of *jaxp.jar* is listed on the CLASSPATH earlier than the newer version. This happens more often than developers expect, because many commercial and open source development tools ship with XML parsers and XSLT processors. The installation routines for these tools may install JAR files without informing developers or asking for their consent.

The simple fix is to locate and remove old versions of JAR files. This is easier said than done, because in many cases (such as JAXP), the version number is not part of the JAR filename. Since many tools ignore or modify the CLASSPATH when they are executed, simply removing older JAR files from the CLASSPATH will not eradicate all problems. Instructions for fixing this problem in Ant, Tomcat, and JBuilder are coming up.

Some JAR files are beginning to include version information inside of the *META-INF/MANIFEST.MF* file. This is called the manifest and can be extracted with the following command, where *filename.jar* is the name of the JAR file:

```
jar -xf filename.jar META-INF/MANIFEST.MF
```

---

* Commonly referred to as the blue screen of death.

Once extracted, the manifest can be viewed with any text editor. Example 9-1 shows the content of the manifest from Version 1.0 of *jaxp.jar*.

Example 9-1. Version 1.0 jaxp.jar manifest contents

```
Manifest-Version: 1.0
Specification-Title:  Java API for XML Parsing Interfaces
Specification-Vendor: Sun Microsystems
Created-By: 1.2.2 (Sun Microsystems Inc.)
Specification-Version: 1.0.0

Name: javax/xml/parsers
Package-Version: 1.0.0
Specification-Title:  Java API for XML Parsing
Specification-Vendor: Sun Microsystems
Sealed: true
Specification-Version: 1.0.0
Package-Vendor: Sun Microsystems, Inc.
Package-Title: javax.xml.parsers
```

This manifest makes it quite easy to identify the contents of this JAR file. Although Sun's products tend to be very good about this, the manifest contents are entirely optional, and many other products omit all manifest information.

Sealing violations

The dreaded "sealing violation" is one of the more cryptic exceptions encountered. Example 9-2 shows a stack trace that is displayed when a sealing violation occurs.

Example 9-2. Sealing violation stack trace

```
Exception in thread "main" java.lang.SecurityException: sealing violation
    at java.net.URLClassLoader.defineClass(URLClassLoader.java:234)
    at java.net.URLClassLoader.access$100(URLClassLoader.java:56)
    at java.net.URLClassLoader$1.run(URLClassLoader.java:195)
    at java.security.AccessController.doPrivileged(Native Method)
    at java.net.URLClassLoader.findClass(URLClassLoader.java:188)
    at java.lang.ClassLoader.loadClass(ClassLoader.java:297)
    at sun.misc.Launcher$AppClassLoader.loadClass(Launcher.java:286)
    at java.lang.ClassLoader.loadClass(ClassLoader.java:253)
    at java.lang.ClassLoader.loadClassInternal(ClassLoader.java:313)
    at java.lang.Class.forName0(Native Method)
    at java.lang.Class.forName(Class.java:120)
    at javax.xml.transform.TransformerFactory.newInstance(TransformerFactory.java:117)
    at Test.main(Test.java:17)
```

This exception is hard to diagnose because the error message is not very descriptive, and the stack trace consists mostly of internal Java classes. According to the stack trace, line 17 of *Test.java* caused the problem. Here it is:

```
TransformerFactory transFact = TransformerFactory.newInstance();
```

Actually, this line of code is perfectly correct. The problem lies in the CLASSPATH instead. The key to understanding this error is the sealing violation description. This indicates that one or more *sealed* JAR files are on the CLASSPATH in the wrong order.

A sealed JAR file has a manifest entry `Sealed: true`, as shown in Example 9-1.* The package sealing mechanism was introduced in Java Version 1.2 to enforce version consistency. Whenever a package is sealed, all classes in that package must be loaded from the same JAR file. If some of the classes are loaded from one JAR file and others from another, an instance of `java.lang.SecurityException` is thrown. Figure 9-2 illustrates the problem.

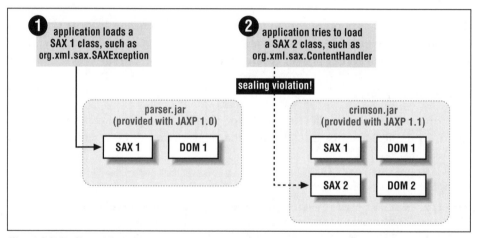

Figure 9-2. Sealing violation

In this diagram, *parser.jar* is listed on the CLASSPATH before *crimson.jar*. This is a problem because Java applications search JAR files in the order in which they appear on the CLASSPATH. Once the `org.xml.sax.SAXException` class has been loaded by the JVM, any additional classes or interfaces in the `org.xml.sax` package must be loaded from *parser.jar* because it is sealed. When the application requests an instance of `ContentHandler`, the class loader attempts to load the requested class file from *crimson.jar*, which triggers the `SecurityException`

---

* It is also possible to seal individual packages within a JAR file. Refer to the Java 2 Standard Edition documentation for more information.

shown in Example 9-2. The simple fix to this problem is to remove *parser.jar* from the CLASSPATH, which will load all classes in the org.xml.sax package from *crimson.jar.*

Other exceptions and errors

Other various "configuration" exceptions defined by JAXP are javax.xml. transform.TransformerConfigurationException and javax.xml. parsers.Factory-ConfigurationError. These may occur when an older version of *jaxp.jar* is still listed on the CLASSPATH. Since JAXP 1.0 is not aware of SAX 2, DOM 2, or XSLT transformations, applications requesting any of these new features may see one of these exceptions when JAXP 1.0 is installed instead of JAXP 1.1.

As mentioned earlier, the filename *jaxp.jar* is used with Versions 1.0 and 1.1 of JAXP. Therefore, special care must be taken to ensure that the newer copy is present instead of the old one. Since JAXP 1.1 is backwards-compatible with Version 1.0, the older version can be safely replaced without breaking currently installed applications that depend on it.

The easiest exception to debug is java.lang.ClassNotFoundException. This may occur when JAXP 1.1 is listed on the CLASSPATH. However, an XSLT processor or XML parser is not listed. To remedy this situation, merely add a JAXP-compliant parser and XSLT processor to the CLASSPATH.

Java optional packages

The Java VM does not simply load classes based on the CLASSPATH environment variable. Before searching the CLASSPATH, the VM attempts to load classes from an optional package directory. An *installed* optional package is a JAR file located in the Java 2 Runtime Environment's *lib/ext* directory or in the *jre/lib/ext* directory of the Java 2 SDK.

If an installed optional package is not located, the VM then searches for *download* optional packages. These are JAR files that are explicitly referenced by the Class-Path manifest header of another JAR file. For example, a manifest might contain the following line:

```
Class-Path: jaxp.jar
```

In this case, the VM would look for *jaxp.jar* in the same directory as the JAR file that contains the manifest entry.

The best way to ensure that the correct version of XML parser, XSLT processor, and JAXP are installed is to manually copy the required JAR files to the installed optional package directory. Software developers should have the Java 2 SDK installed and should place JAR files in the *JAVA_HOME/jre/lib/ext* directory. End users, however, will probably use the Java 2 Runtime Environment instead of the entire SDK. For these users, the JAR files can be installed to the *lib/ext* directory where the JRE is installed.

To uninstall a Java optional package, merely delete the JAR file from the appropriate directory.

Java IDEs

Many developers use tools such as Borland's JBuilder as Java development environments. These tools can introduce problems because they typically include a copy of the Java 2 SDK. When running and compiling within the IDE, the VM uses the tool's own Java directory rather than the Sun Java 2 SDK that is probably already installed elsewhere on the system. Figure 9-3 is a typical directory structure that illustrates this potential problem.

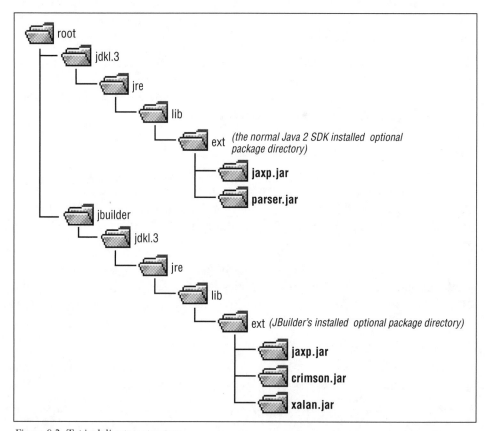

Figure 9-3. Typical directory structure

In this example, JBuilder is properly configured with JAXP 1.1, the Crimson XML parser, and the Xalan 2.0 JAR file. This means that compilation, running, and debugging will all work properly within the JBuilder IDE. But once the application is executed outside of JBuilder, it will probably fail. This is because the Java 2 SDK contains the older JAXP 1.0 JAR file and its older XML parser.

Merely adding the newer JAXP-related JAR files to the CLASSPATH will probably introduce a sealing exception rather than fix the problem, because the VM will still load files from the installed optional package directory before searching the CLASSPATH. One way to fix this problem is to replace *jaxp.jar* and *parser.jar* with the same JAR files found in JBuilder's directory. Another option is to update the JAVA_HOME environment variable and PATH to point to JBuilder's version of Java.

Ant

Configuring JAR files and the CLASSPATH on a single developer's machine can be difficult; keeping an entire team of developers in sync requires support from tools. For this reason, it is critical that every team member use the same build process when testing and integrating code changes. In this section, we take a brief look at Apache's Ant.

As discussed in Chapter 3, Apache's Ant is a Java-based build tool that is an excellent alternative to *make*.* Ant is good for numerous reasons, including:

* Its XML build files are easier to create than Makefiles.

* It is written in Java and is quite portable.

* Builds are extremely fast because the same VM instance is used for most steps in the build process.

Ant can be acquired form *http://jakarta.apache.org/ant*.†

Installing Ant

To install Ant, simply download the binary distribution and uncompress to a convenient directory. Then set the ANT_HOME environment variable to point to this directory and JAVA_HOME to point to the Java installation directory. To test, type **ant -version**. This should display something similar to the following:

```
Ant version 1.3 compiled on March 2 2001
```

---

* These notes apply to Ant 1.3. Newer versions of Ant may handle JAR files differently.

† The original author of Ant is working on a new Java build tool called Amber, available at *http://www. xiyo.org/Amber*.

Since Ant is written in Java, care must be taken to avoid conflicts with Ant's JAR files and JAR files found in the system CLASSPATH. This is a particular concern when using Ant to drive the XSLT transformation process because Ant ships with JAXP 1.0 JAR files that are not compatible with newer JAXP 1.1 implementations.

Once Ant is installed, update *ANT_HOME/lib/jaxp.jar* and *ANT_HOME/lib/parser.jar*, which are part of the older JAXP 1.0 reference implementation. Any JAR files added to the *ANT_HOME/lib* directory are automatically added to Ant's CLASSPATH and will be seen by the various Ant tasks during the build process. Simply adding JAXP 1.1-compatible JAR files to the *ANT_HOME/lib* directory will prevent most conflicts with newer applications that require DOM 2, SAX 2, or support for XSLT transformations.

A typical Ant build file

The best way to learn about Ant is to download it, read the first part of the user manual, and then study several example build files. Example 9-3 presents one such build file, which can be used to compile some of the example code in this chapter as well as perform an XSLT transformation.

Example 9-3. build.xml

```
<?xml version="1.0"?>
<!--
    *********************************************************
    ** Example Ant build file as shown in Chapter 9.
    **
    ** Assumes the following directory structure:
    **    examples
    **      +-chapters
    **      |    +-chap9
    **      |         build.xml (this file)
    **      |         aidan.xml (example XML file)
    **      |         condensePerson.xslt (example XSLT file)
    **      +-common
    **      |    +-src
    **      |         +-com/oreilly/javaxslt/swingtrans/...
    **      |
    **      +-build (created by this build file)
    **
    *********************************************************-->
<project name="chap9" default="help" basedir="../..">

    <!--
    *********************************************************
    ** Global properties.
    *********************************************************-->
    <property name="builddir" value="build"/>
```

Example 9-3. build.xml (continued)

```xml
<path id="thirdparty.class.path">
  <pathelement path="lib/saxon_6.2.2.jar"/>
  <pathelement path="lib/jaxp_1.1.jar"/>
  <pathelement path="lib/servlet_2.3.jar"/>
  <pathelement path="lib/junit_3.5.jar"/>
  <pathelement path="lib/jdom_beta6.jar"/>
</path>

<!--
********************************************************
** Create the output directory structure.
********************************************************-->
<target name="prepare">
  <mkdir dir="${builddir}"/>
</target>

<!--
********************************************************
** Show a brief usage message. This is the default
** target, and shows up when the user types "ant"
********************************************************-->
<target name="help" description="Show a brief help message">
  <echo message="Chapter 9 Example Ant Build File"/>
  <echo message="Type 'ant -projecthelp' for more assistance..."/>
</target>

<!--
********************************************************
** Remove the entire build directory
********************************************************-->
<target name="clean"
      description="Remove all generated code">
  <delete dir="${builddir}"/>
</target>

<!--
********************************************************
** Compile the com.oreilly.javaxslt.swingtrans package
********************************************************-->
<target name="compile" depends="prepare"
      description="Compile the SwingTransformer application">
  <javac srcdir="common/src" destdir="${builddir}"
         includes="com/oreilly/javaxslt/swingtrans/**">
    <classpath refid="thirdparty.class.path"/>
  </javac>
</target>
```

Example 9-3. build.xml (continued)

```
<!--
*********************************************************
** Run com.oreilly.javaxslt.swingtrans.SwingTransformer
*********************************************************-->
<target name="run" depends="compile"
      description="Run the SwingTransformer application">
  <java fork="yes"
        classname="com.oreilly.javaxslt.swingtrans.SwingTransformer">
    <classpath>
      <pathelement path="${builddir}"/>
    </classpath>
    <classpath refid="thirdparty.class.path"/>
  </java>
</target>


<!--
*********************************************************
** Performs an XSLT transformation. If either the XML
** file or the XSLT stylesheet change, the transformation
** is performed again.
**
** basedir - specifies the location of the XSLT
** destdir - a required attribute, however Ant 1.3 is
**           ignoring this. The messages on the console
**           indicate that the destdir is being used,
**           however it was found that the "out"
**           attribute also has to specify the output
**           directory.
*********************************************************-->
<target name="transform"
      description="Perform an XSLT transformation">
  <style processor="trax"
      basedir="chapters/chap9"
      destdir="${builddir}"
      style="condensePerson.xslt"
      in="chapters/chap9/aidan.xml"
      out="${builddir}/aidan_condensed.xml">

    <!-- pass a stylesheet parameter -->
    <param name="includeMiddle" expression="yes"/>
  </style>
</target>
</project>
```

All Ant build files are XML and have a <project> root element. This specifies the default target, as well as the base directory. Each of the targets is specified using

<target> elements, which can have dependencies on each other. Targets, in turn, contain tasks, which are responsible for performing individual units of work.

The CLASSPATH used by various tasks can be defined once and reused throughout the build file. The <path> element is emphasized in Example 9-3, including several JAR files from the *lib* directory. For instance:

```
<pathelement path="lib/servlet_2.3.jar"/>
```

This illustrates two key points about defining a consistent development environment. First, it is a good idea to rename JAR files to include version numbers. This is a great way to avoid conflicts and unexpected errors, because different versions of most tools use the same filenames for JAR files. By renaming them, it is easier to keep track of what is installed on the system. The only drawback to this approach is that build files must be manually updated whenever new versions of JAR files are installed.

Second, this particular Ant build file defines its own CLASSPATH, rather than relying on the developer's CLASSPATH. Relying on the CLASSPATH environment variable introduces problems because each developer on a team may have a completely different set of JAR files defined in his environment. By encoding everything in the Ant build file, everyone will compile and test with the same setup.

The following target shows how the build file compiles the application:

```
<target name="compile" depends="prepare"
      description="Compile the SwingTransformer application">
  <javac srcdir="common/src" destdir="${builddir}"
          includes="com/oreilly/javaxslt/swingtrans/**">
    <classpath refid="thirdparty.class.path"/>
  </javac>
</target>
```

So, to execute this target, simply type **ant compile** from the command prompt. Since this target depends on the prepare target, the *build* directory will be created before the code is compiled. Fortunately, the <javac> task is smart enough to compile only source code files that have changes since the last build, making Ant much faster than manually typing **javac *.java**.

The srcdir and destdir attributes are relative to the basedir that was specified in the <project> element. Since Ant always uses forward slashes (/) as path separators, these relative directories will work on Windows and Unix/Linux systems. As you might guess, the includes attribute defines a filter that limits which files are included in the build.

The last target in this build file performs an XSLT transformation using Ant's <style> task, which is described next.

Transforming using Ant's style task

Of particular interest to XSLT developers is Ant's `<style>` task. This is a core task that performs one or more XSLT transformations. Ant's JAXP JAR files must be updated as described earlier for this task to work. Here is a simple example of this task:

```
<style basedir="." destdir="." style="sample.xslt" processor="trax"
    in="company.xml" out="report.txt"/>
```

This will look in the project's base directory for the specified XML and XSLT files, placing the output into *report.txt*. The processor is `trax`, which means the same thing as JAXP 1.1. Ant will use the first JAXP-compliant processor found on the CLASSPATH. Table 9-2 lists the complete set of attributes for the `style` task.

Table 9-2. Ant style attributes

Attribute	Description	Required?
basedir	The directory where XML files are located.	yes
destdir	The directory where the result tree should be placed.	yes
extension	The default filename extension for the result of the transformation(s).	no
style	The XSLT stylesheet filename.	yes
processor	Specifies which XSLT processor is used. Legal values are "trax" for a TrAX-compliant processor, "xslp" for the XSL:P processor, and "xalan" for Xalan Version 1.x. May also contain the name of a class that implements `org.apache.tools.ant.taskdefs.XSLTLiaison`. When omitted, defaults to "trax."	no
includes	The comma-separated list of file patterns to include.	no
includesfile	The name of a file that contains include patterns.	no
excludes	The comma-separated list of file patterns to exclude.	no
excludesfile	The name of a file that contains exclude patterns.	no
defaultexcludes	May be "yes" or "no," defaults to "yes."	no
in	A single XML file input.	no
out	A single output filename.	no

The pattern attributes, such as `includes` and `excludes`, work just like other patterns in Ant. Basically, these allow the task to filter which files are included and excluded from the transformations. When omitted, all files in the base directory are included. Here is how an entire directory of XML files can be transformed:

```
<style basedir="xmlfiles" includes="*.xml" destdir="build/doc" style="report.xslt"
    extension="html"/>
```

As shown back in Example 9-3, parameters can be passed using nested <param> elements. This element has required name and expression attributes:

```
<style basedir="xmlfiles" includes="*.xml" destdir="build/doc" style="report.xslt"
    extension="html">
  <param name="reportType" expression="'detailed'"/>
</style>
```

Tomcat

Apache's Tomcat is a Servlet and JSP container and has been mentioned throughout this book. It is available from *http://jakarta.apache.org/tomcat*. Tomcat is fairly easy to install and configure:

- Download the latest Tomcat release build for your operating system.

- Uncompress the distribution to a directory.

- Set the TOMCAT_HOME environment variable to point to this directory.

- Set the JAVA_HOME environment variable to point to your Java distribution.

Since web applications are required to read configuration information from their XML deployment descriptors (*web.xml*), all current versions of Tomcat ship with an XML parser.

Configuring Tomcat 3.2.x

Tomcat 3.2.x includes several JAR files in its *$TOMCAT_HOME/lib* directory. Among these are *jaxp.jar* and *parser.jar*, which support JAXP Version 1.0 along with a SAX 1.0 and DOM 1.0 XML parser. Any JAR file added to the *lib* directory becomes available to every web application. Tomcat uses a simple script to locate **.jar* in the *lib* directory, adding each JAR file to the CLASSPATH as it is encountered. The order of inclusion depends on how the operating system lists files, which is generally alphabetically. The complete CLASSPATH used by Tomcat 3.2.x includes the following:

- *$TOMCAT_HOME/classes*

- *$TOMCAT_HOME/lib/*.jar*

- Any existing CLASSPATH

- *$JAVA_HOME/jre/lib/tools.jar*

Although the *lib* directory provides a convenient way to install utility code that all web applications must use, conflicts arise when individual applications require different versions of SAX, DOM, or JAXP. If Tomcat finds an older version of one of these tools before it finds a newer version, exceptions typically occur. For instance, a sealing violation exception may occur if the existing CLASSPATH contains the newer *crimson.jar*, but an older version of *parser.jar* is still present.

The best approach to fully configure Tomcat 3.2.x for XML support is as follows:

- Remove *jaxp.jar* and *parser.jar* from the *$TOMCAT_HOME/lib* directory.

- Install the following files from the JAXP 1.1 distribution into the *$TOMCAT_HOME/lib* directory: *jaxp.jar*, *crimson.jar*, and *xalan.jar*.

Of course, JAXP 1.1 supports other tools besides Crimson and Xalan. If you prefer, simply replace *crimson.jar* and *xalan.jar* with competing products that are JAXP 1.1–compatible.

Configuring Tomcat 4.0.x

Tomcat 4.0 improves upon Tomcat 3.2.x configuration issues in two key ways. First, the user's existing CLASSPATH is no longer appended to Tomcat's CLASSPATH. This helps to avoid situations where code works for one developer (who happens to have some critical file on her CLASSPATH) but fails for other developers who have slightly different personal CLASSPATH configurations.

Secondly, Tomcat 4.0 no longer places JAXP JAR files in a location visible to web applications. This means that if XML support is required, you must install the proper XML JAR files before anything will work. This is far better than the old Tomcat model, because it avoids unexpected collisions with XML libraries used internally by Tomcat. Instead, if you forget to install XML support, you simply see a `java.lang.NoClassDefFoundError`.

To install XML support into Tomcat 4.0, simply install the required JAR files into the *$TOMCAT_HOME/lib* directory. These will then be available to all web applications. The other option is to install JAR files into the *WEB-INF/lib* directory of individual web applications. With this approach, each application can use different versions of various packages without fear of conflicts.

Testing and Debugging

The software development community has shown a renewed interest in testing during the past few years. Much of this has been driven by the eXtreme Programming methodology, which emphasizes lightweight processes and constant unit testing to promote quality.* To demonstrate how to test XSLT transformations, a few simple files will be used. The XML data is shown first in Example 9-4.

---

* See *http://www.xprogramming.com* for more information on eXtreme Programming.

Example 9-4. aidan.xml

```
<?xml version="1.0" encoding="UTF-8"?>
<person>
    <firstName>Aidan</firstName>
    <middleName>Garrett</middleName>
    <lastName>Burke</lastName>
    <birthDate month="6" day="25" year="1999"/>
</person>
```

Although this data is trivial, the same concepts apply to larger, more realistic examples. The sample XSLT stylesheet is shown in Example 9-5.

Example 9-5. condensePerson.xslt

```
<?xml version="1.0" encoding="UTF-8"?>
<!--
***********************************************************
** Transforms an XML file representing a person into a
** more concise format.
***********************************************************-->
<xsl:stylesheet version="1.0" xmlns:xsl="http://www.w3.org/1999/XSL/Transform">
  <xsl:param name="includeMiddle" select="'yes'"/>

  <xsl:output method="xml" version="1.0" encoding="UTF-8" indent="yes"
      doctype-system="condensed.dtd"/>

  <!-- match an existing <person> element -->
  <xsl:template match="person">
    <!-- produce a new <person> element in a condensed form -->
    <xsl:element name="person">
      <xsl:element name="name">
        <xsl:value-of select="firstName"/>
        <xsl:text> </xsl:text>
        <xsl:if test="$includeMiddle = 'yes'">
          <xsl:value-of select="middleName"/>
          <xsl:text> </xsl:text>
        </xsl:if>
        <xsl:value-of select="lastName"/>
      </xsl:element>

      <xsl:element name="birthDate">
        <xsl:value-of select="birthDate/@month"/>
        <xsl:text>/</xsl:text>
        <xsl:value-of select="birthDate/@day"/>
        <xsl:text>/</xsl:text>
        <xsl:value-of select="birthDate/@year"/>
      </xsl:element>
    </xsl:element>
  </xsl:template>
</xsl:stylesheet>
```

The job of this stylesheet is to transform XML data into a more concise format as shown in Example 9-6.

Example 9-6. Expected output

```
<?xml version="1.0" encoding="UTF-8"?>

<!DOCTYPE person
  SYSTEM "condensed.dtd">
<person>
    <name>Aidan Garrett Burke</name>
    <birthDate>6/25/1999</birthDate>
</person>
```

Finally, the DTD for the condensed XML file is shown in Example 9-7.

Example 9-7. condense.dtd

```
<!ELEMENT person (name, birthDate)>
<!ELEMENT birthDate (#PCDATA)>
<!ELEMENT name (#PCDATA)>
```

By providing a DTD for the expected XML output, a unit test can easily validate the result tree after performing one or more transformations. Such a test simply writes the transformation results to a file and then attempts to parse them using a validating XML parser.

JUnit

JUnit is an open source testing framework available from *http://www.junit.org*. It is a lightweight tool designed to be used by programmers specifically for unit tests. Other tools are generally better for integration testing and functional testing, but these are not discussed here.

Since XSLT transformations can be performed independently of the remainder of an application, they are a perfect candidate for automated unit testing. A technology such as JSP, however, is quite difficult to test in an automated fashion because JSPs must be executed within the context of a JSP container and web browser.

An automated test is one that reports "success" or "failure" after execution and does not require a human being to interact as the test is running. For instance, requiring a user to type in specific values into HTML form fields and then look at the resulting web page is clearly not automated. Also, a test that merely displays a long text report is not automated because it requires a knowledgeable person to read over the report and inspect it for errors.

By automating tests, every developer can run an entire suite of tests by executing a command-line program. The test suite then reports exactly which tests failed and where, so the problems can be fixed immediately.

A key philosophy behind a successful unit testing methodology is the idea that every test must always run at 100 percent success. Now, when programmers change an XSLT stylesheet or XML code and a test suddenly fails, they know that their changes were likely the source of the problem. When "broken" tests are left in the project for long periods of time, developers will probably stop running the testing suite because it becomes too difficult to manually filter through all of the error reports caused by the broken tests.

WARNING   It is important to adopt a policy in which every developer runs the suite of unit tests before checking any modified code into a shared code repository such as CVS.

For XSLT transformations, performing a transformation and then validating against a DTD or Schema is the easiest kind of testing. Once the structure of the result is validated, additional tests can be performed to determine if the semantic content of the result is correct. For instance, a DTD can report that a <firstName> element is present, but it takes additional testing to determine if the content of <firstName> is actually the correct name.

An example unit test

Example 9-8 shows how to write a simple test *fixture* using the JUnit framework. JUnit describes fixtures as a group of unit tests.

Example 9-8. Sample test fixture

```
package chap9;

import java.io.*;
import java.net.*;
import java.util.*;

// JAXP used for XSLT transformations
import javax.xml.transform.*;
import javax.xml.transform.stream.*;

// JDOM used for XML parsing and validation
import org.jdom.*;
import org.jdom.input.*;

// JUnit classes
import junit.framework.Test;
```

Example 9-8. Sample test fixture (continued)

```java
import junit.framework.TestCase;
import junit.framework.TestSuite;
import junit.textui.TestRunner;

/**
 * An example JUnit test. This class performs an XSLT transformation
 * and validates the result.
 */
public class SampleUnitTest extends TestCase {
    private String workingDir;

    // input XML files
    private File aidanXMLFile;
    private File johnXMLFile;

    // a stylesheet that condenses the XML data
    private File condenseXSLTFile;

    // the transformation results
    private File aidanCondensedXMLFile;
    private File johnCondensedXMLFile;

    private TransformerFactory transFact;

    /**
     * All JUnit tests have a constructor that takes the test name.
     */
    public SampleUnitTest(String name) {
        super(name);
    }

    /**
     * Initialization before each test[...] method is called.
     */
    public void setUp() {
        // locate a file named test.properties in the chap9 package
        ResourceBundle rb = ResourceBundle.getBundle("chap9.test");
        this.workingDir = rb.getString("chap9.workingDir");

        assertNotNull(workingDir);
        assert("Unable to locate " + this.workingDir,
                new File(this.workingDir).exists());

        this.aidanXMLFile = new File(workingDir + File.separator
                + "aidan.xml");
        this.johnXMLFile = new File(workingDir + File.separator
                + "john.xml");
```

Example 9-8. Sample test fixture (continued)

```
        this.condenseXSLTFile = new File(workingDir + File.separator
                + "condensePerson.xslt");

        this.aidanCondensedXMLFile = new File(this.workingDir + File.separator
                + "aidanCondensed.xml");
        this.johnCondensedXMLFile = new File(this.workingDir + File.separator
                + "johnCondensed.xml");

        this.transFact = TransformerFactory.newInstance();
    }

    /**
     * Clean up after each test[...] method
     */
    public void tearDown() {
        // the transformation results could be deleted here, but the
        // cleanup code is intentionally commented out so the
        // developer can see the generated files:

        // this.aidanCondensedXMLFile.delete();
        // this.johnCondensedXMLFile.delete();
    }

    /**
     * An individual unit test.
     */
    public void testTransformWithTemplates() throws Exception {
        Templates templates = this.transFact.newTemplates(
                new StreamSource(this.condenseXSLTFile));

        Transformer trans = templates.newTransformer();

        // do two transformations using the same Transformer
        trans.transform(new StreamSource(this.aidanXMLFile),
                new StreamResult(this.aidanCondensedXMLFile));
        trans.transform(new StreamSource(this.johnXMLFile),
                new StreamResult(this.johnCondensedXMLFile));

        // validate both files
        validateCondensedFile(this.aidanCondensedXMLFile,
                "Aidan Garrett Burke", "6/25/1999");
        validateCondensedFile(this.johnCondensedXMLFile,
                "John Fitzgerald Kennedy", "5/29/1917");
    }

    /**
     * Another unit test.
     */
```

Example 9-8. Sample test fixture (continued)

```java
public void testTransformer() throws Exception {
    Transformer trans = this.transFact.newTransformer(
            new StreamSource(this.condenseXSLTFile));

    trans.transform(new StreamSource(this.aidanXMLFile),
            new StreamResult(this.aidanCondensedXMLFile));

    validateCondensedFile(this.aidanCondensedXMLFile,
            "Aidan Garrett Burke", "6/25/1999");
}

// a helper method used by each of the unit tests
private void validateCondensedFile(File file, String expectedName,
        String expectedBirthDate) {
    try {
        // first do a simple validation against the DTD
        SAXBuilder builder = new SAXBuilder(true); // validate
        Document doc = builder.build(file);

        // now perform some additional checks
        Element nameElem = doc.getRootElement().getChild("name");
        assertEquals("Name was not correct",
                expectedName, nameElem.getText());

        Element birthDateElem = doc.getRootElement().getChild("birthDate");
        assertEquals("Birth date was not correct",
                expectedBirthDate, birthDateElem.getText());

    } catch (JDOMException jde) {
        fail("XML was not valid: " + jde.getMessage());
    }
}

/**
 * @return a TestSuite, which is a composite of Test objects.
 */
public static Test suite() {
    // uses reflection to locate each method named test[...]
    return new TestSuite(SampleUnitTest.class);
}

/**
 * Allow the unit tests to be invoked from the command line
 * in text-only mode.
 */
```

Example 9-8. Sample test fixture (continued)

```
    public static void main(String[] args) {
        TestRunner.run(suite());
    }
}
```

First, notice that `SampleUnitTest` extends from `junit.framework.TestCase`. Each subclass of `TestCase` defines a fixture and can contain multiple individual unit tests. Each method that begins with the word "test" is a unit test. All of the private fields in `SampleUnitTest` are specific to our particular needs and are not part of the JUnit framework.

The constructor takes the name of a unit test as an argument:

```
    public SampleUnitTest(String name) {
        super(name);
    }
```

The `name` argument is the test method name, and JUnit uses the Java reflection API to locate and instantiate the correct method. As we will see in a moment, this constructor is rarely called directly.

The `setUp()` method is called before each unit test is executed. As expected, this method is used to set up preconditions before a test is executed. Its counterpart is the `tearDown()` method, which is called just after each test is executed. If a fixture contains four unit test methods, then `setUp()` and `tearDown()` will each be called four times.

For our purposes, the `setUp()` method locates all of the files that will be used for XSLT transformations. These include XML input files, the XSLT stylesheet, and the XSLT result targets. It also performs some simple testing:

```
    assertNotNull(workingDir);
    assert("Unable to locate " + this.workingDir,
        new File(this.workingDir).exists());
```

These `assert()` methods are part of the JUnit framework, causing test failures when the tested condition is not true.[*] These are the heart of what programmers write when creating unit tests and can be used in any of the test methods or in the `setUp()` and `tearDown()` methods. When an assertion is not true, JUnit reports an error message and the line number where the failure occurred. This is known as a test failure, which is different than a test error. An error is reported when JUnit catches an exception that one of the unit tests throws.

---

[*] JUnit 3.7 renamed the `assert()` method `assertTrue()` to avoid conflicts with the new JDK 1.4 assertion facility.

This first unit test in our example is the `testTransformWithTemplates()` method. Because this method name begins with "test," JUnit can use reflection to locate it. The job of this test is to merely perform an XSLT transformation using JAXP's `Templates` interface, delegating to the `validateCondensedFile()` method to do the actual testing. This approach is taken because the same testing code can be shared among a group of individual unit tests.

The `validateCondensedFile()` method performs two levels of testing. First, the result of the transformation is validated against its DTD. If an exception is thrown, the test fails:

```
fail("XML was not valid: " + jde.getMessage());
```

JUnit will intercept this failure and display the error message to the programmer running the test. If the validation succeeds, the unit test then uses the `assertEquals()` method to test some of the actual XML content:

```
assertEquals("Name was not correct",
        expectedName, nameElem.getText());
```

In this method, if the second two arguments are not equal, the provided error message is displayed and the test fails.

One key additional method is `suite()`:

```
public static Test suite() {
    // uses reflection to locate each method named test[...]
    return new TestSuite(SampleUnitTest.class);
}
```

This is useful because it automatically locates all methods whose names begin with "test" and adds them to a test suite. Both `TestCase` and `TestSuite` implement the `Test` interface; `TestSuite` is a composite of many individual `Test` objects. By organizing tests into suites, entire families of tests can be executed by running the suite. As expected with a composite pattern, test suites can also consist of other test suites. At some point, one top-level test suite can directly or indirectly include every other test in the application. Therefore, all tests can be executed with a single command.

Running the test

To run the test from the command line, type the following command:

```
java chap9.SampleUnitTest
```

This works because the fixture contains the following `main()` method:

```
public static void main(String[] args) {
    TestRunner.run(suite());
}
```

The `TestRunner` class is a command-line tool that reports the following output when all tests succeed:

```
Time: 1.081


OK (2 tests)
```

The two dots in the first line of output represent each of the test methods. As each unit test executes, a new dot appears. If a test fails, JUnit reports a stack trace, a (sometimes) descriptive message, and the line number of the failure. At the end, the number of tests, failures, and errors are reported.

JUnit also has a Swing GUI client that can be executed with the following command:

```
java junit.swingui.TestRunner chap9.SampleUnitTest
```

Figure 9-4 shows the graphical output when errors occur.

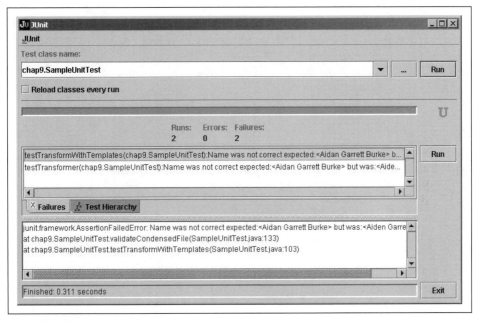

Figure 9-4. JUnit output with errors

The rectangular area to the left of "U" is a progress bar that expands as tests are executed. When dozens or hundreds of tests are executed, the progress bar gives a good visual indication of how many tests have executed. It also changes from green to red when errors or failures occur, so programmers know exactly when something went wrong. The scrolling list in the middle of the screen shows individual test errors and failures, and the text area near the bottom of the screen shows details for the selected error.

The GUI interface is great for interactive testing, while the command-line interface is more appropriate for batch-mode, automated tests. These are the sorts of tests that execute as part of a nightly build process. We now move past unit testing software into the realm of custom application error handling using JAXP error listeners.

JAXP 1.1 Error Listeners

When performing XSLT transformations using JAXP, errors are typically reported to `System.err`. While this is sufficient for command-line transformations, some custom applications require more control over the error-reporting process. For this class of applications, the `javax.xml.transform.ErrorListener` interface is provided.

By implementing this interface, an application can capture and report detailed information about where transformation errors occur and why. In Example 9-9, a custom Swing table model is presented. This class implements the `javax.xml.transform.ErrorListener` interface and is used by a `JTable` to display errors graphically. Later, in Example 9-11, we show how to register this error listener with a `TransformerFactory` and `Transformer`.

Example 9-9. ErrorListenerModel

```
package com.oreilly.javaxslt.swingtrans;

import java.io.*;
import java.util.*;
import javax.swing.table.*;

// XML-related imports
import javax.xml.transform.ErrorListener;
import javax.xml.transform.SourceLocator;
import javax.xml.transform.TransformerException;

/**
 * A JTable data model that provides detail information about a list
 * of javax.xml.transform.TransformerException objects.
 */
public class ErrorListenerModel extends AbstractTableModel
        implements ErrorListener {

    // column positions in the table
    private static final int LINE_COL = 0;
    private static final int COLUMN_COL = 1;
    private static final int PUBLIC_ID_COL = 2;
    private static final int SYSTEM_ID_COL = 3;
    private static final int MESSAGE_AND_LOC_COL = 4;
    private static final int LOCATION_COL = 5;
```

Example 9-9. ErrorListenerModel (continued)

```
    private static final int EXCEPTION_COL = 6;
    private static final int CAUSE_COL = 7;

    private static final String[] COLUMN_NAMES = {
        "Line",
        "Column",
        "Public ID",
        "System ID",
        "Message & Location",
        "Location",
        "Exception",
        "Cause"
    };

    // the actual data
    private List exceptionList = null;

    /**
     * @return a detailed text report of the exception at the specified row.
     */
    public String getDetailReport(int row) {
        if (this.exceptionList == null
                || row < 0 || row >= this.exceptionList.size()) {
            return "";
        }

        TransformerException te = (TransformerException)
                this.exceptionList.get(row);
        SourceLocator loc = te.getLocator(); // may be null

        // buffer the report
        StringWriter sw = new StringWriter();
        PrintWriter pw = new PrintWriter(sw);

        pw.println(te.getClass().getName());
        pw.println("-------------------------------------------------------");
        if (loc == null) {
            pw.println("Line Number   : [null SourceLocator]");
            pw.println("Column Number: [null SourceLocator]");
            pw.println("Public ID     : [null SourceLocator]");
            pw.println("System ID     : [null SourceLocator]");
        } else {
            pw.println("Line Number   : " + loc.getLineNumber());
            pw.println("Column Number: " + loc.getColumnNumber());
            pw.println("Public ID     : " + loc.getPublicId());
            pw.println("System ID     : " + loc.getSystemId());
        }
```

Example 9-9. ErrorListenerModel (continued)

```
        pw.println("Message & Location : " + te.getMessageAndLocation());
        pw.println("Location            : " + te.getLocationAsString());

        pw.println("Exception           : " + te.getException());
        if (te.getException() != null) {
            te.getException().printStackTrace(pw);
        }

        pw.println("Cause               : " + te.getCause());
        if (te.getCause() != null && (te.getCause() != te.getException())) {
            te.getCause().printStackTrace(pw);
        }

        return sw.toString();
    }

    /**
     * Part of the TableModel interface.
     */
    public Object getValueAt(int row, int column) {
        if (this.exceptionList == null) {
            return "No errors or warnings";
        } else {
            TransformerException te = (TransformerException)
                    this.exceptionList.get(row);
            SourceLocator loc = te.getLocator();

            switch (column) {
            case LINE_COL:
                return (loc != null)
                        ? String.valueOf(loc.getLineNumber()) : "N/A";
            case COLUMN_COL:
                return (loc != null)
                        ? String.valueOf(loc.getColumnNumber()) : "N/A";
            case PUBLIC_ID_COL:
                return (loc != null) ? loc.getPublicId() : "N/A";
            case SYSTEM_ID_COL:
                return (loc != null) ? loc.getSystemId() : "N/A";
            case MESSAGE_AND_LOC_COL:
                return te.getMessageAndLocation();
            case LOCATION_COL:
                return te.getLocationAsString();
            case EXCEPTION_COL:
                return te.getException();
            case CAUSE_COL:
                return te.getCause();
            default:
                return "[error]"; // shouldn't happen
            }
```

Example 9-9. ErrorListenerModel (continued)

```
        }
    }

    /**
     * Part of the TableModel interface.
     */
    public int getRowCount() {
        return (this.exceptionList == null) ? 1 :
                this.exceptionList.size();
    }

    /**
     * Part of the TableModel interface.
     */
    public int getColumnCount() {
        return (this.exceptionList == null) ? 1 :
                COLUMN_NAMES.length;
    }

    /**
     * Part of the TableModel interface.
     */
    public String getColumnName(int column) {
        return (this.exceptionList == null)
                ?  "Transformation Problems"
                : COLUMN_NAMES[column];
    }

    /**
     * @return true if any errors occurred.
     */
    public boolean hasErrors() {
        return this.exceptionList != null;
    }

    /**
     * This is part of the javax.xml.transform.ErrorListener interface.
     * Indicates that a warning occurred. Transformers are required to
     * continue processing after warnings, unless the application
     * throws TransformerException.
     */
    public void warning(TransformerException te) throws TransformerException {
        report(te);
    }

    /**
     * This is part of the javax.xml.transform.ErrorListener interface.
     * Indicates that a recoverable error occurred.
```

Example 9-9. ErrorListenerModel (continued)

```
  */
 public void error(TransformerException te) throws TransformerException {
     report(te);
 }


 /**
  * This is part of the javax.xml.transform.ErrorListener interface.
  * Indicates that a non-recoverable error occurred.
  */
 public void fatalError(TransformerException te) throws TransformerException {
     report(te);
 }


 // adds the exception to exceptionList and notifies the JTable that
 // the content of the table has changed.
 private void report(TransformerException te) {
     if (this.exceptionList == null) {
         this.exceptionList = new ArrayList();
         this.exceptionList.add(te);
         fireTableStructureChanged();
     } else {
         this.exceptionList.add(te);
         int row = this.exceptionList.size()-1;
         super.fireTableRowsInserted(row, row);
     }
   }
 }
}
```

Code related to the `ErrorListener` interface is emphasized; the remaining code is used to present errors in a Swing table. The Swing `JTable` component displays rows and columns of data, getting its information from an underlying `javax.swing.table.TableModel` interface. `javax.swing.table.AbstractTableModel` is an abstract class that implements `TableModel`, serving as the base class for application-defined table models as shown here. As you can see, `ErrorListenerModel` extends from `AbstractTableModel`.

Since our table model implements the `ErrorListener` interface, it can be attached to a JAXP `Transformer`. When transformation problems occur, `warning()`, `error()`, or `fatalError()` is called. Since these methods have the same signature, they all delegate to the `report()` method. Comments in the code indicate which types of problems are supposed to call each method, although XSLT processors are not consistent in the way they report errors.

The `report()` method simply adds the `TransformerException` object to a private list of exceptions and then triggers a Swing event to indicate that the `JTable` should redraw its contents. When the JTable receives this event, it asks the ErrorListenerModel for the row count, column count, and values at individual cells within the table model. This functionality is contained within the getRowCount(), getColumnCount(), and getValueAt() methods, all of which are defined in the TableModel interface.

Our class also has an additional method called getDetailReport(), which is used to produce a text report of a TransformerException object. This method is worth studying because it shows which methods are available when dealing with transformation problems. As the code in Example 9-9 shows, many of the fields may be null. Some XSLT processors may provide a lot of detailed error reporting, while others may simply leave these fields null.

A Custom XSLT Transformer GUI

In this section, an XSLT transformer GUI is developed. This is a simple Swing application that allows an XML file to be transformed using an XSLT stylesheet. The results of the transformation are then shown in a text area, along with a JTable that shows all errors using the ErrorListenerModel class shown in Example 9-9.

XML validation of the transformation result is also provided. Given that the stylesheet produces XML, this tool will attempt to parse and validate the result tree. This is a great way to make sure that your XSLT is producing valid XHTML, for example, because the result can be validated against one of the XHTML DTDs as soon as each transformation is performed.

The Ant build file shown earlier in Example 9-3 contains a "run" target that can be used to execute this application by typing **ant run**.

Screen shots

The first window to appear is shown in Figure 9-5. This window is always displayed and allows the user to select the XML and XSLT input files.*

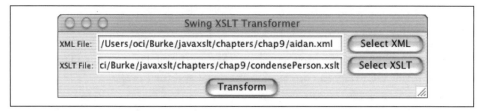

Figure 9-5. SwingTransformer frame

---

* These screen shots show the Macintosh OS/X Aqua look and feel using Java Swing.

When the Transform button is clicked, the window shown in Figure 9-6 appears. Subsequent transformations can be performed, and each one will cause an additional window to appear. Since the XML and XSLT files are parsed with each transformation, this application does not have to be restarted to see changes to those files.

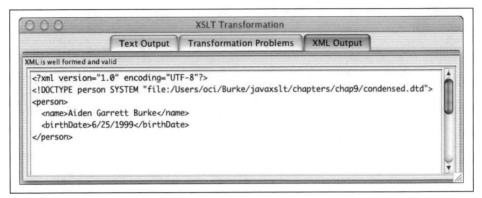

Figure 9-6. XML output panel

The first tab, Text Output, is actually the first one to be displayed. It is not shown here because it merely shows the raw text contents of the XSLT result tree, which includes any whitespace produced by the transformation. When the user clicks on the XML Output tab, the result tree is parsed and validated against its DTD. The XML is then displayed in the GUI using JDOM's XMLOutputter class, which removes ignorable whitespace and pretty-prints the XML.

If errors occur during the transformation process, the text and XML output panels are blank. Instead, the user is presented with the display shown in Figure 9-7.

This display shows how the ErrorListenerModel presented in Example 9-9 is used. The JTable at the top of the screen shows a tabular view of all errors, and the text area at the bottom of the screen shows the output from ErrorListenerModel's getDetailReport() method. In the error shown, a select attribute was intentionally misspelled in an XSLT stylesheet as seelect.

Source code

The source code for the main window is shown in Example 9-10. This is a subclass of JFrame that allows the user to select XML and XSLT filenames. This class is almost entirely GUI-related code and is not discussed further.

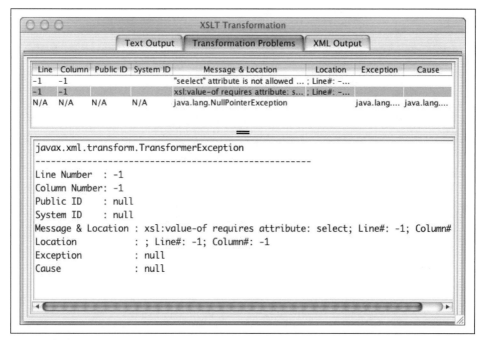

Figure 9-7. Transformation problems

Example 9-10. SwingTransformer.java

```
package com.oreilly.javaxslt.swingtrans;

import java.awt.*;
import java.awt.event.*;
import java.io.*;
import javax.swing.*;

/**
 * The entry point into this application. This class displays the main
 * window, allowing the user to select an XML file and an XSLT file.
 */
public class SwingTransformer extends JFrame {
    private JTextField xmlFileFld = new JTextField(30);
    private JTextField xsltFileFld = new JTextField(30);

    // file filters used with the JFileChooser class
    private XMLFileFilter xmlFilter = new XMLFileFilter();
    private XSLTFileFilter xsltFilter = new XSLTFileFilter();
    private JFileChooser fileChooser = new JFileChooser();

    // actions are hooked up to the JButtons
    private Action loadXMLAction =
            new javax.swing.AbstractAction("Select XML") {
```

Example 9-10. SwingTransformer.java (continued)

```
    public void actionPerformed(ActionEvent evt) {
        selectXMLFile();
    }
};

private Action loadXSLTAction =
        new javax.swing.AbstractAction("Select XSLT") {
    public void actionPerformed(ActionEvent evt) {
        selectXSLTFile();
    }
};

private Action transformAction =
        new javax.swing.AbstractAction("Transform") {
    public void actionPerformed(ActionEvent evt) {
        File xmlFile = new File(xmlFileFld.getText());
        File xsltFile = new File(xsltFileFld.getText());

        if (!xmlFile.exists() || !xmlFile.canRead()) {
            showErrorDialog("Unable to read XML file");
            return;
        }
        if (!xsltFile.exists() || !xsltFile.canRead()) {
            showErrorDialog("Unable to read XSLT file");
            return;
        }

        // show the results of the transformation in a new window
        new TransformerWindow().transform(xmlFile, xsltFile);
    }
};

/**
 * The entry point into the application; shows the main window.
 */
public static void main(String[] args) {
    new SwingTransformer().setVisible(true);
}

/**
 * Construct the main window and layout the GUI.
 */
public SwingTransformer() {
    super("Swing XSLT Transformer");

    // note: this line requires Java 2 v1.3
    setDefaultCloseOperation(JFrame.EXIT_ON_CLOSE);
```

Example 9-10. SwingTransformer.java (continued)

```
        Container cp = getContentPane();
        cp.setLayout(new GridBagLayout());

        GridBagConstraints gbc = new GridBagConstraints();
        gbc.anchor = GridBagConstraints.WEST;
        gbc.fill = GridBagConstraints.HORIZONTAL;
        gbc.gridx = GridBagConstraints.RELATIVE;
        gbc.gridy = 0;
        gbc.insets.top = 2;
        gbc.insets.left = 2;
        gbc.insets.right = 2;

        cp.add(new JLabel("XML File:"), gbc);
        gbc.weightx = 1.0;
        cp.add(this.xmlFileFld, gbc);
        gbc.weightx = 0.0;
        cp.add(new JButton(this.loadXMLAction), gbc);

        gbc.gridy++;
        cp.add(new JLabel("XSLT File:"), gbc);
        gbc.weightx = 1.0;
        cp.add(this.xsltFileFld, gbc);
        gbc.weightx = 0.0;
        cp.add(new JButton(this.loadXSLTAction), gbc);

        gbc.gridy++;
        gbc.gridx = 0;
        gbc.gridwidth = GridBagConstraints.REMAINDER;
        gbc.anchor = GridBagConstraints.CENTER;
        gbc.fill = GridBagConstraints.NONE;
        cp.add(new JButton(this.transformAction), gbc);

        pack();
    }


    /**
     * Show the file chooser, listing all XML files.
     */
    private void selectXMLFile() {
        this.fileChooser.setDialogTitle("Select XML File");
        this.fileChooser.setFileFilter(this.xmlFilter);
        int retVal = this.fileChooser.showOpenDialog(this);
        if (retVal == JFileChooser.APPROVE_OPTION) {
            this.xmlFileFld.setText(
                    this.fileChooser.getSelectedFile().getAbsolutePath());
        }
    }
```

Example 9-10. SwingTransformer.java (continued)

```java
    /**
     * Show the file chooser, listing all XSLT files.
     */
    private void selectXSLTFile() {
        this.fileChooser.setDialogTitle("Select XSLT File");
        this.fileChooser.setFileFilter(this.xsltFilter);
        int retVal = this.fileChooser.showOpenDialog(this);
        if (retVal == JFileChooser.APPROVE_OPTION) {
            this.xsltFileFld.setText(
                    this.fileChooser.getSelectedFile().getAbsolutePath());
        }
    }

    private void showErrorDialog(String msg) {
        JOptionPane.showMessageDialog(this, msg, "Error",
                JOptionPane.ERROR_MESSAGE);
    }
}

/**
 * Used with JFileChooser to only show files ending with .xml or .XML.
 */
class XMLFileFilter extends javax.swing.filechooser.FileFilter {
    public boolean accept(File f) {
        String name = f.getName();
        return f.isDirectory() || name.endsWith(".xml")
                || name.endsWith(".XML");
    }

    public String getDescription() {
        return "XML Files";
    }

}

/**
 * Used with JFileChooser to only show files ending with .xslt or .XSLT.
 */
class XSLTFileFilter extends javax.swing.filechooser.FileFilter {
    public boolean accept(File f) {
        String name = f.getName();
        return f.isDirectory() || name.endsWith(".xsl")
                || name.endsWith(".xslt") || name.endsWith(".XSL")
                || name.endsWith(".XSLT");
    }
```

Example 9-10. SwingTransformer.java (continued)

```
    public String getDescription() {
        return "XSLT Files";
    }
}
```

The next class, shown in Example 9-11, creates the window shown in Figures 9-5 and 9-6. Much of this code is responsible for arranging the JTabbedPane component, which contains the three folder tabs that make up the window. This class also does the actual XSLT transformation; these lines are emphasized.

Example 9-11. TransformerWindow.java

```
package com.oreilly.javaxslt.swingtrans;

import java.awt.*;
import java.awt.event.*;
import java.io.*;
import javax.swing.*;
import javax.swing.table.*;
import javax.swing.event.*;

// XML-related imports
import javax.xml.transform.SourceLocator;
import javax.xml.transform.Transformer;
import javax.xml.transform.TransformerConfigurationException;
import javax.xml.transform.TransformerException;
import javax.xml.transform.TransformerFactory;
import javax.xml.transform.stream.StreamResult;
import javax.xml.transform.stream.StreamSource;

/**
 * A secondary JFrame that shows the result of a single XSLT
 * transformation. This frame has a JTabbedPane interface, showing
 * the transformation result, error messages, and the XML output.
 */
public class TransformerWindow extends JFrame {
    // the result of the XSLT transformation as text
    private String resultText;

    private JTabbedPane tabPane = new JTabbedPane();
    private JTextArea textOutputArea = new JTextArea(30, 70);
    private XMLOutputPanel xmlOutputPanel = new XMLOutputPanel();
    private ErrorListenerModel errModel = new ErrorListenerModel();
    private JTable errorTable = new JTable(this.errModel);
    private JTextArea errorDetailArea = new JTextArea(10, 70);
    private String xsltURL;
```

Example 9-11. TransformerWindow.java (continued)

```java
/**
 * Construct a new instance and layout the GUI components.
 */
public TransformerWindow() {
    super("XSLT Transformation");

    // add the tab pane to the frame
    Container cp = getContentPane();
    cp.add(this.tabPane, BorderLayout.CENTER);

    // add individual tabs
    this.tabPane.add("Text Output", new JScrollPane(this.textOutputArea));
    this.tabPane.add("Transformation Problems",
            createErrorPanel());
    this.tabPane.add("XML Output", this.xmlOutputPanel);

    // listen to new tab selections
    this.tabPane.addChangeListener(new ChangeListener() {
        public void stateChanged(ChangeEvent evt) {
            tabChanged();
        }
    });

    this.textOutputArea.setEditable(false);

    // listen to selection changes on the table of errors
    this.errorTable.getSelectionModel().addListSelectionListener(
        new ListSelectionListener() {
            public void valueChanged(ListSelectionEvent evt) {
                if (!evt.getValueIsAdjusting()) {
                    showErrorDetails();
                }
            }
        });
    pack();
}

/**
 * Show details for the currently selected error.
 */
private void showErrorDetails() {
    int selRow = this.errorTable.getSelectedRow();
    this.errorDetailArea.setText(this.errModel.getDetailReport(selRow));
}

/**
 * Perform an XSLT transformation.
 */
```

Example 9-11. TransformerWindow.java (continued)

```java
public void transform(File xmlFile, File xsltFile) {
    setVisible(true);
    try {
        // figure out the directory of the XSLT file. This will be
        // used to locate the DTD
        if (xsltFile != null) {
            File xsltDir = xsltFile.getParentFile();
            if (xsltDir.isDirectory()) {
                this.xsltURL = xsltDir.toURL().toExternalForm();
            }
        }

        TransformerFactory transFact = TransformerFactory.newInstance();

        // register the table model as an error listener
        transFact.setErrorListener(this.errModel);

        Transformer trans = transFact.newTransformer(
                new StreamSource(xsltFile));

        // check for null, because the factory might not throw
        // exceptions when the call to newTransformer() fails. This
        // is because we registered an error listener that does not
        // throw exceptions.
        if (trans != null) {
            trans.setErrorListener(this.errModel);

            // capture the result of the XSLT transformation
            StringWriter sw = new StringWriter();
            trans.transform(new StreamSource(xmlFile),
                    new StreamResult(sw));

            // show the results
            this.resultText = sw.toString();
            this.textOutputArea.setText(this.resultText);
        }

    } catch (TransformerConfigurationException tce) {
        try {
            this.errModel.fatalError(tce);
        } catch (TransformerException ignored) {
        }
    } catch (TransformerException te) {
        try {
            this.errModel.fatalError(te);
        } catch (TransformerException ignored) {
        }
```

Example 9-11. TransformerWindow.java (continued)

```java
        } catch (Exception unexpected) {
            System.err.println(
                    "The XSLT processor threw an unexpected exception");
            unexpected.printStackTrace();
        }

        // show the error tab
        if (this.errModel.hasErrors()) {
            this.tabPane.setSelectedIndex(1);
        }
    }

    // the user clicked on a different tab
    private void tabChanged() {
        try {
            setCursor(Cursor.getPredefinedCursor(Cursor.WAIT_CURSOR));
            int selIndex = this.tabPane.getSelectedIndex();
            String selTab = this.tabPane.getTitleAt(selIndex);

            // when the XML tab is selected, set the text on the XML panel.
            // Although the text may not be XML, we won't know that until
            // it is parsed.
            if ("XML Output".equals(selTab)) {
                this.xmlOutputPanel.setXML(this.resultText,
                        this.xsltURL);
            }
        } finally {
            setCursor(Cursor.getPredefinedCursor(Cursor.DEFAULT_CURSOR));
        }
    }

    // a helper method to create the panel that displays errors
    private JComponent createErrorPanel() {
        JSplitPane splitPane = new JSplitPane(JSplitPane.VERTICAL_SPLIT);
        this.errorTable.setAutoResizeMode(JTable.AUTO_RESIZE_OFF);
        int size = this.errorDetailArea.getFont().getSize();
        this.errorDetailArea.setEditable(false);
        this.errorDetailArea.setFont(
                new Font("Monospaced", Font.PLAIN, size+2));

        splitPane.setTopComponent(new JScrollPane(this.errorTable));
        splitPane.setBottomComponent(new JScrollPane(this.errorDetailArea));
        return splitPane;
    }
}
```

As the emphasized code shows, the error listener table model is registered on the
`TransformerFactory` as well as the `Transformer` instance. In addition to

registering the error listener, exceptions also have to be caught because XSLT processors may still throw exceptions and errors even though an error listener is registered. Generally, errors on the `TransformerFactory` indicate problems while parsing the XSLT stylesheet, while `Transformer` error listeners are notified of problems with the actual transformation or in the XML data.

The final class, `XMLOutputPanel`, is shown in Example 9-12.

Example 9-12. XMLOutputPanel.java

```
package com.oreilly.javaxslt.swingtrans;

import java.awt.*;
//import java.awt.event.*;
import java.io.*;
import javax.swing.*;

// XML-related imports
import org.jdom.Document;
import org.jdom.input.SAXBuilder;
import org.jdom.output.XMLOutputter;

/**
 * Displays XML text in a scrolling text area. A status label indicates
 * whether or not the XML is well formed and valid.
 */
public class XMLOutputPanel extends JPanel {
    // displays the XML
    private JTextArea xmlArea = new JTextArea(20,70);
    private String xml;
    private JLabel statusLabel = new JLabel();

    /**
     * Construct the panel and layout the GUI components.
     */
    public XMLOutputPanel() {
        super(new BorderLayout());
        add(new JScrollPane(this.xmlArea), BorderLayout.CENTER);
        add(this.statusLabel, BorderLayout.NORTH);
    }

    /**
     * @param xml the actual XML data to display.
     * @param uri the location of the XML, thus allowing the parser
     * to locate the DTD.
     */
    public void setXML(String xml, String uri) {
        // return quickly if the XML has already been set
        if (xml == null || xml.equals(this.xml)) {
```

Example 9-12. XMLOutputPanel.java (continued)

```java
        return;
    }
    this.xml = xml;

    // use JDOM to parse the XML
    Document xmlDoc = null;
    try {
        // attempt to validate the XML
        SAXBuilder saxBuilder = new SAXBuilder(true);
        xmlDoc = saxBuilder.build(new StringReader(this.xml), uri);
        this.statusLabel.setText("XML is well formed and valid");
    } catch (Exception ignored) {
        // the data is not valid, but we should parse it again
        // to see if it is well formed
    }

    if (xmlDoc == null) {
        try {
            // don't validate
            SAXBuilder saxBuilder = new SAXBuilder(false);
            xmlDoc = saxBuilder.build(new StringReader(this.xml));
            this.statusLabel.setText("XML is well formed, but not valid");
        } catch (Exception ex) {
            this.statusLabel.setText("Data is not well formed XML");

            // show the stack trace in the text area
            StringWriter sw = new StringWriter();
            ex.printStackTrace(new PrintWriter(sw));
            this.xmlArea.setText(sw.toString());
        }
    }

    // if the document was parsed, show it
    if (xmlDoc != null) {
        try {
            // pretty-print the XML by indenting two spaces
            XMLOutputter xmlOut = new XMLOutputter("  ", true);
            StringWriter sw = new StringWriter();
            xmlOut.output(xmlDoc, sw);
            this.xmlArea.setText(sw.toString());
        } catch (Exception ex) {
            this.statusLabel.setText("Data could not be displayed.");

            // show the stack trace in the text area
            StringWriter sw = new StringWriter();
            ex.printStackTrace(new PrintWriter(sw));
            this.xmlArea.setText(sw.toString());
```

Example 9-12. XMLOutputPanel.java (continued)

```
            }
        }
    }
}
```

`XMLOutputPanel` is responsible for parsing the result tree to determine if it is well-formed and valid XML. It starts by parsing the text using a validating parser, simply ignoring errors. If no errors occur, the document is well-formed, valid XML and can be displayed in the text area. Otherwise, the document is parsed again, only without any validation. This allows the code to determine if the XML is at least well-formed.

If the document is not well-formed or valid, the parser's stack trace is displayed in the GUI. For many XSLT transformations, the result tree may not be XML, and this message can simply be ignored. When errors do occur, however, this should make it much easier to locate the problems.

Performance Techniques

One common criticism of XSLT is its performance. The overhead of transformation from XML to another format is the price paid for clean separation between data and programming logic, as well as the ability to customize transformations for different clients. In this section, we look at strategies for improving performance without giving up the benefits that XSLT offers.

The actual XSLT transformation is not always the root of performance problems. XML parsers have a significant impact on performance, along with many other factors such as database access time, time spent processing business logic, and network latency.

Obsessing over performance can be a dangerous trap to fall into. Focusing too heavily on optimization techniques often results in code that is difficult or impossible to understand and maintain. From a strictly technical viewpoint, the fastest technology sounds great. From a business viewpoint, time to market and maintainability are often far more important than runtime performance metrics. An application that meets performance requirements and is easy to maintain over the years makes better business sense than a highly tuned, cryptic application that runs fast but cannot be modified because the original author quit the company and nobody can figure out the code.

Stress Testing with JMeter

One good way to measure overall application throughput is to simulate how real users use an application. Apache's JMeter is designed to perform this task for web applications, measuring response time as the number of concurrent users increases. JMeter is written in Java and can display response time graphically as shown in Figure 9-8.

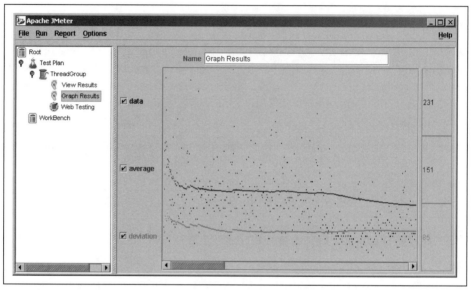

Figure 9-8. JMeter output

It should be noted that this is the output from Version 1.6 Alpha of JMeter, so later versions may change significantly. The GUI interface has been completely rewritten for Version 1.6, and many features are unfinished as this book is being written. On this display, the dots represent actual response times, the top line represents the average response time, and the bottom line represents the standard deviation from average.

Of the measurements shown on the graph, the average response time is the most useful. The numbers to the right are in milliseconds, so we can see that the average response time for this web application is 151 milliseconds. When using a tool such as JMeter, it is best to leave the stress test running for several minutes until the average response time stabilizes. It generally takes much longer for the first few tests to run because Java is loading classes, starting threads, and allocating memory. Over time, performance will fluctuate as the garbage collector runs and VMs such as HotSpot optimize code. Unless the application has memory leaks or simply cannot keep up with demand, the response time should eventually level off.

Table 9-3 shows how the View Month page from the discussion forum example in Chapter 7 fared when tested with JMeter. In this table, worst case and best case scenarios are shown. Other combinations of servlet container, XSLT processor, and database are not shown. The number of threads in the fourth column indicates the number of simulated users. In the final column, lower numbers are better.

Table 9-3. View month response time

Servlet container	XSLT processor	Database	Threads	Average response time (ms)
Tomcat 3.2.1	Xalan 2.0	Access 2000	1	130
"	"	"	5	320
"	"	"	10	760
"	"	"	20	1600
Tomcat 4.0	SAXON 6.2.2	MySQL	1	18
"	"	"	5	150
"	"	"	10	320
"	"	"	20	610

This table does not paint the complete picture. However, it should illustrate the point that in many cases, merely changing to different tools and libraries can dramatically improve performance. For the measurements shown, JMeter was instructed to simulate up to 20 concurrent users with absolutely zero delay between requests. JMeter can also be configured to insert fixed or random delays between requests, which tends to be much more representative of real-world conditions.

The goal of this test was not to benchmark the performance of the discussion forum, but rather to compare the relative performance when switching to different tools.* Over a period of many hours, the discussion forum was restarted with various combinations of servlet containers, XSLT processors, and databases. Although Tomcat 4.0 and SAXON 6.2.2 tend to be slightly faster than Tomcat 3.2.1 and Xalan 2.0, the most dramatic performance delta occurs when switching from Microsoft Access to MySQL.

More Detailed Measurements

In the previous example, the overall performance of an application was measured with Apache's JMeter. This is a great way to prove that an application scales well under stress, and it allows for comparisons between different software, hardware, and database configurations. If you reach a point where an application is simply not scaling as required, however, additional techniques must be employed to isolate bottlenecks within Java code. Tools such as JMeter show performance from an end user's perspective, rather than on a per-method basis within a Java application.

---

* Because XSLT processors and servlet containers are changing so fast, the actual tool names are not listed here.

Commercial options

One approach is to purchase a commercial profiling tool such as Sitraka's JProbe, available from *http://www.sitraka.com*, or VMGear's OptimizeIt from *http://www. vmgear.com*. Among other things, these tools can report how many times each method in an application is called, how much time is spent in each method, and how much memory is allocated. The huge advantage of tools such as these is their unique ability to tell you exactly where the hotspots are within Java code. In general, a small fraction of methods consumes a vast majority of resources.* Optimizing these specific methods often yields the biggest performance gains with the least amount of effort.

JVMPI

Sun's Java 2 SDK offers a set of command-line options that enable the Java Virtual Machine Profiling Interface (JVMPI), which can write detailed profiling information to a log file as an application runs. Example 9-13 shows the Help page reported by typing the command: **java -Xrunhprof:help**.

Example 9-13. JVMPI command-line options

```
C:\>java -Xrunhprof:help
Hprof usage: -Xrunhprof[:help]|[<option>=<value>, ...]

Option Name and Value     Description            Default
---------------------     -----------            -------
heap=dump|sites|all       heap profiling         all
cpu=samples|times|old     CPU usage              off
monitor=y|n               monitor contention     n
format=a|b                ascii or binary output a
file=<file>               write data to file     java.hprof(.txt for ascii)
net=<host>:<port>         send data over a socket write to file
depth=<size>              stack trace depth      4
cutoff=<value>            output cutoff point    0.0001
lineno=y|n                line number in traces? y
thread=y|n                thread in traces?      n
doe=y|n                   dump on exit?          y

Example: java -Xrunhprof:cpu=samples,file=log.txt,depth=3 FooClass
```

Although this is only an experimental feature of the JVM, it is useful when other tools are not available. To locate processor bottlenecks, the `cpu` option should be set to `samples`, which uses statistical estimates based on periodic samples of performance. It defaults to `off` because this feature can significantly decrease performance.

---

* Typically referred to as the 80/20 rule.

Example 9-14 lists a very small portion of the output from a single run of a Java application using the JVMPI feature. This section ranks the methods according to which consume the most time. For instance, a method that takes 20 ms to execute but is called millions of times will probably rank very high on this list, while a method that consumes one second but is only called once will be much further down on the list.

Example 9-14. Partial JVMPI output

```
rank   self   accum   count trace method
   1 13.70% 13.70%      20      31 java.lang.ClassLoader.defineClass0
   2  7.53% 21.23%      11      19 java.util.zip.ZipFile.getEntry
   3  5.48% 26.71%       8      35 java.io.Win32FileSystem.getBooleanAttributes
   4  4.11% 30.82%       6      26 java.util.zip.ZipFile.read
   5  3.42% 34.25%       5      92 java.util.zip.Inflater.inflateBytes
   6  3.42% 37.67%       5       6 java.lang.ClassLoader.findBootstrapClass
   7  2.74% 40.41%       4      22 java.util.zip.ZipFile.getEntry
   8  2.74% 43.15%       4     143 org.apache.xalan.templates
                                   StylesheetRootnewTransformer
   9  2.74% 45.89%       4      14 java.util.zip.ZipFile.open
  10  1.37% 47.26%       2       4 java.net.URLClassLoader.defineClass
```

The actual file will grow to many megabytes in size, depending on how large an application is and how long the profiler runs. As expected, a difficult task is filtering through a file of this size to find bottlenecks that are actually caused by an application's code rather than by the Java class libraries.

A majority of the JVMPI output file consists of stack traces. A number identifies each trace, and the depth command-line option affects how many lines are displayed for each stack trace. The fifth column of data in Example 9-14 contains the trace number, making it possible to search through the file for the actual stack trace:

```
TRACE 31:
    java.lang.ClassLoader.defineClass0(ClassLoader.java:Native method)
    java.lang.ClassLoader.defineClass(ClassLoader.java:486)
    java.security.SecureClassLoader.defineClass(SecureClassLoader.java:111)
    java.net.URLClassLoader.defineClass(URLClassLoader.java:248)
    java.net.URLClassLoader.access$100(URLClassLoader.java:56)
    java.net.URLClassLoader$1.run(URLClassLoader.java:195)
```

By making the stack trace depth larger, it is more likely that some of your code will show up somewhere in the report. This makes the report much larger, however. These traces are useful because they show which methods are called leading up to each hotspot.

Companies that have the budget to do so should definitely consider purchasing a tool such as JProbe or OptimizeIt. Although the JVMPI interface offers much of the same functionality that these tools offer, JVMPI output is entirely textual, requiring quite a bit of manual detective work to isolate problems. The commercial profiling tools also require some analysis but present the results in a graphical format that is substantially easier to navigate.

Unit testing

The effectiveness of simpler approaches to measurement should not be dismissed. Often, the easiest technique is to simply write a 15-line Java program that tests a specific piece of functionality. For instance, you might want to start with a short Java program that performs an XSLT transformation as shown in Chapter 5. Next, use `System.currentTimeInMillis()` to measure the time immediately before and after each transformation. Then simply experiment with different XSLT stylesheets to see which approaches offer the best performance.

Similar standalone tests can be written for various database access routines, key pieces of business logic, and code that generates XML. Since JUnit reports the time spent in each unit test, you may want to combine these performance metrics with meaningful unit tests.

Regardless of how these individual test routines are written, it is critical that the first runs are ignored. This is because the results will be greatly skewed by Java class loading and initialization time. A good approach is to execute the unit test once before recording the system time. Then execute the test many thousands of times, recording the overall time at the end of the runs. The average response time, calculated by dividing the total time by the number of runs, will be much more accurate than taking a few isolated measurements.

Another point to consider is caching. In a real application, data may change with every single request, making it difficult to cache the transformation result. Unit tests that repeatedly transform the same file are not a good representation of real-world behavior because the processor may cache the transformation result and report artificially high performance.

Using XSLT Processors Effectively

Measuring performance is the first step towards making Java and XSLT applications faster. Once the bottlenecks have been located, it is time to fix the problems.

Stylesheet caching

As mentioned several times in this book, caching XSLT stylesheets is an essential performance technique. JAXP includes the `Templates` interface for this purpose, and we already saw the implementation of a stylesheet cache in Chapter 5. Table 9-4 illustrates the performance gains seen when using the `Templates` interface to transform a small XML file repeatedly. For this test, the same transformation is performed 100 times using various programming techniques.

Table 9-4. Benefits of caching

Processor	No templates	Templates	Templates and cached XML
Xalan 2.0	71.8ms	45.9ms	39.2ms
SAXON 6.2.2	52.7ms	37.3ms	34.2ms

In the "No templates" column, the `Templates` interface was not used for transformations. As you can see, this resulted in the slowest performance because the stylesheet had to be parsed from a file with each transformation. In the next column, a Templates instance was created once and reused for each transformation. As you can see, the performance increased substantially.

In the final column of the table, the XML data was read into memory and cached as a DOM Document. Instead of reparsing the XML file with each request, the same DOM tree was cached and reused for each of the transformations. This yielded a slight performance gain because the XML file did not have to be read from the file system with each transformation.

Although these results seem to imply that SAXON is faster than Xalan, this may be a faulty assumption. Performance can vary greatly depending on how large the input files are and which features of XSLT are used. It is wise to test performance with your application before choosing one set of tools over another.

Result caching

When the XML is highly dynamic and changes with each request, XSLT caching may be the best one can hope for. But when the same data is requested repeatedly, such as on the home page for your company, it makes sense to cache the result of the transformation rather than the XSLT stylesheet. This way, the transformation is performed only when the XML or XSLT actually change.

Example 9-15 presents a utility class that caches the results of XSLT transformations. In this implementation, both the XML data and XSLT stylesheet must come from static files. If the timestamp of either file changes, the transformation is performed again. Otherwise, a cached copy of the transformation result is returned to the caller.

Example 9-15 . ResultCache.java

```
package com.oreilly.javaxslt.util;

import java.io.*;
import java.util.*;
import javax.xml.transform.*;
```

Example 9-15 . ResultCache.java (continued)

```java
import javax.xml.transform.stream.*;

/**
 * A utility class that caches XSLT transformation results in memory.
 *
 * @author Eric M. Burke
 */
public class ResultCache {
    private static Map cache = new HashMap();

    /**
     * Flush all results from memory, emptying the cache.
     */
    public static synchronized void flushAll() {
        cache.clear();
    }

    /**
     * Perform a single XSLT transformation.
     */
    public static synchronized String transform(String xmlFileName,
            String xsltFileName) throws TransformerException {

        MapKey key = new MapKey(xmlFileName, xsltFileName);

        File xmlFile = new File(xmlFileName);
        File xsltFile = new File(xsltFileName);

        MapValue value = (MapValue) cache.get(key);
        if (value == null || value.isDirty(xmlFile, xsltFile)) {
            // this step performs the transformation
            value = new MapValue(xmlFile, xsltFile);
            cache.put(key, value);
        }

        return value.result;
    }

    // prevent instantiation of this class
    private ResultCache() {
    }

    ///////////////////////////////////////////////////////////////////
    // a helper class that represents a key in the cache map
    ///////////////////////////////////////////////////////////////////
    static class MapKey {
        String xmlFileName;
        String xsltFileName;
```

Example 9-15 . ResultCache.java (continued)

```java
        MapKey(String xmlFileName, String xsltFileName) {
            this.xmlFileName = xmlFileName;
            this.xsltFileName = xsltFileName;
        }

        public boolean equals(Object obj) {
            if (obj instanceof MapKey) {
                MapKey rhs = (MapKey) obj;
                return this.xmlFileName.equals(rhs.xmlFileName)
                        && this.xsltFileName.equals(rhs.xsltFileName);
            }
            return false;
        }

        public int hashCode() {
            return this.xmlFileName.hashCode() ^ this.xsltFileName.hashCode();
        }
    }

    /////////////////////////////////////////////////////////////////////
    // a helper class that represents a value in the cache map
    /////////////////////////////////////////////////////////////////////
    static class MapValue {
        long xmlLastModified;   // when the XML file was modified
        long xsltLastModified;  // when the XSLT file was modified
        String result;

        MapValue(File xmlFile, File xsltFile) throws TransformerException {
            this.xmlLastModified = xmlFile.lastModified();
            this.xsltLastModified = xsltFile.lastModified();

            TransformerFactory transFact = TransformerFactory.newInstance();
            Transformer trans = transFact.newTransformer(
                    new StreamSource(xsltFile));

            StringWriter sw = new StringWriter();
            trans.transform(new StreamSource(xmlFile), new StreamResult(sw));

            this.result = sw.toString();
        }

        /**
         * @return true if either the XML or XSLT file has been
         * modified more recently than this cache entry.
         */
        boolean isDirty(File xmlFile, File xsltFile) {
```

Example 9-15 . ResultCache.java (continued)

```
        return this.xmlLastModified < xmlFile.lastModified()
            || this.xsltLastModified < xsltFile.lastModified();
    }
  }
}
```

The key to this class is its `transform()` method. This method takes filenames of an XML file and XSLT stylesheet as arguments and returns the transformation result as a `String`. If any error occurs, a `TransformerException` is thrown:

```
public static synchronized String transform(String xmlFileName,
        String xsltFileName) throws TransformerException {
```

The cache is implemented using a `java.util.Map` data structure, which requires key/value pairs of data. The `MapKey` helper class is used as the key:

```
MapKey key = new MapKey(xmlFileName, xsltFileName);

File xmlFile = new File(xmlFileName);
File xsltFile = new File(xsltFileName);
```

Next, the value is retrieved from the cache. Another helper class, `MapValue`, keeps track of the transformation result and when each file was last modified. If this is the first request, the value will be `null`. Otherwise, the `isDirty()` method determines if either file has been updated:

```
        MapValue value = (MapValue) cache.get(key);
        if (value == null || value.isDirty(xmlFile, xsltFile)) {
            // this step performs the transformation
            value = new MapValue(xmlFile, xsltFile);
            cache.put(key, value);
        }

        return value.result;
    }
```

As the comment indicates, constructing a new `MapValue` causes the XSLT transformation to occur. Unless exceptions are thrown, the result of the transformation is returned to the caller.

When compared to the results shown earlier in Table 9-4, this approach to caching is much faster. In fact, the average response time is less than a millisecond once the initial transformation has been performed.

This approach is quite easy to implement for applications based on a collection of static files but is significantly more difficult for database-driven applications. Since more dynamic applications may generate new XML with each invocation, a generic utility class cannot simply cache the result of the transformation. Stale data is the biggest problem with dynamic caching. When the result of an XSLT transformation is stored in memory and the underlying database changes, the cache must be refreshed for users to see the correct data.

Let's suppose that we want to add result caching to the discussion forum application presented in Chapter 7. Since messages cannot be modified once they have been posted, this should be fairly easy to implement for the View Message page. One easy approach is to keep a cache of a fixed number of messages. Whenever a user views a message, the generated web page is added to the cache. If the cache exceeds a specified number of messages, the oldest entries can be flushed.

For more dynamic pages, such as the Month View page, the database must be queried to determine when the most recent message was posted for that particular message board. If the most recently posted message is newer than the cached web page, the transformation must be performed again using the updated data. As you might guess, this sort of caching must be done on a case-by-case basis, because it is very tightly coupled to the database design.

WARNING   Web applications relying on URL rewriting for session tracking may
             not be able to cache transformation results. This is because, as out-
             lined in Chapter 8, every URL must be dynamically encoded with the
             jsessionid when cookies are disabled.

As with any other type of optimization, the benefits of caching must be carefully weighed against the costs of added complexity. The best approach is to analyze log files to see which pages are requested most often and to focus optimization efforts there.

Writing Effective XSLT

A big performance hit can be incurred during the XSLT transformation process. For large XML documents in particular, try to avoid situations where large portions of the tree must be processed repeatedly. The `//` operator can be particularly dangerous:

```
<xsl:apply-templates select="/.//name"/>
```

In this statement, the entire document is recursively searched for all <name> elements, beginning at the root. The XSLT processor has no way of knowing where <name> might appear, so it must check every node in the document. If the specific path is known, a more efficient approach is:

```
<xsl:apply-templates select="/company/employee/name"/>
```

Variables can also be used to improve performance. For example, key pieces of data may be copied to the result tree several times. Do not do this each time the company owner's name must be displayed:

```
<xsl:value-of select="/company/owner/name/last"/>
<xsl:text> </xsl:text>
<xsl:value-of select="/company/owner/name/first"/>
```

Instead, assign the name to a variable once and reuse that variable throughout the stylesheet. This has the added benefit of making the XSLT more readable:

```
<!-- output the value of the companyOwner variable -->
<xsl:value-of select="$companyOwner"/>
```

Another common tip is to write inline code wherever possible. Instead of using `<xsl:apply-templates>` to recursively process XML data, use `<xsl:value-of>` to directly output the current node. This approach may result in duplicate code, however; a key reason to use templates is to modularize a stylesheet into reusable pieces of functionality. This is a good example of the tradeoff between code maintenance and raw performance that developers are often faced with.

Sorting within the XSLT may introduce performance problems, primarily because the entire node set must be sorted before any content can be output to the result tree. If it is easy to pre-sort the XML content using Java code, the XSLT processor may be able to transform the document using less memory by outputting some of the result tree before the entire document is processed.

Finally, writing smaller XSLT stylesheets is a great way to improve performance. Cascading style sheets (CSS) should be used whenever possible, because the CSS style instructions can be stored in a separate file, thus keeping the XSLT and result tree much smaller. JavaScript functions can also be placed in a separate file, eliminating the need to embed the JavaScript code within the stylesheet.

CSS was used in this manner back in Chapter 7 for the discussion forum example. It is worth mentioning again that CSS is used only for defining styles, such as font colors, indentation, alignment, and colors. Many of these styles can also be defined directly in HTML, for instance:

```
<h1 align="center">Some Heading</h1>
```

By defining the alignment in a separate CSS file, however, the HTML is reduced to:

```
<h1>Some Heading</h1>
```

Because the HTML is now simplified, the XSLT stylesheet is also simplified. This is why CSS complements XSLT so nicely and should be used whenever possible.

Interacting with EJB

Enterprise JavaBeans (EJB) objects are server-side components that encapsulate business logic and access to data. Because EJBs execute inside of application servers, they are typically accessed remotely using Java Remote Method Invocation (RMI) interfaces. This implies that method calls to EJB components occur over a network connection; they are much slower than local method calls within the same VM. For this reason, care must be taken when sending data to and from the application server.

Sending XML from EJBs

From the perspective of Java and XSLT, the critical issue is determining where to produce XML. There are basically two options available. The first is to produce the XML within the EJB container, thus providing a pure XML interface to any client wishing to use the beans. For instance, a bean may have the following additional methods that know how to produce XML:

```
public String getLeaderXML() throws RemoteException;
public String getTeamMembersXML() throws RemoteException;
public String getProjectInformation() throws RemoteException;
```

Each of these methods simply returns a `String` that contains XML content. Figure 9-9 illustrates how this model works.

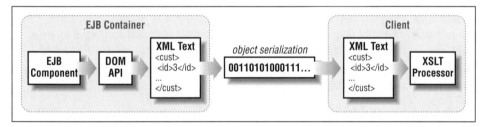

Figure 9-9. Generating XML in the EJB tier

TIP   Another variation on this theme is to use a helper class whose sole responsibility is to produce XML from a bean, rather than embedding the XML production directly in the bean.

The EJB component is responsible for generating XML before sending a response to the client. Although DOM is shown in the figure, JDOM or any other XML generation API may be used. The client, whether a servlet container or a standalone Java client, sees XML only from the server.

At one extreme, each of these XML strings is a well-formed XML document. Another option, perhaps more useful, is returning fragments of XML. The client can then assemble many of these XML fragments into more complex XML documents. While this does put slightly more burden on the client to assemble the pieces properly, it does offer significantly more flexibility.

This approach may seem like it offers the cleanest interface to the EJB tier. As long as the structure of the XML remains the same, both client and server can change their internal object models without affecting the other.

WARNING   Many DOM implementations are not comprised of `Serializable` Java objects. Furthermore, the client may not use the same DOM implementation that the server uses. For these reasons, it is rarely a good idea to try sending DOM trees directly from an EJB to a client.

Producing XML on the EJB tier has significant drawbacks, however. First, the size of XML text is typically quite large. Compression of the text is essential, particularly as the size of the XML gets larger. While compression reduces bandwidth requirements, it increases the processor workload on both client and server for compression and decompression. This is supported by `java.util.zip.` `GZIPInputStream` and `java.util.zip.GZIPOutputStream`.

The second drawback is that 100 percent of an application's business logic can rarely be placed inside of EJB components. Although this is an admirable goal, it means that the client must make a remote network call to the server for every operation. By simply returning XML to the client, it is much harder for some of the business logic to be offloaded to the client machine.

Sending objects from EJBs

The second option is to leave XML out of the EJB components altogether. Instead, each bean method returns instances of helper classes such as `Employee` and `ProjectInfo`. With this approach, the client can perform some business logic by invoking methods locally on the returned objects. Figure 9-10 illustrates where XML production occurs in this model.

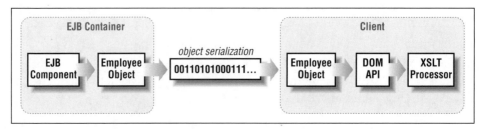

Figure 9-10. Generating XML on the client tier

As shown, the `Employee` object is serialized, and the serialized object is sent from the EJB container to the client, rather than a big text string of XML. On the client machine, the DOM API is used to convert the Employee into an XML representation, which is fed directly into an XSLT processor. By using DOM on the client, the XML never has to be completely converted to text, which tends to be slightly faster for transformations.

TIP   While custom XML production using DOM is common today, more automated XML data-binding technologies are becoming increasingly popular. Sun's Java Architecture for XML Data Binding (JAXB) provides a standard Java API for mapping to and from XML documents and Java objects.

Although the bandwidth requirements for serialized objects are comparable to compressed XML, more finely grained requests are easier when returning objects instead of XML text. Consider an online benefit processing application. In this type of application, an employee may have a spouse, children, beneficiaries, and benefit elections. As the user moves from page to page in this application, the `Employee` object can be cached in the `HttpSession`. As new pages require additional data, they merely call methods on this cached `Employee` object:

```
// somewhere in a servlet...
if (employee.isMarried()) {
    // request the Spouse, which will make a call to the EJB tier
    // unless the spouse was requested earlier and is cached
    Person spouse = employee.getSpouse();
    // generate XML for the spouse...
} else {
    // simply generate XML for the employee; do not call the EJB tier
}
```

As the code fragment shows, when an employee does not have a spouse, no additional call to the EJB tier is required. If the EJB tier returns pure XML, then additional calls to the EJB tier are almost certainly required for each web page that is displayed. This is because the web tier sees only big blocks of XML text from the EJB tier, making it much more difficult to add any business logic to the web tier.

The biggest advantage of returning objects instead of XML is the ability to keep presentation logic out of the EJB tier. Most web applications combine data from several EJBs onto each web page. End user requirements for the user interface tend to change much more frequently than data requirements. It makes sense to keep the EJB tier stable while changing the XML generation code in the web tier more frequently.

10

Wireless Applications

Cellular phones, personal digital assistants (PDAs), and various other forms of wireless devices are taking the world by storm, opening new avenues for development as well as a whole host of challenges for developers. These devices are tiny compared to PCs, both in terms of physical size and processing power. This means that traditional HTML web pages are unacceptable, opening the door for new markup languages based on XML to take center stage.

This chapter introduces key concepts behind wireless technologies with particular emphasis on Wireless Markup Language (WML), a concise alternative to HTML that is custom made for wireless devices. The role of XSLT and servlets will also be explored though an example application that allows wireless users to browse movie theaters and showtimes.

Wireless Technologies

The family of technologies used by wireless devices is in its infancy, just a few years old. Because of this, there are a few competing markup languages in use today. In Japan, the i-mode protocol is the market leader. i-mode is defined by a company named NTT DoCoMo, utilizing a subset of HTML known as Compact HTML (cHTML). This markup language shares much of the same syntax as HTML but is essentially proprietary and is not based on XML.

In Europe and the United States, Wireless Access Protocol (WAP) is more popular. WAP currently utilizes WML, which is quite different from HTML and cHTML. In coming years, it is likely that most vendors will consolidate around XHTML Basic, although existing markup languages will need to be supported for quite some time. WML and cHTML will be seen as transitional technologies that allowed us to start experimenting with wireless services. At any rate, XSLT offers an excellent way to minimize risk as vendors work through their differences and technology progresses.

Phone Simulators

A variety of cell phone simulators are illustrated throughout this chapter. All of these tools run on a PC, allowing developers to test various devices without purchasing actual phones and subscribing to wireless Internet access services. Here are some products and URLs to start with:

- Ericsson WapIDE (*http://www.ericsson.com*)
- Motorola Mobile Application Development Kit (*http://www.motorola.com*)
- Nokia WAP Toolkit (*http://www.nokia.com*)
- Openwave Software Development Kit (*http://developer.openwave.com*)

Why Not HTML?

HTML is used by nearly every web site and can theoretically be used by wireless devices as well. All that is needed is a web browser, a big display, lots of processing power, and sufficient bandwidth. Maybe not!

Problems with HTML

Consider this web page:

```
<boDY>
  <h1 align=center>Welcome to our home page!</h1>
  <ul>
    <LI>first item
    <LI>second item
    <Li>third item
```

Believe it or not, Netscape 4.x, Netscape 6, and IE 5.5 all display this page perfectly, without a single warning or error. Browsers are incredibly forgiving of errors in HTML, because vendors and end users want these browsers to display all web pages properly. Since only a tiny fraction of web sites are written using well-formed HTML, browsers must be written to silently recover from a wide range of errors. A browser that fails to display poorly written HTML is not acceptable in the marketplace because it fails on so many pages.

Nonprogrammers may view this as a benefit, because it allows them to create web sites without too much concern for capitalization, quotes, or properly nested tags. What they do not realize is that browsers are much more complex than they really need to be. Writing HTML parsers to handle every conceivable form of poorly written HTML results in huge, complex browsers that require far too many resources to execute on a handheld device.

Until all web pages are written using well-formed HTML or XHTML, browsers must support poorly written HTML. Until browsers are more stringent, however, web authors will continue writing sloppy code.

Limitations of current devices

Another blow against HTML is the simple fact that current wireless devices have tiny displays, small amounts of memory, and very slow network connections. Devices with five line displays simply cannot display HTML tables, framesets, and large fonts. Instead, these devices demand entirely new markup languages that are far smaller and make more efficient use of available resources.

The Wireless Architecture

Although wireless users want to access the internet, they cannot simply dial a phone number and expect to browse web sites. This is because wireless devices use protocols based on WAP, rather than traditional web-based protocols such as HTTP. Figure 10-1 shows how a typical web server fits into the wireless architecture.

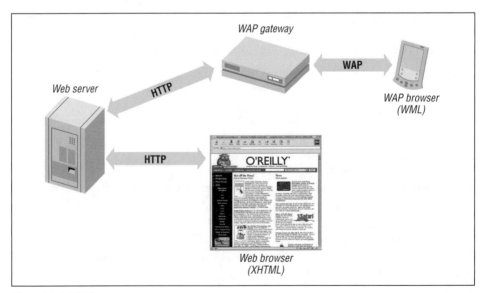

Figure 10-1. WAP gateways

As shown, a new type of server called a *WAP gateway* is introduced into the equation. This is a server that converts HTTP traffic into WAP traffic, using protocols appropriate to the given wireless service. The details of this are well beyond the scope of this chapter and are generally unimportant to most developers. This is because cell phone companies and other wireless portals provide these gateways, allowing their customers to access the entire Internet via their wireless devices. Typical web application developers can deploy servlets and WML content onto normal web servers, and the content will be available to wireless users automatically.

Java, XSLT, and WML

Unless a web application is limited to a corporate intranet, it must be designed to support a wide variety of device types. As the upcoming examples will demonstrate, wireless devices are far less consistent than web browsers. This amplifies the need for the clean separation between data and presentation that XML and XSLT offer, because many different presentation styles may be needed to take advantage of specific devices. Java servlets are used to tie everything together, detecting the type of client device and driving the XSLT transformation process.

A WML Example

WML is a relatively new XML-based markup language specifically designed for wireless devices. As such, it is compact, easy to parse, and optimized for small displays. WML is the product of the WAP Forum, an association consisting of over 500 member companies that defines specifications for wireless devices. You can learn more about WML by downloading the specification from *http://www. wapforum.org* or by reading *Learning WML and WMLScript* by Martin Frost (O'Reilly).

First of all, WML is an XML-based markup language.* This means that, unlike HTML, all WML documents must be well-formed and valid. For instance, all tags must be lowercase and nested properly, and attribute values must be quoted. Example 10-1 lists a WML document.

Example 10-1. A very simple WML page

```
<?xml version="1.0" encoding="UTF-8"?>
<!DOCTYPE wml PUBLIC "-//WAPFORUM//DTD WML 1.1//EN"
        "http://www.wapforum.org/DTD/wml_1.1.xml">
<wml>
  <card id="home" title="Name Entry">
    <p>Enter your first name:
      <input name="firstName"/>
```

---

* WML documents are XML documents that conform to one of the WML DTDs.

Example 10-1. A very simple WML page (continued)

```
    </p>
    <p>Enter your age:
      <input name="age" format="*N"/>
    </p>
    <do type="accept">
      <go href="#hello"/>
    </do>
  </card>
  <card id="hello" title="Hello">
    <p>
    Hello there, $(firstName:e)!
    </p>
    <p>
    You claim to be <em>$(age:e)</em> years
    old...can this possibly be true?
    </p>
    <p>Click <a href="#home">here</a> to
       change your answer.</p>
  </card>
</wml>
```

This particular WML document adheres to Version 1.1 of the WML specification, as indicated by the document type declaration. Unlike HTML, the root element is <wml>, which is commonly known as a *deck*. The WML deck contains one or more <card> elements, each of which represents a single screen that is displayed on the device. Grouping cards into decks increases performance because the wireless device can make fewer requests to the server as the user navigates from card to card.

The first card in this example prompts the user to enter his first name and age. Unlike HTML form techniques, these values are stored in the WML variables firstName and age. This is much better than posting a form to the server because of the limited bandwidth available to wireless devices. The age field illustrates another interesting feature of WML that does not exist in HTML:

```
    <input name="age" format="*N"/>
```

The format attribute shown here indicates that the user can enter any number of numeric digits or decimal points.* Formats for date entry, telephone numbers, and other known patterns can also be configured using simple pattern strings defined by the WML specification. This is a big advantage over traditional web techniques that require scripting language support to perform client-side validation. Table 10-1 lists all of the format patterns supported by WML 1.1.

---

* Not all devices support this feature.

Table 10-1. WML format strings

Format	Displays
A	Uppercase letters, symbols, and punctuation characters; not numbers.
a	Lowercase letters, symbols, and punctuation characters; not numbers.
N	Any number.
n	Any number, symbol, or punctuation character.
X	Same as A, but includes numbers.
x	Same as a, but includes numbers.
M	Any character, but the device should try to default to uppercase entry.
m	Any character, but the device should try to default to lowercase entry.
*f	Any number of the specified characters; f is one of the format codes shown in this table. Must appear at the end of the format string.
nf	n is a number from 1 to 9, specifying the number of characters that can be entered. f is one of the format codes shown in this table. Must appear at the end of the format string.
\c	Displays a specific character in the field. For instance, NNN\-NN\-NNNN specifies a data format for U.S. social security numbers, allowing the user to enter a number such as 333-22-4444.

The first card in Example 10-1 finishes with a `<do>` tag:

```
<do type="accept">
  <go href="#hello"/>
</do>
```

This causes a button to appear, which acts like a hyperlink to the #hello URL when the user clicks on it. This is a reference to the second card in the deck. Therefore, the server is not contacted when this particular button is clicked. Figure 10-2 shows how one particular device displays the first and second cards.

As you can see in the picture, the second card displays the values that were entered in the first card.* Here is some of the code again:

```
Hello there, $(firstName:e)!
```

This demonstrates how to utilize WML variables, something that is not possible with HTML. The :e at the end of the variable name is optional and instructs the device to perform URL escaping of the text before displaying it. This is useful if the user enters spaces and other characters such as < that may cause problems with the WML.

Hyperlinks in WML look just like hyperlinks in HTML:

---

* Notice that this particular device does not honor the `<em>` tag when the age is displayed.

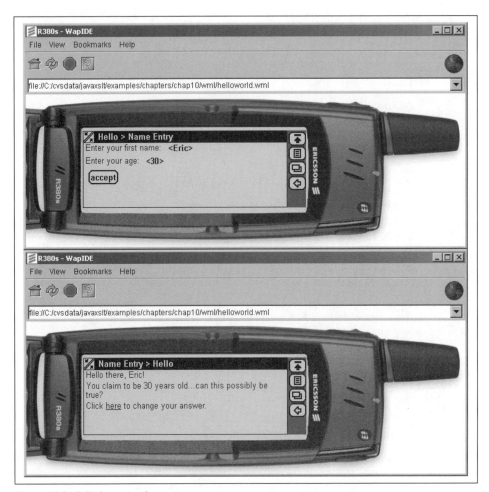

Figure 10-2. Cell phone simulator

```
<p>Click <a href="#home">here</a> to
```

The trickiest part about WML is the wide variety of devices that may be in use. Figure 10-3 shows these same two cards on a cellular phone that has a smaller display.

As you can see, the first card does not fit on the display, so the user has to scroll. On the second card, the phone honors the emphasis (<em>) tag when displaying the age, while the first browser in Figure 10-2 does not. While differences like these should diminish as vendors have more time to implement the complete WML specification, there are no guarantees as to how buttons and <input> fields will be displayed. In many cases, <do> tags are mapped to physical buttons on the cell phone keypad rather than displayed as buttons on the screen.

Figure 10-3. Another cell phone simulator

WMLScript and WBMP

Because of bandwidth constraints, scripting capability is critical for wireless devices. WAP defines a scripting language called WMLScript, which is tightly integrated with WML and features a syntax that is very similar to JavaScript. With WMLScript, form validation and lightweight processing can be performed on the client device, greatly reducing the number of requests to a server.

Wireless Bitmap (WBMP) is a very simple image format that, as expected, is optimized for small devices. WBMP files are black and white and can be created with a number of free tools. There is even a free web site at *http://www.teraflops.com/wbmp* that will convert GIF, JPEG, and BMP images to WBMP using a browser-based interface.

Again, refer to *Learning WML & WMLScript* for the complete story on these technologies.

Servlets and WML

Servlets are important to wireless developers because they can detect the type of client device. Different XSLT stylesheets can then be selected for regular web browsers, sophisticated PDAs, and simple cell phones.

Identifying the client

Detecting the type of client is the most important role of the servlet. There are two HTTP header values that are typically used for this purpose: User-Agent and Accept. The text in Example 10-2 shows what an HTTP header looks like for the Ericsson R520m cell phone simulator.

Example 10-2. Example HTTP header

```
GET / HTTP/1.1
Host: 25.12.44.22
Accept: application/vnd.wap.wmlc, application/vnd.wap.wbxml,
application/vnd.wap.wmlscriptc, */*, text/vnd.wap.wml, application/xml, text/xml,
text/vnd.wap.wmlscript
User-Agent: EricssonR520/R1A
Accept-Charset: *
```

The HTTP header is text, and each line after the first consists of a name:value pair. The Accept header indicates the MIME content types that this device knows how to display, so searching for text/vnd.wap.wml is a simple way to detect if the client device supports WML. If the client accepts this MIME type, it could be a wireless device.

WARNING   Some browsers may also know how to display *text/vnd.wap.wml*. The Accept header is not a completely reliable way to determine the client type.

The User-Agent header definitively identifies the device. However, vendors do not consistently follow standards. Table 10-2 lists several user agents reported by various cell phone simulators.

Table 10-2. Sample user agents

Simulator type	User-Agent
Ericsson R320s	EricssonR320/R1A
Ericsson R380s	R380 2.1 WAP1.1
Ericsson R520m	EricssonR520/R1A
Motorola	Motorola VoxGateway/2.0
Nokia	Nokia-WAP-Toolkit/2.1
Openwave	OWG1 UP/4.1.20a UP.Browser/4.1.20a-XXXX UP.Link/4.1.HTTP-DIRECT

In general, a model number follows the vendor name. However, the Ericsson R380s does not follow this convention. As mentioned in Chapter 8, almost every web browser reports a `User-Agent` that begins with the text "Mozilla," which can be used to identify a web browser rather than a wireless device.

From the servlet, it is quite easy to get to these HTTP headers:

```
protected void doGet(HttpServletRequest req, HttpServletResponse res)
        throws IOException, ServletException {
    String userAgent = req.getHeader("User-Agent");
    String accept = req.getHeader("Accept");

    if (userAgent != null) {
        ...
```

A more complete example is presented in the section "Movie Theater Example."

Setting the content type

Once the client type has been identified as either a web browser or a specific type of wireless device, the response must be sent back. Table 10-3 lists the three most common content types a servlet will encounter.

Table 10-3. MIME content types

MIME type	Extension	Description
text/vnd.wap.wml	.wml	WML source code
text/vnd.wap.wmlscript	.wmls	WMLScript source code
image/vnd.wap.wbmp	.wmlc	Wireless Bitmaps

This simply means that before sending a WML response back to the client device, the following code must be present in the servlet:

```
public void doGet(HttpServletRequest req, HttpServletResponse res) ... {
    res.setContentType("text/vnd.wap.wml");
    // now obtain a PrintWriter or OutputStream and perform
```

```
// the XSLT transformation...
```

For dynamically generated pages, this is all that must be done. If a web application also consists of static resources such as WMLScript files and WBMP images, the web application deployment descriptor should also be updated. Example 10-3 lists some additional content that should be added to the deployment descriptor.

Example 10-3. Deployment descriptor MIME mappings

```
<mime-mapping>
  <extension>.wml</extension>
  <mime-type>text/vnd.wap.wml</mime-type>
</mime-mapping>
<mime-mapping>
  <extension>.wmls</extension>
  <mime-type>text/vnd.wap.wmlscript</mime-type>
</mime-mapping>
<mime-mapping>
  <extension>.wmlc</extension>
  <mime-type>image/vnd.wap.wbmp</mime-type>
</mime-mapping>
```

This effectively tells the web server to use the specified MIME type whenever the client requests files with the listed extensions.

Movie Theater Example

Admittedly, this is a crash course introduction to WML; hopefully a more complete example will clarify some of the concepts.

Storyboard

This example consists of three WML decks and several cards. Through this interface, users can select their city, select a particular movie theater within that city, and finally view showtimes for that theater. The diagram in Figure 10-4 contains the storyboard for this application, showing how each screen links to the next.

As the illustration indicates, the first deck contains a splash screen that displays for 1.5 seconds. This takes advantage of a WML timer, automatically displaying the city selection page after the timer expires. From this page, the user can select from a list of cities.

The second deck consists of a single card, which shows a list of theaters for the current city. Once the user clicks on a particular city, the third deck is displayed. This deck may have many cards, depending on how many movies are showing in that particular theater. The user can browse from movie to movie without requesting additional data from the server.

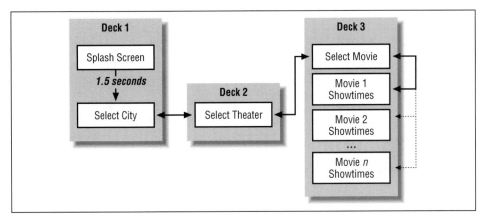

Figure 10-4. Storyboard

For the servlet to dynamically build the appropriate decks and cards, each page requires certain parameters. These parameters are passed along to the XSLT stylesheet so it can select the appropriate data from the XML file. Table 10-4 lists the required parameters for each deck. These will appear in each of the WML files, as well as in the servlet and XSLT stylesheets. If any parameter is invalid or missing, the application merely returns the user to the home page.

Table 10-4. Required parameters

Deck	Parameters	Notes
1	none	Shows all cities
2	action=theaters city=*city_id*	Shows theaters for a single city
3	action=showtimes city=*city_id* theater=*theater_id*	Shows all movies for a specific theater in the given city

XML data

To keep things simple for the theater owners, this application produces all pages from a single XML datafile on the server. The DTD for this file is shown in Example 10-4.

Example 10-4. Movie theater DTD

```
<!ELEMENT movies (moviedef+, city+)>
<!ELEMENT moviedef (shortName, longName)>
<!ELEMENT city (name, theater+)>
<!ELEMENT name (#PCDATA)>
<!ELEMENT shortName (#PCDATA)>
<!ELEMENT longName (#PCDATA)>
```

Example 10-4. Movie theater DTD (continued)

```
<!ELEMENT theater (name, movie+)>
<!ELEMENT movie (times)>
<!ELEMENT times (#PCDATA)>
<!ATTLIST city
  id ID #REQUIRED
>
<!ATTLIST movie
  ref IDREF #REQUIRED
>
<!ATTLIST moviedef
  id ID #REQUIRED
>
<!ATTLIST theater
  id ID #REQUIRED
>
```

It is worth pointing out the difference between a <moviedef> and <movie> element. Basically, a <moviedef> defines a short and long description for a movie in a single place. Since the same movie is likely to be listed in many different theaters, it makes sense to define the <moviedef> once, and then refer to it from other parts of the document using <movie> elements.

Example 10-5 contains a portion of an example XML datafile that adheres to this DTD. This is the data displayed in the upcoming screen shots.

Example 10-5. Movie theater XML datafile

```
<?xml version="1.0" encoding="UTF-8"?>
<?xml-stylesheet type="text/xsl" href="../xslt/wml/showtimes.xslt"?>
<movies>
  <!-- all movies -->
  <moviedef id="star_wars1">
    <shortName>Star Wars Ep 1</shortName>
    <longName>Star Wars Episode I: The Phantom Menace</longName>
  </moviedef>
  <moviedef id="star_wars4">
    <shortName>Star Wars</shortName>
    <longName>Star Wars: A New Hope</longName>
  </moviedef>
  <moviedef id="star_wars5">
    <shortName>Emp Strikes Back</shortName>
    <longName>The Empire Strikes Back</longName>
  </moviedef>
  ...additional moviedef elements

  <city id="stl">
    <name>St. Louis</name>
    <theater id="westolive16">
```

Example 10-5. Movie theater XML datafile (continued)

```
      <name>West Olive 16</name>
      <movie ref="star_wars1">
        <times>10:15a, 3:30, 12:30, 5:45, 7:15, 10:30</times>
      </movie>
      <movie ref="star_wars4">
        <times>1:30, 4:00, 6:00</times>
      </movie>
      <movie ref="star_wars5">
        <times>2:30, 4:10, 6:20</times>
      </movie>
      <movie ref="back2future3">
        <times>4:00, 6:00, 8:00, 10:00</times>
      </movie>
    </theater>
    <theater id="stcharles18">
      <name>St. Charles 18</name>
      <movie ref="star_wars4">
        <times>10:15a, 3:30, 12:30, 5:45, 7:15, 10:30</times>
      </movie>
      <movie ref="star_wars5">
        <times>1:30, 4:00, 6:00</times>
      </movie>
      <movie ref="back2future2">
        <times>4:00, 6:00, 8:00, 10:00</times>
      </movie>
    </theater>

    ... additional theater elements
  </city>

  ... additional city elements

</movies>
```

As you can see in the XML, nothing in the data indicates that the output must be
WML. In fact, this application can support both XHTML and WML output via different XSLT stylesheets. Of course, WML support is the primary goal of this application. Therefore, <shortName> is included to support wireless devices. If this
were targeted towards only web browsers, this element would not be required.

WML prototypes and screen shots

When using XSLT to produce XHTML or WML, it is a good idea to start with prototypes. This is because XSLT adds a level of indirection that makes it hard to visualize the result. It is much easier to simply create static WML first, test it using a
simulator, and then develop the XSLT stylesheets once everything is working.

Example 10-6 lists the first WML deck used in this example. As mentioned earlier, this deck contains two cards, the first of which is a splash screen that displays for 1.5 seconds.

Example 10-6. Home page WML

```
<?xml version="1.0" encoding="UTF-8"?>
<!DOCTYPE wml PUBLIC "-//WAPFORUM//DTD WML 1.1//EN"
"http://www.wapforum.org/DTD/wml_1.1.xml">
<wml>
  <card ontimer="#home" title="ABC Theaters" id="splash">
    <timer value="15"/>
    <p align="center">
      <big>Welcome to ABC Theaters</big>
    </p>
    <p>Mmmm...Popcorn...</p>
    <do type="accept">
      <go href="#home"/>
    </do>
  </card>
  <card newcontext="true" title="Home" id="home">
    <p align="center">Please select your city:
      <select multiple="false" name="city">
        <option value="chi">Chicago</option>
        <option value="stl">St. Louis</option>
        <option value="seb">Sebastopol</option>
      </select>
    </p>
    <p>
      <em>
        <a href="movieguide?action=theaters&amp;city=$(city)">Show Theaters...</a>
      </em>
    </p>
  </card>
</wml>
```

The `ontimer` attribute of the first card indicates the URL to load when the `<timer>` element expires. The timer value is 15, meaning 15 tenths of a second, or 1.5 seconds. This first card also contains a `<do>` element, allowing the user to click on a button to jump to the home page if she does not want to wait for the timer to expire. Like XHTML, the `<p>` element indicates a paragraph of text, causing text to appear on the next line of the display.

The next card contains a `<select>` element, allowing the user to select from a list of cities. The value of the selection is assigned to the `city` variable, making it easy to submit the information to the server with the `<a>` tag:

```
<a href="movieguide?action=theaters&amp;city=$(city)">Show Theaters...</a>
```

This is actually the final URL used by the finished application, rather than a proto-type URL. During the prototyping phase, the following link is more appropriate:

```
<a href="theaters.wml">Show Theaters...</a>
```

By using URLs to static WML files, it is at least possible to navigate from page to page before the servlet is written. Figure 10-5 shows how these first two pages look on a cell phone simulator.

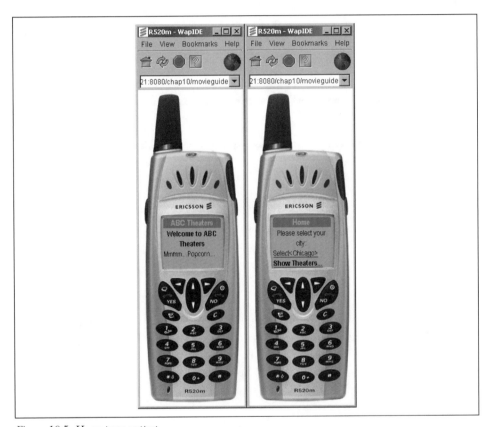

Figure 10-5. Home page output

The image to the left shows the splash screen, which is replaced by the image on the right after 1.5 seconds. On this particular phone, the user navigates with the up and down arrows, making selections by clicking on the telephone's YES button.

The next WML page, shown in Example 10-7, shows a list of theaters for the current city. In this example, the list uses a series of hyperlinks. This can also be done using a `<select>` tag, as shown in the previous example. However, the user can see the entire list when hyperlinks and `<br/>` tags are used. Of course, on smaller displays the user will typically have to scroll down to see all items.

Example 10-7. Theater listing WML

```
<?xml version="1.0" encoding="UTF-8"?>
<!DOCTYPE wml PUBLIC "-//WAPFORUM//DTD WML 1.1//EN"
    "http://www.wapforum.org/DTD/wml_1.1.xml">
<wml>
  <card title="Theaters" id="theaters">
    <p>
      <big>St. Louis</big>
    </p>
    <p>Select a theater:</p>
    <p>
      <a href="movieguide?action=showtimes&amp;city=stl&amp;theater=westolive16">
          West Olive 16</a>
      <br/>
      <a href="movieguide?action=showtimes&amp;city=stl&amp;theater=stcharles18">
          St. Charles 18</a>
      <br/>
      <a href="movieguide?action=showtimes&amp;city=stl&amp;theater=ofallon">
          O'Fallon Cine</a>
      <br/>
    </p>
    <p>
      <em>
        <a href="movieguide">Change city...</a>
      </em>
    </p>
  </card>
</wml>
```

This WML file is shown on the left side of Figure 10-6 using a different cell phone simulator. On the right side of this figure, an XHTML representation of the same data is shown in a web browser. These images were generated using the same servlet and XML datafile but different XSLT stylesheets.

Figure 10-6. Theater listing output

The final deck is shown in Example 10-8. As mentioned earlier, this consists of several cards, one per movie.

Example 10-8. Showtimes WML

```
<?xml version="1.0" encoding="UTF-8"?>
<!DOCTYPE wml PUBLIC "-//WAPFORUM//DTD WML 1.1//EN" "http://www.wapforum.org/DTD/wml_
1.1.xml">
<wml>
  <template>
    <do name="common_prev" label="Back" type="prev">
      <prev/>
    </do>
  </template>
  <card title="Movies" id="movies">
    <do name="common_prev" type="prev">
      <noop/>
    </do>
    <p>
      <big>O'Fallon Cine</big>
```

Example 10-8. Showtimes WML (continued)

```
      </p>
      <p>Select a movie:</p>
      <p>
        <a href="#jones1">Raiders Lost Ark</a>
        <br/>
        <a href="#jones2">Temple of Doom</a>
        <br/>
        <a href="#back2future2">Back 2 Future 2</a>
        <br/>
      </p>
      <p>
        <em>
          <a href="movieguide?action=theaters&amp;city=stl">Change theater...</a>
        </em>
      </p>
    </card>
    <card title="Showtimes" id="jones1">
      <p>
        <em>Raiders of the Lost Ark</em>
      </p>
      <p>10:15a, 3:30, 12:30, 5:45, 7:15, 10:30</p>
    </card>
    <card title="Showtimes" id="jones2">
      <p>
        <em>Indiana Jones and The Temple of Doom</em>
      </p>
      <p>1:30, 4:00, 6:00</p>
    </card>
    <card title="Showtimes" id="back2future2">
      <p>
        <em>Back to the Future 2</em>
      </p>
      <p>4:00, 6:00, 8:00, 10:00</p>
    </card>
</wml>
```

This WML file illustrates how to define and use a `<template>`, which is a piece of reusable markup that can be shared by all cards in the deck. This particular template defines a Back button displayed on each instance of the `Showtimes` card, allowing the user to easily return to the list of movies.

Since the Back button should not appear on the movie list card, it is *shadowed* as follows:

```
<do name="common_prev" type="prev">
  <noop/>
</do>
```

The <noop/> element stands for "No Operation" and effectively removes the <do> element defined by the common_prev template. When cards define elements with the same names as templates, the card elements take precedence. The card can choose to modify the behavior of the template or simply suppress it with the <noop/> tag as shown here.

The screen shot shown in Figure 10-7 illustrates how these cards look in a cell phone. As shown, the Back button does not appear in the list of movies but does appear in the Showtimes card.

Figure 10-7. Showtimes WML output

The final screen shot, shown in Figure 10-8, shows how a web browser takes advantage of its large display area by displaying all of the information in a single table. Once again, this is accomplished with a different XSLT stylesheet that converts the XML to XHTML instead of WML.

Although WML does define a <table> element, it has almost no chance of fitting on a cell phone display and is not widely supported by currently available devices.

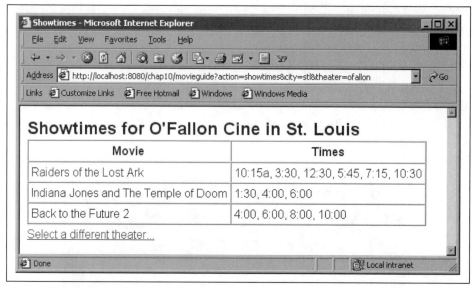

Figure 10-8. Showtimes XHTML output

Servlet implementation

This application uses a single servlet, listed in Example 10-9. This servlet has three primary functions:

- Parse request parameters and determine which page to display next.
- Identify the client type.
- Perform the appropriate XSLT transformation.

Example 10-9. MovieServlet.java

```
package chap10;

import java.io.*;
import javax.servlet.*;
import javax.servlet.http.*;
import javax.xml.transform.*;
import javax.xml.transform.stream.*;

/**
 * A servlet that shows schedules for movie theaters in various
 * cities. Supports normal web browser clients as well as WAP-enabled
 * PDAs and cell phones.
 */
public class MovieServlet extends HttpServlet {

    // currently supports two types of clients; could be expanded later
```

Example 10-9. MovieServlet.java (continued)

```java
private static final int XHTML_CLIENT_TYPE = 1;
private static final int WML_CLIENT_TYPE = 2;

// three pages in this web app
private static final int HOME_PAGE = 100;
private static final int THEATERS_PAGE = 101;
private static final int SHOWTIMES_PAGE = 102;


/**
 * This servlet supports GET and POST.
 */
public void doGet(HttpServletRequest req, HttpServletResponse res)
        throws IOException, ServletException {
    doPost(req, res);
}


public void doPost(HttpServletRequest req, HttpServletResponse res)
        throws IOException, ServletException {
    try {
        String action = req.getParameter("action");
        String city = req.getParameter("city");
        String theater = req.getParameter("theater");

        // default to the home page
        int pageToShow = HOME_PAGE;

        if ("theaters".equals(action) && city != null) {
            // city is a required parameter for a theater list
            pageToShow = THEATERS_PAGE;
        } else if ("showtimes".equals(action) && city != null
                && theater != null) {
            // city and theater are required parameters for showtimes
            pageToShow = SHOWTIMES_PAGE;
        }

        // set the content type of the response
        int clientType = determineClientType(req);
        switch (clientType) {
        case XHTML_CLIENT_TYPE:
            res.setContentType("text/html");
            break;
        case WML_CLIENT_TYPE:
            res.setContentType("text/vnd.wap.wml");
            break;
        default:
            res.sendError(HttpServletResponse.SC_INTERNAL_SERVER_ERROR);
            return;
        }
```

Example 10-9. MovieServlet.java (continued)

```java
        File xsltFile = locateStylesheet(req, clientType, pageToShow);

        // prepare for the transformation using JAXP
        TransformerFactory transFact = TransformerFactory.newInstance();
        Transformer trans = transFact.newTransformer(
                new StreamSource(xsltFile));

        // pass parameters to the XSLT stylesheet
        if (city != null) {
            trans.setParameter("city_id", city);
        }
        if (theater != null) {
            trans.setParameter("theater_id", theater);
        }

        // all pages, both WML and XHTML, share the exact same
        // XML data file
        InputStream xmlIn = getServletContext().getResourceAsStream(
                "/WEB-INF/xml/movies.xml");

        // do the transformation
        trans.transform(new StreamSource(xmlIn),
                new StreamResult(res.getOutputStream())));
    } catch (TransformerException te) {
        throw new ServletException(te);
    }
}

/**
 * @param clientType one of the constants defined in this class, either
 *         WML_CLIENT_TYPE or XHTML_CLIENT_TYPE.
 * @param pageToShow one of the _PAGE constants defined by this class.
 * @return a file representing the appropriate XSLT stylesheet.
 */
private File locateStylesheet(HttpServletRequest req,
        int clientType, int pageToShow) {
    String xsltDir = null;
    switch (clientType) {
    case WML_CLIENT_TYPE:
        xsltDir = "wml";
        break;
    case XHTML_CLIENT_TYPE:
        xsltDir = "xhtml";
        break;
    default:
        throw new IllegalArgumentException("Illegal clientType: "
                + clientType);
```

Example 10-9. MovieServlet.java (continued)

```java
        }

        String xsltName = null;
        switch (pageToShow) {
        case HOME_PAGE:
            xsltName = "home.xslt";
            break;
        case THEATERS_PAGE:
            xsltName = "theaters.xslt";
            break;
        case SHOWTIMES_PAGE:
            xsltName = "showtimes.xslt";
            break;
        default:
            throw new IllegalArgumentException("Illegal pageToShow: "
                    + pageToShow);
        }

        // locate a platform-dependent path
        String fullPath = getServletContext().getRealPath(
                "/WEB-INF/xslt/" + xsltDir + "/" + xsltName);
        return new File(fullPath);
    }

    /**
     * Determines the type of user agent.
     *
     * @return either XHTML_CLIENT_TYPE or WML_CLIENT_TYPE.
     */
    private int determineClientType(HttpServletRequest req) {
        // first check for normal web browsers that claim to be
        // mozilla-compliant
        String userAgent = req.getHeader("User-Agent");
        if (userAgent != null
                && userAgent.toLowerCase().startsWith("mozilla")) {
            return XHTML_CLIENT_TYPE;
        }

        // if the client accepts wml, it must be a WAP-compatible device
        String accept = req.getHeader("Accept");
        if (accept != null && accept.indexOf("text/vnd.wap.wml") > -1) {
            return WML_CLIENT_TYPE;
        }

        // otherwise, default to XHTML
        return XHTML_CLIENT_TYPE;
    }
}
```

This servlet determines the client type by looking at the HTTP User-Agent and Accept headers. This logic is encapsulated in the determineClientType() method, which first checks the User-Agent for Mozilla-compatible browsers such as Microsoft Internet Explorer and Netscape Navigator. If the client is not one of these browsers, it then checks the Accept header for text/vnd.wap.wml. If both tests fail, the servlet defaults to XHTML because the device did not claim to accept the WML content type.

Once the client browser type is identified, the HTTP Content-Type response header is set to the appropriate MIME type:

```
switch (clientType) {
case XHTML_CLIENT_TYPE:
    res.setContentType("text/html");
    break;
case WML_CLIENT_TYPE:
    res.setContentType("text/vnd.wap.wml");
    break;
default:
    res.sendError(HttpServletResponse.SC_INTERNAL_SERVER_ERROR);
    return;
}
```

The default case will occur only if the servlet has a bug. Therefore, it simply causes the code to fail with an internal server error. A helper method called locateStylesheet() is then used to locate the appropriate XSLT stylesheet:

```
File xsltFile = locateStylesheet(req, clientType, pageToShow);
```

In this application, there are two sets of XSLT stylesheets. One resides in a directory named *wml*, and another resides in a directory named *xhtml*. Just like examples shown in previous chapters, ServletContext is utilized to locate these files in a portable manner:

```
String fullPath = getServletContext().getRealPath(
        "/WEB-INF/xslt/" + xsltDir + "/" + xsltName);
```

Last but not least, the XSLT transformation is performed using the JAXP API.

XSLT stylesheets

This application consists of six XSLT stylesheets. Three of these stylesheets are listed here and are used to generate the three WML decks. The other three are used to generate XHTML and can be downloaded along with the rest of the examples in this book. The first stylesheet, shown in Example 10-10, is responsible for creating the home deck.

Example 10-10. Home page XSLT

```
<?xml version="1.0" encoding="UTF-8"?>
<!--
**********************************************************************
** Produces the home page for WML-enabled devices.
**********************************************************************-->
<xsl:stylesheet version="1.0"
    xmlns:xsl="http://www.w3.org/1999/XSL/Transform">
  <xsl:output method="xml"
  version="1.0" encoding="UTF-8" indent="yes"
  doctype-public="-//WAPFORUM//DTD WML 1.1//EN"
  doctype-system="http://www.wapforum.org/DTD/wml_1.1.xml"/>
  <!--
**********************************************************************
** The main template; creates the deck and the home card.
**********************************************************************-->
<xsl:template match="/movies">
  <wml>

    <!-- call a template to produce the splash screen -->
    <xsl:call-template name="createSplashCard"/>

    <card id="home" title="Home" newcontext="true">
      <p align="center">
        Please select your city:
        <select name="city" multiple="false">
          <xsl:apply-templates select="city"/>
        </select>
      </p>

      <p>
        <em>
          <a href="movieguide?action=theaters&amp;city=$(city)"
             >Show Theaters...</a>
        </em>
      </p>
    </card>
  </wml>
</xsl:template>


<!--
**********************************************************************
** Produce a single <option> element for a city
**********************************************************************-->
<xsl:template match="city">
  <option value="{@id}">
    <xsl:value-of select="name"/>
  </option>
</xsl:template>
```

Example 10-10. Home page XSLT (continued)

```
<!--
************************************************************************
** Create the splash screen.
************************************************************************-->
<xsl:template name="createSplashCard">
  <card id="splash" title="ABC Theaters" ontimer="#home">
    <timer value="15"/>
    <p align="center">
      <big>Welcome to ABC Theaters</big>
    </p>
    <p>Mmmm...Popcorn...</p>
    <do type="accept">
      <go href="#home"/>
    </do>
  </card>
</xsl:template>

</xsl:stylesheet>
```

This is actually a very simple stylesheet. The critical feature is the `<xsl:output>` element, which specifies the XML output method and the WML DTD. This application adheres to Version 1.1 of WML for maximum compatibility with existing cell phones, although newer versions of WML are available. For these versions, use the newer DTDs found at *http://www.wapforum.org*.

The only marginally difficult part of the stylesheet is the following line:

```
<a href="movieguide?action=theaters&amp;city=$(city)">
    Show Theaters...</a>
```

This creates the hyperlink to the next deck, passing parameters for the `action` and `city`. The ampersand character (&) must be written as `&amp;` for the XML parser to handle this attribute correctly. Although the `$(city)` syntax looks a lot like an XSLT Attribute Value Template, it is actually a WML variable.[*] This is how the selected city is sent to the servlet when the user clicks on the hyperlink. With ordinary XHTML, this can only be accomplished using a form or a scripting language.

The stylesheet shown in Example 10-11 is responsible for creating a list of theaters in a city.

---

[*] Recall from Chapter 2 that XSLT AVTs are written like `{$var}`.

Example 10-11. Movie listing XSLT

```xml
<?xml version="1.0" encoding="UTF-8"?>
<!--
*************************************************************************
** Produces a list of theaters for WML-enabled devices.
*************************************************************************-->
<xsl:stylesheet version="1.0" xmlns:xsl="http://www.w3.org/1999/XSL/Transform">
  <xsl:param name="city_id" select="'stl'"/>

  <xsl:output method="xml"
  version="1.0" encoding="UTF-8" indent="yes"
   doctype-public="-//WAPFORUM//DTD WML 1.1//EN"
   doctype-system="http://www.wapforum.org/DTD/wml_1.1.xml"/>

  <!--
*************************************************************************
** The main template; creates the deck and the theaters card.
*************************************************************************-->
  <xsl:template match="/movies">
    <wml>
      <card id="theaters" title="Theaters">
        <!-- select the appropriate city -->
        <xsl:apply-templates select="city[@id=$city_id]"/>
        <p>
          <em>
            <a href="movieguide">Change city...</a>
          </em>
        </p>
      </card>
    </wml>
  </xsl:template>

  <!--
*************************************************************************
** Show details for a city.
*************************************************************************-->
  <xsl:template match="city">
    <p>
      <big><xsl:value-of select="name"/></big>
    </p>
    <p>Select a theater:</p>
    <p>
      <!-- show a list of all theaters in this city -->
      <xsl:apply-templates select="theater"/>
    </p>
  </xsl:template>

  <!--
*************************************************************************
```

Example 10-11. Movie listing XSLT (continued)

```
 ** Create a link for an individual theater.
 **********************************************************************-->
<xsl:template match="theater">
    <a href="movieguide?action=showtimes&amp;city={
            $city_id}&amp;theater={@id}">
      <xsl:value-of select="name"/>
    </a>
    <br/>
 </xsl:template>
</xsl:stylesheet>
```

Unlike the first stylesheet, this one requires a parameter for the city:

```
<xsl:param name="city_id" select="'stl'"/>
```

For testing purposes, the parameter defaults to `stl`, but in the real application it should always be passed from the servlet. This is necessary because one big XML file contains data for all cities. This parameter allows the stylesheet to extract information from this file for a single city. For example, the first `<xsl:apply-templates>` uses a predicate to select the city whose `id` attribute matches the `city_id` stylesheet parameter:

```
<xsl:apply-templates select="city[@id=$city_id]"/>
```

The remainder of this stylesheet is very basic, simply outputting a list of theaters in the city. The final stylesheet, shown in Example 10-12, creates a list of showtimes for a movie theater. This is the most complex stylesheet merely because it produces multiple cards.

Example 10-12. Showtimes XSLT

```
<?xml version="1.0" encoding="UTF-8"?>
<!--
**********************************************************************
** Produces a list of showtimes for WML-enabled devices.
**********************************************************************-->
<xsl:stylesheet version="1.0" xmlns:xsl="http://www.w3.org/1999/XSL/Transform">
  <xsl:param name="city_id" select="'stl'"/>
  <xsl:param name="theater_id" select="'ofallon'"/>

  <xsl:output method="xml"
  version="1.0" encoding="UTF-8" indent="yes"
   doctype-public="-//WAPFORUM//DTD WML 1.1//EN"
   doctype-system="http://www.wapforum.org/DTD/wml_1.1.xml"/>

  <!--
**********************************************************************
** The main template; creates the deck and the movies card.
```

Example 10-12. Showtimes XSLT (continued)

```
********************************************************************-->
<xsl:template match="/movies">
  <wml>
    <!-- generate the WML template -->
    <template>
      <do type="prev" label="Back" name="common_prev">
        <prev/>
      </do>
    </template>

    <card id="movies" title="Movies">
      <!-- shadow the template in this card -->
      <do type="prev" name="common_prev">
        <noop/>
      </do>

      <!-- select the theater that matches the city_id and
           theater_id stylesheet parameters -->
      <xsl:apply-templates
        select="city[@id=$city_id]/theater[@id=$theater_id]"/>
    </card>

    <!-- generate more cards, one per movie -->
    <xsl:apply-templates
        select="city[@id=$city_id]/theater[@id=$theater_id]/movie"
          mode="createCard"/>

  </wml>
</xsl:template>

<!--
********************************************************************
** Show more information about a theater.
********************************************************************-->
<xsl:template match="theater">
  <p>
    <big>
      <xsl:value-of select="name"/>
    </big>
  </p>
  <p>Select a movie:</p>
  <p>
    <xsl:apply-templates select="movie"/>
  </p>

  <p>
    <em>
      <a href="movieguide?action=theaters&amp;city={$city_id}">
```

Example 10-12. Showtimes XSLT (continued)

```
                  Change theater...</a>
      </em>
    </p>
  </xsl:template>

  <!--
  *********************************************************************
  ** Show more information about a movie in the main card.
  *******************************************************************-->
  <xsl:template match="movie">
   <xsl:variable  name="curId" select="@ref"/>
   <!-- the hyperlink text is the shortName from the <moviedef> -->
   <a href="#{$curId}">
     <xsl:value-of select="/movies/moviedef[@id=$curId]/shortName"/>
   </a>
   <br/>
  </xsl:template>

  <!--
  *********************************************************************
  ** Create a card for a movie that lists showtimes.
  *******************************************************************-->
  <xsl:template match="movie" mode="createCard">
    <xsl:variable  name="curId" select="@ref"/>

    <card id="{$curId}" title="Showtimes">
      <p>
        <em>
          <xsl:value-of select="/movies/moviedef[@id=$curId]/longName"/>
        </em>
      </p>
      <p>
        <xsl:value-of select="times"/>
      </p>
    </card>
  </xsl:template>
</xsl:stylesheet>
```

As described earlier in this chapter, this deck creates a template that defines a Back button visible on all but the first card. The template is produced just before the first card, which also happens to be the one card that shadows the template with a <noop/> element.

The following <xsl:apply-templates> element selects the correct city and theater based on the stylesheet parameters city_id and theater_id:

```
<xsl:apply-templates
    select="city[@id=$city_id]/theater[@id=$theater_id]"/>
```

Although this syntax was covered in detail back in Chapter 2, here is a quick review of how it works:

1. Select all <city> children of the <movies> element.

2. Use the predicate [@id=$city_id] to narrow this list down to the correct city.

3. Select all <theater> children of the <city>.

4. Use the predicate [@id=$theater_id] to narrow this list down to a single <theater>.

After the home card is created, <xsl:apply-templates> is used to create one card per movie:

```
<xsl:apply-templates
    select="city[@id=$city_id]/theater[@id=$theater_id]/movie"
    mode="createCard"/>
```

This uses template modes, a technique covered in Chapter 3. It causes the following template to be instantiated, since it has a matching mode:

```
<xsl:template match="movie" mode="createCard">
  ...produce a card containing showtimes for a movie
</xsl:template>
```

The Future of Wireless

Looking toward the future, two things are inevitable. First, device capabilities will improve. Color displays, increased screen resolution, increased memory, and faster processors can be expected. Second, bandwidth will improve. Migration to Third Generation (3G) wireless networks is already underway in many countries, offering bandwidth anywhere from 128Kbps to 2Mbps.

Partly because of these two advancements, the WAP Forum and NTT DoCoMo have agreed to migrate towards XHTML Basic for future devices. XHTML Basic uses a subset of XHTML. Therefore, it is far more familiar to web developers than WML. Existing web browsers can already display XHTML Basic, which is not the case with WML or cHTML. XHTML Basic also utilizes CSS to define colors, fonts, and other presentation styles. Newer, more capable devices should be able to take advantage of far more style instructions than currently available devices.

The migration to XHTML Basic will not eliminate the need for technologies such as XSLT, however. Even though normal web browsers can display the same XHTML Basic web pages that wireless devices use, devices such as cellular phones and pagers will always have tiny displays. Most web applications will still need to maintain a simplified interface for these devices to minimize the amount of scrolling the user has to do. Therefore, XSLT will continue to be important.

A

Discussion Forum Code

This appendix contains all of the remaining code from the discussion forum example presented in Chapter 7. These are the "simple" files that did not merit a lot of explanation in the text. All of the source code can be downloaded from this book's companion web site at *http://www.oreilly.com/catalog/javaxslt.*

BoardSummaryImpl.java(1) (shown in Example A-1) provides a default implementation of the BoardSummary interface.

Example A-1. BoardSummaryImpl.java(1)

```
package com.oreilly.forum.domain;

import com.oreilly.forum.domain.*;
import java.util.*;

/**
 * An implementation of the BoardSummary interface.
 */
public class BoardSummaryImpl implements BoardSummary {
    private long id;
    private String name;
    private String description;
    private List monthsWithMessages;

    /**
     * @param monthsWithMessages a list of MonthYear objects.
     */
    public BoardSummaryImpl(long id, String name, String description,
            List monthsWithMessages) {
        this.id = id;
        this.name = name;
        this.description = description;
```

Example A-1. BoardSummaryImpl.java(1) (continued)

```
        this.monthsWithMessages = monthsWithMessages;

    }

    public long getID() {
        return this.id;
    }

    public String getName() {
        return this.name;
    }

    public String getDescription() {
        return this.description;
    }

    /**
     * @return an iterator of <code>MonthYear</code> objects.
     */
    public Iterator getMonthsWithMessages() {
        return this.monthsWithMessages.iterator();
    }
}
```

BoardSummaryImpl.java(2) (shown in Example A-2) is an alternate implementation of the `BoardSummary` interface. This class is used by the fake data implementation, which is useful for testing purposes when a database is not available.

Example A-2. BoardSummaryImpl.java(2)

```
package com.oreilly.forum.fakeimpl;

import com.oreilly.forum.domain.*;

import java.util.*;

public class BoardSummaryImpl implements BoardSummary {
    private long id;
    private String name;
    private String description;
    // a list of MonthYear objects
    private List monthsWithMessages;

    public BoardSummaryImpl(long id, String name, String description) {
        this.id = id;
        this.name = name;
        this.description = description;
        this.monthsWithMessages = new ArrayList();
    }
```

Example A-2. BoardSummaryImpl.java(2) (continued)

```java
public void messageAdded(Message msg) {
    DayMonthYear createDate = msg.getCreateDate();

    // update the monthsWithMessages list
    Iterator iter = this.monthsWithMessages.iterator();
    while (iter.hasNext()) {
        MonthYear curMonth = (MonthYear) iter.next();
        if (createDate.getMonth() == curMonth.getMonth()
                && createDate.getYear() == curMonth.getYear()) {
            return;
        }
    }

    this.monthsWithMessages.add(createDate);
}

public long getID() {
    return this.id;
}

public String getName() {
    return this.name;
}

public String getDescription() {
    return this.description;
}

public Iterator getMonthsWithMessages() {
    return this.monthsWithMessages.iterator();
}
}
```

DataException.java (shown in Example A-3) is a generic exception that occurs when something goes wrong with the underlying database. This prevents database-specific code from creeping into the application, making it possible to migrate to other data sources in the future.

Example A-3. DataException.java

```java
package com.oreilly.forum.adapter;

/**
 * An exception that indicates some operation with the back-end
 * data source failed.
 */
public class DataException extends Exception {
    private Throwable rootCause;
```

Example A-3. DataException.java (continued)

```
    /**
     * Wrap a DataException around another throwable.
     */
    public DataException(Throwable rootCause) {
        super(rootCause.getMessage());
        this.rootCause = rootCause;
    }


    /**
     * Construct an exception with the specified detail message.
     */
    public DataException(String message) {
        super(message);
    }


    /**
     * @return a reference to the root exception or null.
     */
    public Throwable getRootCause() {
        return this.rootCause;
    }
}
```

DateUtil.java (shown in Example A-4) is a simple utility method that deals with dates.

Example A-4. DateUtil.java

```
package com.oreilly.forum.domain;

import java.util.*;

/**
 * Misc utility functions for dates. Methods are synchronized because
 * the same Calendar instance is shared.
 */
public final class DateUtil {

    private static Calendar cal = Calendar.getInstance();

    /**
     * @return the day of the month for a given date.
     */
    public synchronized static int getDayOfMonth(Date date) {
        cal.setTime(date);
        return cal.get(Calendar.DAY_OF_MONTH);
    }
```

Example A-4. DateUtil.java (continued)

```java
    /**
     * @return the month number for a given date.
     */
    public synchronized static int getMonth(Date date) {
        cal.setTime(date);
        return cal.get(Calendar.MONTH);
    }

    /**
     * @return the year number for the given date.
     */
    public synchronized static int getYear(Date date) {
        cal.setTime(date);
        return cal.get(Calendar.YEAR);
    }

    private DateUtil() {
    }
}
```

DayMonthYear.java (shown in Example A-5) is a helper class that groups a day, month, and year together. It also supports comparisons for sorting purposes.

Example A-5. DayMonthYear.java

```java
package com.oreilly.forum.domain;

import java.util.Date;

/**
 * Represents a day, month, and year.
 */
public class DayMonthYear extends MonthYear {
    private int day;

    public DayMonthYear() {
        this(new Date());
    }

    public DayMonthYear(Date date) {
        super(date);
        this.day = DateUtil.getDayOfMonth(date);
    }

    public DayMonthYear(int day, int month, int year) {
        super(month, year);
        this.day = day;
    }
```

Example A-5. DayMonthYear.java (continued)

```java
    public int getDay() {
        return this.day;
    }

    public boolean equals(Object obj) {
        if (obj instanceof DayMonthYear) {
            DayMonthYear rhs = (DayMonthYear) obj;
            return super.equals(obj) && this.day == rhs.day;
        }
        return false;
    }

    public int hashCode() {
        return super.hashCode() ^ this.day;
    }

    public int compareTo(Object obj) {
        DayMonthYear rhs = (DayMonthYear) obj;
        int comparison = super.compareTo(obj);
        if (comparison == 0) {
            if (this.day < rhs.day) {
                return -1;
            } else if (this.day > rhs.day) {
                return 1;
            }
        }
        return comparison;
    }

    public String toString() {
        return getMonth() + "/" + getDay() + "/" + getYear();
    }
}
```

FakeDataAdapter.java (shown in Example A-6) allows the discussion forum to be executed without any database. This class was written before the database was implemented, and is useful for testing purposes only.

Example A-6. FakeDataAdapter.java

```java
package com.oreilly.forum.fakeimpl;

import com.oreilly.forum.*;
import com.oreilly.forum.adapter.*;
import com.oreilly.forum.domain.*;
import java.util.*;

public class FakeDataAdapter extends DataAdapter {
    // a list of BoardSummary objects
```

Example A-6. FakeDataAdapter.java (continued)

```java
    private List allBoards;
    private static long nextMessageID = 0;
    private Map messageMap = new HashMap();

    public FakeDataAdapter() throws DataException {
        this.allBoards = new ArrayList();

        BoardSummary bs0 = new BoardSummaryImpl(0L,
                "Java Programming",
                "General programming questions about Java.");
        BoardSummary bs1 = new BoardSummaryImpl(1L,
                "XSLT Stylesheet Techniques",
                "Writing effective XSLT stylesheets.");
        this.allBoards.add(bs0);
        this.allBoards.add(bs1);

        this.postNewMessage(0L, "First subject in Java Prog",
                "burke_e@yahoo.com", "Sample message text");

    }

    /**
     * @param msgID must be a valid message identifier.
     * @return the message with the specified id.
     * @throws DataException if msgID does not exist or a database
     * error occurs.
     */
    public Message getMessage(long msgID) throws DataException {
        Message msg = (Message) this.messageMap.get(new Long(msgID));
        if (msg != null) {
            return msg;
        }
        throw new DataException("Invalid msgID");
    }

    /**
     * If no messages exist for the specified board and month, return
     * an empty iterator.
     * @return an iterator of <code>MessageSummary</code> objects.
     * @throws DataException if the boardID is illegal or a database
     * error occurs.
     */
    public Iterator getAllMessages(long boardID, MonthYear month)
            throws DataException {
        // this is slow, but works fine for a fake implementation
        List msgs = new ArrayList();
        Iterator iter = this.messageMap.values().iterator();
        while (iter.hasNext()) {
```

Example A-6. FakeDataAdapter.java (continued)

```java
        MessageSummary curMsg = (MessageSummary) iter.next();
        if (curMsg.getBoard().getID() == boardID
                && month.containsInMonth(curMsg.getCreateDate())) {
            msgs.add(curMsg);
        }
    }
    return msgs.iterator();
}


/**
 * Add a reply to an existing message.
 *
 * @throws DataException if a database error occurs, or if any
 * parameter is illegal.
 */
public Message replyToMessage(long origMsgID, String msgSubject,
        String authorEmail, String msgText) throws DataException {
    MessageSummary origMsg = getMessage(origMsgID);
    long msgID = getNextMessageID();

    Message msg = new MessageImpl(msgID, new DayMonthYear(), origMsg.getBoard(),
            msgSubject, authorEmail, msgText, origMsgID);

    this.messageMap.put(new Long(msg.getID()), msg);
    return msg;
}


/**
 * Post a new message.
 *
 * @return the newly created message.
 * @throws DataException if a database error occurs, or if any
 * parameter is illegal.
 */
public Message postNewMessage(long boardID, String msgSubject,
        String authorEmail, String msgText) throws DataException {
    BoardSummary boardSum = getBoardSummary(boardID);
    long msgID = getNextMessageID();

    Message msg = new MessageImpl(msgID, new DayMonthYear(), boardSum,
            msgSubject, authorEmail, msgText, -1);
    this.messageMap.put(new Long(msg.getID()), msg);

    ((BoardSummaryImpl) boardSum).messageAdded(msg);

    return msg;
}
```

Example A-6. FakeDataAdapter.java (continued)

```java
    /**
     * @return an iterator of <code>BoardSummary</code> objects.
     */
    public Iterator getAllBoards() throws DataException {
        return this.allBoards.iterator();
    }

    public BoardSummary getBoardSummary(long boardID)
            throws DataException {
        Iterator iter = getAllBoards();
        while (iter.hasNext()) {
            BoardSummary curBoard = (BoardSummary) iter.next();
            if (curBoard.getID() == boardID) {
                return curBoard;
            }
        }
        throw new DataException("Illegal boardID: " + boardID);
    }

    private synchronized static long getNextMessageID() {
        nextMessageID++;
        return nextMessageID;
    }
}
```

MessageImpl.java (shown in Example A-7) is an implementation of the Message interface.

Example A-7. MessageImpl.java

```java
package com.oreilly.forum.domain;

import java.util.*;

/**
 * An implementation of the Message interface.
 */
public class MessageImpl extends MessageSummaryImpl implements Message {
    private String text;

    /**
     * Construct a new instance of this class.
     */
    public MessageImpl(long id, DayMonthYear createDate,
            BoardSummary board, String subject, String authorEmail,
            String text, long inReplyTo) {
        super(id, createDate, board, subject, authorEmail, inReplyTo);
        this.text = text;
    }
```

Example A-7. MessageImpl.java (continued)

```java
    /**
     * @return the text of this message.
     */
    public String getText() {
        return this.text;
    }
}
```

MessageSummaryImpl.java (shown in Example A-8) is an implementation of the `MessageSummary` interface.

Example A-8. MessageSummaryImpl.java

```java
package com.oreilly.forum.domain;

import java.util.*;

/**
 * Implementation of the MessageSummary interface.
 */
public class MessageSummaryImpl implements MessageSummary {
    private long id;
    private BoardSummary board;
    private String subject;
    private String authorEmail;
    private DayMonthYear createDate;
    private long inReplyTo;

    public MessageSummaryImpl(long id, DayMonthYear createDate,
            BoardSummary board, String subject, String authorEmail,
            long inReplyTo) {
        this.id = id;
        this.createDate = createDate;
        this.board = board;
        this.subject = subject;
        this.authorEmail = authorEmail;
        this.inReplyTo = inReplyTo;
    }

    public long getInReplyTo() {
        return this.inReplyTo;
    }

    public long getID() {
        return this.id;
    }

    public DayMonthYear getCreateDate() {
        return this.createDate;
```

Example A-8. MessageSummaryImpl.java (continued)

```
    }

    public BoardSummary getBoard() {
        return this.board;
    }

    public String getSubject() {
        return this.subject;
    }

    public String getAuthorEmail() {
        return this.authorEmail;
    }

    public boolean equals(Object obj) {
        if (obj instanceof MessageSummaryImpl) {
            MessageSummaryImpl rhs = (MessageSummaryImpl) obj;
            return this.id == rhs.id;
        }
        return false;
    }

    public int hashCode() {
        return (int) this.id;
    }

    /**
     * Sorts by create date followed by message subject.
     */
    public int compareTo(Object obj) {
        if (this == obj) {
            return 0;
        }
        MessageSummaryImpl rhs = (MessageSummaryImpl) obj;

        int comparison = this.createDate.compareTo(rhs.createDate);
        if (comparison != 0) {
            return comparison;
        }

        comparison = this.subject.compareTo(rhs.subject);
        if (comparison != 0) {
            return comparison;
        }

        return 0;
    }
}
```

MonthYear.java (shown in Example A-9) groups a month and year together. It also supports sorting.

Example A-9. MonthYear.java

```
package com.oreilly.forum.domain;

import java.io.Serializable;
import java.util.*;

/**
 * Represents a month and a year.
 */
public class MonthYear implements Comparable, Serializable {
    private int month;
    private int year;

    /**
     * Construct a new object representing the current instant in time.
     */
    public MonthYear() {
        this(new Date());
    }

    /**
     * Construct a new object with the given date.
     */
    public MonthYear(Date date) {
        this(DateUtil.getMonth(date), DateUtil.getYear(date));
    }

    /**
     * Construct a new object with the given month and year.
     * @param month a zero-based month, just like java.util.Calendar.
     */
    public MonthYear(int month, int year) {
        this.month = month;
        this.year = year;
    }

    /**
     * Compare this MonthYear object to another.
     */
    public int compareTo(Object obj) {
        MonthYear rhs = (MonthYear) obj;
        // first compare year
        if (this.year < rhs.year) {
            return -1;
        } else if (this.year > rhs.year) {
```

Example A-9. MonthYear.java (continued)

```
            return 1;
        }
        // then month
        if (this.month < rhs.month) {
            return -1;
        } else if (this.month > rhs.month) {
            return 1;
        }

        return 0;
    }

    /**
     * @return true if the specified date occurs sometime during this month.
     */
    public boolean containsInMonth(DayMonthYear date) {
        return date.getMonth() == this.month
                && date.getYear() == this.year;
    }

    /**
     * @return the month number, starting with 0 for January.
     */
    public int getMonth() {
        return this.month;
    }

    /**
     * @return the year number.
     */
    public int getYear() {
        return this.year;
    }

    public boolean equals(Object obj) {
        if (obj instanceof MonthYear) {
            MonthYear rhs = (MonthYear) obj;
            return this.month == rhs.month
                    && this.year == rhs.year;
        }
        return false;
    }

    public int hashCode() {
        return this.month ^ this.year;
    }
}
```

The `viewMsg.xslt` XSLT stylesheet (shown in Example A-10) displays a web page for a single message.

Example A-10. viewMsg.xslt

```
<?xml version="1.0" encoding="UTF-8"?>
<!--
************************************************************
** viewMsg.xslt
**
** Shows details for a specific message.
************************************************************
-->
<xsl:stylesheet version="1.0"
  xmlns:xsl="http://www.w3.org/1999/XSL/Transform">
  <xsl:import href="utils.xslt"/>
  <xsl:param name="rootDir" select="'../docroot/'"/>
  <xsl:output method="xml" version="1.0" encoding="UTF-8"
    indent="yes"
    doctype-public="-//W3C//DTD XHTML 1.0 Strict//EN"
    doctype-system="http://www.w3.org/TR/xhtml1/DTD/xhtml1-strict.dtd"/>

  <!--
  ************************************************************
  ** Create the XHTML web page
  ************************************************************-->
  <xsl:template match="/">
    <html xmlns="http://www.w3.org/1999/xhtml">
      <head>
        <title>View Message</title>
        <link href="{$rootDir}forum.css"
            rel="stylesheet" type="text/css"/>
      </head>
      <body>
        <div class="box1">
          <h1>View Message</h1>
          <div>
            <xsl:value-of select="message/board/name"/>
          </div>
        </div>
        <!-- ===== Quick Actions ====== -->
        <h3>Quick Actions</h3>
        <ul>
          <li>Return to
                        <!-- long line wrapped -->
          <a href="viewMonth?boardID={message/board/@id}&amp;month={
              message/@month}&amp;year={message/@year}">
              <xsl:call-template name="utils.printLongMonthName">
                <xsl:with-param name="monthNumber" select="message/@month"/>
```

Example A-10. viewMsg.xslt (continued)

```
                  </xsl:call-template>,
            <xsl:value-of select="message/@year"/>
              </a> messages for <xsl:value-of select="message/board/name"/>
            </li>
            <li>Return to the <a href="home">home page</a>
            </li>
            <li>
              <a href="postMsg?mode=replyToMsg&amp;origMsgID={message/@id}">Reply</a>
                to this message</li>
        </ul>
        <h3>Message</h3>
        <div class="box2">
          <xsl:apply-templates select="message"/>
        </div>
      </body>
    </html>
</xsl:template>

<!--
***********************************************************
** Show details for the <message> element
***********************************************************-->
<xsl:template match="message">
  <div>
    <div style="font-weight: bold;">
      <xsl:value-of select="subject"/>
    </div>
    <xsl:text> posted by </xsl:text>
    <a href="mailto:{authorEmail}">
      <xsl:value-of select="authorEmail"/>
    </a>
    <xsl:text> on </xsl:text>
    <xsl:call-template name="utils.printShortMonthName">
      <xsl:with-param name="monthNumber" select="@month"/>
    </xsl:call-template>
    <xsl:text> </xsl:text>
    <xsl:value-of select="@day"/>
    <xsl:text>, </xsl:text>
    <xsl:value-of select="@year"/>
    <xsl:apply-templates select="inResponseTo"/>
  </div>
  <pre>
    <xsl:value-of select="text"/>
  </pre>
</xsl:template>
```

Example A-10. viewMsg.xslt (continued)

```
<!--
**********************************************************
** Show a link to the message that this one is in
** response to.
**********************************************************-->
<xsl:template match="inResponseTo">
  <div style="text-indent: 2em;">
    <xsl:text>In response to </xsl:text>
    <a href="viewMsg?msgID={@id}">
      <xsl:value-of select="subject"/>
    </a>
  </div>
</xsl:template>
</xsl:stylesheet>
```

B

JAXP API Reference

This appendix summarizes Version 1.1 of the Java API for XML Processing (JAXP).* JAXP provides a standard way for Java programs to interact with XML parsers and XSLT processors and is freely available from *http://java.sun.com/xml.* JAXP also includes classes and interfaces for DOM and SAX; these are not listed here.

The biggest changes from JAXP 1.0 to JAXP 1.1 are support for level 2 of DOM and SAX, as well as an entirely new plugability layer for performing transformations. JAXP 1.1 also refines the algorithm used for locating implementation classes for the three supported plugability layers. This algorithm is discussed in Chapter 5, in the "Introduction to JAXP 1.1" section.

Package: javax.xml.parsers

The classes in this package support parsing using Simple API for XML (SAX) 2 and Document Object Model (DOM) Level 2. These classes do not perform the actual parsing work; instead, they delegate to plugable parser implementations such as Apache's Crimson or Xerces.

DocumentBuilder

Instances of this class define an API for parsing XML from a variety of input sources, as well as for creating new DOM Document objects from scratch. The DocumentBuilder instance should be obtained from the DocumentBuilderFactory instance. Once an instance has been obtained, the newDocument() method can be used to construct new DOM Document objects without resorting to the implementation of specific code.

---

* Before transformation support was added, JAXP stood for "Java API for XML Parsing."

```
public abstract class DocumentBuilder {
    protected DocumentBuilder();
    public abstract DOMImplementation getDOMImplementation();
    public abstract boolean isNamespaceAware();
    public abstract boolean isValidating();
    public abstract Document newDocument();
    public Document parse(InputStream is, String systemId)
        throws SAXException, IOException;
    public Document parse(String uri)
        throws SAXException, IOException;
    public Document parse(File f)
        throws SAXException, IOException;
    public abstract Document parse(InputSource is)
        throws SAXException, IOException;
    public Document parse(InputStream is)
        throws SAXException, IOException;
    public abstract void setEntityResolver(EntityResolver er);
    public abstract void setErrorHandler(ErrorHandler eh);
}
```

DocumentBuilderFactory

This class allows instances of `DocumentBuilder` to be constructed using a factory pattern,
insulating application code from specific DOM implementations. Various methods in this
class allow programs to specify which features the parser will support. If these features are
not available, the `newDocumentBuilder()` throws a `ParserConfigurationException`.
The various accessor methods, such as `isNamespaceAware()`, do not indicate whether the
underlying parser actually supports a given feature. Instead, these methods indicate whether
the application configured those features on this `DocumentBuilderFactory` instance.
Before using this class, call the `newInstance()` method to create an instance of it. This
object is then used to construct an instance of `DocumentBuilder` using the
`newDocumentBuilder()` method.

```
public abstract class DocumentBuilderFactory {
    protected DocumentBuilderFactory();
    public abstract Object getAttribute(String name)
        throws IllegalArgumentException;
    public boolean isCoalescing();
    public boolean isExpandEntityReferences();
    public boolean isIgnoringComments();
    public boolean isIgnoringElementContentWhitespace();
    public boolean isNamespaceAware();
    public boolean isValidating();
    public abstract DocumentBuilder newDocumentBuilder()
        throws ParserConfigurationException;
    public static DocumentBuilderFactory newInstance();
    public abstract void setAttribute(String name, Object value)
        throws IllegalArgumentException;
    public void setCoalescing(boolean coalescing);
    public void setExpandEntityReferences(boolean expandEntityRef);
```

```
        public void setIgnoringComments(boolean ignoreComments);
        public void setIgnoringElementContentWhitespace(boolean whitespace);
        public void setNamespaceAware(boolean awareness);
        public void setValidating(boolean validating);
    }
```

FactoryConfigurationError

This indicates that the class for a parser factory could not be located or instantiated. If this error occurs, something is not installed correctly on the system. Refer to Chapter 5 for information on the algorithm that JAXP uses to locate parser implementations.

```
    public class FactoryConfigurationError
            extends Error {
        public FactoryConfigurationError(String msg);
        public FactoryConfigurationError(Exception e);
        public FactoryConfigurationError(Exception e, String msg);
        public FactoryConfigurationError();
        public Exception getException();
        public String getMessage();
    }
```

ParserConfigurationException

According to the API specification, represents "a serious configuration error." Generally, this means that the factory cannot provide a parser with the requested features. For instance, a programmer may ask for a namespace-aware parser, but the only parser available does not support namespaces.[*]

```
    public class ParserConfigurationException
            extends Exception {
        public ParserConfigurationException(String msg);
        public ParserConfigurationException();
    }
```

SAXParser

This class defines a wrapper around an underlying SAX parser implementation. It was part of JAXP 1.0 and supports both SAX 1 and SAX 2 features. If possible, programmers should avoid methods that use `HandlerBase`, because this is a deprecated SAX 1 interface. Instead, use the methods that deal with `DefaultHandler`.

```
    public abstract class SAXParser {
        protected SAXParser();
        public abstract Parser getParser()
            throws SAXException;
        public abstract Object getProperty(String name)
            throws SAXNotRecognizedException, SAXNotSupportedException;
        public abstract XMLReader getXMLReader()
            throws SAXException;
```

---

* XSLT processing requires namespace-aware XML parsers.

```
        public abstract boolean isNamespaceAware();
        public abstract boolean isValidating();
        public void parse(InputStream is, DefaultHandler dh, String systemId)
            throws SAXException, IOException;
        public void parse(InputStream is, DefaultHandler p1)
            throws SAXException, IOException;
        public void parse(InputStream is, HandlerBase hb, String systemId)
            throws SAXException, IOException;
        public void parse(File f, HandlerBase hb)
            throws SAXException, IOException;
        public void parse(InputStream is, HandlerBase hb)
            throws SAXException, IOException;
        public void parse(String uri, HandlerBase hb)
            throws SAXException, IOException;
        public void parse(InputSource is, HandlerBase hb)
            throws SAXException, IOException;
        public void parse(InputSource is, DefaultHandler dh)
            throws SAXException, IOException;
        public void parse(String systemId, DefaultHandler dh)
            throws SAXException, IOException;
        public void parse(File f, DefaultHandler dh)
            throws SAXException, IOException;
        public abstract void setProperty(String name, Object value)
            throws SAXNotRecognizedException, SAXNotSupportedException;
    }
```

SAXParserFactory

This class defines a factory for creating instances of SAX parsers. Before creating these instances, use the **setFeature()** method to define which parsing features are required of the parser to be created. See *http://www.megginson.com/SAX/Java/features.html* for a list of core SAX 2 features.

```
    public abstract class SAXParserFactory {
        protected SAXParserFactory();
        public abstract boolean getFeature(String name)
            throws ParserConfigurationException, SAXNotRecognizedException,
            SAXNotSupportedException;
        public boolean isNamespaceAware();
        public boolean isValidating();
        public static SAXParserFactory newInstance();
        public abstract SAXParser newSAXParser()
            throws ParserConfigurationException, SAXException;
        public abstract void setFeature(String name, boolean value)
            throws ParserConfigurationException, SAXNotRecognizedException,
            SAXNotSupportedException;
        public void setNamespaceAware(boolean awareness);
        public void setValidating(boolean validating);
    }
```

Package: javax.xml.transform

This package defines an API for performing transformations. Although these are common XSLT transformations, the API is flexible enough to support other transformation technologies. Like the `javax.xml.parsers` package, the classes and interfaces in this package hide vendor-specific implementation code. JAXP 1.1 ships with Xalan as its reference implementation for transformations; different processors can be plugged in.

ErrorListener

This interface allows applications to implement custom error handling. If an error listener is not registered, errors are written to `System.err`. More details on this interface can be found in Chapter 9.

```
public interface ErrorListener {
    void error(TransformerException exception)
        throws TransformerException;
    void fatalError(TransformerException exception)
        throws TransformerException;
    void warning(TransformerException exception)
        throws TransformerException;
}
```

OutputKeys

These are constant definitions for legal output property settings on the `Transformer` interface. They map directly to the legal attributes for the `<xsl:output>` element. Programmatically specified output properties take priority over output properties specified in the XSLT stylesheet.

```
public class OutputKeys {
    public static final String CDATA_SECTION_ELEMENTS = "cdata-section-elements";
    public static final String DOCTYPE_PUBLIC = "doctype-public";
    public static final String DOCTYPE_SYSTEM = "doctype-system";
    public static final String ENCODING = "encoding";
    public static final String INDENT = "indent";
    public static final String MEDIA_TYPE = "media-type";
    public static final String METHOD = "method";
    public static final String OMIT_XML_DECLARATION = "omit-xml-declaration";
    public static final String STANDALONE = "standalone";
    public static final String VERSION = "version";
}
```

Result

This is a common interface for classes that produce a transformation result. `DOMResult`, `SAXResult`, and `StreamResult` are implementing classes. The two constants in this interface are used when specifying whether output escaping is performed, as discussed in section 16.4 of the XSLT specification at *http://www.w3.org/TR/xslt*. The system id is optional but can be helpful when displaying error messages or warnings.

```
public interface Result {
    public static final String PI_DISABLE_OUTPUT_ESCAPING =
        "javax.xml.transform.disable-output-escaping";
    public static final String PI_ENABLE_OUTPUT_ESCAPING =
        "javax.xml.transform.enable-output-escaping";
    String getSystemId();
    void setSystemId(String systemId);
}
```

Source

This is a generic interface implemented by DOMSource, SAXSource, and StreamSource. The system id is particularly important for Source because it allows the processor to resolve relative URI references within the XML and XSLT inputs.[*]

```
public interface Source {
    String getSystemId();
    void setSystemId(String systemId);
}
```

SourceLocator

Instances of this interface are useful when reporting locations of error messages and warnings. Application programmers retrieve SourceLocator instances from TransformerException's getLocator() method.

```
public interface SourceLocator {
    int getColumnNumber();
    int getLineNumber();
    String getPublicId();
    String getSystemId();
}
```

Templates

These instances represent "compiled" transformation instructions. Whether a particular XSLT processor actually compiles stylesheets is implementation-dependent. However, Templates objects are guaranteed to be thread-safe. This makes them ideal for servlet environments, where it is desirable to parse an XSLT stylesheet once then cache it in memory as a Templates object. The output properties are a read-only representation of the <xsl: output> stylesheet element.

```
public interface Templates {
    Properties getOutputProperties();
    Transformer newTransformer()
        throws TransformerConfigurationException;
}
```

---

* URI references are found in elements such as <xsl:import> and <xsl:include>.

Transformer

Instances of this class perform one or more transformations. Although `Transformer` objects can be reused, they are not thread-safe and therefore cannot be used concurrently. Output property names are defined by the `OutputKeys` class and map to the `<xsl:output>` stylesheet element. Parameters, on the other hand, are stylesheet parameters and map to top-level `<xsl:param>` elements. The `getParameter()` method returns only parameters that have been programmatically set.

```
public abstract class Transformer {
    protected Transformer();
    public abstract void clearParameters();
    public abstract ErrorListener getErrorListener();
    public abstract Properties getOutputProperties();
    public abstract String getOutputProperty(String name)
        throws IllegalArgumentException;
    public abstract Object getParameter(String name);
    public abstract URIResolver getURIResolver();
    public abstract void setErrorListener(ErrorListener listener)
        throws IllegalArgumentException;
    public abstract void setOutputProperties(Properties oformat)
        throws IllegalArgumentException;
    public abstract void setOutputProperty(String name, String value)
        throws IllegalArgumentException;
    public abstract void setParameter(String name, Object value);
    public abstract void setURIResolver(URIResolver resolver);
    public abstract void transform(Source xmlSource, Result outputTarget)
        throws TransformerException;
}
```

TransformerConfigurationException

This exception indicates a serious problem and may occur when an XSLT stylesheet has syntax errors that prevent instantiation of a `Transformer` instance. This class can wrap around other exceptions. For example, an underlying parser exception may be wrapped by an instance of this class.

```
public class TransformerConfigurationException
        extends TransformerException {
    public TransformerConfigurationException(String msg);
    public TransformerConfigurationException(Throwable e);
    public TransformerConfigurationException(String msg, Throwable e);
    public TransformerConfigurationException(String msg, SourceLocator locator);
    public TransformerConfigurationException(String msg, SourceLocator locator,
        Throwable e);
    public TransformerConfigurationException();
}
```

TransformerException

This is a general-purpose exception that occurs during transformation. If an `ErrorListener` is registered, the processor should try to report exceptions there first.

Otherwise, exceptions are written to System.err. The quality of error messages varies widely across different XSLT processors. This class can wrap around other exceptions.

```
public class TransformerException
        extends Exception {
    public TransformerException(String msg, Throwable e);
    public TransformerException(String msg, SourceLocator locator);
    public TransformerException(Throwable e);
    public TransformerException(String msg);
    public TransformerException(String msg, SourceLocator locator, Throwable e);
    public Throwable getCause();
    public Throwable getException();
    public String getLocationAsString();
    public SourceLocator getLocator();
    public String getMessageAndLocation();
    public synchronized Throwable initCause(Throwable cause);
    public void printStackTrace(PrintStream ps);
    public void printStackTrace(PrintWriter pw);
    public void printStackTrace();
    public void setLocator(SourceLocator locator);
}
```

TransformerFactory

This defines a portable way to access different TransformerFactory instances and is the key abstraction that masks differences between XSLT processors from different vendors.

```
public abstract class TransformerFactory {
    protected TransformerFactory();
    public abstract Source getAssociatedStylesheet(Source source, String media,
        String title, String charset) throws TransformerConfigurationException;
    public abstract Object getAttribute(String name)
        throws IllegalArgumentException;
    public abstract ErrorListener getErrorListener();
    public abstract boolean getFeature(String name);
    public abstract URIResolver getURIResolver();
    public static TransformerFactory newInstance()
        throws TransformerFactoryConfigurationError;
    public abstract Templates newTemplates(Source source)
        throws TransformerConfigurationException;
    public abstract Transformer newTransformer(Source source)
        throws TransformerConfigurationException;
    public abstract Transformer newTransformer()
        throws TransformerConfigurationException;
    public abstract void setAttribute(String name, Object value)
        throws IllegalArgumentException;
    public abstract void setErrorListener(ErrorListener listener)
        throws IllegalArgumentException;
    public abstract void setURIResolver(URIResolver resolver);
}
```

TransformerFactoryConfigurationError

This error is typically seen when a transformer factory class cannot be instantiated. This is a good indicator of CLASSPATH problems.

```
public class TransformerFactoryConfigurationError
        extends Error {
    public TransformerFactoryConfigurationError(String msg);
    public TransformerFactoryConfigurationError(Exception e);
    public TransformerFactoryConfigurationError(Exception e, String msg);
    public TransformerFactoryConfigurationError();
    public Exception getException();
    public String getMessage();
}
```

URIResolver

In most cases, the JAXP provides a `URIResolver` instance. By creating a custom implementation, however, applications can define how relative URI references in XSLT stylesheets are resolved. For instance, the `URIResolver` defines how `<xsl:include href="header. xslt"/>` locates *header.xslt*.

```
public interface URIResolver {
    Source resolve(String href, String base)
        throws TransformerException;
}
```

Package: javax.xml.transform.dom

This package defines how to perform transformations using DOM.

DOMLocator

This interface allows applications to locate the DOM node where an error occurs. Since `TransformerException` returns instances of `SourceLocator`, applications must downcast to obtain `DOMLocator` objects.

```
public interface DOMLocator
        extends SourceLocator {
    Node getOriginatingNode();
}
```

DOMResult

This class allows transformation results to be stored in a DOM tree. If the default constructor is used, the XSLT processor creates a DOM `Document` node. Otherwise, applications can specify a DOM `Document`, `DocumentFragment`, or `Element` node as the constructor parameter.

The `FEATURE` constant is used with `TransformerFactory.getFeature()` to determine if the factory supports `DOMResult`.

```
public class DOMResult
        implements Result {
    public static final String FEATURE =
        "http://javax.xml.transform.dom.DOMResult/feature";
    public DOMResult(Node node);
    public DOMResult(Node node, String systemId);
    public DOMResult();
    public Node getNode();
    public String getSystemId();
    public void setNode(Node node);
    public void setSystemId(String systemId);
}
```

DOMSource

This class allows a DOM tree to be used as an input source. In practice, the node parameter is usually an instance of a DOM Document. However, XSLT processors may also support any other type of DOM Node. The system id is still important for resolving relative URI references.

```
public class DOMSource
        implements Source {
    public static final String FEATURE =
        "http://javax.xml.transform.dom.DOMSource/feature";
    public DOMSource(Node node);
    public DOMSource(Node node, String systemId);
    public DOMSource();
    public Node getNode();
    public String getSystemId();
    public void setNode(Node node);
    public void setSystemId(String systemId);
}
```

Package: javax.xml.transform.sax

This package defines how to perform transformations using SAX. Example usages can be found in Chapter 5.

SAXResult

This class makes it possible to emit SAX events as the result of a transformation. The ContentHandler parameter receives these events.

```
public class SAXResult
        implements Result {
    public static final String FEATURE =
        "http://javax.xml.transform.sax.SAXResult/feature";
    public SAXResult(ContentHandler handler);
    public SAXResult();
```

```
        public ContentHandler getHandler();
        public LexicalHandler getLexicalHandler();
        public String getSystemId();
        public void setHandler(ContentHandler handler);
        public void setLexicalHandler(LexicalHandler handler);
        public void setSystemId(String systemId);
    }
```

SAXSource

This allows output from a SAX parser to be fed into an XSLT processor for transformation. It
is also used to build Templates or Transformer objects using TransformerFactory.

```
    public class SAXSource
            implements Source {
        public static final String FEATURE =
            "http://javax.xml.transform.sax.SAXSource/feature";
        public SAXSource(XMLReader reader, InputSource inputSource);
        public SAXSource(InputSource inputSource);
        public SAXSource();
        public InputSource getInputSource();
        public String getSystemId();
        public XMLReader getXMLReader();
        public void setInputSource(InputSource inputSource);
        public void setSystemId(String systemId);
        public void setXMLReader(XMLReader reader);
        public static InputSource sourceToInputSource(Source source);
    }
```

SAXTransformerFactory

This is a subclass of TransformerFactory that adds SAX-specific methods. To create an
instance of this class, create a TransformerFactory instance and downcast if transFact.
getFeature(SAXTransformerFactory.FEATURE) returns true.

```
    public abstract class SAXTransformerFactory
            extends TransformerFactory {
        public static final String FEATURE =
            "http://javax.xml.transform.sax.SAXTransformerFactory/feature";
        public static final String FEATURE_XMLFILTER =
            "http://javax.xml.transform.sax.SAXTransformerFactory/feature/xmlfilter";
        protected SAXTransformerFactory();
        public abstract TemplatesHandler newTemplatesHandler()
            throws TransformerConfigurationException;
        public abstract TransformerHandler newTransformerHandler(Templates templates)
            throws TransformerConfigurationException;
        public abstract TransformerHandler newTransformerHandler()
            throws TransformerConfigurationException;
        public abstract TransformerHandler newTransformerHandler(Source src)
            throws TransformerConfigurationException;
        public abstract XMLFilter newXMLFilter(Templates templates)
            throws TransformerConfigurationException;
```

```
        public abstract XMLFilter newXMLFilter(Source src)
            throws TransformerConfigurationException;
}
```

TemplatesHandler

This acts as a SAX 2 `ContentHandler`, which receives SAX events as a document is parsed. Once parsing is complete, it returns a `Templates` object. Instances are constructed using `SAXTransformerFactory`.

```
    public interface TemplatesHandler
            extends ContentHandler {
        String getSystemId();
        Templates getTemplates();
        void setSystemId(String systemId);
    }
```

TransformerHandler

Instances of this interface receive SAX events and produce `Transformer` objects once parsing is complete. Instances are constructed using `SAXTransformerFactory`.

```
    public interface TransformerHandler
            extends ContentHandler, LexicalHandler, DTDHandler {
        String getSystemId();
        Transformer getTransformer();
        void setResult(Result result)
            throws IllegalArgumentException;
        void setSystemId(String systemId);
    }
```

Package: javax.xml.transform.stream

This package defines how to perform transformations using Java I/O streams.

StreamResult

This allows transformation results to be sent to a `File`, `Writer`, or `OutputStream`.

```
    public class StreamResult
            implements Result {
        public static final String FEATURE =
            "http://javax.xml.transform.stream.StreamResult/feature";
        public StreamResult(OutputStream outputStream);
        public StreamResult(Writer writer);
        public StreamResult(String systemId);
        public StreamResult(File f);
        public StreamResult();
        public OutputStream getOutputStream();
        public String getSystemId();
```

```
        public Writer getWriter();
        public void setOutputStream(OutputStream outputStream);
        public void setSystemId(File f);
        public void setSystemId(String systemId);
        public void setWriter(Writer writer);
    }
```

StreamSource

This supports input from a URL, File, Reader, or InputStream. The system id is used to resolve relative URLs in the XML and XSLT.

```
    public class StreamSource
            implements Source {
        public static final String FEATURE =
            "http://javax.xml.transform.stream.StreamSource/feature";
        public StreamSource(InputStream inputStream);
        public StreamSource(InputStream inputStream, String systemId);
        public StreamSource(Reader reader);
        public StreamSource(Reader reader, String systemId);
        public StreamSource(String systemId);
        public StreamSource(File f);
        public StreamSource();
        public InputStream getInputStream();
        public String getPublicId();
        public Reader getReader();
        public String getSystemId();
        public void setInputStream(InputStream inputStream);
        public void setPublicId(String systemId);
        public void setReader(Reader reader);
        public void setSystemId(File f);
        public void setSystemId(String systemId);
    }
```

C

XSLT Quick Reference

This appendix provides a quick reference to the XSLT markup language. Each element is listed in alphabetical order, along with a reference to the appropriate section in Version 1.0 of the XSLT specification available at *http://www.w3.org/TR/xslt.*

Attributes are shown along with their allowable values, and square brackets indicate optional attributes. Values enclosed in curly braces are treated as attribute value templates, and quoted values are literals. XML-style comments indicate which elements allow content and the allowable type of that content.

<xsl:apply-imports>

```
<xsl:apply-imports/>
```

See XSLT specification section 5.6: "Overriding Template Rules."

<xsl:apply-templates>

```
<xsl:apply-templates
    [select = node-set-expression]
    [mode = qname]>
  <!-- Content: Any number of <xsl:sort> or <xsl:with-param> -->
</xsl:apply-templates>
```

See XSLT specification section 5.4: "Applying Template Rules."

<xsl:attribute>

```
<xsl:attribute
    name = {qname}
    [namespace = {uri-reference}]>
  <!-- Content: template -->
</xsl:attribute>
```

See XSLT specification section 7.1.3: "Creating Attributes with <xsl:attribute>."

<xsl:attribute-set>

```
<xsl:attribute-set
    name = qname
    [use-attribute-sets = qnames]>
  <!-- Content: Any number of <xsl:attribute> -->
</xsl:attribute-set>
```

See XSLT specification section 7.1.4: "Named Attribute Sets."

<xsl:call-template>

```
<xsl:call-template
    name = qname>
  <!-- Content: Any number of <xsl:with-param> -->
</xsl:call-template>
```

See XSLT specification section 6: "Named Templates."

<xsl:choose>

```
<xsl:choose>
  <!-- Content: One or more <xsl:when>, followed by an optional <xsl:
otherwise> -->
</xsl:choose>
```

See XSLT specification section 9.2: "Conditional Processing with <xsl:choose>."

<xsl:comment>

```
<xsl:comment>
  <!-- Content: template -->
</xsl:comment>
```

See XSLT specification section 7.4: "Creating Comments."

<xsl:copy>

```
<xsl:copy
    [use-attribute-sets = qnames]>
  <!-- Content: template -->
</xsl:copy>
```

See XSLT specification section 7.5: "Copying."

<xsl:copy-of>

```
<xsl:copy-of
    select = expression/>
```

See XSLT specification section 11.3: "Using Values of Variables and Parameters with <xsl: copy-of>."

<xsl:decimal-format>

```
<xsl:decimal-format
    [name = qname]
    [decimal-separator = char]
    [grouping-separator = char]
    [infinity = string]
    [minus-sign = char]
    [NaN = string]
    [percent = char]
    [per-mille = char]
    [zero-digit = char]
    [digit = char]
    [pattern-separator = char]/>
```

See XSLT specification section 12.3: "Number Formatting."

<xsl:element>

```
<xsl:element
    name = {qname}
    [namespace = {uri-reference}]
    [use-attribute-sets = qnames]>
  <!-- Content: template -->
</xsl:element>
```

See XSLT specification section 7.1.2: "Creating Elements with <xsl:element>."

<xsl:fallback>

```
<xsl:fallback>
  <!-- Content: template -->
</xsl:fallback>
```

See XSLT specification section 15: "Fallback."

<xsl:for-each>

```
<xsl:for-each
    select = node-set-expression>
  <!-- Content: Any number of <xsl:sort>, followed by template -->
</xsl:for-each>
```

See XSLT specification section 8: "Repetition."

<xsl:if>

```
<xsl:if
    test = boolean-expression>
  <!-- Content: template -->
</xsl:if>
```

See XSLT specification section 9.1: "Conditional Processing with <xsl:if>."

<xsl:import>

```
<xsl:import
    href = uri-reference/>
```

See XSLT specification section 2.6.2: "Stylesheet Import."

<xsl:include>

```
<xsl:include
    href = uri-reference/>
```

See XSLT specification section 2.6.1: "Stylesheet Inclusion."

<xsl:key>

```
<xsl:key
    name = qname
    match = pattern
    use = expression/>
```

See XSLT specification section 12.2: "Keys."

<xsl:message>

```
<xsl:message
    [terminate = "yes" or "no"]>
  <!-- Content: template -->
</xsl:message>
```

See XSLT specification section 13: "Messages."

<xsl:namespace-alias>

```
<xsl:namespace-alias
    stylesheet-prefix = prefix or "#default"
    result-prefix = prefix or "#default"/>
```

See XSLT specification section 7.1.1: "Literal Result Elements."

<xsl:number>

```
<xsl:number
    [level = "single" or "multiple" or "any"]
    [count = pattern]
    [from = pattern]
    [value = number-expression]
    [format = {string}]
    [lang = {nmtoken}]
    [letter-value = {"alphabetic" or "traditional"}]
    [grouping-separator = {char}]
    [grouping-size = {number}]/>
```

See XSLT specification section 7.7: "Numbering."

<xsl:otherwise>

```
<xsl:otherwise>
  <!-- Content: template -->
</xsl:otherwise>
```

See XSLT specification section 9.2: "Conditional Processing with <xsl:choose>."

<xsl:output>

```
<xsl:output
    [method = "xml" or "html" or "text" or qname-but-not-ncname]
    [version = nmtoken]
    [encoding = string]
    [omit-xml-declaration = "yes" or "no"]
    [standalone = "yes" or "no"]
    [doctype-public = string]
    [doctype-system = string]
    [cdata-section-elements = qnames]
    [indent = "yes" or "no"]
    [media-type = string]/>
```

See XSLT specification section 16: "Output."

<xsl:param>

```
<xsl:param
    name = qname
    [select = expression]>
  <!-- Content: template -->
</xsl:param>
```

See XSLT specification section 11: "Variables and Parameters."

<xsl:preserve-space>

```
<xsl:preserve-space
    elements = tokens/>
```

See XSLT specification section 3.4: "Whitespace Stripping."

<xsl:processing-instruction>

```
<xsl:processing-instruction
    name = {ncname}>
  <!-- Content: template -->
</xsl:processing-instruction>
```

See XSLT specification section 7.3: "Creating Processing Instructions."

<xsl:sort>

```
<xsl:sort
    [select = string-expression]
    [lang = {nmtoken}]
    [data-type = {"text" or "number" or qname-but-not-ncname}]
    [order = {"ascending" or "descending"}]
    [case-order = {"upper-first" or "lower-first"}]/>
```

See XSLT specification section 10: "Sorting."

<xsl:strip-space>

```
<xsl:strip-space
    elements = tokens/>
```

See XSLT specification section 3.4: "Whitespace Stripping."

<xsl:stylesheet>

```
<xsl:stylesheet
    version = number
    [id = id]
    [extension-element-prefixes = tokens]
    [exclude-result-prefixes = tokens]>
  <!-- Content: Any number of <xsl:import>, followed by top-level-elements -
->
</xsl:stylesheet>
```

See XSLT specification section 2.2: "Stylesheet Element."

<xsl:template>

```
<xsl:template
    [match = pattern]
    [name = qname]
    [priority = number]
    [mode = qname]>
  <!-- Content: Any number of <xsl:param>, followed by template -->
</xsl:template>
```

See XSLT specification section 5.3: "Defining Template Rules."

<xsl:text>

```
<xsl:text
    [disable-output-escaping = "yes" or "no"]>
  <!-- Content: #PCDATA -->
</xsl:text>
```

See XSLT specification section 7.2: "Creating Text."

<xsl:transform>

```
<xsl:transform
    version = number
    [id = id]
    [extension-element-prefixes = tokens]
    [exclude-result-prefixes = tokens]>
  <!-- Content: Any number of <xsl:import>, followed by top-level-elements -
->
</xsl:transform>
```

See XSLT specification section 2.2: "Stylesheet Element."

<xsl:value-of>

```
<xsl:value-of
    select = string-expression
    [disable-ouput-escaping = "yes" or "no"]/>
```

See XSLT specification section 7.6.1: "Generating Text with <xsl:value-of>."

<xsl:variable>

```
<xsl:variable
    name = qname
    [select = expression]>
  <!-- Content: template -->
</xsl:variable>
```

See XSLT specification section 11: "Variables and Parameters."

<xsl:when>

```
<xsl:when
    test = boolean-expression>
  <!-- Content: template -->
</xsl:when>
```

See XSLT specification section 9.2: "Conditional Processing with xsl:choose."

<xsl:with-param>

```
<xsl:with-param
    name = qname
    [select = expression]>
  <!-- Content: template -->
</xsl:with-param>
```

See XSLT specification section 11.6: "Passing Parameters to Templates."

Index

We'd like to hear yor suggestions for improving our indexes. Send email to *index@oreilly.com.*

About the Author

Eric M. Burke is a Java consultant with extensive training and mentoring experience. Before moving to Java, he was a C++ programmer specializing in X-Windows/Motif GUI development on various Unix platforms. He now focuses exclusively on Java and XML technologies, particularly XSLT, servlets, Swing, and EJB.

Eric has a Bachelor of Science degree in Computer Science from Southern Illinois University at Carbondale and is currently a Principal Software Engineer with Object Computing, Inc. (OCI) in St. Louis, MO. He spends most days consulting and teaches a few courses per month. He has also written and contributed to numerous courses, covering topics such as object-oriented concepts, Java servlets, JSPs, and JavaBeans. When he is not working at the computer, Eric enjoys woodworking and home remodeling projects. He can be contacted at *burke_e@yahoo.com.*

Colophon

Our look is the result of reader comments, our own experimentation, and feedback from distribution channels. Distinctive covers complement our distinctive approach to technical topics, breathing personality and life into potentially dry subjects.

The animals on the cover of *Java and XSLT* are ermines, also known as stoats or short-tailed weasels. *Mustela erminea* are found around the world between the Arctic Circle and approximately 40° north latitude. Their body length, not including tail, ranges from 7 to 12 inches, with proportionately sized tails from 3 to 6 inches long. They weigh between 1.5 and 11.5 ounces. Males are, on average, larger than females.

Ermines can both swim and climb trees, and though they live in such diverse habitats as grasslands, tundra, and deep forests, they tend to prefer rocky or brushy areas. They are carnivores and eat mostly rodents, but they also enjoy small rabbits and birds, fish, bugs, and eggs. (Whether they take their eggs sunny-side-up or over-easy is still a matter of great debate.)

Female ermines give birth to only one litter per year. The mating season is in the late spring, but after fertilization, the ermine embryos stop developing and do not implant in the uterus for several months. Once implantation occurs, gestation takes only about a month, and the babies are born in the spring of the year following fertilization.

Ermines can live up to eight years, but their lifespan in the wild tends to be only a year or less. Their main killer is starvation, dependent as they are on fluctuating rodent populations, but they are also preyed upon by hawks, owls, and humans.

Ermine fur, which is harvested from both *M. erminea* and its cousin, *M. frenata*, the long-tailed weasel, is specifically the fur of an ermine in winter. At this time of year, their fur is stark white except for a small black tip on the tail, leading to the black-flecked, white-fur robes favored by stylish monarchs all over the world.

Matt Hutchinson was the production editor and copyeditor for *Java and XSLT*. Susan Carlson Greene proofread the book, and Leanne Soylemez and Emily Quill provided quality control. John Bickelhaupt wrote the index. James Carter provided production assistance.

Ellie Volckhausen designed the cover of this book, based on a series design by Edie Freedman. The cover image is a 19th-century engraving from the Dover Pictorial Archive. Emma Colby produced the cover layout with QuarkXPress 4.1 using Adobe's ITC Garamond font.

David Futato designed the interior layout, based on a series design by Nancy Priest. Neil Walls converted the files from Microsoft Word to FrameMaker 5.5.6 using tools created by Mike Sierra. The heading font is Bitstream Bodoni, the text font is ITC New Baskerville, and the code font is Constant Willison. The illustrations that appear in the book were produced by Robert Romano and Jessamyn Read using Macromedia FreeHand 9 and Adobe Photoshop 6. This colophon was written by Leanne Soylemez.

Whenever possible, our books use a durable and flexible lay-flat binding. If the page count exceeds this binding's limit, perfect binding is used.